WITHDRAWN

THE
COMPLETE
VOLUME ONE
FIRST
VOLUME

LADY MECHANIKA™

Volume 1: The Mystery of the Mechanical Corpse

SPECIAL THANKS:

M M Chen *for Writing Assists*
Martin Montiel *for Pencil Assists, Chapter 5*
Mike Garcia *for Color Assists, Chapters 4 & 5*

Editors, Original Series:

Vince Hernandez, Frank Mastromauro, & Marcia Chen

For This Edition:

Supervising Editor: Marcia Chen

Book Design and Production: Mark Roslan, Marcia Chen, & Peter Steigerwald

Lady Mechanika Logo by: Peter Steigerwald

Cover Illustration and Original Covers by:
Joe Benitez & Peter Steigerwald
(except where noted otherwise)

Originally published in single magazine form as Lady Mechanika #0-5 by Aspen MLT, Inc. and Benitez Productions.

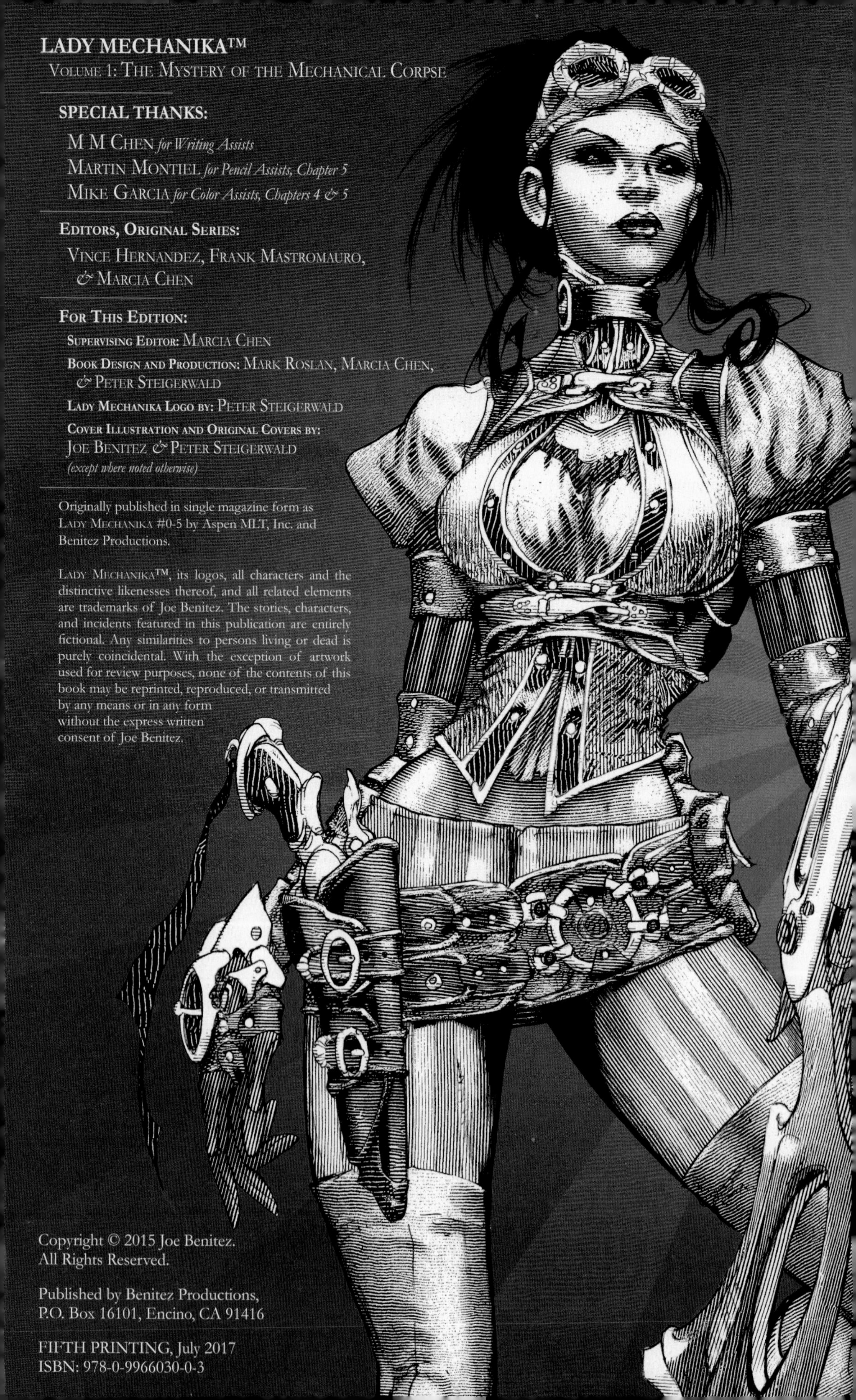

Published by Benitez Productions,
P.O. Box 16101, Encino, CA 91416

FIFTH PRINTING, July 2017
ISBN: 978-0-9966030-0-3

Created, Written & Drawn
by JOE
BENITEZ

Colors
by PETER
STEIGERWALD

Letters
by JOSH
REED

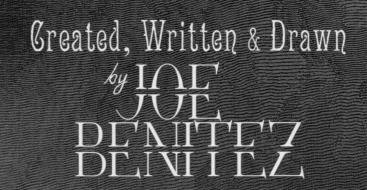

Joe Benitez's
Lady Mechanika
in

The
MYSTERY of the
MECHANICAL
CORPSE

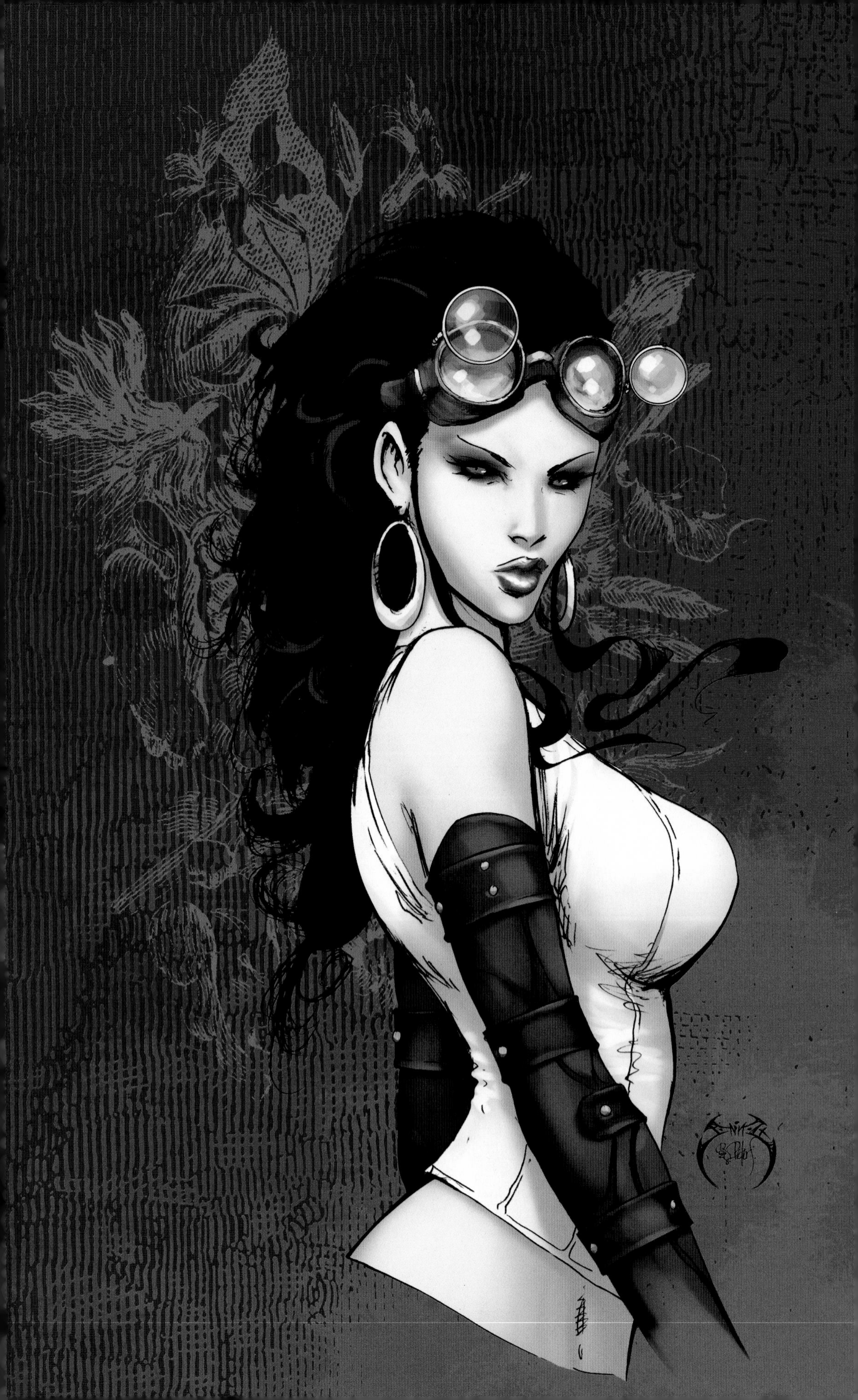

Chapter Zero
The Demon of Satan's Alley

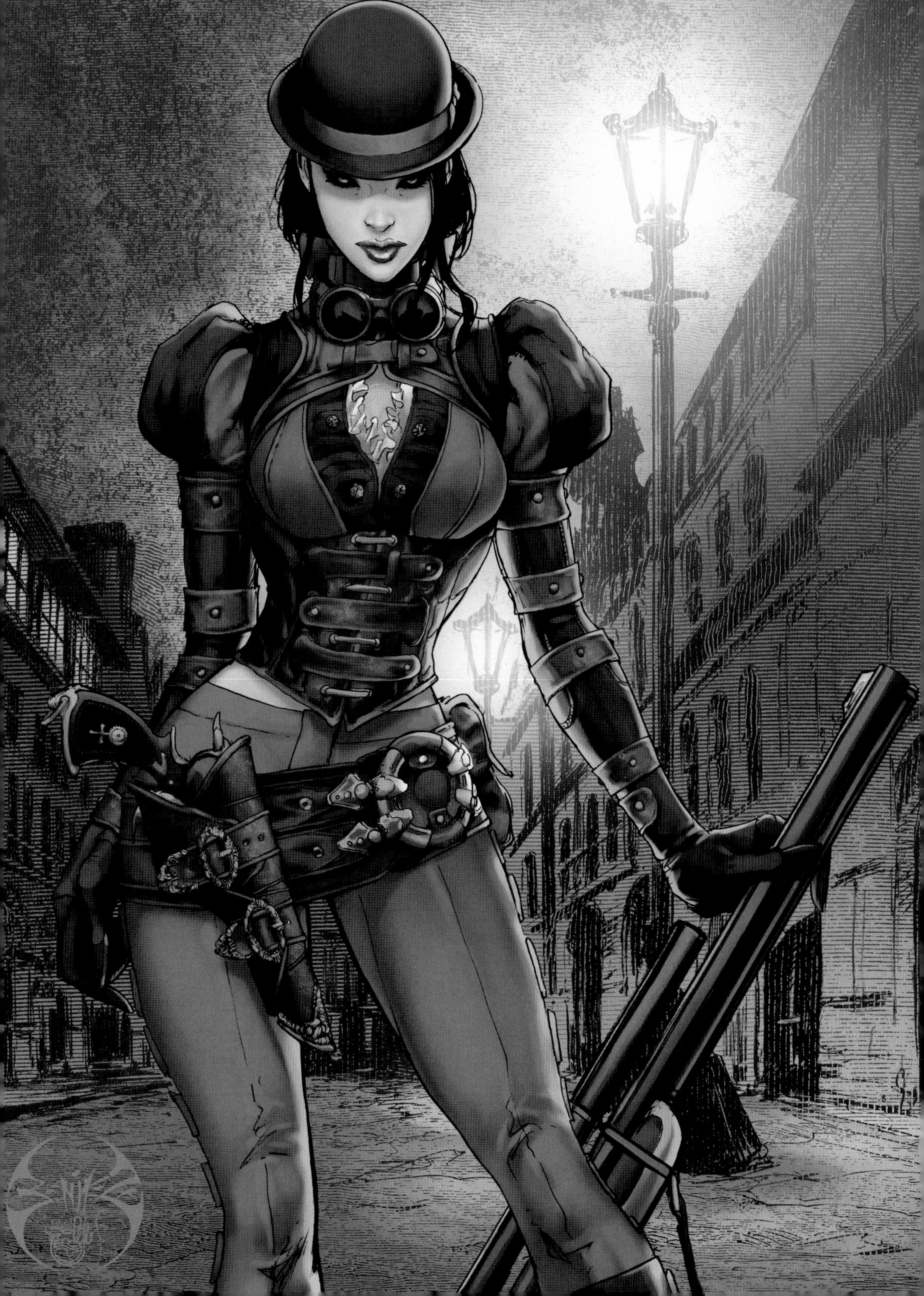

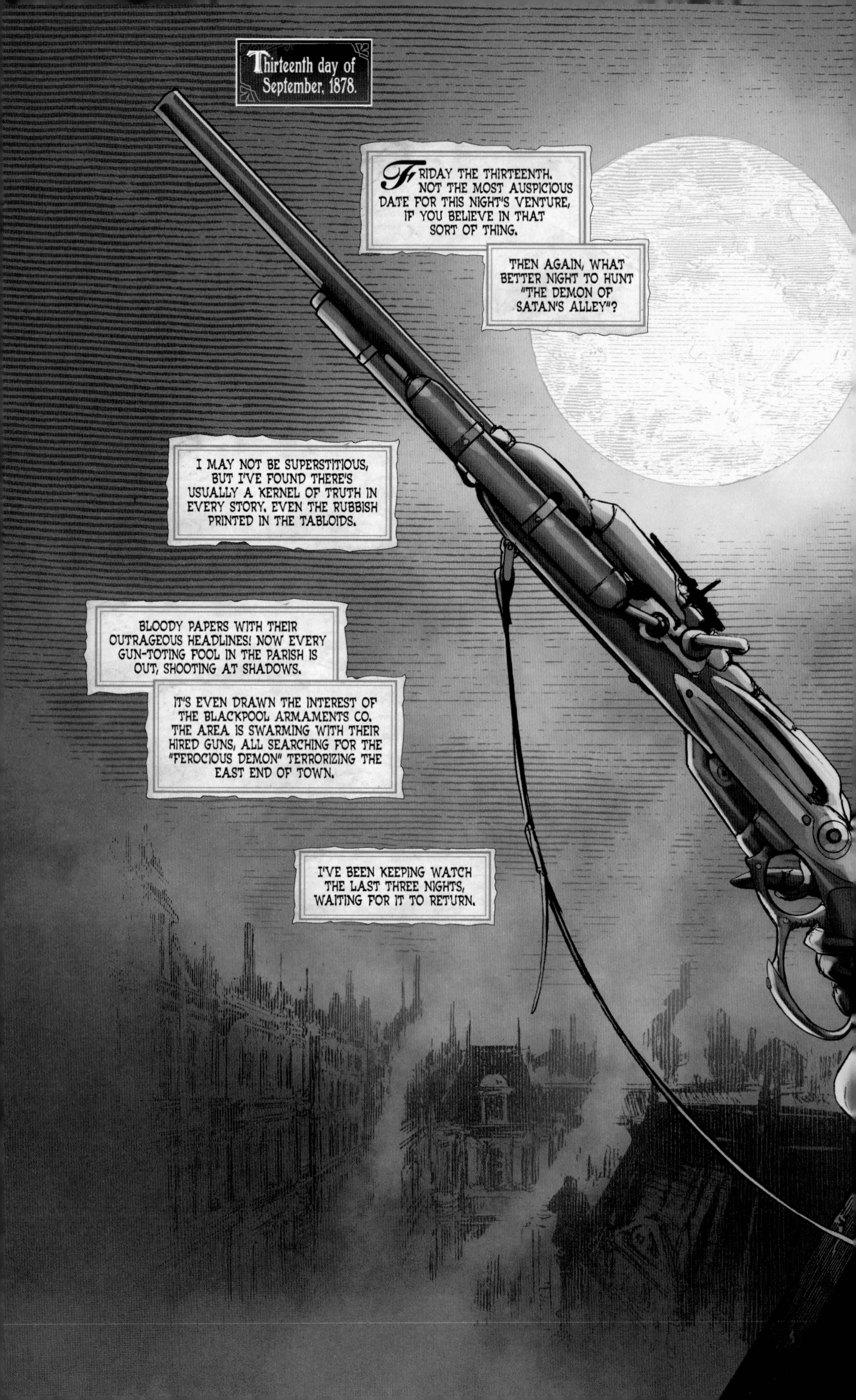
Thirteenth day of September, 1878.
FRIDAY THE THIRTEENTH. NOT THE MOST AUSPICIOUS DATE FOR THIS NIGHT'S VENTURE, IF YOU BELIEVE IN THAT SORT OF THING.
THEN AGAIN, WHAT BETTER NIGHT TO HUNT "THE DEMON OF SATAN'S ALLEY"?
I MAY NOT BE SUPERSTITIOUS, BUT I'VE FOUND THERE'S USUALLY A KERNEL OF TRUTH IN EVERY STORY, EVEN THE RUBBISH PRINTED IN THE TABLOIDS.
BLOODY PAPERS WITH THEIR OUTRAGEOUS HEADLINES! NOW EVERY GUN-TOTING FOOL IN THE PARISH IS OUT, SHOOTING AT SHADOWS.
IT'S EVEN DRAWN THE INTEREST OF THE BLACKPOOL ARMAMENTS CO. THE AREA IS SWARMING WITH THEIR HIRED GUNS, ALL SEARCHING FOR THE "FEROCIOUS DEMON" TERRORIZING THE EAST END OF TOWN.
I'VE BEEN KEEPING WATCH THE LAST THREE NIGHTS, WAITING FOR IT TO RETURN.

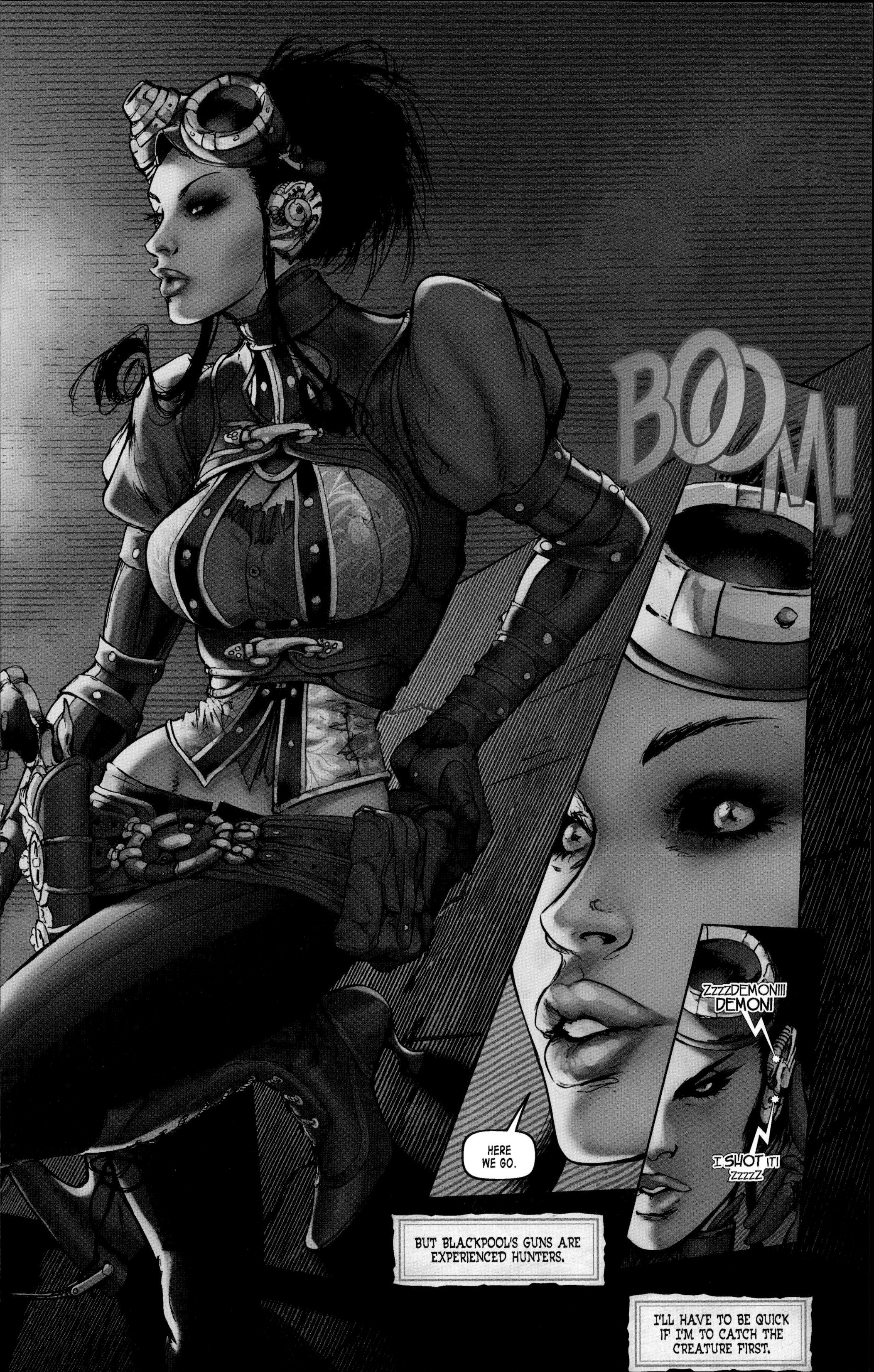
BOOM!
ZzzzDEMON!!!
DEMON!
I SHOT IT!
ZzzzZ
HERE WE GO.
BUT BLACKPOOL'S GUNS ARE EXPERIENCED HUNTERS.
I'LL HAVE TO BE QUICK IF I'M TO CATCH THE CREATURE FIRST.

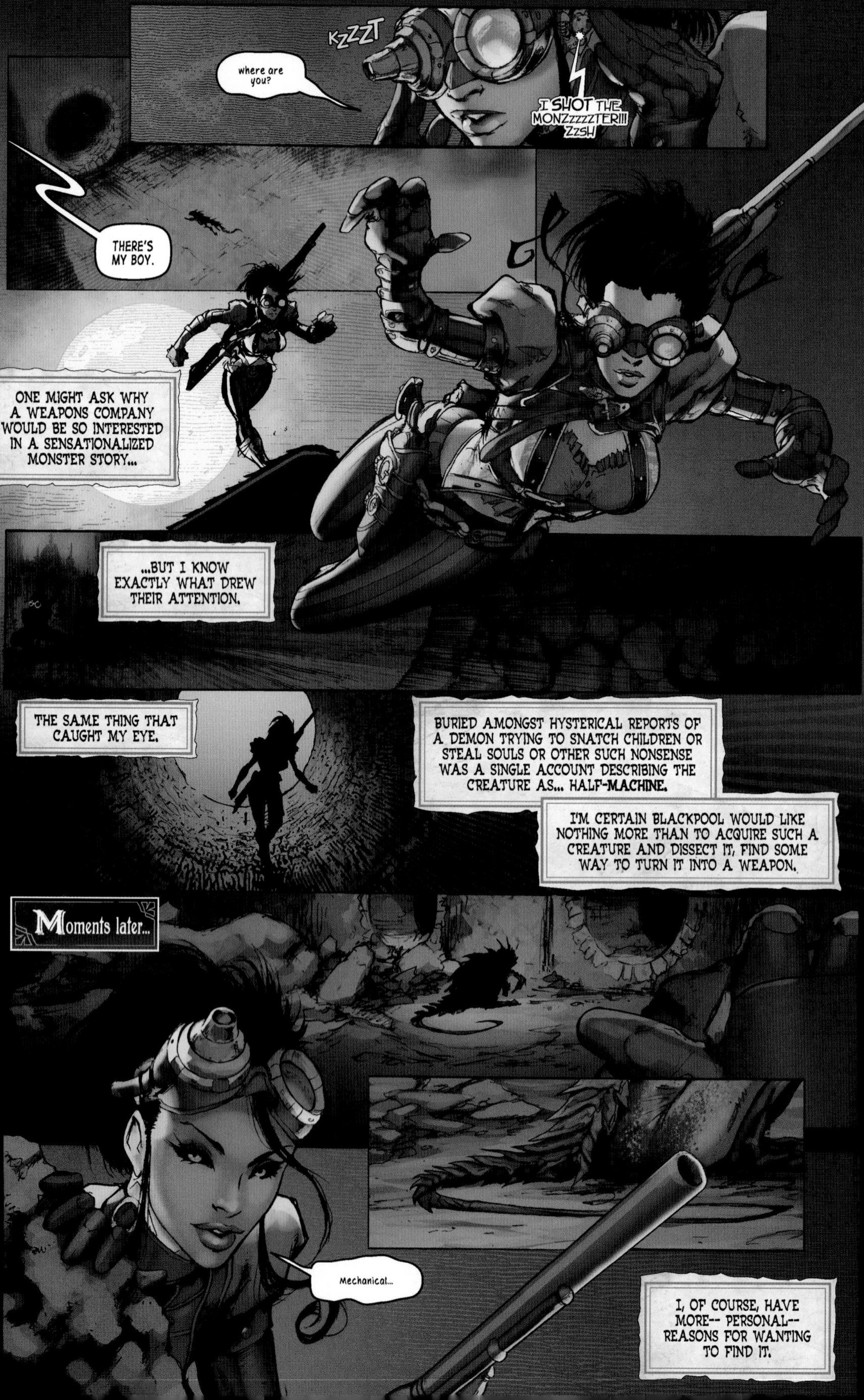
KZZZT
where are you?
I SHOT THE MONZzzzzTER!!! ZZSH
THERE'S MY BOY.
ONE MIGHT ASK WHY A WEAPONS COMPANY WOULD BE SO INTERESTED IN A SENSATIONALIZED MONSTER STORY...
...BUT I KNOW EXACTLY WHAT DREW THEIR ATTENTION.
THE SAME THING THAT CAUGHT MY EYE.
BURIED AMONGST HYSTERICAL REPORTS OF A DEMON TRYING TO SNATCH CHILDREN OR STEAL SOULS OR OTHER SUCH NONSENSE WAS A SINGLE ACCOUNT DESCRIBING THE CREATURE AS... HALF-MACHINE.
I'M CERTAIN BLACKPOOL WOULD LIKE NOTHING MORE THAN TO ACQUIRE SUCH A CREATURE AND DISSECT IT, FIND SOME WAY TO TURN IT INTO A WEAPON.
Moments later...
Mechanical...
I, OF COURSE, HAVE MORE-- PERSONAL-- REASONS FOR WANTING TO FIND IT.

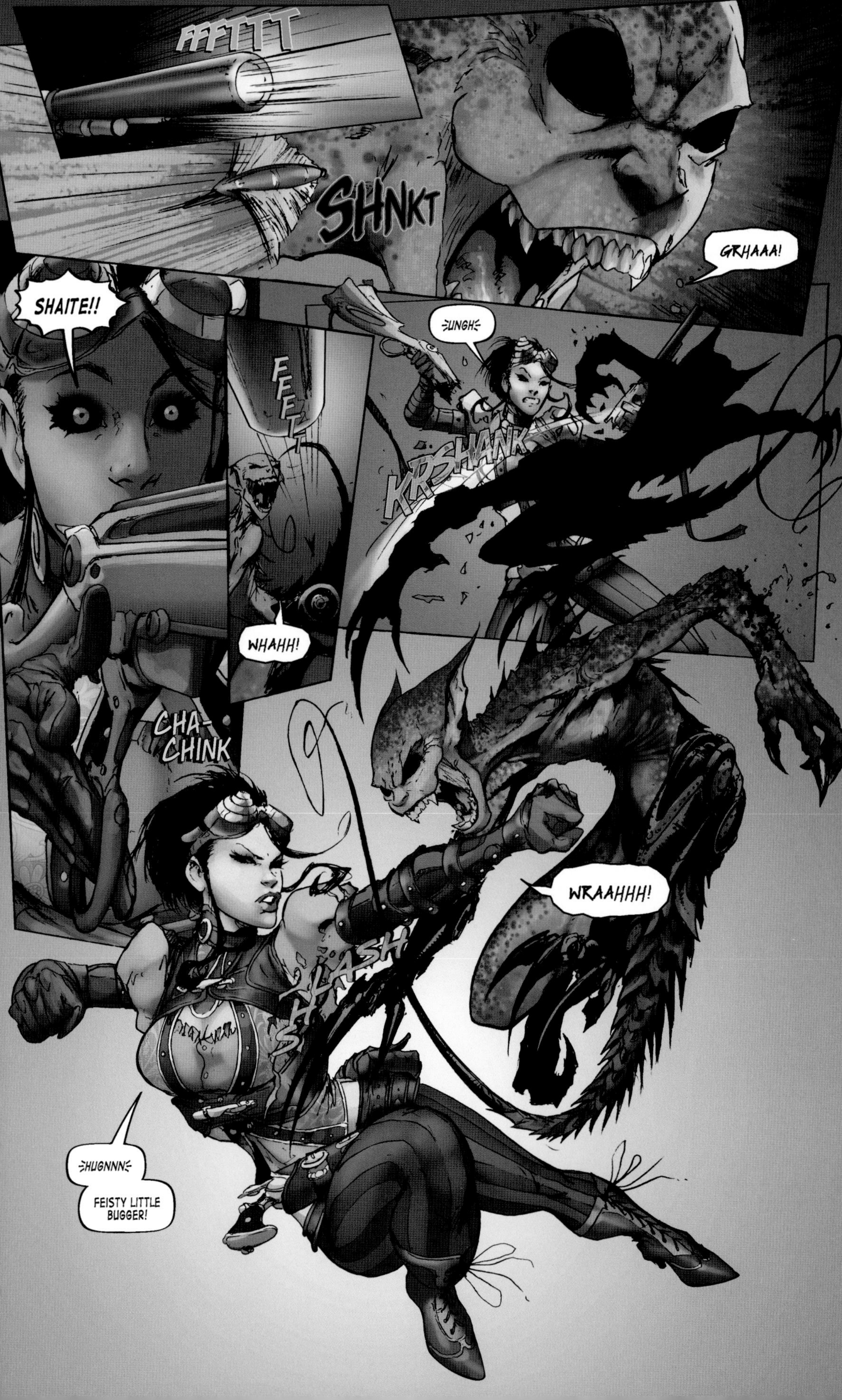
FFFTTT
SHNKT
GRHAAA!
SHAITE!!
FFFT
WHAHH!
UNGH
KRSHANK
CHA-CHINK
WRAAHHH!
SHLASH
HUGNNN
FEISTY LITTLE BUGGER!

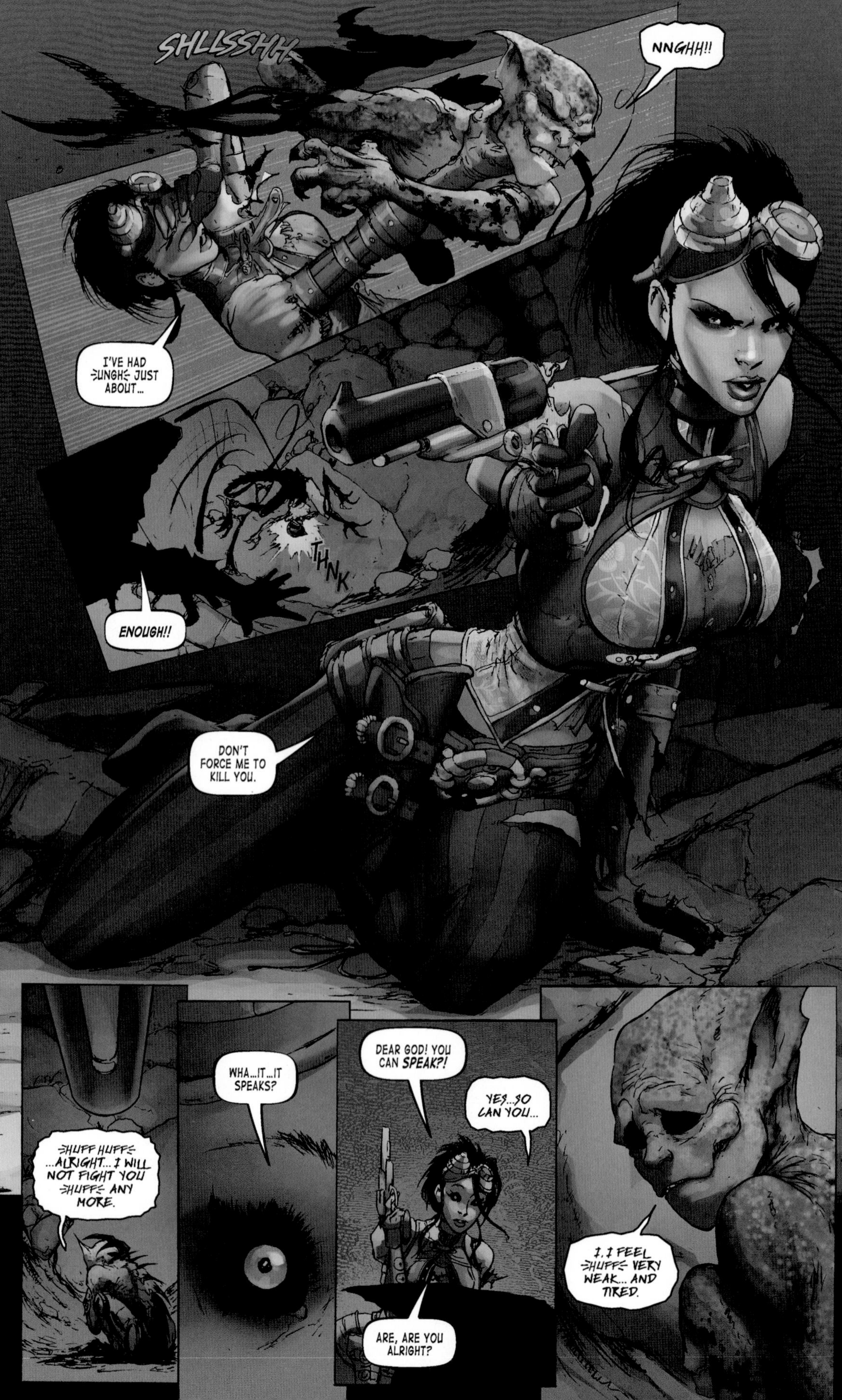
SHLLSSHH
NNGHH!!
I'VE HAD
=UNGH= JUST
ABOUT...
THNK
ENOUGH!!
DON'T
FORCE ME TO
KILL YOU.
=HUFF HUFF=
...ALRIGHT... I WILL
NOT FIGHT YOU
=HUFF= ANY
MORE.
WHA...IT...IT
SPEAKS?
DEAR GOD! YOU
CAN SPEAK?!
YES...SO
CAN YOU...
ARE, ARE YOU
ALRIGHT?
I, I FEEL
=HUFF= VERY
WEAK... AND
TIRED.

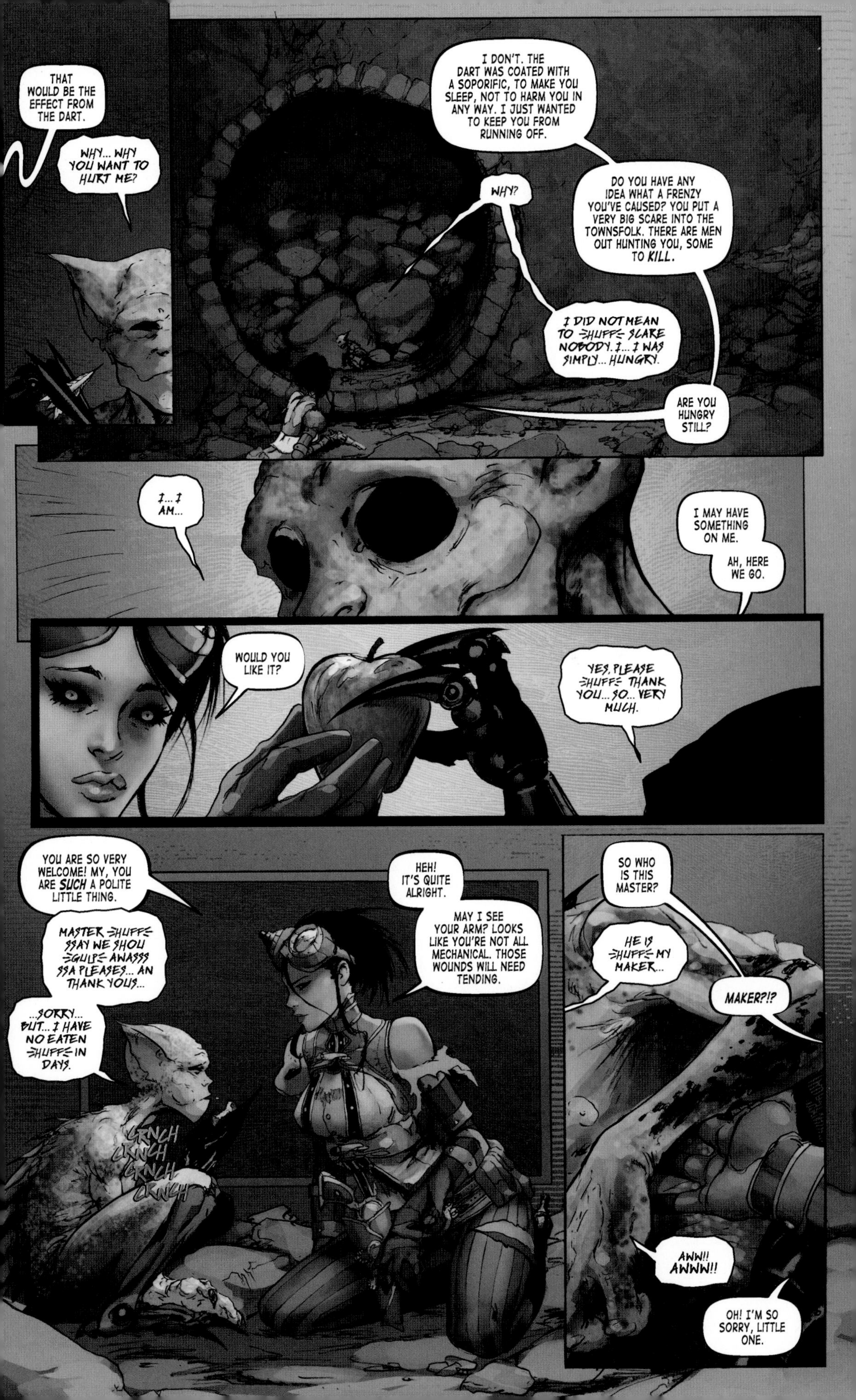
THAT WOULD BE THE EFFECT FROM THE DART.
WHY... WHY YOU WANT TO HURT ME?
I DON'T. THE DART WAS COATED WITH A SOPORIFIC, TO MAKE YOU SLEEP, NOT TO HARM YOU IN ANY WAY. I JUST WANTED TO KEEP YOU FROM RUNNING OFF.
WHY?
DO YOU HAVE ANY IDEA WHAT A FRENZY YOU'VE CAUSED? YOU PUT A VERY BIG SCARE INTO THE TOWNSFOLK. THERE ARE MEN OUT HUNTING YOU, SOME TO KILL.
I DID NOT MEAN TO =HUFF= SCARE NOBODY. I... I WAS SIMPLY... HUNGRY.
ARE YOU HUNGRY STILL?
I... I AM...
I MAY HAVE SOMETHING ON ME.
AH, HERE WE GO.
WOULD YOU LIKE IT?
YES, PLEASE =HUFF= THANK YOU... SO... VERY MUCH.
YOU ARE SO VERY WELCOME! MY, YOU ARE SUCH A POLITE LITTLE THING.
MASTER =HUFF= SSAY WE SHOU =GULP= AWASSS SSA PLEASES... AN THANK YOUS...
...SORRY... BUT... I HAVE NO EATEN =HUFF= IN DAYS.
CRNCH CRNCH CRNCH CRNCH
HEH! IT'S QUITE ALRIGHT.
MAY I SEE YOUR ARM? LOOKS LIKE YOU'RE NOT ALL MECHANICAL. THOSE WOUNDS WILL NEED TENDING.
SO WHO IS THIS MASTER?
HE IS =HUFF= MY MAKER...
MAKER?!?
AWW!! AWWW!!
OH! I'M SO SORRY, LITTLE ONE.

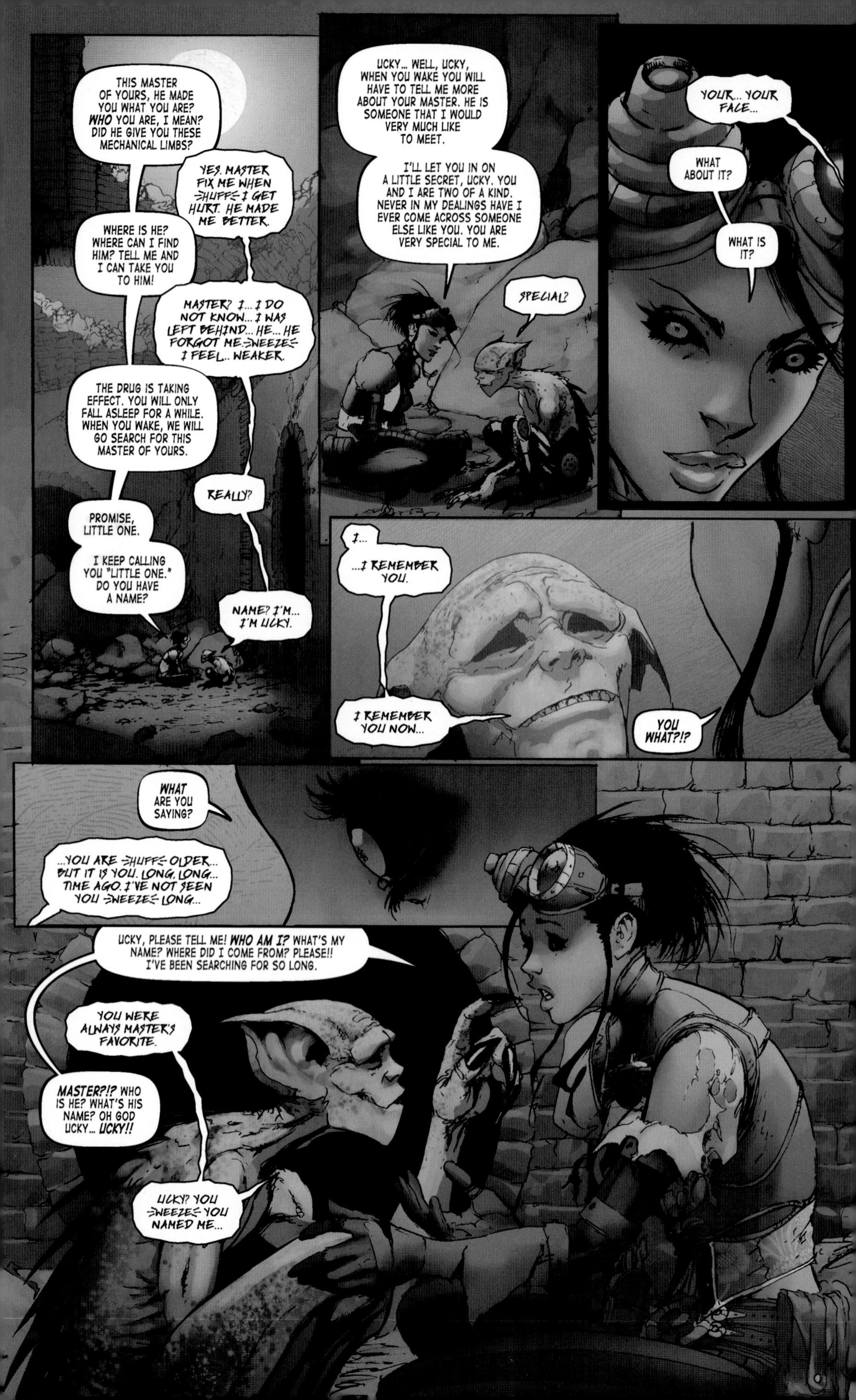
THIS MASTER OF YOURS, HE MADE YOU WHAT YOU ARE? WHO YOU ARE, I MEAN? DID HE GIVE YOU THESE MECHANICAL LIMBS?
YES. MASTER FIX ME WHEN =HUFF= I GET HURT. HE MADE ME BETTER.
WHERE IS HE? WHERE CAN I FIND HIM? TELL ME AND I CAN TAKE YOU TO HIM!
MASTER? I... I DO NOT KNOW... I WAS LEFT BEHIND... HE... HE FORGOT ME. =WEEZE= I FEEL... WEAKER.
THE DRUG IS TAKING EFFECT. YOU WILL ONLY FALL ASLEEP FOR A WHILE. WHEN YOU WAKE, WE WILL GO SEARCH FOR THIS MASTER OF YOURS.
REALLY?
PROMISE, LITTLE ONE.
I KEEP CALLING YOU "LITTLE ONE." DO YOU HAVE A NAME?
NAME? I'M... I'M UCKY.
UCKY... WELL, UCKY, WHEN YOU WAKE YOU WILL HAVE TO TELL ME MORE ABOUT YOUR MASTER. HE IS SOMEONE THAT I WOULD VERY MUCH LIKE TO MEET.
I'LL LET YOU IN ON A LITTLE SECRET, UCKY. YOU AND I ARE TWO OF A KIND. NEVER IN MY DEALINGS HAVE I EVER COME ACROSS SOMEONE ELSE LIKE YOU. YOU ARE VERY SPECIAL TO ME.
SPECIAL?
YOUR... YOUR FACE...
WHAT ABOUT IT?
WHAT IS IT?
I...
...I REMEMBER YOU.
I REMEMBER YOU NOW...
YOU WHAT?!?
WHAT ARE YOU SAYING?
...YOU ARE =HUFF= OLDER... BUT IT IS YOU. LONG, LONG... TIME AGO. I'VE NOT SEEN YOU =WEEZE= LONG...
UCKY, PLEASE TELL ME! WHO AM I? WHAT'S MY NAME? WHERE DID I COME FROM? PLEASE!! I'VE BEEN SEARCHING FOR SO LONG.
YOU WERE ALWAYS MASTER'S FAVORITE.
MASTER?!? WHO IS HE? WHAT'S HIS NAME? OH GOD UCKY... UCKY!!
UCKY? YOU =WEEZE= YOU NAMED ME...

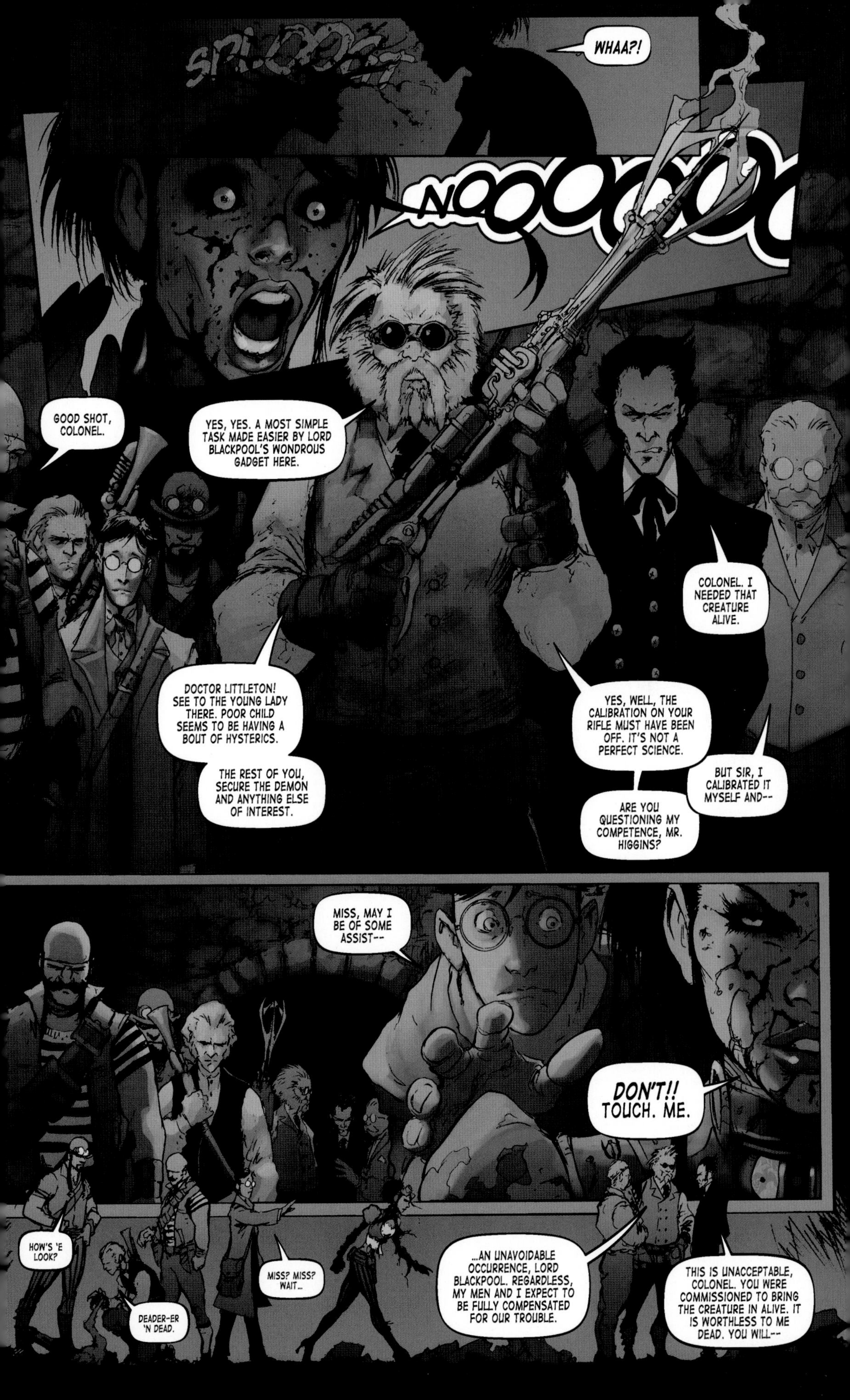
WHAA?!
NOOOOOOO
GOOD SHOT, COLONEL.
YES, YES. A MOST SIMPLE TASK MADE EASIER BY LORD BLACKPOOL'S WONDROUS GADGET HERE.
COLONEL. I NEEDED THAT CREATURE ALIVE.
DOCTOR LITTLETON! SEE TO THE YOUNG LADY THERE. POOR CHILD SEEMS TO BE HAVING A BOUT OF HYSTERICS.
THE REST OF YOU, SECURE THE DEMON AND ANYTHING ELSE OF INTEREST.
YES, WELL, THE CALIBRATION ON YOUR RIFLE MUST HAVE BEEN OFF. IT'S NOT A PERFECT SCIENCE.
BUT SIR, I CALIBRATED IT MYSELF AND--
ARE YOU QUESTIONING MY COMPETENCE, MR. HIGGINS?
MISS, MAY I BE OF SOME ASSIST--
DON'T!! TOUCH. ME.
HOW'S 'E LOOK?
DEADER-ER 'N DEAD.
MISS? MISS? WAIT...
THIS IS UNACCEPTABLE, COLONEL. YOU WERE COMMISSIONED TO BRING THE CREATURE IN ALIVE. IT IS WORTHLESS TO ME DEAD. YOU WILL--
...AN UNAVOIDABLE OCCURRENCE, LORD BLACKPOOL. REGARDLESS, MY MEN AND I EXPECT TO BE FULLY COMPENSATED FOR OUR TROUBLE.

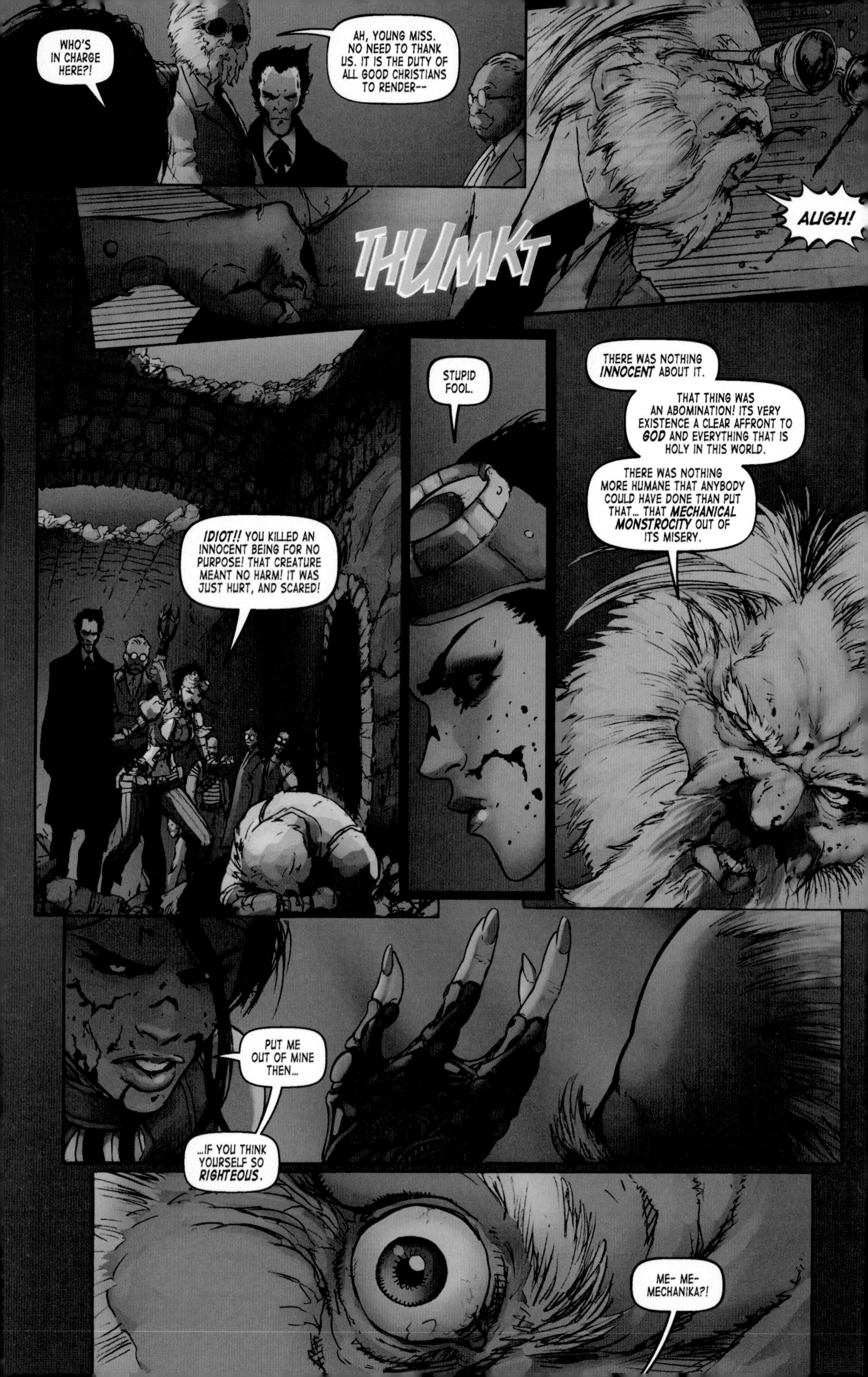
WHO'S IN CHARGE HERE?!
AH, YOUNG MISS. NO NEED TO THANK US. IT IS THE DUTY OF ALL GOOD CHRISTIANS TO RENDER--
THUMKT
AUGH!
IDIOT!! YOU KILLED AN INNOCENT BEING FOR NO PURPOSE! THAT CREATURE MEANT NO HARM! IT WAS JUST HURT, AND SCARED!
STUPID FOOL.
THERE WAS NOTHING INNOCENT ABOUT IT.
THAT THING WAS AN ABOMINATION! ITS VERY EXISTENCE A CLEAR AFFRONT TO GOD AND EVERYTHING THAT IS HOLY IN THIS WORLD.
THERE WAS NOTHING MORE HUMANE THAT ANYBODY COULD HAVE DONE THAN PUT THAT... THAT MECHANICAL MONSTROCITY OUT OF ITS MISERY.
PUT ME OUT OF MINE THEN...
...IF YOU THINK YOURSELF SO RIGHTEOUS.
ME- ME- MECHANIKA?!

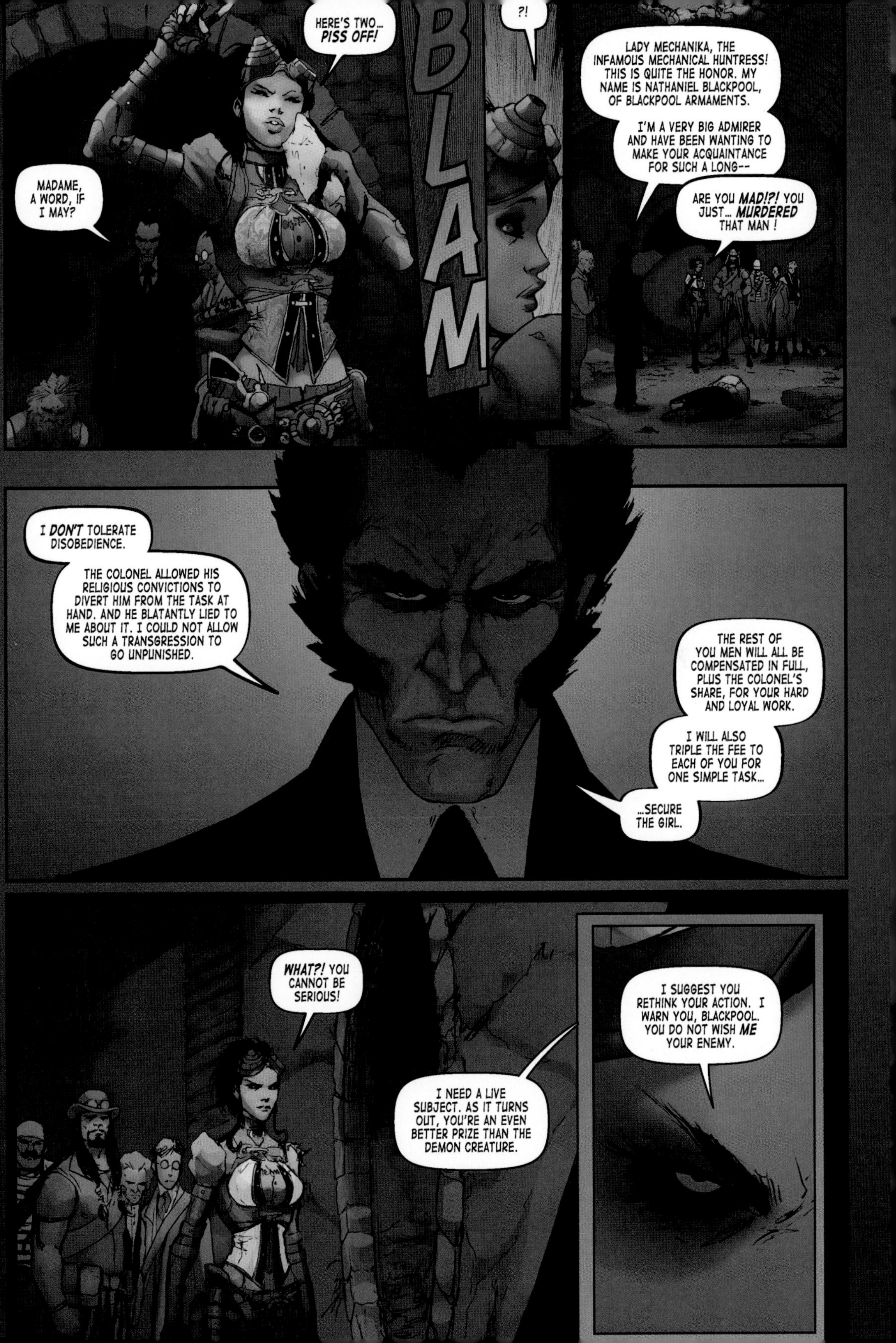
HERE'S TWO... *PISS OFF!*
MADAME, A WORD, IF I MAY?
BLAM
?!
LADY MECHANIKA, THE INFAMOUS MECHANICAL HUNTRESS! THIS IS QUITE THE HONOR. MY NAME IS NATHANIEL BLACKPOOL, OF BLACKPOOL ARMAMENTS.
I'M A VERY BIG ADMIRER AND HAVE BEEN WANTING TO MAKE YOUR ACQUAINTANCE FOR SUCH A LONG--
ARE YOU *MAD!?!* YOU JUST... *MURDERED* THAT MAN !
I *DON'T* TOLERATE DISOBEDIENCE.
THE COLONEL ALLOWED HIS RELIGIOUS CONVICTIONS TO DIVERT HIM FROM THE TASK AT HAND. AND HE BLATANTLY LIED TO ME ABOUT IT. I COULD NOT ALLOW SUCH A TRANSGRESSION TO GO UNPUNISHED.
THE REST OF YOU MEN WILL ALL BE COMPENSATED IN FULL, PLUS THE COLONEL'S SHARE, FOR YOUR HARD AND LOYAL WORK.
I WILL ALSO TRIPLE THE FEE TO EACH OF YOU FOR ONE SIMPLE TASK...
...SECURE THE GIRL.
WHAT?! YOU CANNOT BE SERIOUS!
I NEED A LIVE SUBJECT. AS IT TURNS OUT, YOU'RE AN EVEN BETTER PRIZE THAN THE DEMON CREATURE.
I SUGGEST YOU RETHINK YOUR ACTION. I WARN YOU, BLACKPOOL. YOU DO NOT WISH *ME* YOUR ENEMY.

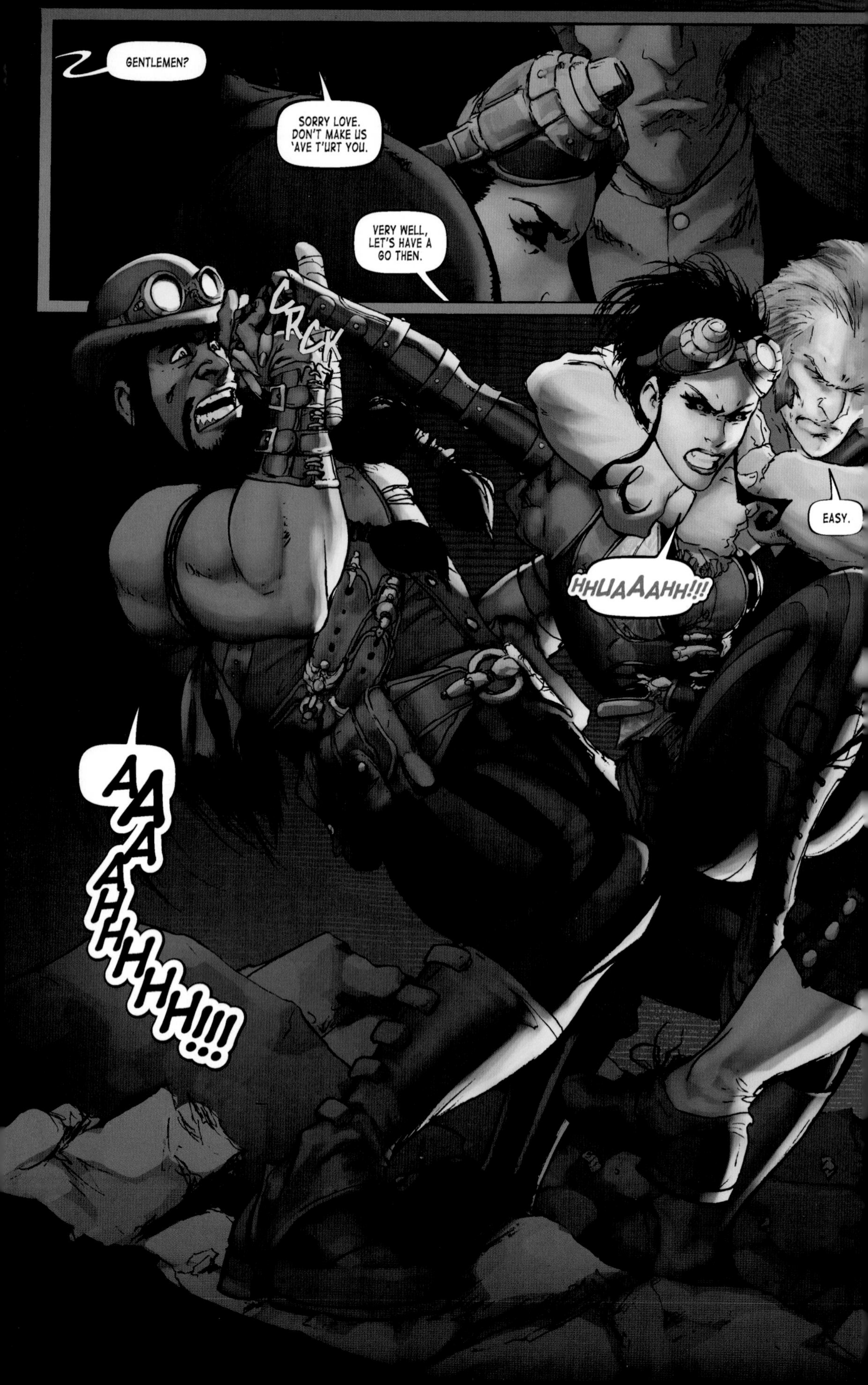
GENTLEMEN?
SORRY LOVE. DON'T MAKE US 'AVE T'URT YOU.
VERY WELL, LET'S HAVE A GO THEN.
CRCK
EASY.
HHUAAAHH!!!
AAAAHHHHH!!!

WHMP
UUNNGHH!!
AAAGGHH!
NRK
NCH
HUNGH!
PERHAPS IT WOULD BE WISEST TO DEPART, YOUR LORDSHIP.
HMMM... PERHAPS.
KRACK
HAUUGGH!
THUNKT
UNGH!

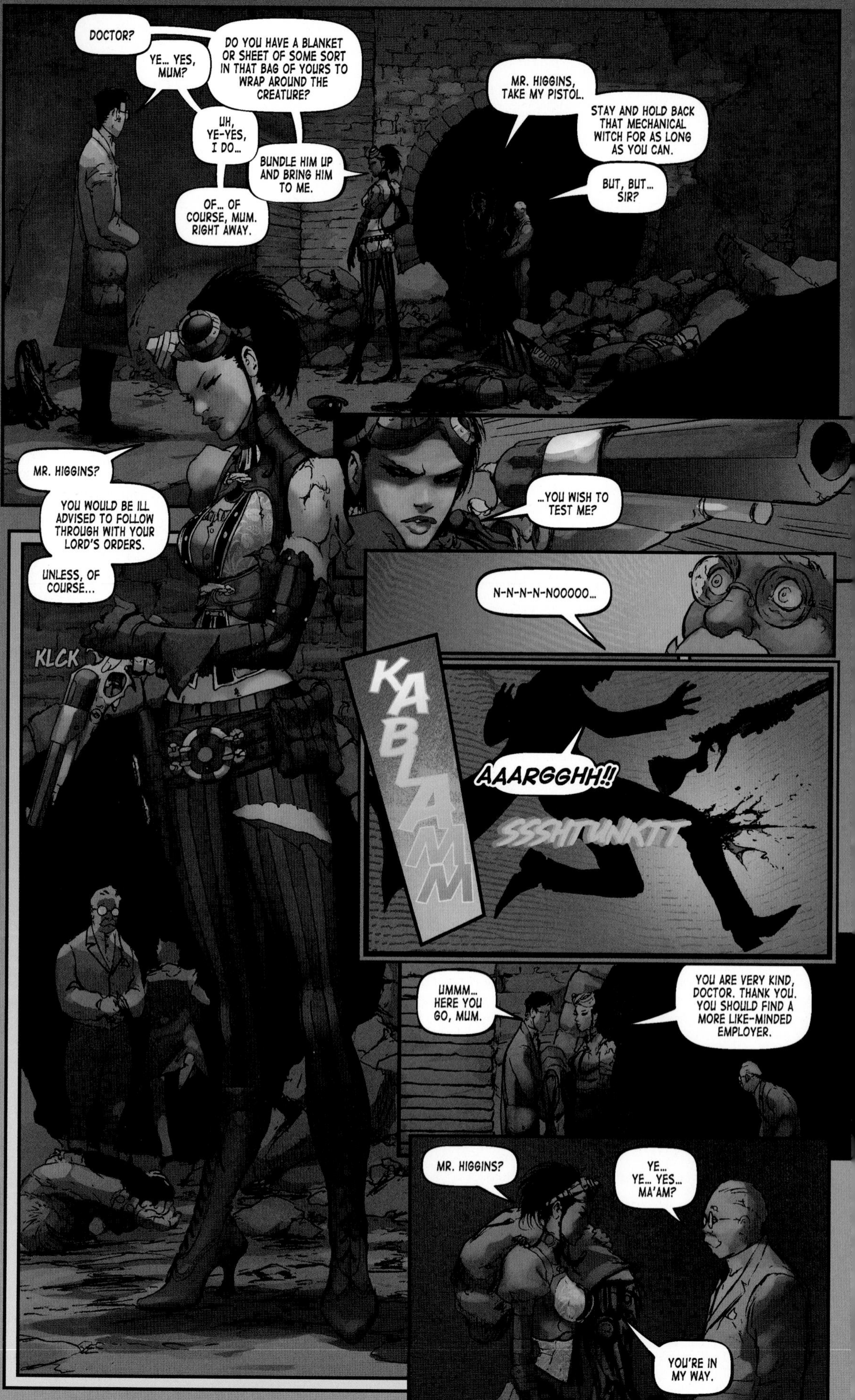
DOCTOR?
YE... YES, MUM?
DO YOU HAVE A BLANKET OR SHEET OF SOME SORT IN THAT BAG OF YOURS TO WRAP AROUND THE CREATURE?
UH, YE-YES, I DO...
BUNDLE HIM UP AND BRING HIM TO ME.
OF... OF COURSE, MUM. RIGHT AWAY.
MR. HIGGINS, TAKE MY PISTOL.
STAY AND HOLD BACK THAT MECHANICAL WITCH FOR AS LONG AS YOU CAN.
BUT, BUT... SIR?
MR. HIGGINS?
YOU WOULD BE ILL ADVISED TO FOLLOW THROUGH WITH YOUR LORD'S ORDERS.
UNLESS, OF COURSE...
KLCK
...YOU WISH TO TEST ME?
N-N-N-N-NOOOOO...
KABLAMM
AAARGGHH!!
SSSHTUNKTT
UMMM... HERE YOU GO, MUM.
YOU ARE VERY KIND, DOCTOR. THANK YOU. YOU SHOULD FIND A MORE LIKE-MINDED EMPLOYER.
MR. HIGGINS?
YE... YE... YES... MA'AM?
YOU'RE IN MY WAY.

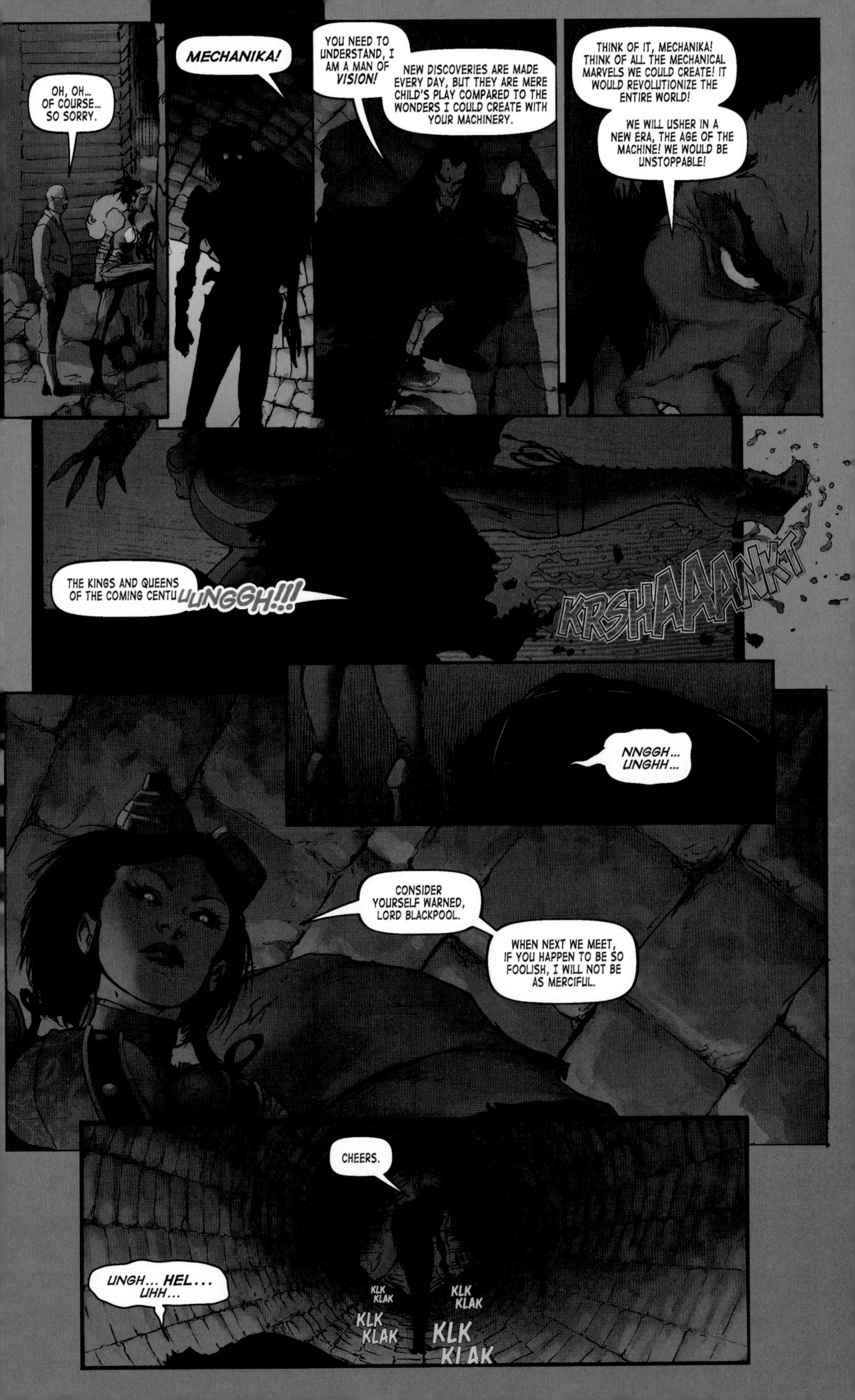
OH, OH... OF COURSE... SO SORRY.
MECHANIKA!
YOU NEED TO UNDERSTAND, I AM A MAN OF VISION!
NEW DISCOVERIES ARE MADE EVERY DAY, BUT THEY ARE MERE CHILD'S PLAY COMPARED TO THE WONDERS I COULD CREATE WITH YOUR MACHINERY.
THINK OF IT, MECHANIKA! THINK OF ALL THE MECHANICAL MARVELS WE COULD CREATE! IT WOULD REVOLUTIONIZE THE ENTIRE WORLD!
WE WILL USHER IN A NEW ERA, THE AGE OF THE MACHINE! WE WOULD BE UNSTOPPABLE!
THE KINGS AND QUEENS OF THE COMING CENTUUUNGGH!!!
KRSHAAAANKT
NNGGH... UNGHH...
CONSIDER YOURSELF WARNED, LORD BLACKPOOL.
WHEN NEXT WE MEET, IF YOU HAPPEN TO BE SO FOOLISH, I WILL NOT BE AS MERCIFUL.
CHEERS.
UNGH... HEL... UHH...
KLK KLAK
KLK KLAK
KLK KLAK
KLK KLAK

Chapter One

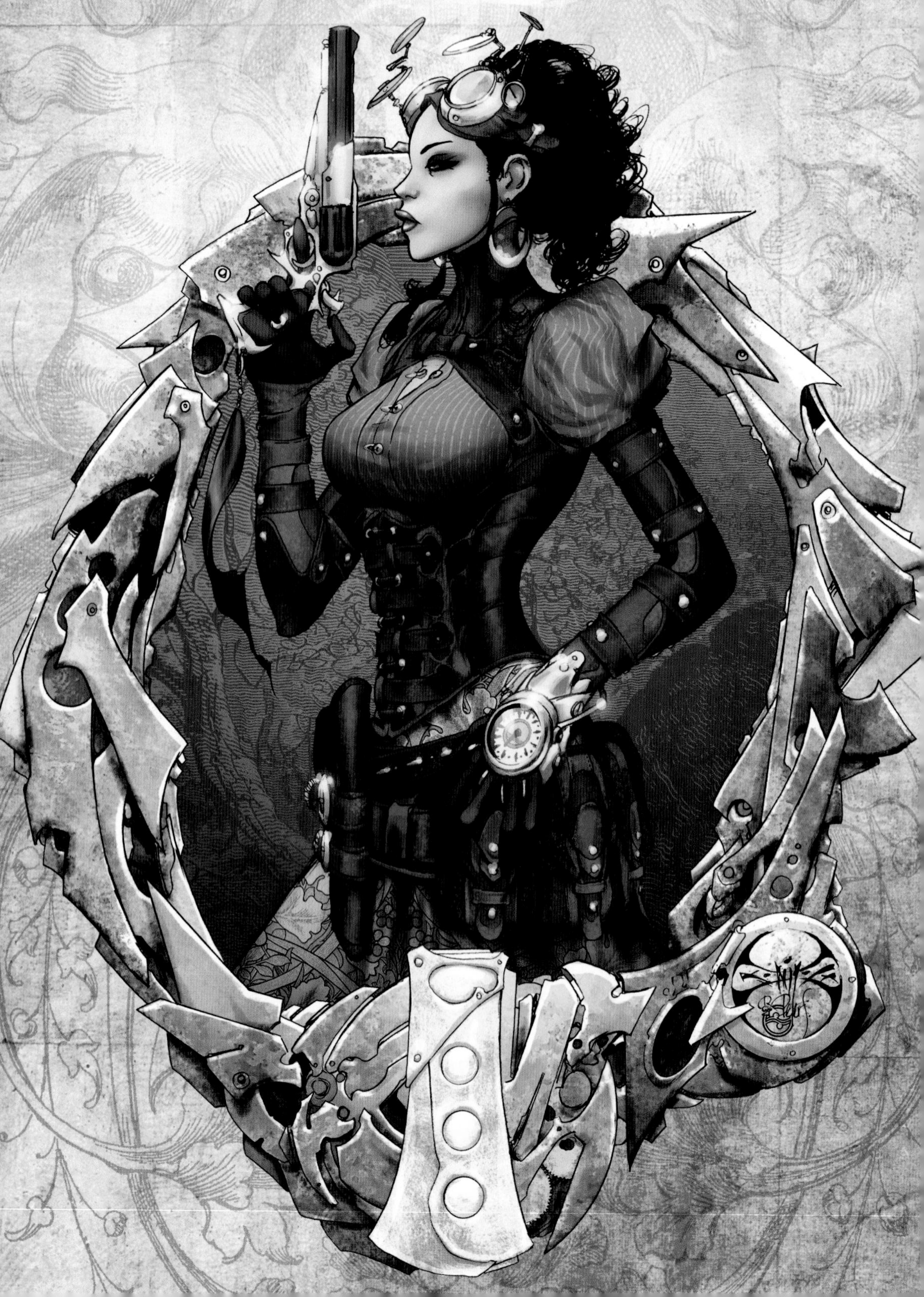

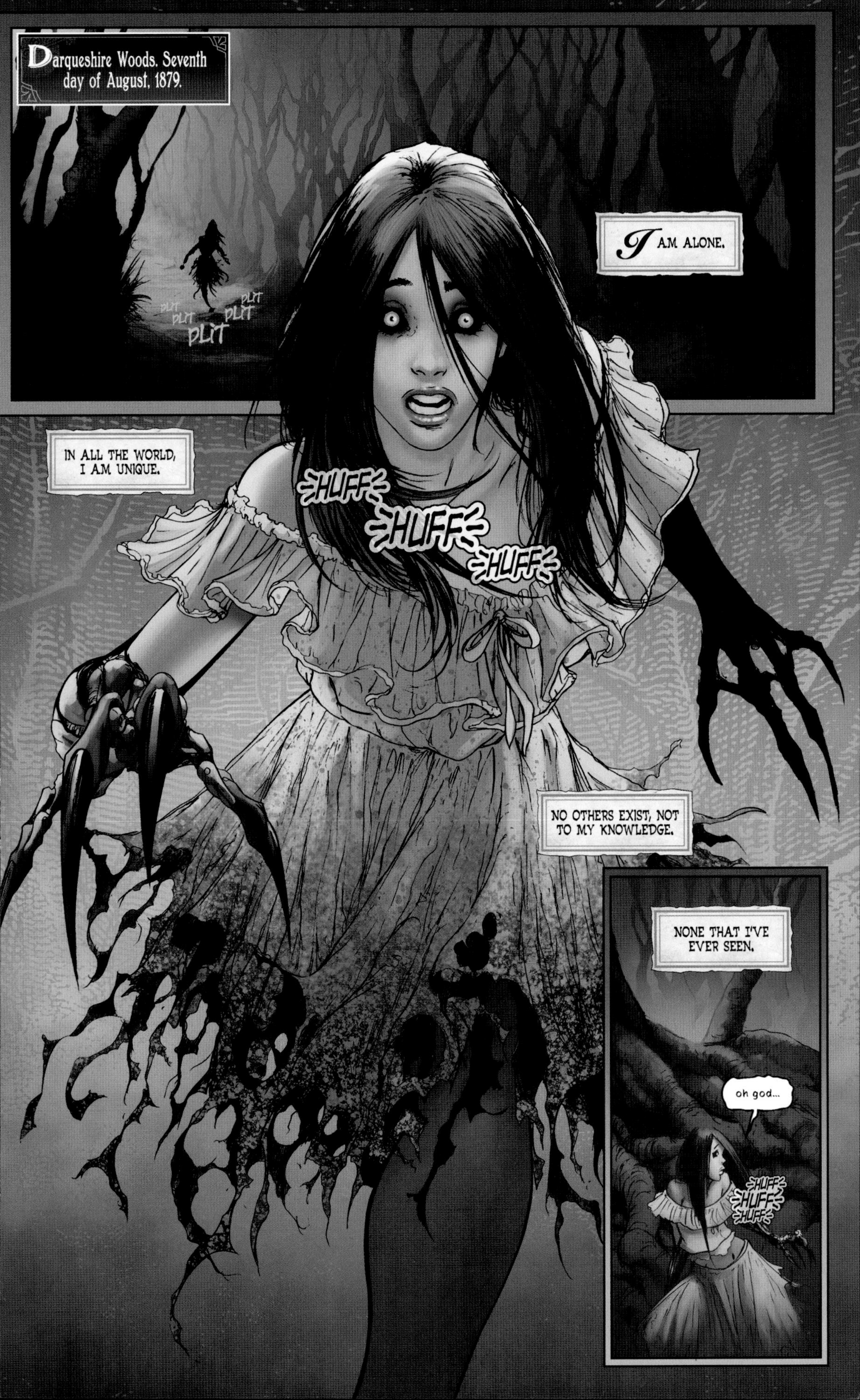
Darqueshire Woods. Seventh day of August, 1879.
I AM ALONE.
PLIT
PLIT
PLIT
PLIT
PLIT
IN ALL THE WORLD, I AM UNIQUE.
HUFF
HUFF
HUFF
NO OTHERS EXIST, NOT TO MY KNOWLEDGE.
NONE THAT I'VE EVER SEEN.
oh god...
HUFF
HUFF
HUFF

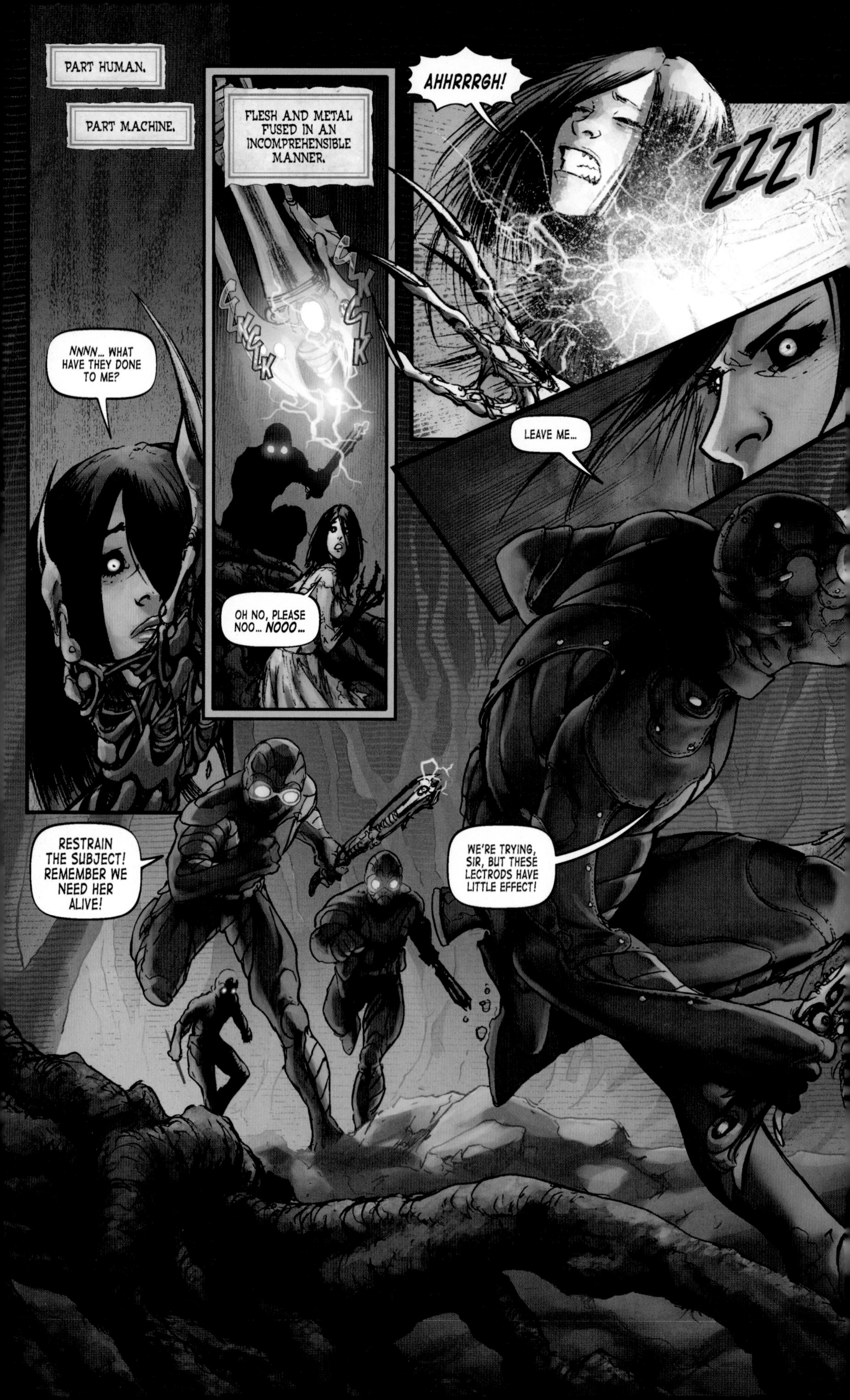
PART HUMAN.
PART MACHINE.
FLESH AND METAL FUSED IN AN INCOMPREHENSIBLE MANNER.
AHHRRRGH!
ZZZT
NNNN... WHAT HAVE THEY DONE TO ME?
OH NO, PLEASE NOO... NOOO...
LEAVE ME...
RESTRAIN THE SUBJECT! REMEMBER WE NEED HER ALIVE!
WE'RE TRYING, SIR, BUT THESE LECTRODS HAVE LITTLE EFFECT!

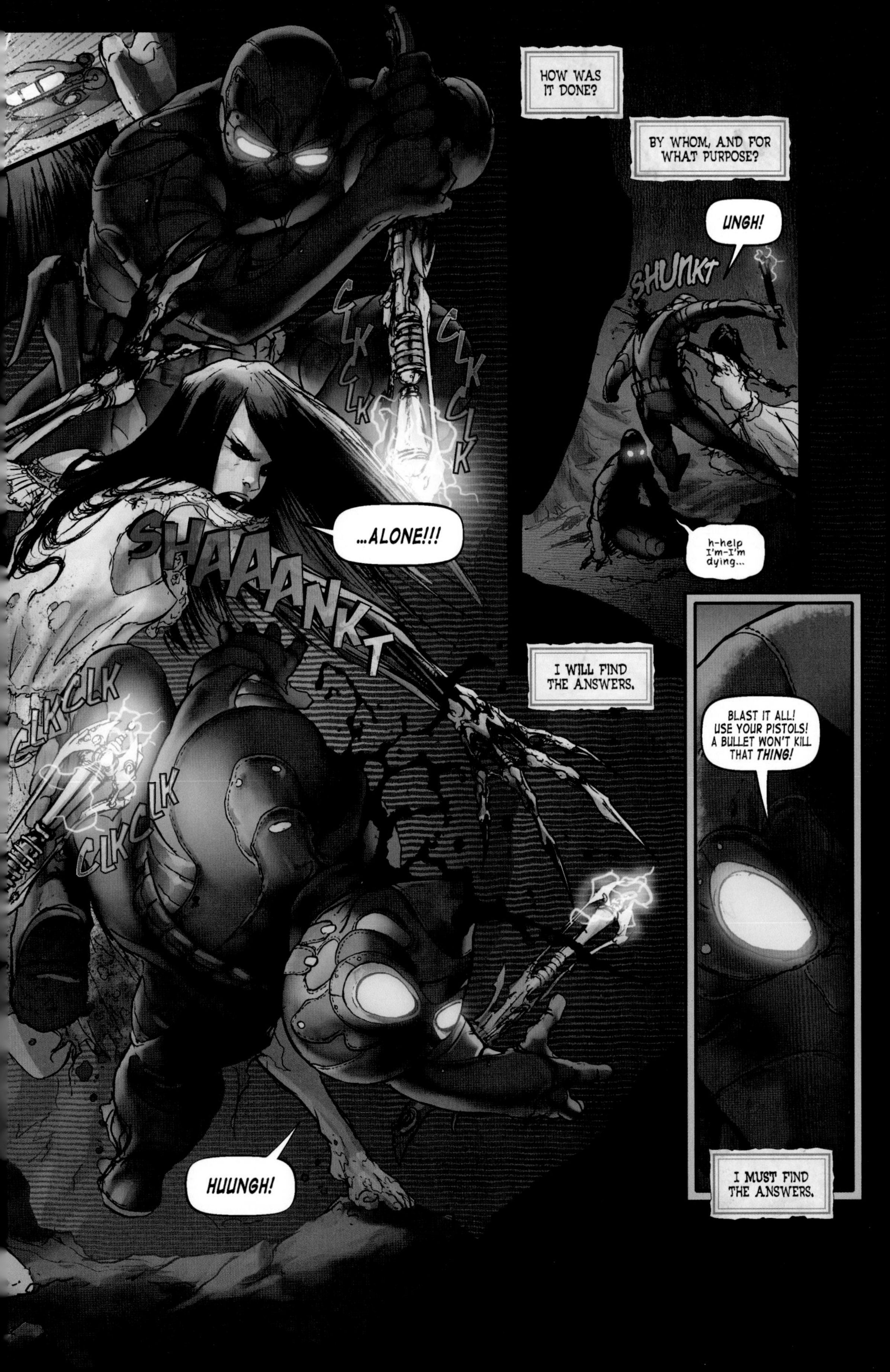

HOW WAS IT DONE?
BY WHOM, AND FOR WHAT PURPOSE?
CLK CLK
CLK CLK
...ALONE!!!
SHAAAANKT
UNGH!
SHUNKT
h-help I'm-I'm dying...
I WILL FIND THE ANSWERS.
BLAST IT ALL! USE YOUR PISTOLS! A BULLET WON'T KILL THAT THING!
CLKCLK
CLKCLK
HUUNGH!
I MUST FIND THE ANSWERS.

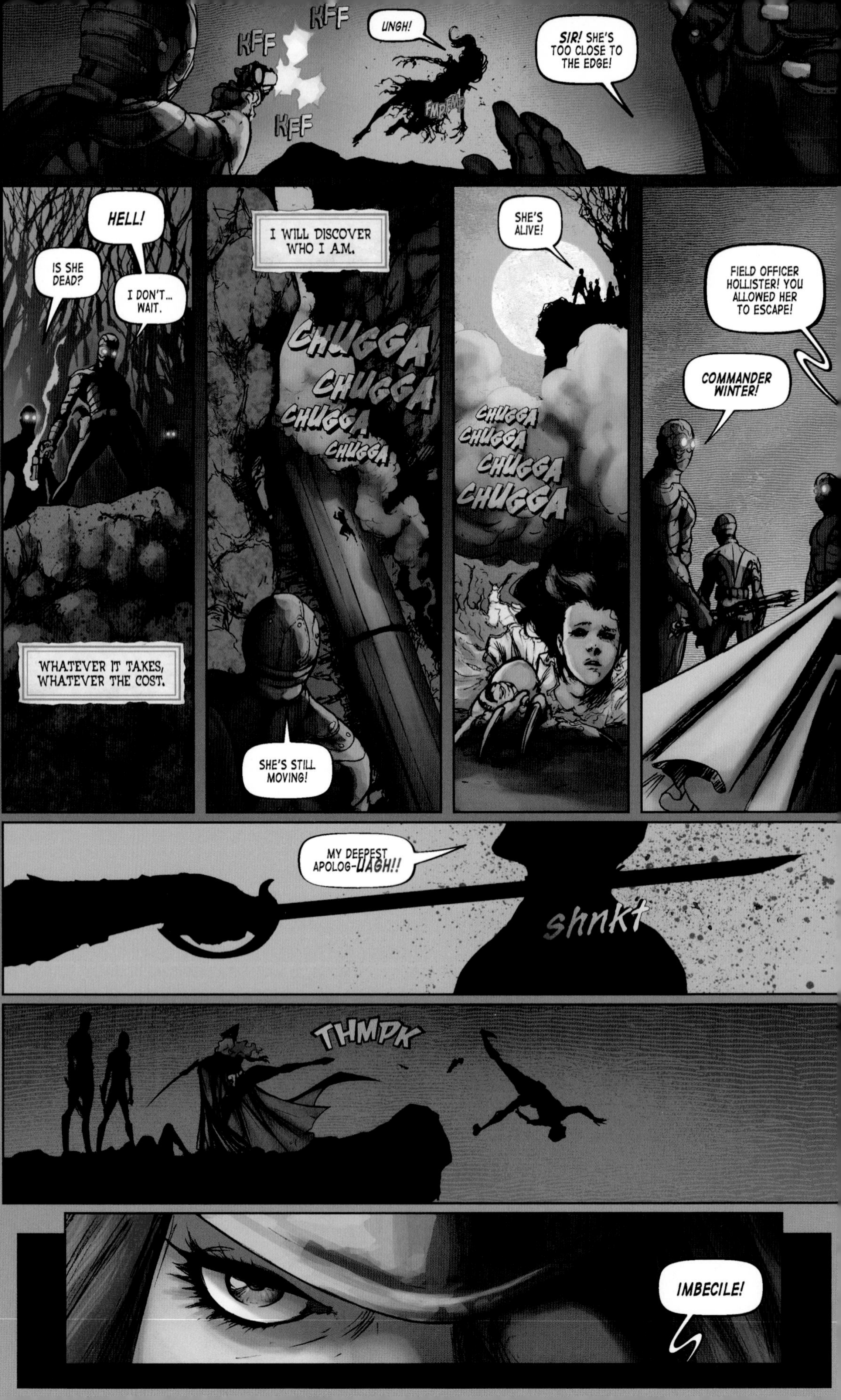
KFF
KFF
UNGH!
KFF
FMP FMP
SIR! SHE'S TOO CLOSE TO THE EDGE!
HELL!
IS SHE DEAD?
I DON'T... WAIT.
WHATEVER IT TAKES, WHATEVER THE COST.
I WILL DISCOVER WHO I AM.
CHUGGA
CHUGGA
CHUGGA
CHUGGA
SHE'S STILL MOVING!
SHE'S ALIVE!
CHUGGA
CHUGGA
CHUGGA
CHUGGA
FIELD OFFICER HOLLISTER! YOU ALLOWED HER TO ESCAPE!
COMMANDER WINTER!
MY DEEPEST APOLOG-UAGH!!
shnkt
THMPK
IMBECILE!

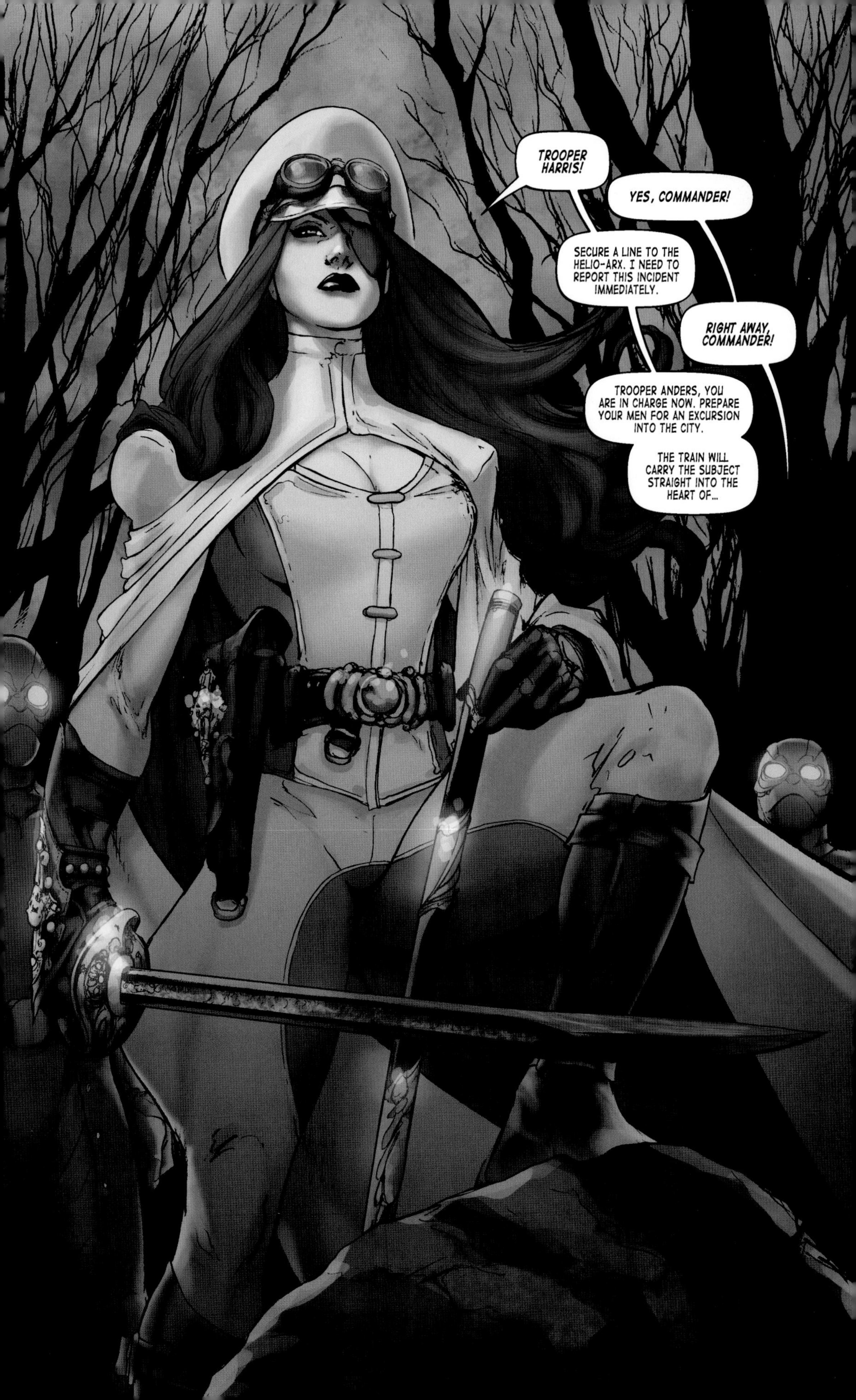
TROOPER HARRIS!
YES, COMMANDER!
SECURE A LINE TO THE HELIO-ARX. I NEED TO REPORT THIS INCIDENT IMMEDIATELY.
RIGHT AWAY, COMMANDER!
TROOPER ANDERS, YOU ARE IN CHARGE NOW. PREPARE YOUR MEN FOR AN EXCURSION INTO THE CITY.
THE TRAIN WILL CARRY THE SUBJECT STRAIGHT INTO THE HEART OF...

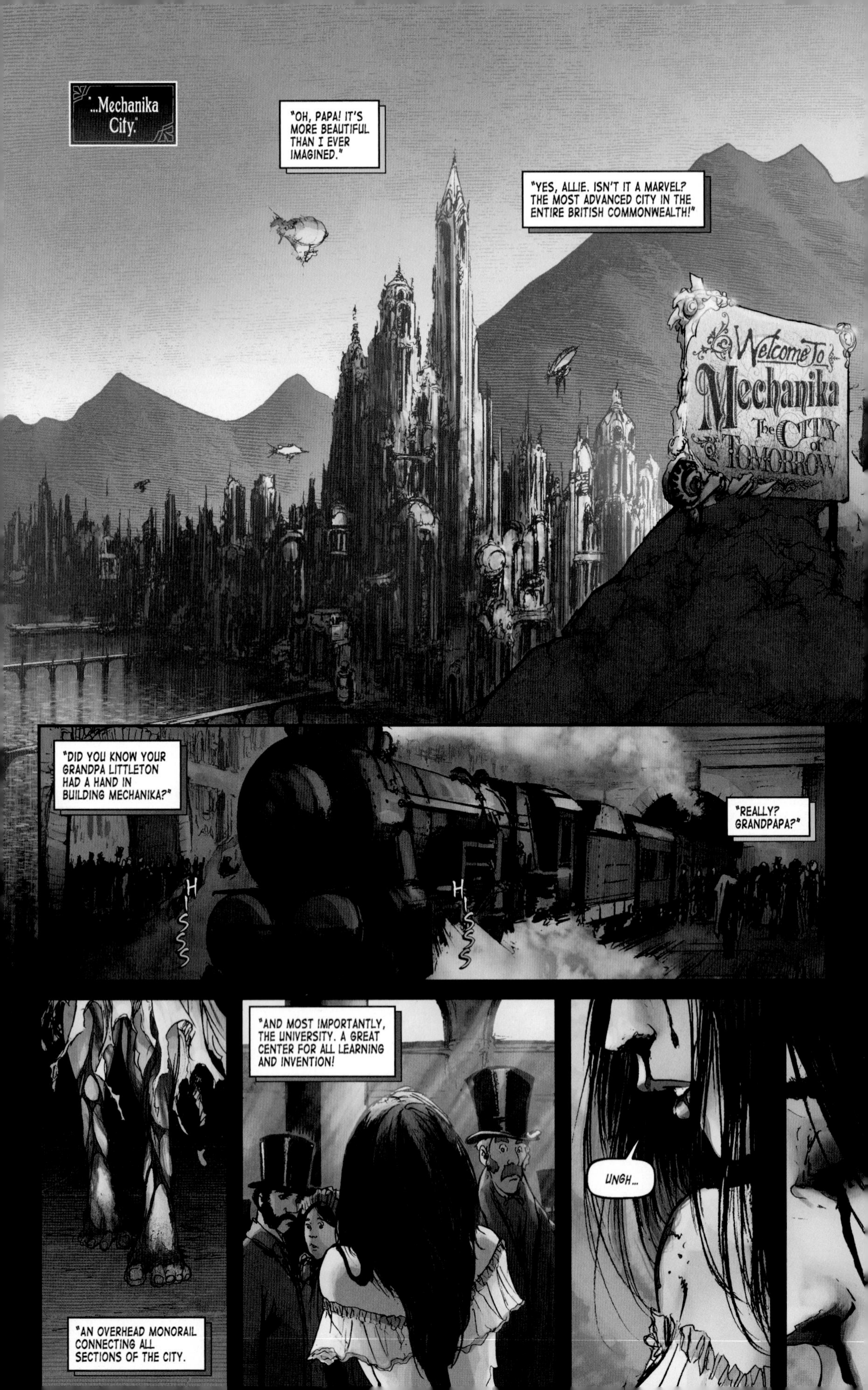
"...Mechanika City."
"OH, PAPA! IT'S MORE BEAUTIFUL THAN I EVER IMAGINED."
"YES, ALLIE. ISN'T IT A MARVEL? THE MOST ADVANCED CITY IN THE ENTIRE BRITISH COMMONWEALTH!"
Welcome To Mechanika The CITY of TOMORROW
"DID YOU KNOW YOUR GRANDPA LITTLETON HAD A HAND IN BUILDING MECHANIKA?"
HISSS
HISSS
"REALLY? GRANDPAPA?"
"AN OVERHEAD MONORAIL CONNECTING ALL SECTIONS OF THE CITY.
"AND MOST IMPORTANTLY, THE UNIVERSITY. A GREAT CENTER FOR ALL LEARNING AND INVENTION!
UNGH...

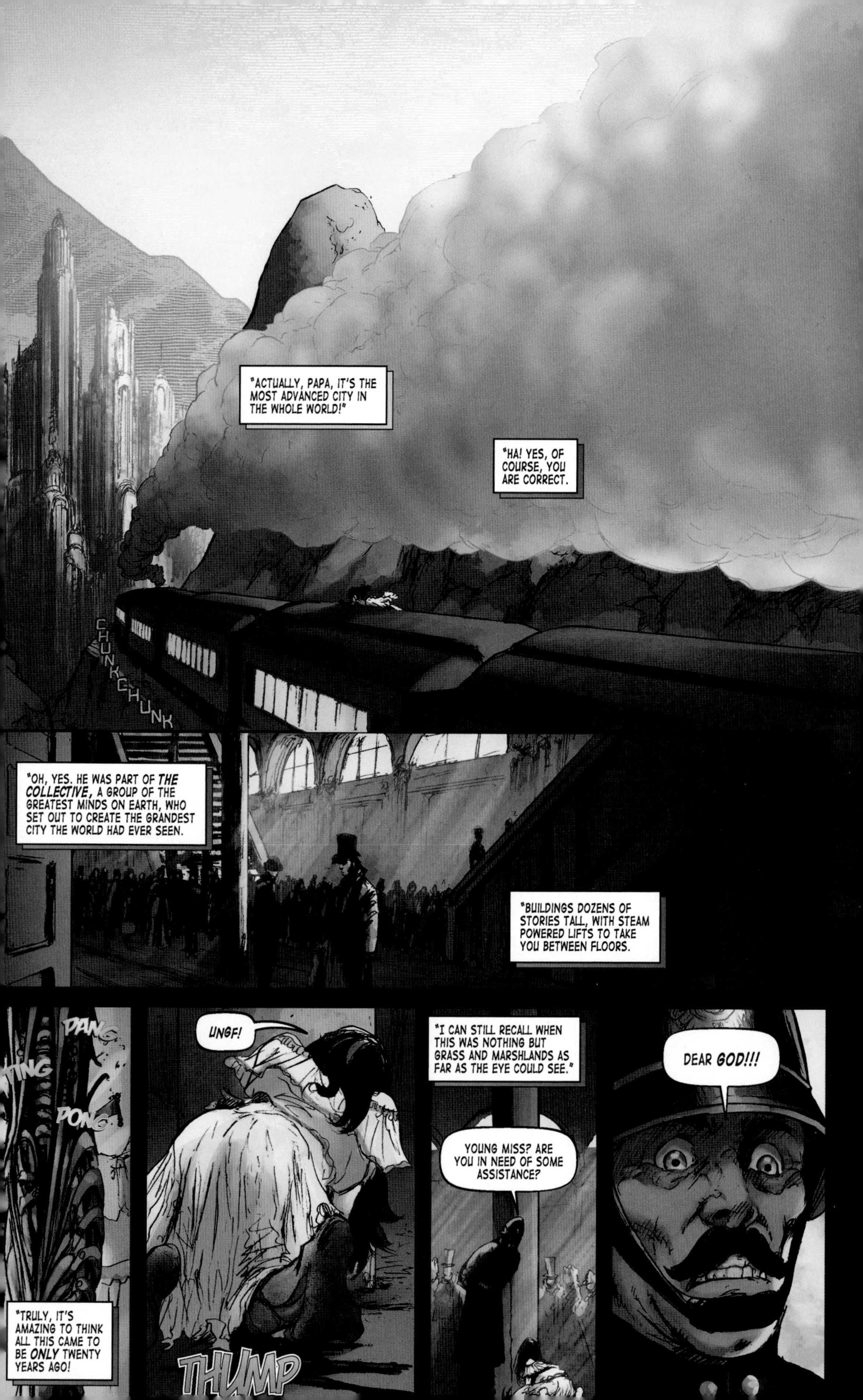
"ACTUALLY, PAPA, IT'S THE MOST ADVANCED CITY IN THE WHOLE WORLD!"
"HA! YES, OF COURSE, YOU ARE CORRECT.
CHUNK CHUNK
"OH, YES. HE WAS PART OF THE COLLECTIVE, A GROUP OF THE GREATEST MINDS ON EARTH, WHO SET OUT TO CREATE THE GRANDEST CITY THE WORLD HAD EVER SEEN.
"BUILDINGS DOZENS OF STORIES TALL, WITH STEAM POWERED LIFTS TO TAKE YOU BETWEEN FLOORS.
DANG
PONG
"TRULY, IT'S AMAZING TO THINK ALL THIS CAME TO BE ONLY TWENTY YEARS AGO!
UNGF!
THUMP
"I CAN STILL RECALL WHEN THIS WAS NOTHING BUT GRASS AND MARSHLANDS AS FAR AS THE EYE COULD SEE."
YOUNG MISS? ARE YOU IN NEED OF SOME ASSISTANCE?
DEAR GOD!!!

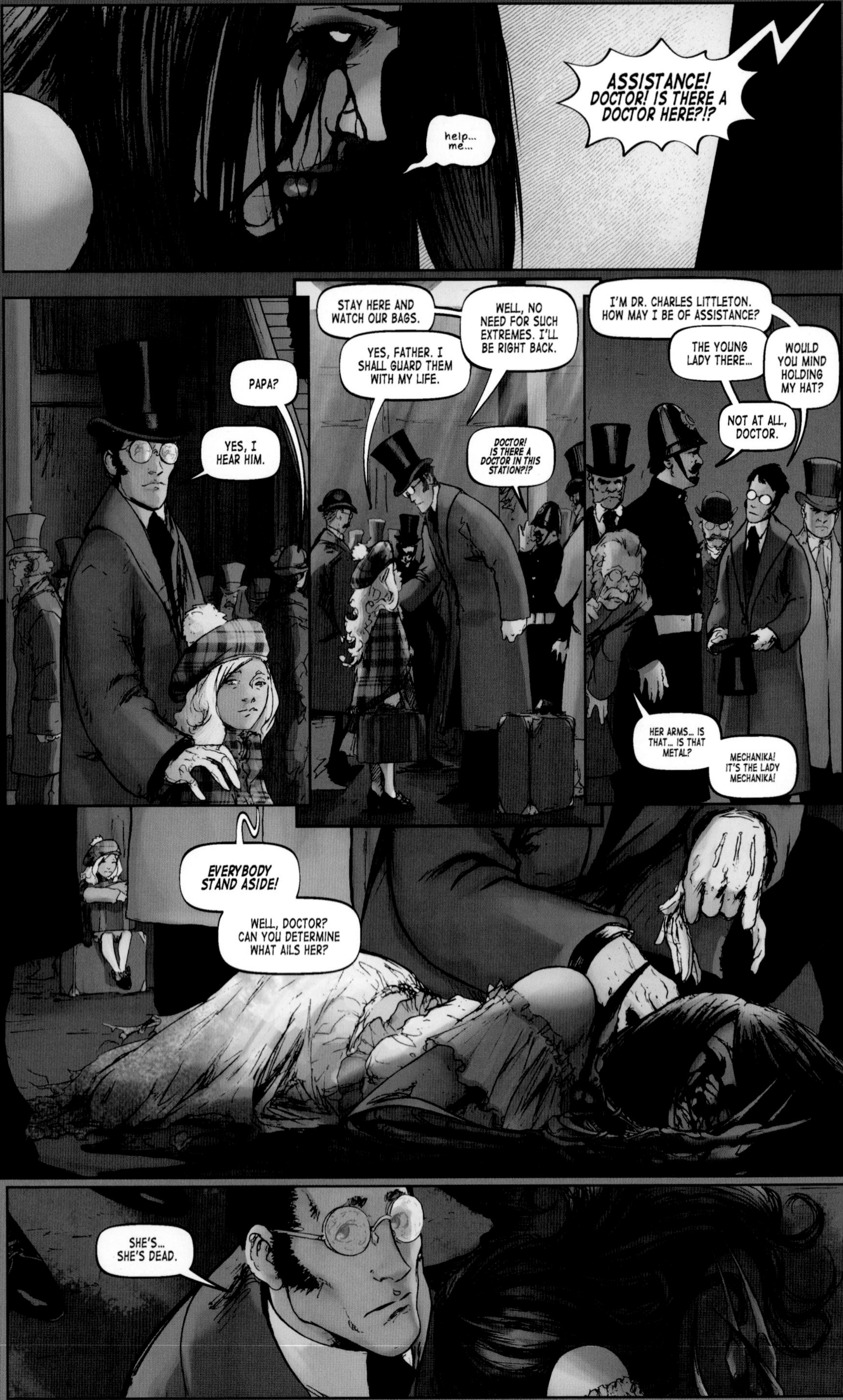
help... me...
ASSISTANCE! DOCTOR! IS THERE A DOCTOR HERE?!?
PAPA?
YES, I HEAR HIM.
STAY HERE AND WATCH OUR BAGS.
YES, FATHER. I SHALL GUARD THEM WITH MY LIFE.
WELL, NO NEED FOR SUCH EXTREMES. I'LL BE RIGHT BACK.
DOCTOR! IS THERE A DOCTOR IN THIS STATION?!?
I'M DR. CHARLES LITTLETON. HOW MAY I BE OF ASSISTANCE?
THE YOUNG LADY THERE...
WOULD YOU MIND HOLDING MY HAT?
NOT AT ALL, DOCTOR.
HER ARMS... IS THAT... IS THAT METAL?
MECHANIKA! IT'S THE LADY MECHANIKA!
EVERYBODY STAND ASIDE!
WELL, DOCTOR? CAN YOU DETERMINE WHAT AILS HER?
SHE'S... SHE'S DEAD.

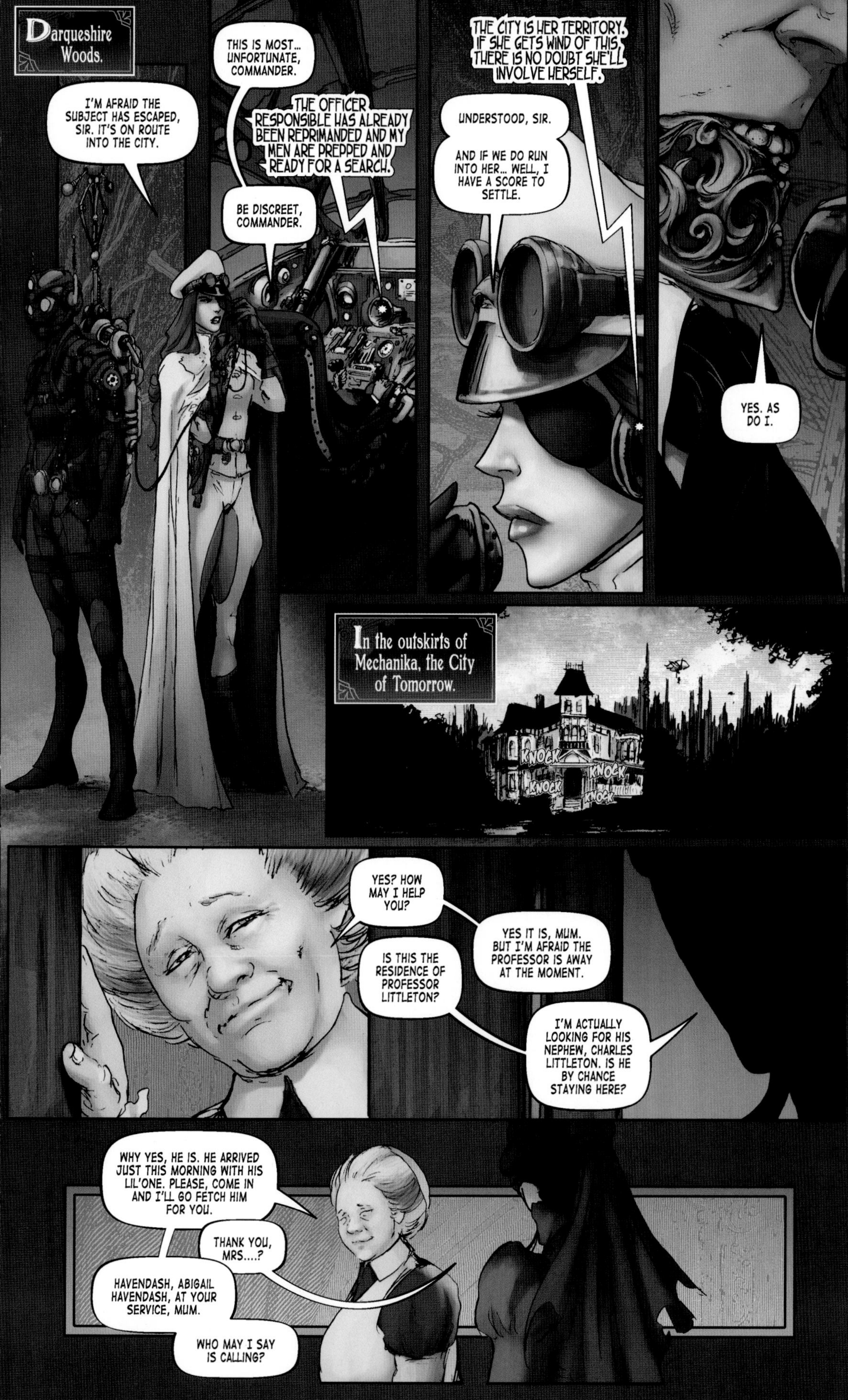
Darqueshire Woods.
I'M AFRAID THE SUBJECT HAS ESCAPED, SIR. IT'S ON ROUTE INTO THE CITY.
THIS IS MOST... UNFORTUNATE, COMMANDER.
THE OFFICER RESPONSIBLE HAS ALREADY BEEN REPRIMANDED AND MY MEN ARE PREPPED AND READY FOR A SEARCH.
BE DISCREET, COMMANDER.
THE CITY IS HER TERRITORY. IF SHE GETS WIND OF THIS, THERE IS NO DOUBT SHE'LL INVOLVE HERSELF.
UNDERSTOOD, SIR.
AND IF WE DO RUN INTO HER... WELL, I HAVE A SCORE TO SETTLE.
YES. AS DO I.
In the outskirts of Mechanika, the City of Tomorrow.
KNOCK KNOCK KNOCK KNOCK
YES? HOW MAY I HELP YOU?
IS THIS THE RESIDENCE OF PROFESSOR LITTLETON?
YES IT IS, MUM. BUT I'M AFRAID THE PROFESSOR IS AWAY AT THE MOMENT.
I'M ACTUALLY LOOKING FOR HIS NEPHEW, CHARLES LITTLETON. IS HE BY CHANCE STAYING HERE?
WHY YES, HE IS. HE ARRIVED JUST THIS MORNING WITH HIS LIL'ONE. PLEASE, COME IN AND I'LL GO FETCH HIM FOR YOU.
THANK YOU, MRS....?
HAVENDASH, ABIGAIL HAVENDASH, AT YOUR SERVICE, MUM.
WHO MAY I SAY IS CALLING?

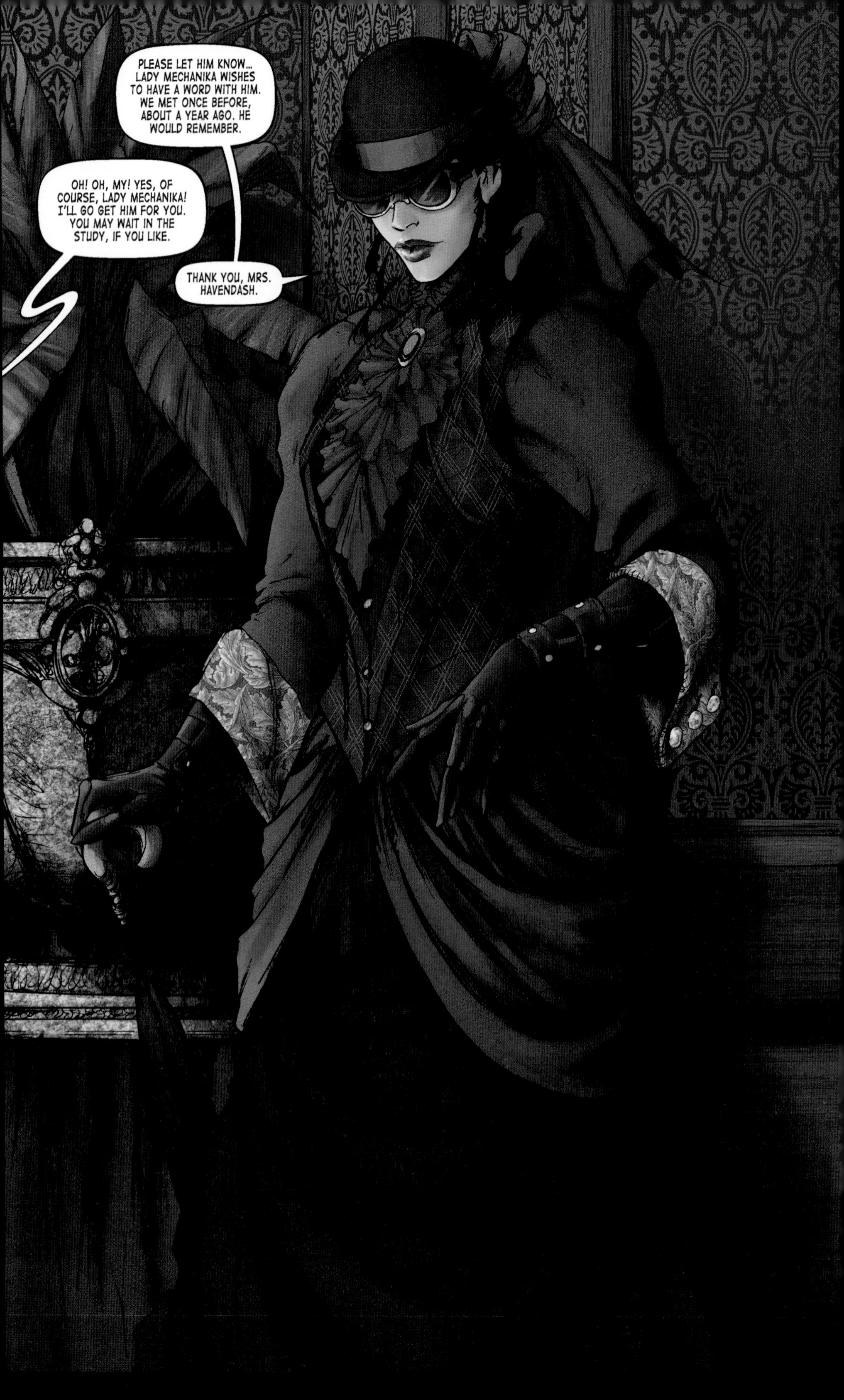
PLEASE LET HIM KNOW... LADY MECHANIKA WISHES TO HAVE A WORD WITH HIM. WE MET ONCE BEFORE, ABOUT A YEAR AGO. HE WOULD REMEMBER.
OH! OH, MY! YES, OF COURSE, LADY MECHANIKA! I'LL GO GET HIM FOR YOU. YOU MAY WAIT IN THE STUDY, IF YOU LIKE.
THANK YOU, MRS. HAVENDASH.

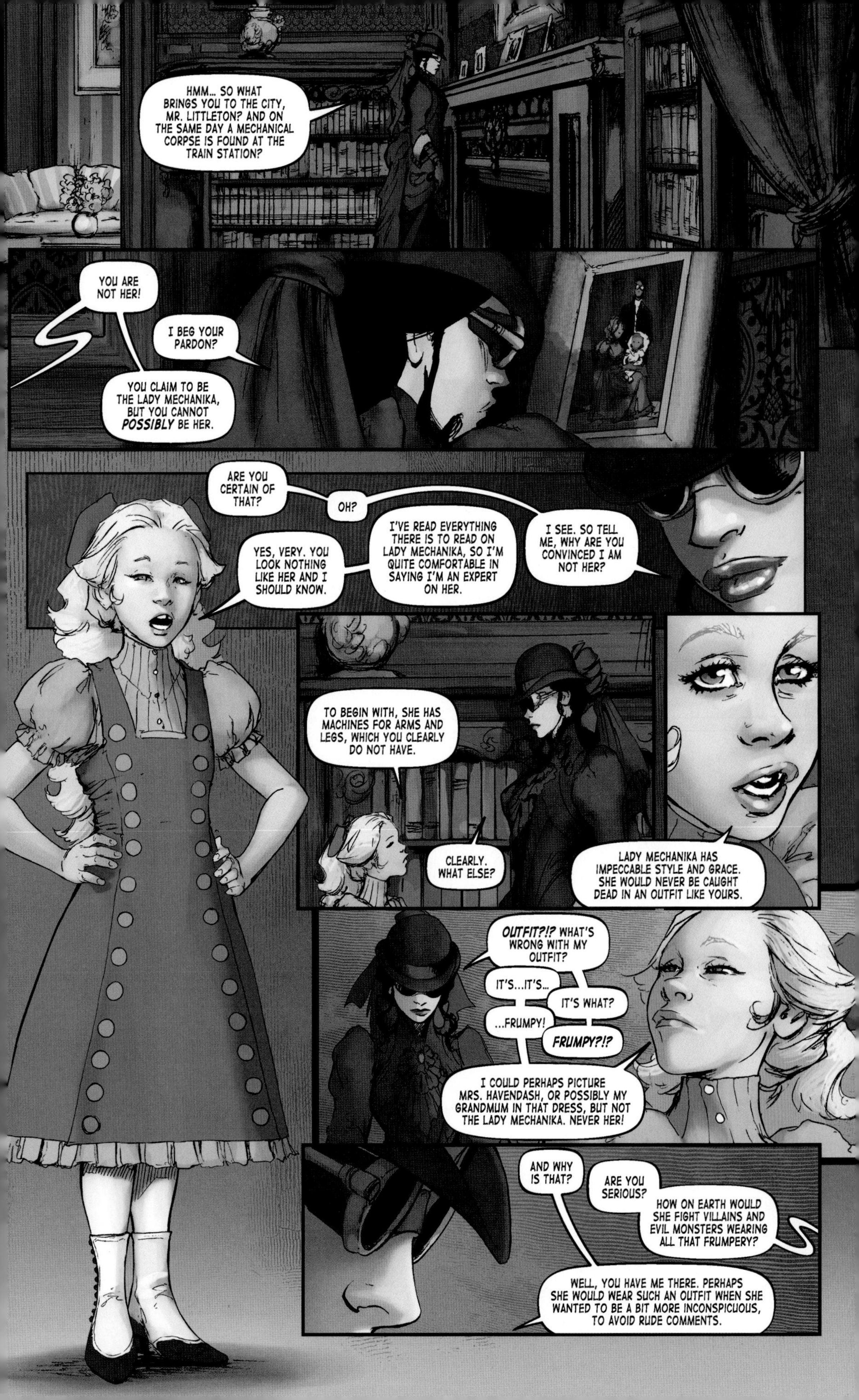
HMM... SO WHAT BRINGS YOU TO THE CITY, MR. LITTLETON? AND ON THE SAME DAY A MECHANICAL CORPSE IS FOUND AT THE TRAIN STATION?
YOU ARE NOT HER!
I BEG YOUR PARDON?
YOU CLAIM TO BE THE LADY MECHANIKA, BUT YOU CANNOT *POSSIBLY* BE HER.
ARE YOU CERTAIN OF THAT?
OH?
YES, VERY. YOU LOOK NOTHING LIKE HER AND I SHOULD KNOW.
I'VE READ EVERYTHING THERE IS TO READ ON LADY MECHANIKA, SO I'M QUITE COMFORTABLE IN SAYING I'M AN EXPERT ON HER.
I SEE. SO TELL ME, WHY ARE YOU CONVINCED I AM NOT HER?
TO BEGIN WITH, SHE HAS MACHINES FOR ARMS AND LEGS, WHICH YOU CLEARLY DO NOT HAVE.
CLEARLY. WHAT ELSE?
LADY MECHANIKA HAS IMPECCABLE STYLE AND GRACE. SHE WOULD NEVER BE CAUGHT DEAD IN AN OUTFIT LIKE YOURS.
OUTFIT?!? WHAT'S WRONG WITH MY OUTFIT?
IT'S...IT'S...
IT'S WHAT?
...FRUMPY!
FRUMPY?!?
I COULD PERHAPS PICTURE MRS. HAVENDASH, OR POSSIBLY MY GRANDMUM IN THAT DRESS, BUT NOT THE LADY MECHANIKA. NEVER HER!
AND WHY IS THAT?
ARE YOU SERIOUS?
HOW ON EARTH WOULD SHE FIGHT VILLAINS AND EVIL MONSTERS WEARING ALL THAT FRUMPERY?
WELL, YOU HAVE ME THERE. PERHAPS SHE WOULD WEAR SUCH AN OUTFIT WHEN SHE WANTED TO BE A BIT MORE INCONSPICUOUS, TO AVOID RUDE COMMENTS.

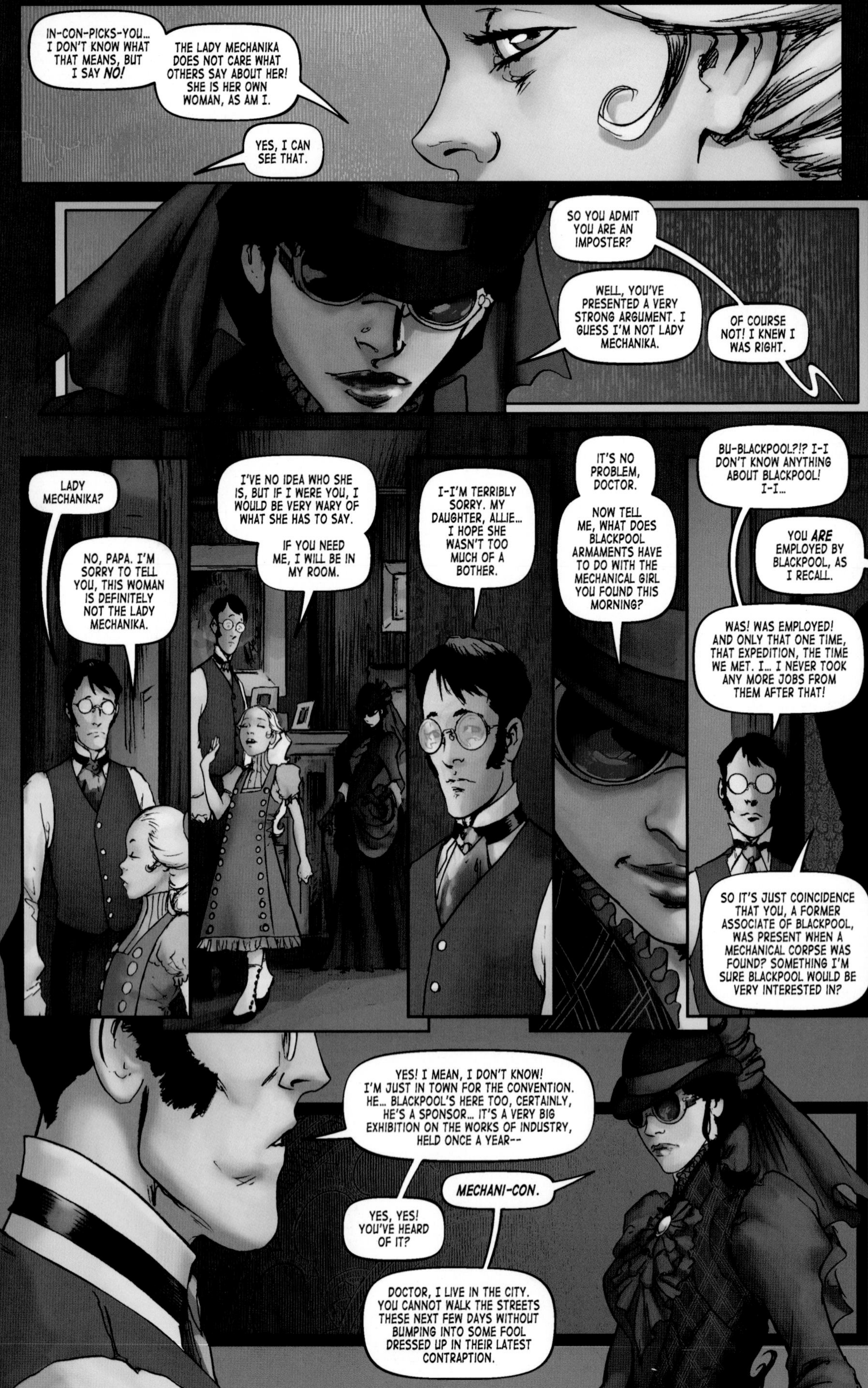
IN-CON-PICKS-YOU... I DON'T KNOW WHAT THAT MEANS, BUT I SAY *NO!*
THE LADY MECHANIKA DOES NOT CARE WHAT OTHERS SAY ABOUT HER! SHE IS HER OWN WOMAN, AS AM I.
YES, I CAN SEE THAT.
SO YOU ADMIT YOU ARE AN IMPOSTER?
WELL, YOU'VE PRESENTED A VERY STRONG ARGUMENT. I GUESS I'M NOT LADY MECHANIKA.
OF COURSE NOT! I KNEW I WAS RIGHT.
LADY MECHANIKA?
NO, PAPA. I'M SORRY TO TELL YOU, THIS WOMAN IS DEFINITELY NOT THE LADY MECHANIKA.
I'VE NO IDEA WHO SHE IS, BUT IF I WERE YOU, I WOULD BE VERY WARY OF WHAT SHE HAS TO SAY.
IF YOU NEED ME, I WILL BE IN MY ROOM.
I-I'M TERRIBLY SORRY. MY DAUGHTER, ALLIE... I HOPE SHE WASN'T TOO MUCH OF A BOTHER.
IT'S NO PROBLEM, DOCTOR.
NOW TELL ME, WHAT DOES BLACKPOOL ARMAMENTS HAVE TO DO WITH THE MECHANICAL GIRL YOU FOUND THIS MORNING?
BU-BLACKPOOL?!? I-I DON'T KNOW ANYTHING ABOUT BLACKPOOL! I-I...
YOU *ARE* EMPLOYED BY BLACKPOOL, AS I RECALL.
WAS! WAS EMPLOYED! AND ONLY THAT ONE TIME, THAT EXPEDITION, THE TIME WE MET. I... I NEVER TOOK ANY MORE JOBS FROM THEM AFTER THAT!
SO IT'S JUST COINCIDENCE THAT YOU, A FORMER ASSOCIATE OF BLACKPOOL, WAS PRESENT WHEN A MECHANICAL CORPSE WAS FOUND? SOMETHING I'M SURE BLACKPOOL WOULD BE VERY INTERESTED IN?
YES! I MEAN, I DON'T KNOW! I'M JUST IN TOWN FOR THE CONVENTION. HE... BLACKPOOL'S HERE TOO, CERTAINLY, HE'S A SPONSOR... IT'S A VERY BIG EXHIBITION ON THE WORKS OF INDUSTRY, HELD ONCE A YEAR--
MECHANI-CON.
YES, YES! YOU'VE HEARD OF IT?
DOCTOR, I LIVE IN THE CITY. YOU CANNOT WALK THE STREETS THESE NEXT FEW DAYS WITHOUT BUMPING INTO SOME FOOL DRESSED UP IN THEIR LATEST CONTRAPTION.

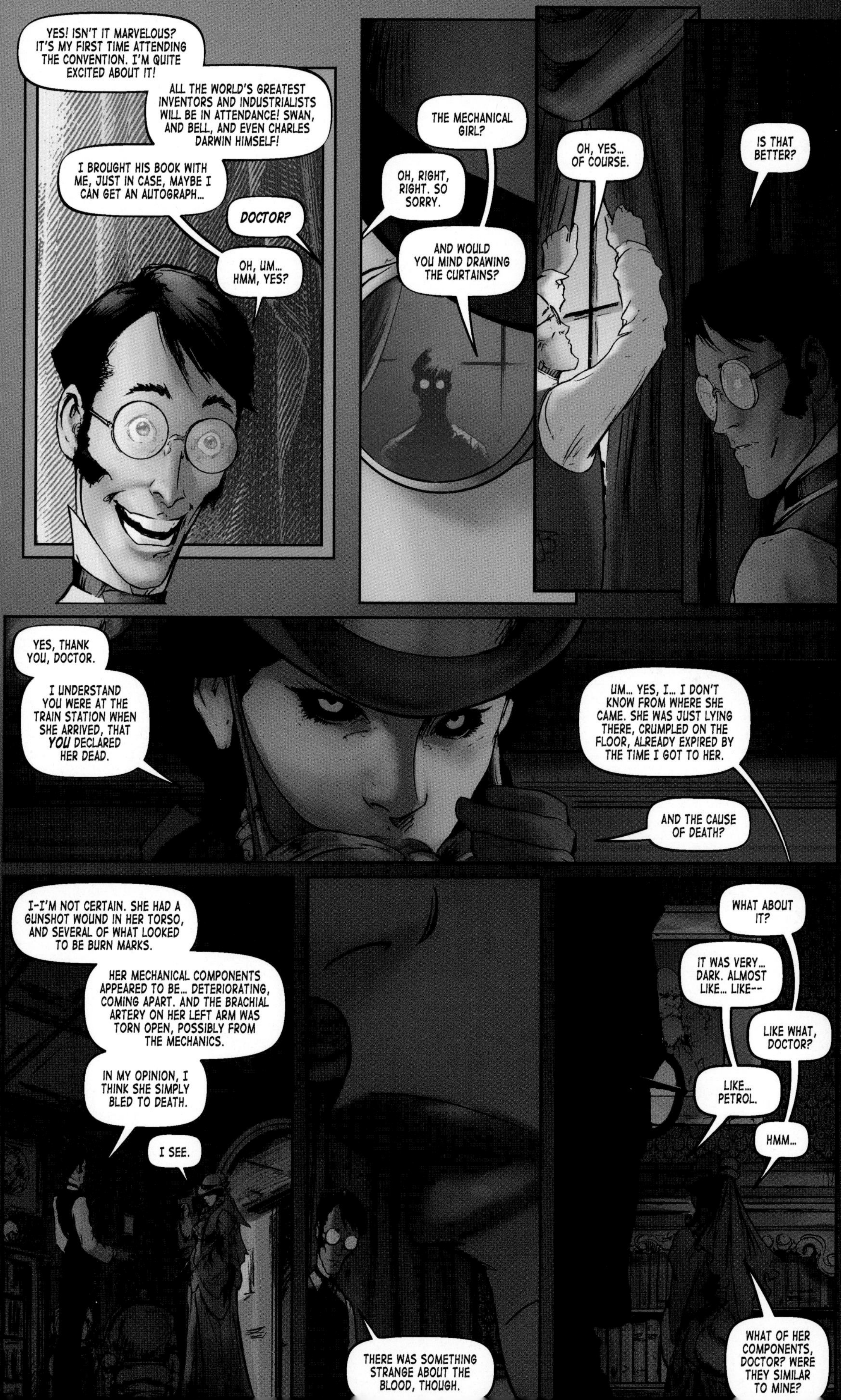
YES! ISN'T IT MARVELOUS? IT'S MY FIRST TIME ATTENDING THE CONVENTION. I'M QUITE EXCITED ABOUT IT!
ALL THE WORLD'S GREATEST INVENTORS AND INDUSTRIALISTS WILL BE IN ATTENDANCE! SWAN, AND BELL, AND EVEN CHARLES DARWIN HIMSELF!
I BROUGHT HIS BOOK WITH ME, JUST IN CASE, MAYBE I CAN GET AN AUTOGRAPH...
DOCTOR?
OH, UM... HMM, YES?
THE MECHANICAL GIRL?
OH, RIGHT, RIGHT. SO SORRY.
AND WOULD YOU MIND DRAWING THE CURTAINS?
OH, YES... OF COURSE.
IS THAT BETTER?
YES, THANK YOU, DOCTOR.
I UNDERSTAND YOU WERE AT THE TRAIN STATION WHEN SHE ARRIVED, THAT *YOU* DECLARED HER DEAD.
UM... YES, I... I DON'T KNOW FROM WHERE SHE CAME. SHE WAS JUST LYING THERE, CRUMPLED ON THE FLOOR, ALREADY EXPIRED BY THE TIME I GOT TO HER.
AND THE CAUSE OF DEATH?
I-I'M NOT CERTAIN. SHE HAD A GUNSHOT WOUND IN HER TORSO, AND SEVERAL OF WHAT LOOKED TO BE BURN MARKS.
HER MECHANICAL COMPONENTS APPEARED TO BE... DETERIORATING, COMING APART. AND THE BRACHIAL ARTERY ON HER LEFT ARM WAS TORN OPEN, POSSIBLY FROM THE MECHANICS.
IN MY OPINION, I THINK SHE SIMPLY BLED TO DEATH.
I SEE.
THERE WAS SOMETHING STRANGE ABOUT THE BLOOD, THOUGH.
WHAT ABOUT IT?
IT WAS VERY... DARK. ALMOST LIKE... LIKE--
LIKE WHAT, DOCTOR?
LIKE... PETROL.
HMM...
WHAT OF HER COMPONENTS, DOCTOR? WERE THEY SIMILAR TO MINE?

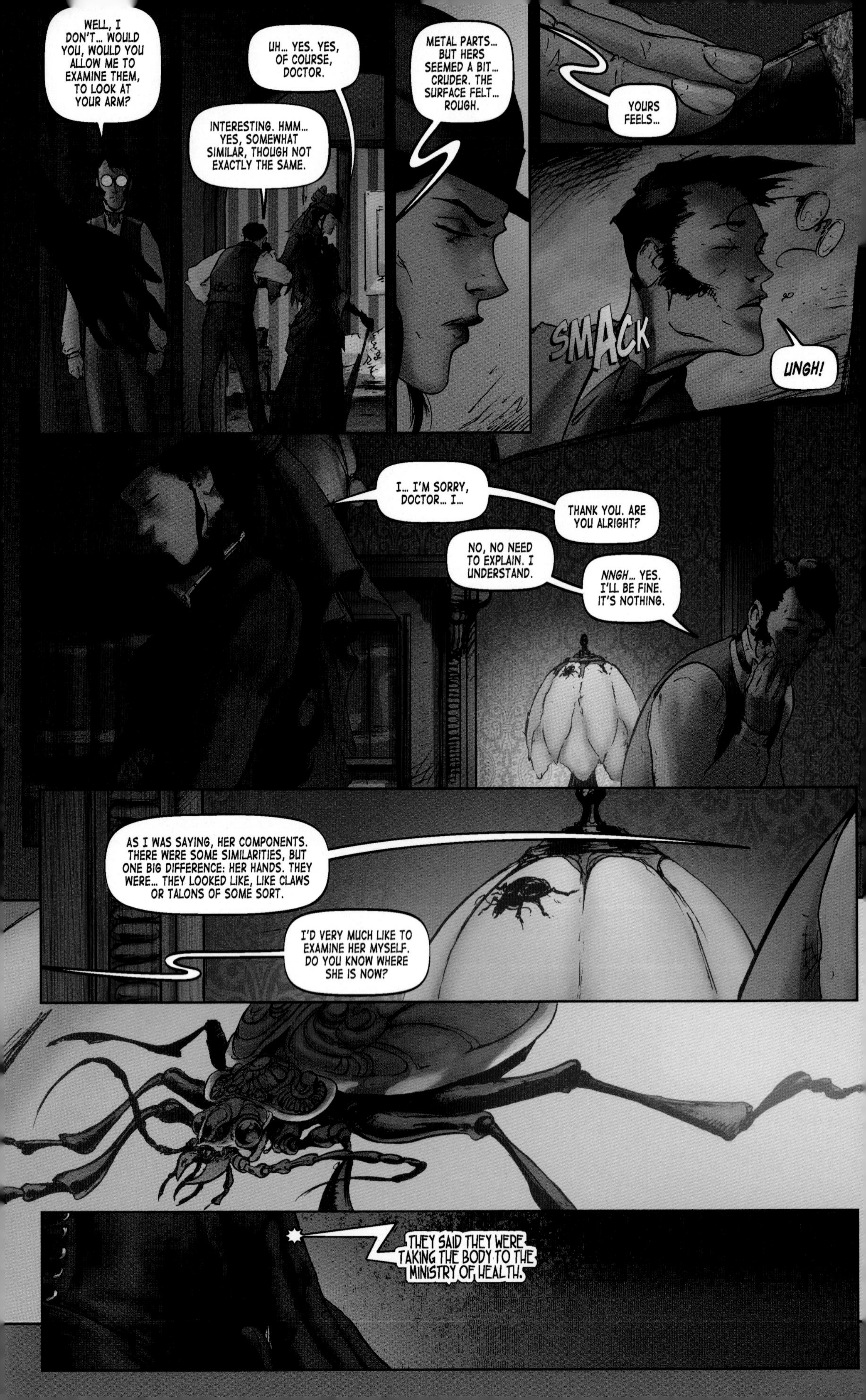
WELL, I DON'T... WOULD YOU, WOULD YOU ALLOW ME TO EXAMINE THEM, TO LOOK AT YOUR ARM?
UH... YES. YES, OF COURSE, DOCTOR.
INTERESTING. HMM... YES, SOMEWHAT SIMILAR, THOUGH NOT EXACTLY THE SAME.
METAL PARTS... BUT HERS SEEMED A BIT... CRUDER. THE SURFACE FELT... ROUGH.
YOURS FEELS...
SMACK
UNGH!
I... I'M SORRY, DOCTOR... I...
THANK YOU. ARE YOU ALRIGHT?
NO, NO NEED TO EXPLAIN. I UNDERSTAND.
NNGH... YES. I'LL BE FINE. IT'S NOTHING.
AS I WAS SAYING, HER COMPONENTS. THERE WERE SOME SIMILARITIES, BUT ONE BIG DIFFERENCE: HER HANDS. THEY WERE... THEY LOOKED LIKE, LIKE CLAWS OR TALONS OF SOME SORT.
I'D VERY MUCH LIKE TO EXAMINE HER MYSELF. DO YOU KNOW WHERE SHE IS NOW?
THEY SAID THEY WERE TAKING THE BODY TO THE MINISTRY OF HEALTH.

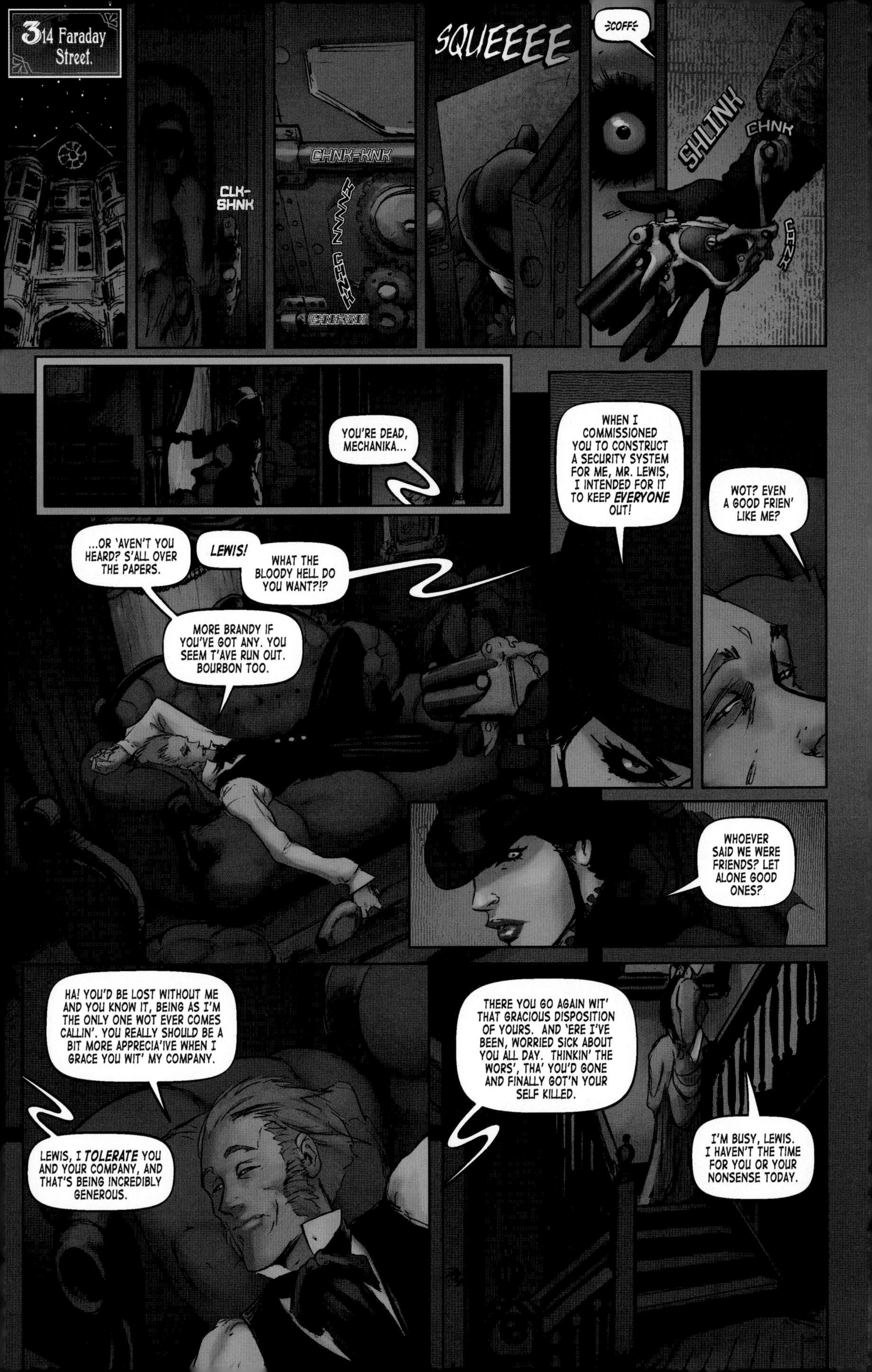
314 Faraday Street.
CLK-SHNK
CHNK-KNK
NNNNN
CHNK
CHNK-KNK
SQUEEEE
COFF
SHLINK
CHNK
CHNK
YOU'RE DEAD, MECHANIKA...
...OR 'AVEN'T YOU HEARD? S'ALL OVER THE PAPERS.
LEWIS!
WHAT THE BLOODY HELL DO YOU WANT?!?
MORE BRANDY IF YOU'VE GOT ANY. YOU SEEM T'AVE RUN OUT. BOURBON TOO.
WHEN I COMMISSIONED YOU TO CONSTRUCT A SECURITY SYSTEM FOR ME, MR. LEWIS, I INTENDED FOR IT TO KEEP EVERYONE OUT!
WOT? EVEN A GOOD FRIEN' LIKE ME?
WHOEVER SAID WE WERE FRIENDS? LET ALONE GOOD ONES?
HA! YOU'D BE LOST WITHOUT ME AND YOU KNOW IT, BEING AS I'M THE ONLY ONE WOT EVER COMES CALLIN'. YOU REALLY SHOULD BE A BIT MORE APPRECIA'IVE WHEN I GRACE YOU WIT' MY COMPANY.
LEWIS, I TOLERATE YOU AND YOUR COMPANY, AND THAT'S BEING INCREDIBLY GENEROUS.
THERE YOU GO AGAIN WIT' THAT GRACIOUS DISPOSITION OF YOURS. AND 'ERE I'VE BEEN, WORRIED SICK ABOUT YOU ALL DAY. THINKIN' THE WORS', THA' YOU'D GONE AND FINALLY GOT'N YOUR SELF KILLED.
I'M BUSY, LEWIS. I HAVEN'T THE TIME FOR YOU OR YOUR NONSENSE TODAY.

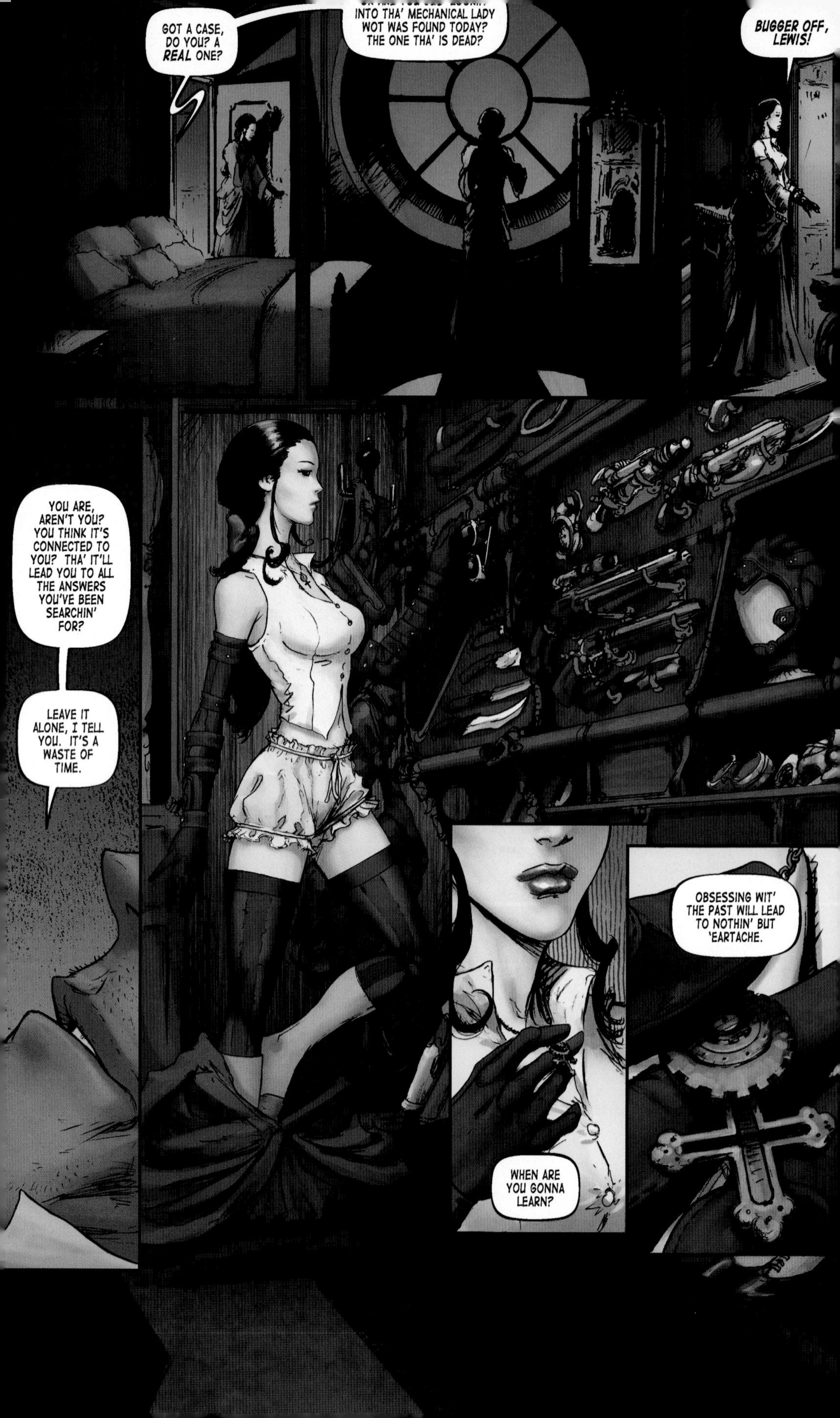
GOT A CASE, DO YOU? A *REAL* ONE?
INTO THA' MECHANICAL LADY WOT WAS FOUND TODAY? THE ONE THA' IS DEAD?
BUGGER OFF, LEWIS!
YOU ARE, AREN'T YOU? YOU THINK IT'S CONNECTED TO YOU? THA' IT'LL LEAD YOU TO ALL THE ANSWERS YOU'VE BEEN SEARCHIN' FOR?
LEAVE IT ALONE, I TELL YOU. IT'S A WASTE OF TIME.
WHEN ARE YOU GONNA LEARN?
OBSESSING WIT' THE PAST WILL LEAD TO NOTHIN' BUT 'EARTACHE.

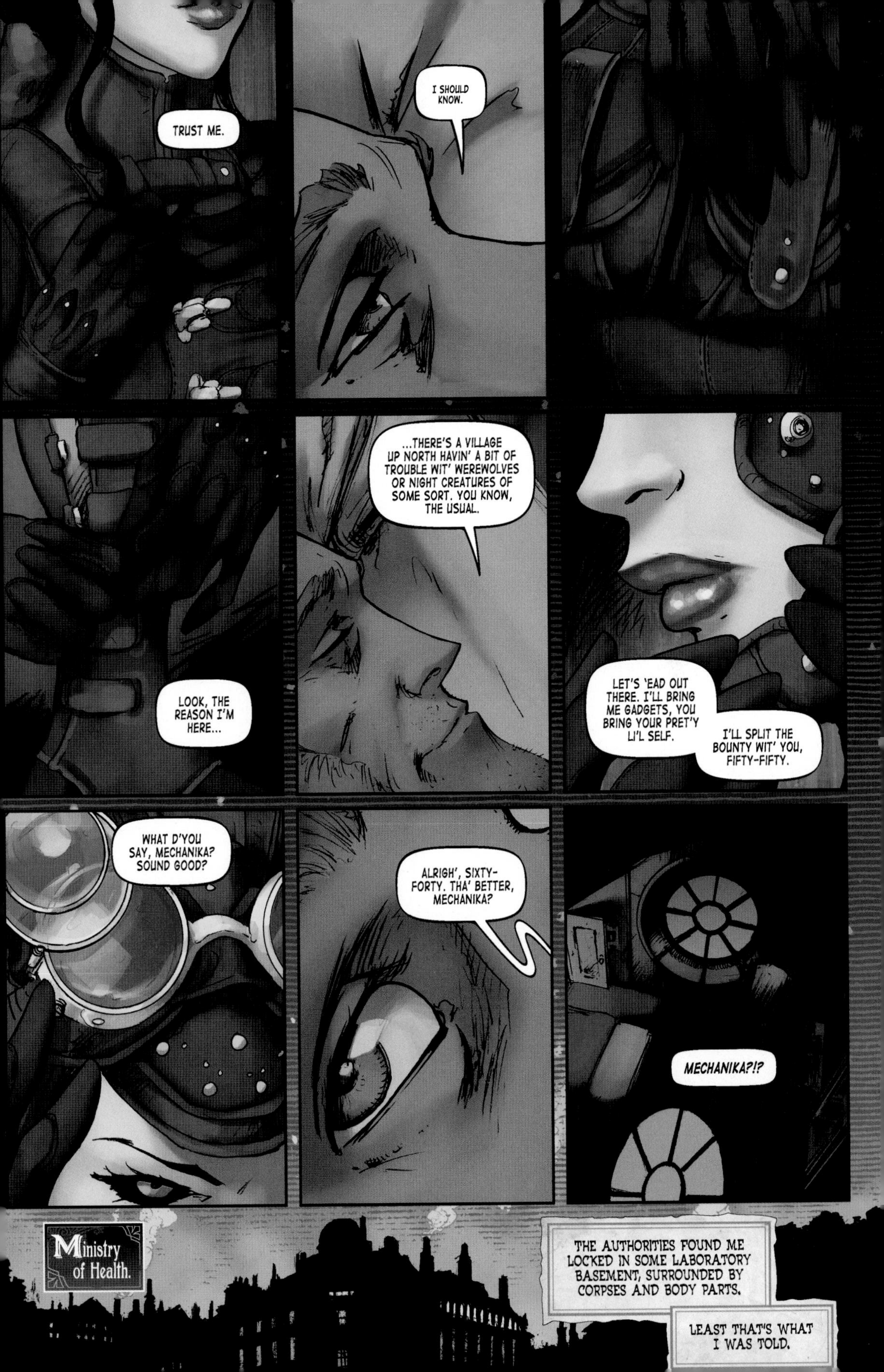
TRUST ME.
I SHOULD KNOW.
LOOK, THE REASON I'M HERE...
...THERE'S A VILLAGE UP NORTH HAVIN' A BIT OF TROUBLE WIT' WEREWOLVES OR NIGHT CREATURES OF SOME SORT. YOU KNOW, THE USUAL.
LET'S 'EAD OUT THERE. I'LL BRING ME GADGETS, YOU BRING YOUR PRET'Y LI'L SELF.
I'LL SPLIT THE BOUNTY WIT' YOU, FIFTY-FIFTY.
WHAT D'YOU SAY, MECHANIKA? SOUND GOOD?
ALRIGH', SIXTY-FORTY. THA' BETTER, MECHANIKA?
MECHANIKA?!?
Ministry of Health.
THE AUTHORITIES FOUND ME LOCKED IN SOME LABORATORY BASEMENT, SURROUNDED BY CORPSES AND BODY PARTS.
LEAST THAT'S WHAT I WAS TOLD.

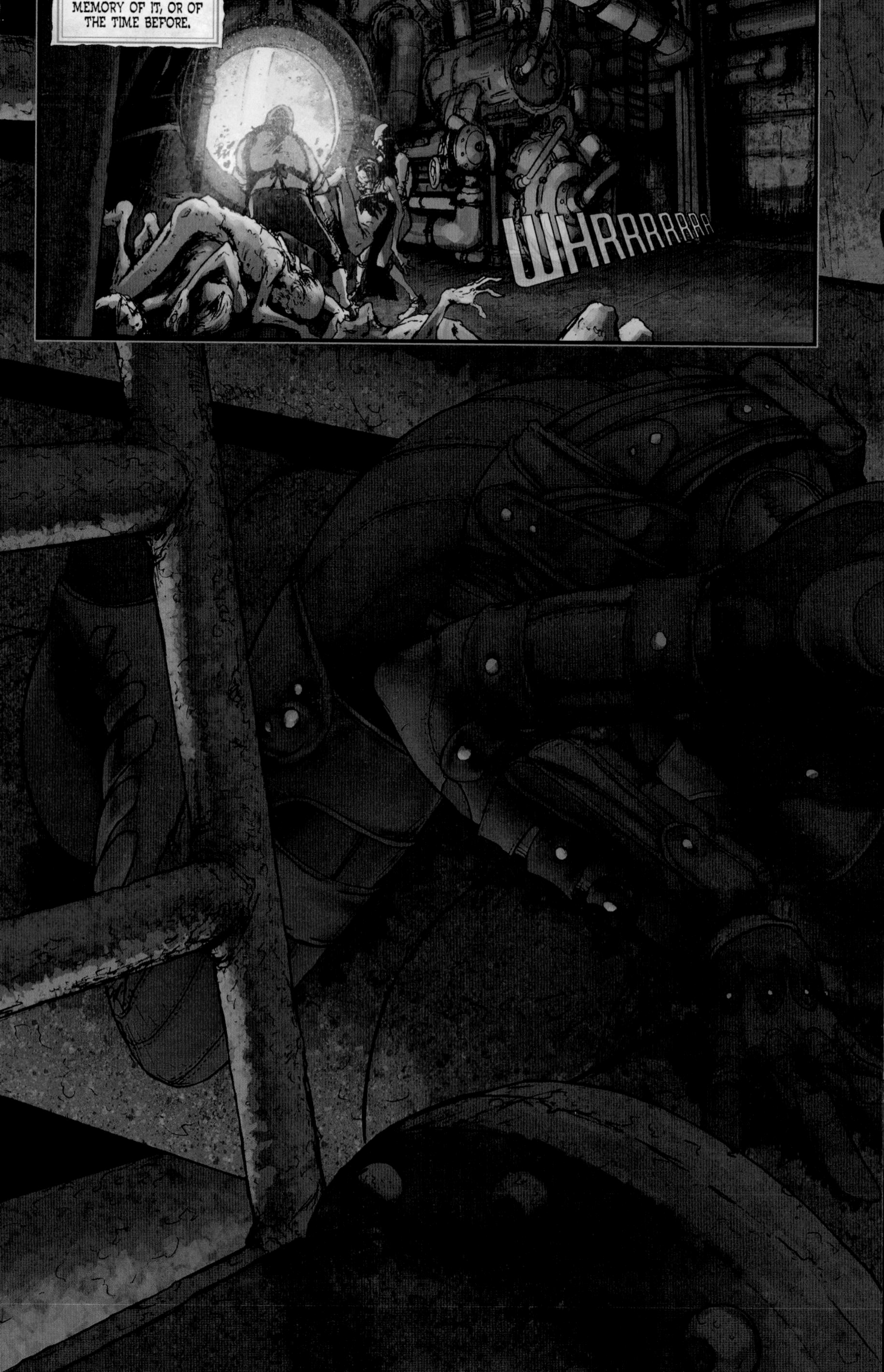
MEMORY OF IT, OR OF
THE TIME BEFORE.
WHRRRRRRRR

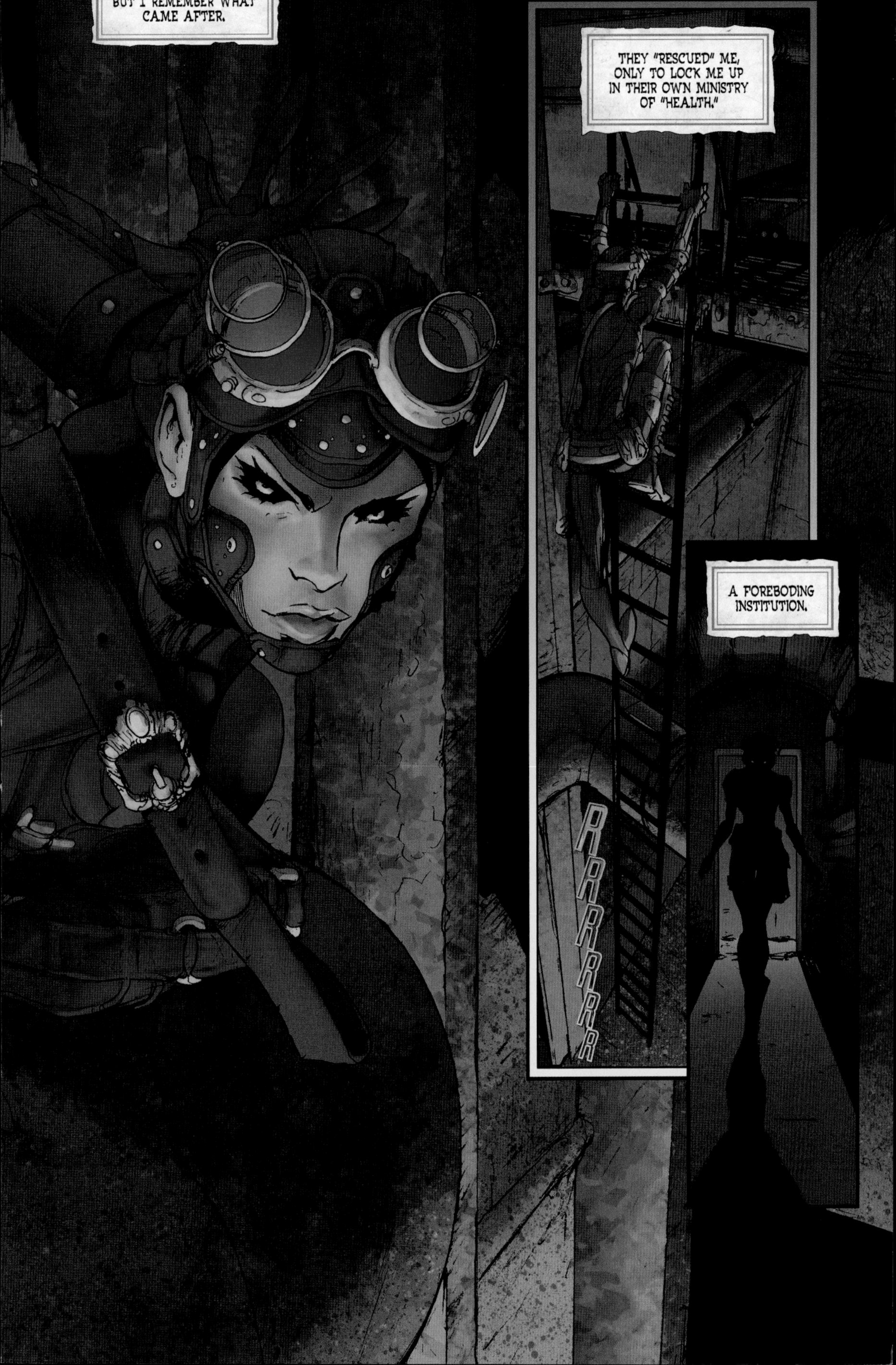
BUT I REMEMBER WHAT CAME AFTER.
THEY "RESCUED" ME, ONLY TO LOCK ME UP IN THEIR OWN MINISTRY OF "HEALTH."
RRRRRR
A FOREBODING INSTITUTION.

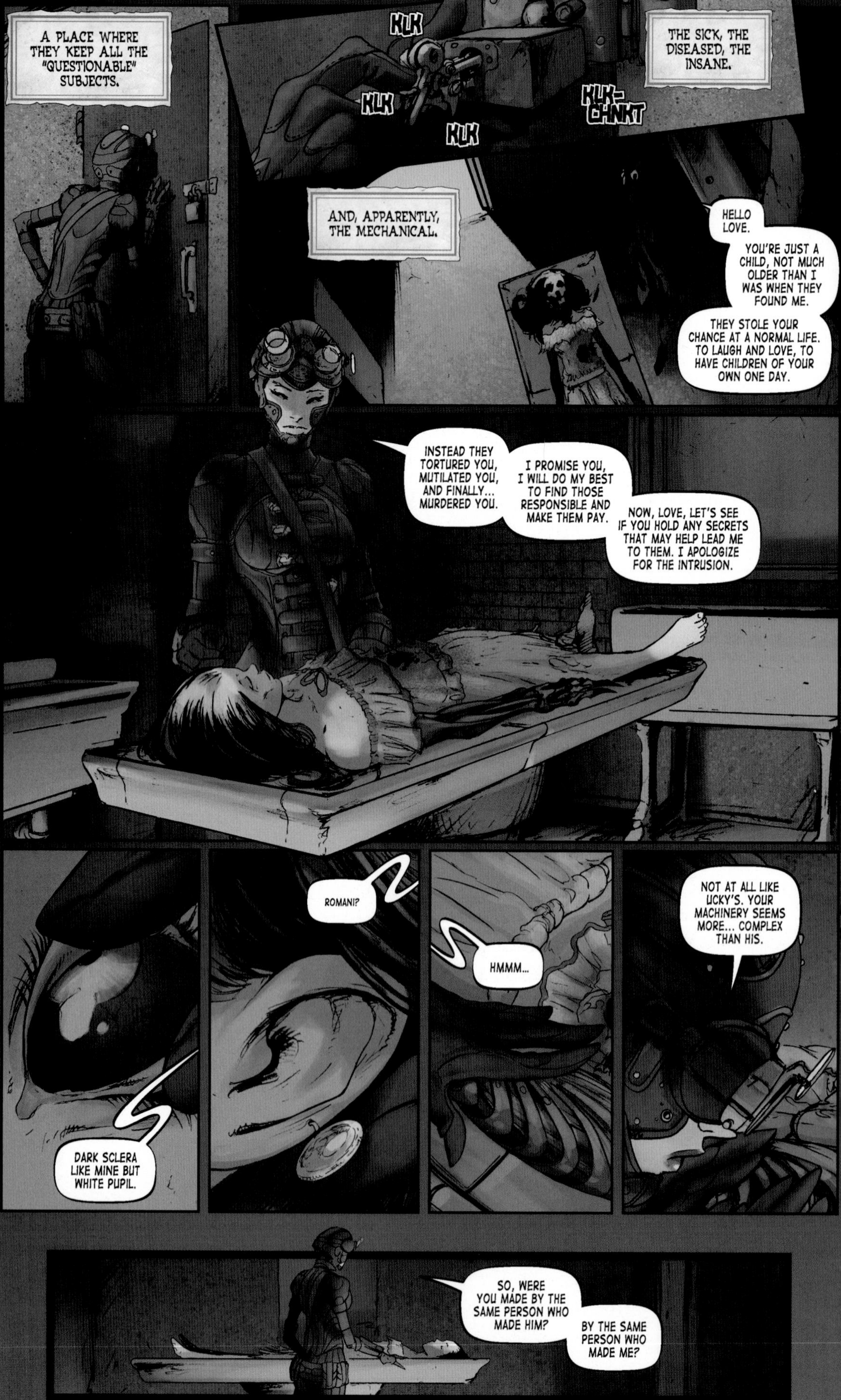
A PLACE WHERE THEY KEEP ALL THE "QUESTIONABLE" SUBJECTS.
KLK
KLK
KLK
KLK-CHNKT
THE SICK, THE DISEASED, THE INSANE.
AND, APPARENTLY, THE MECHANICAL.
HELLO LOVE.
YOU'RE JUST A CHILD, NOT MUCH OLDER THAN I WAS WHEN THEY FOUND ME.
THEY STOLE YOUR CHANCE AT A NORMAL LIFE. TO LAUGH AND LOVE, TO HAVE CHILDREN OF YOUR OWN ONE DAY.
INSTEAD THEY TORTURED YOU, MUTILATED YOU, AND FINALLY... MURDERED YOU.
I PROMISE YOU, I WILL DO MY BEST TO FIND THOSE RESPONSIBLE AND MAKE THEM PAY.
NOW, LOVE, LET'S SEE IF YOU HOLD ANY SECRETS THAT MAY HELP LEAD ME TO THEM. I APOLOGIZE FOR THE INTRUSION.
DARK SCLERA LIKE MINE BUT WHITE PUPIL.
ROMANI?
HMMM...
NOT AT ALL LIKE LICKY'S. YOUR MACHINERY SEEMS MORE... COMPLEX THAN HIS.
SO, WERE YOU MADE BY THE SAME PERSON WHO MADE HIM?
BY THE SAME PERSON WHO MADE ME?

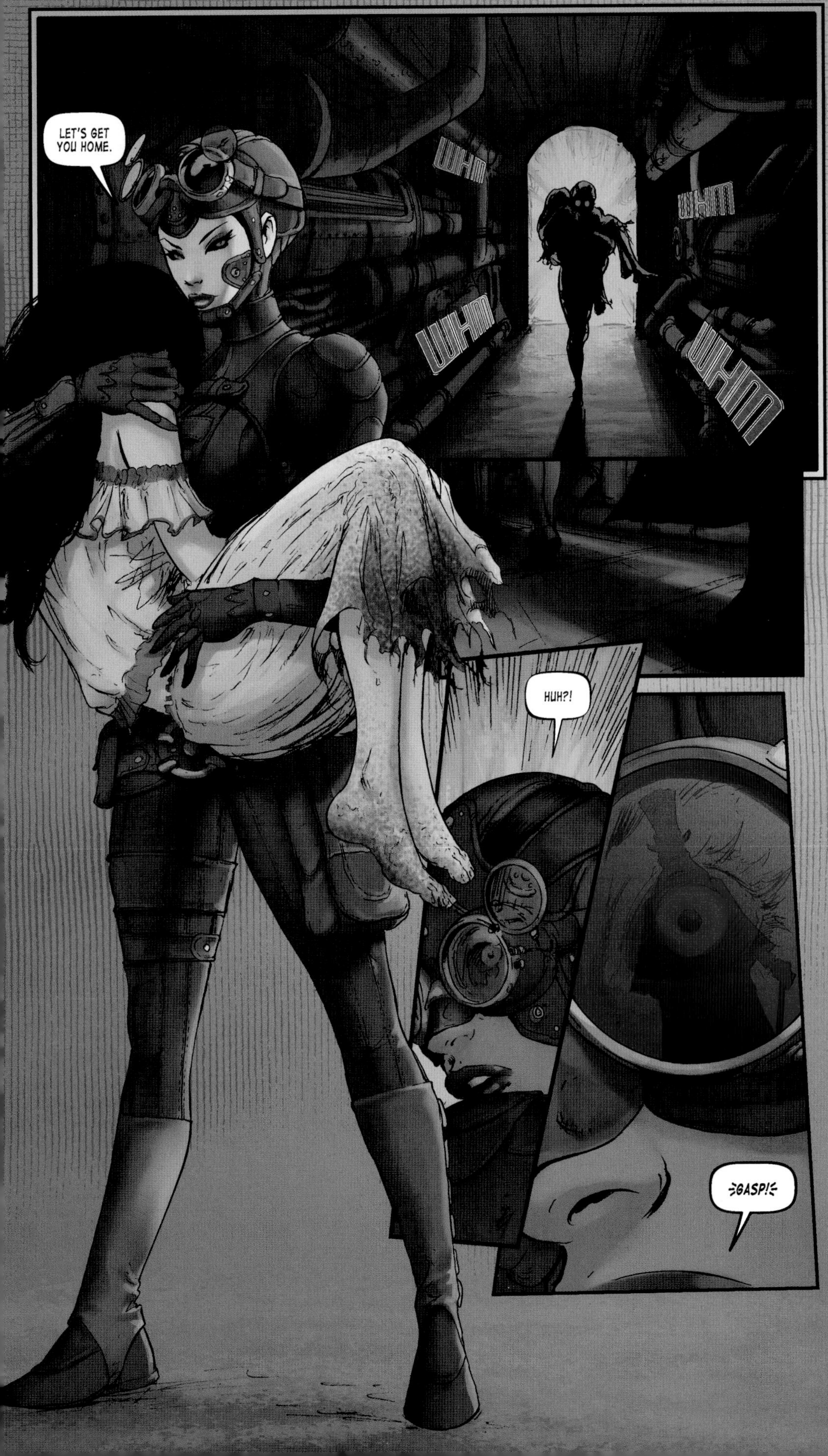
LET'S GET YOU HOME.
WHM
WHM
WHM
WHM
HUH?!
GASP!

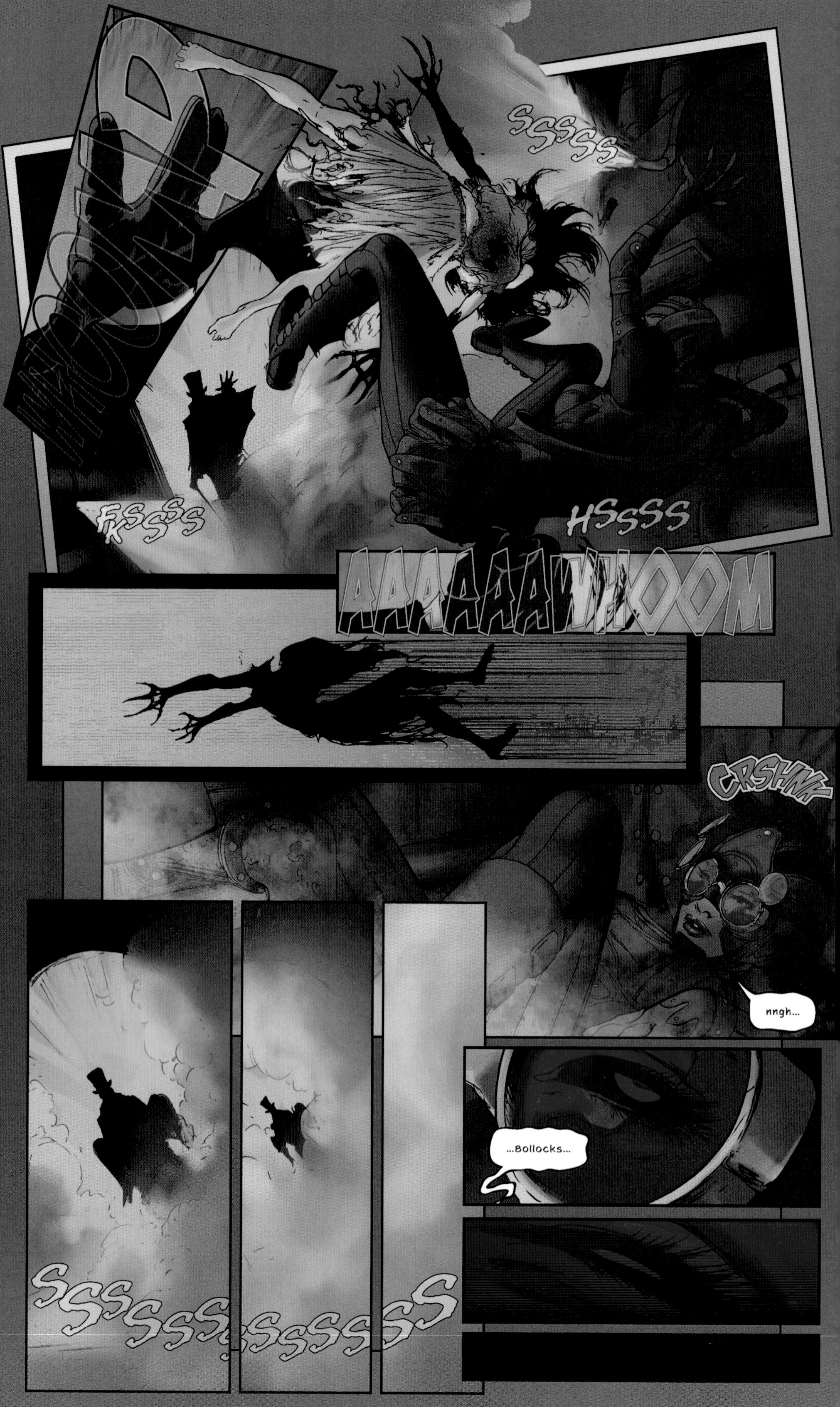
SSSSS
FKSSSS
HSSSS
AAAAAAWHOOM
CRSHNK
nngh...
...Bollocks...
SSSSSSSSSSSSSS

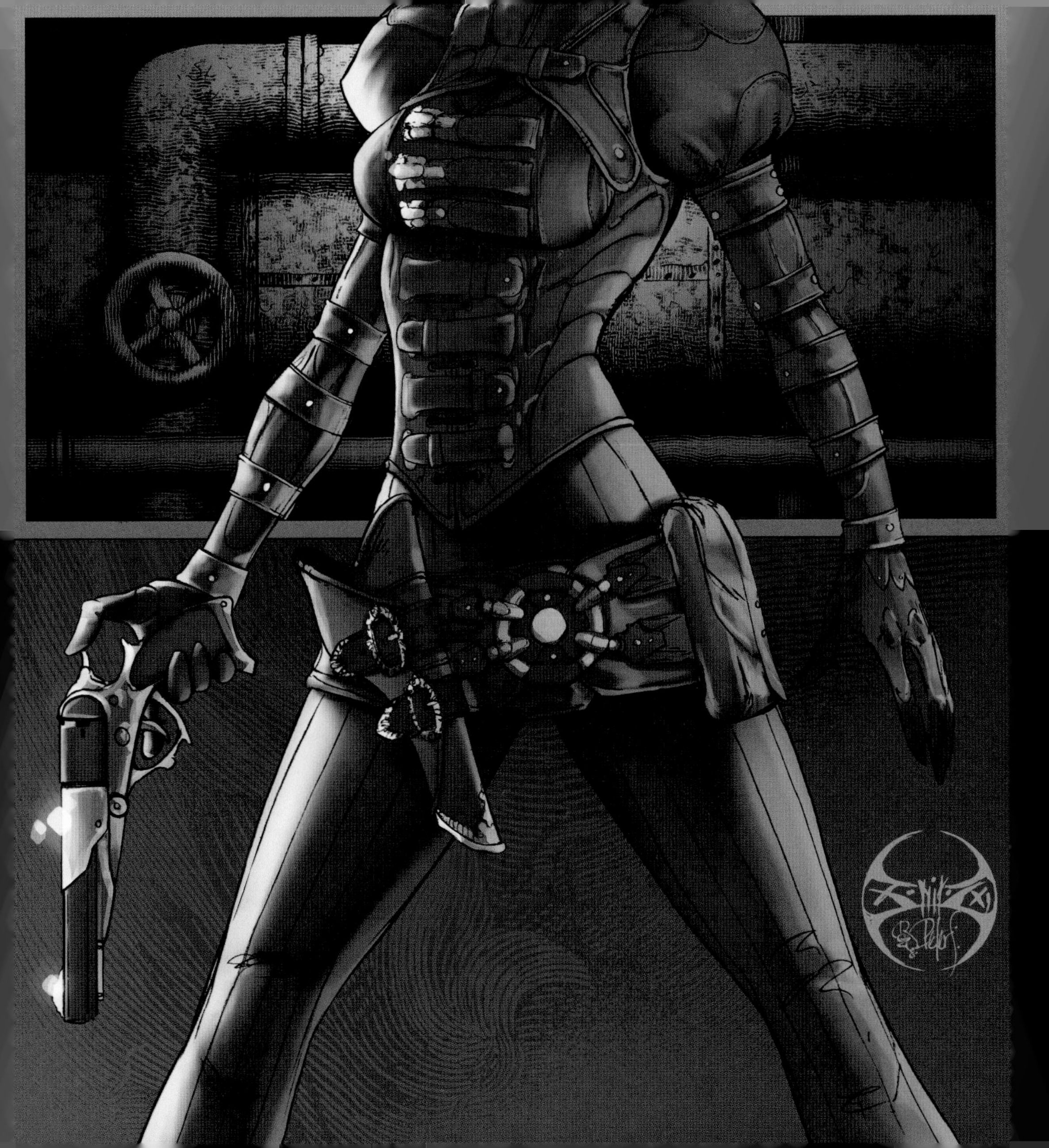

Chapter Two

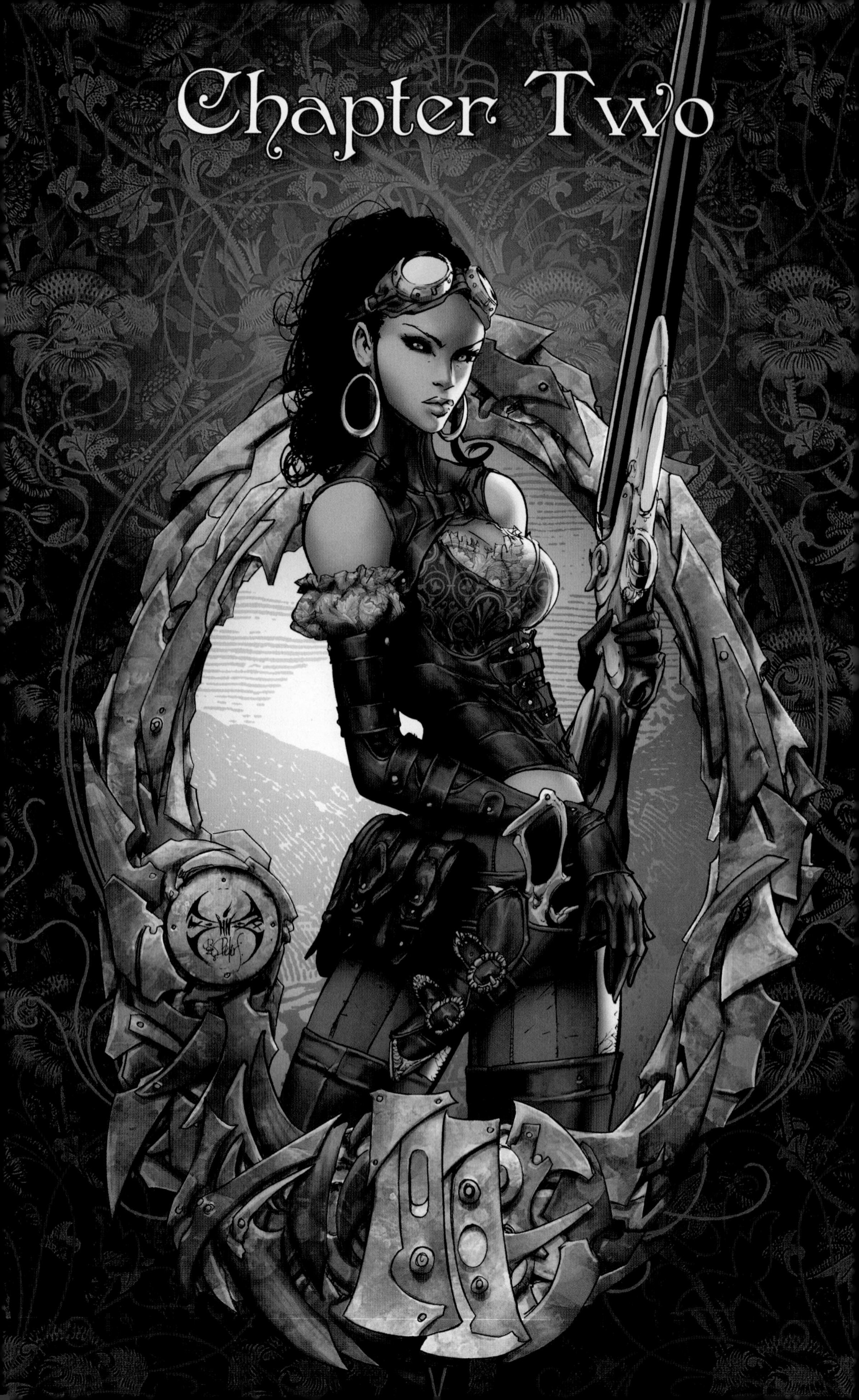

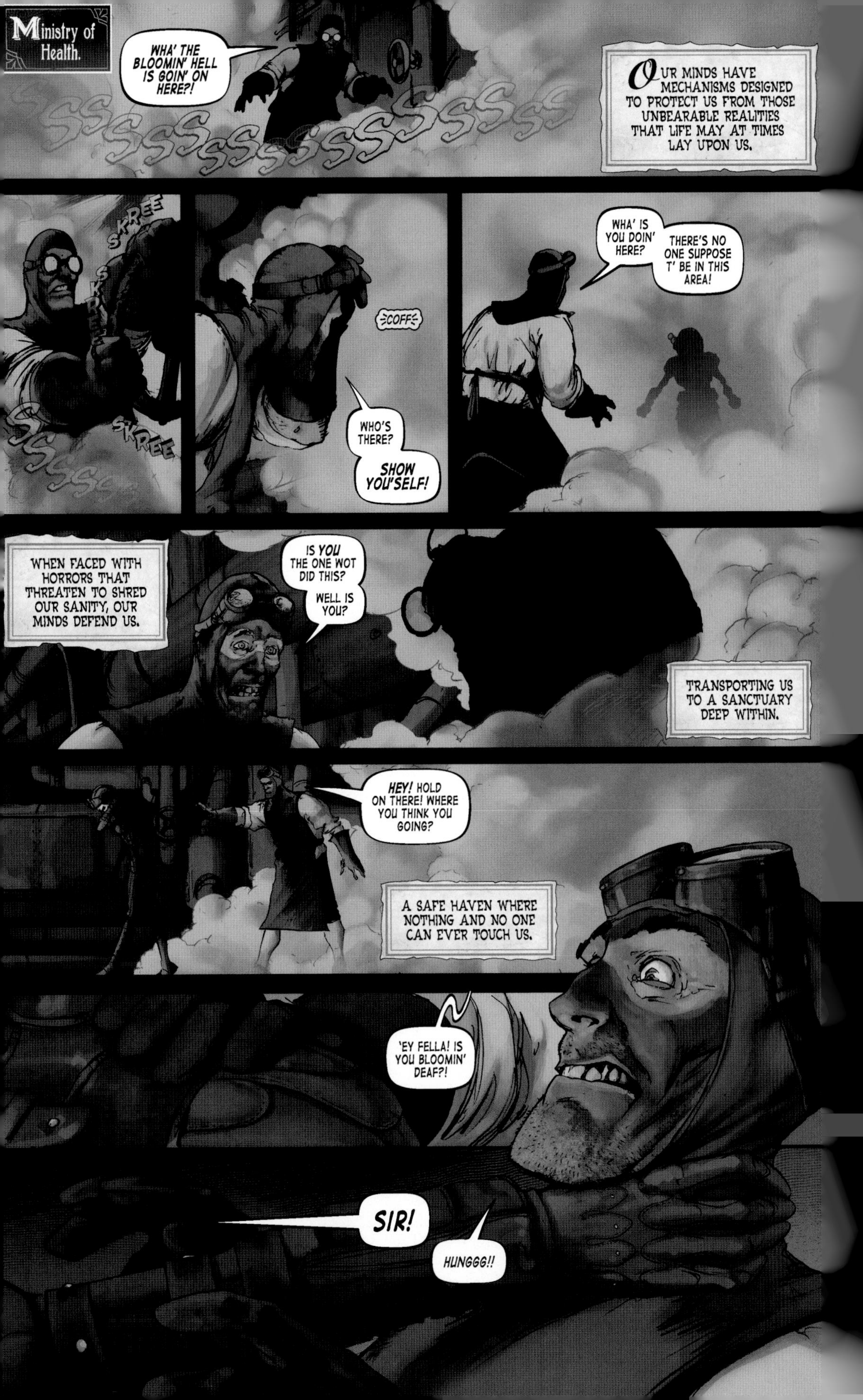

Ministry of Health.
WHA' THE BLOOMIN' HELL IS GOIN' ON HERE?!
SSSSSSSSSSSSSSSSS
OUR MINDS HAVE MECHANISMS DESIGNED TO PROTECT US FROM THOSE UNBEARABLE REALITIES THAT LIFE MAY AT TIMES LAY UPON US.
SKREE
SKREE
SKREE
COFF
WHO'S THERE?
SHOW YOU'SELF!
WHA' IS YOU DOIN' HERE?
THERE'S NO ONE SUPPOSE T' BE IN THIS AREA!
WHEN FACED WITH HORRORS THAT THREATEN TO SHRED OUR SANITY, OUR MINDS DEFEND US.
IS YOU THE ONE WOT DID THIS?
WELL IS YOU?
TRANSPORTING US TO A SANCTUARY DEEP WITHIN.
HEY! HOLD ON THERE! WHERE YOU THINK YOU GOING?
A SAFE HAVEN WHERE NOTHING AND NO ONE CAN EVER TOUCH US.
'EY FELLA! IS YOU BLOOMIN' DEAF?!
SIR!
HUNGGG!!

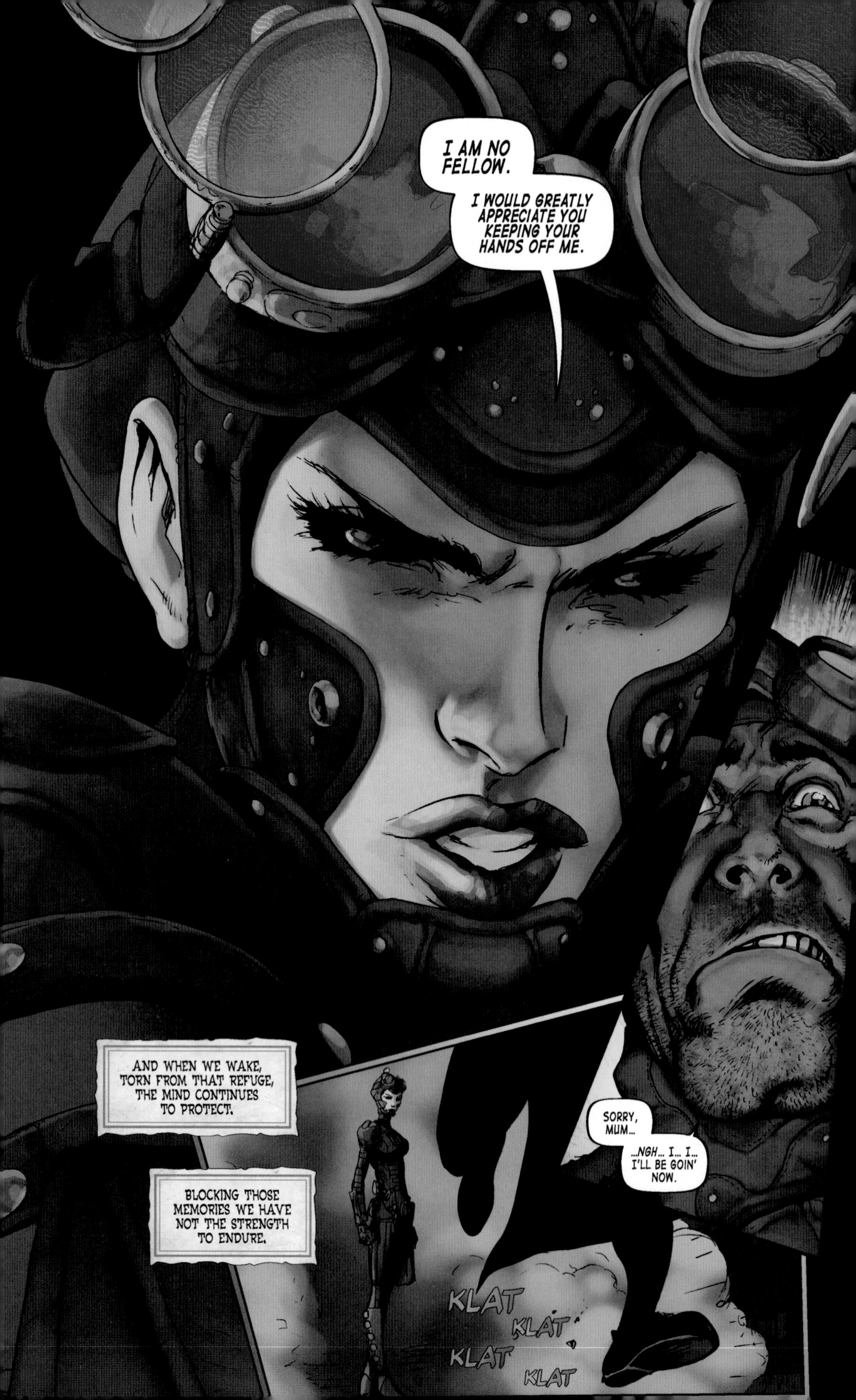
I AM NO FELLOW.
I WOULD GREATLY APPRECIATE YOU KEEPING YOUR HANDS OFF ME.
AND WHEN WE WAKE, TORN FROM THAT REFUGE, THE MIND CONTINUES TO PROTECT.
BLOCKING THOSE MEMORIES WE HAVE NOT THE STRENGTH TO ENDURE.
SORRY, MUM...
...NGH... I... I... I'LL BE GOIN' NOW.
KLAT
KLAT
KLAT
KLAT

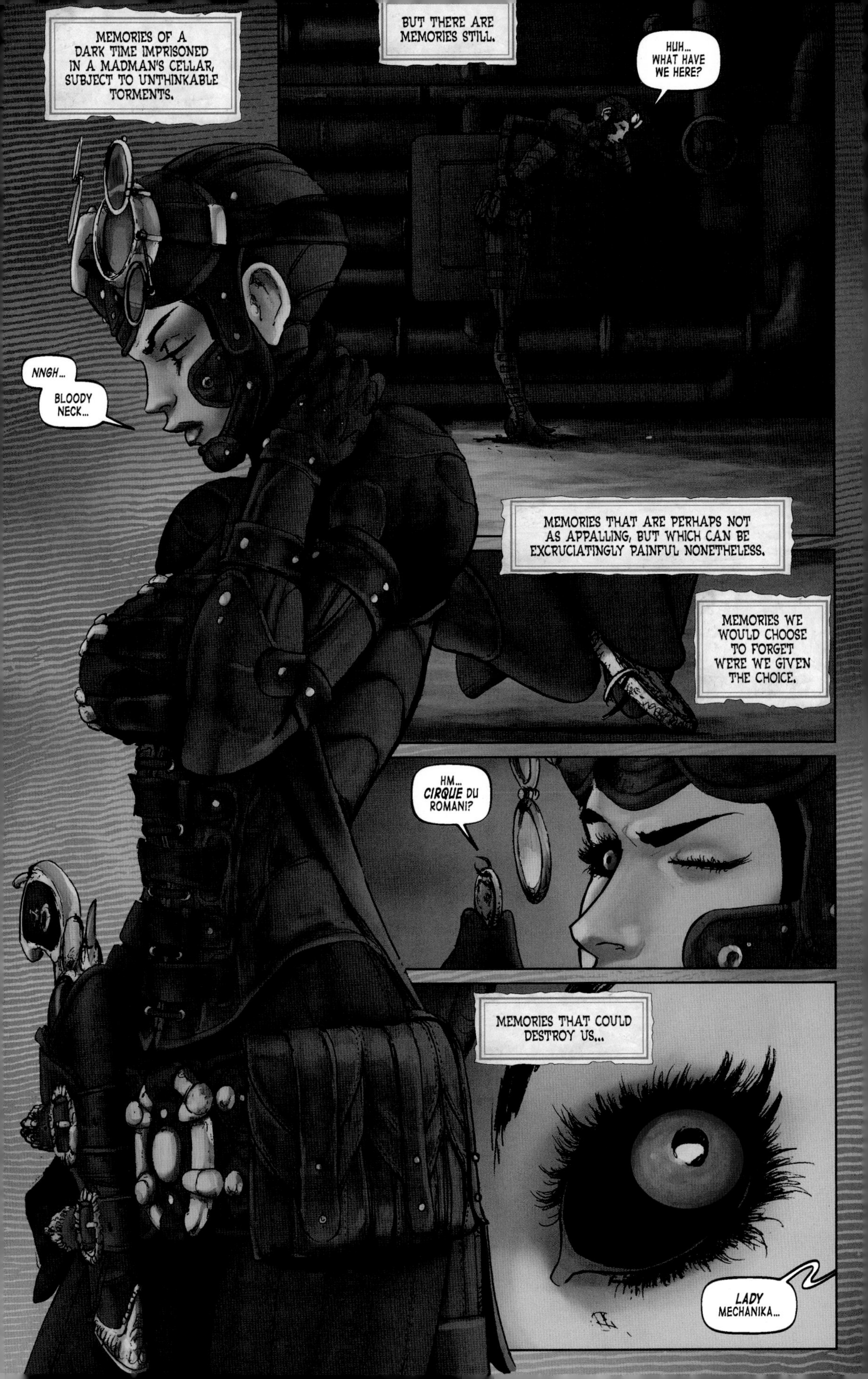
MEMORIES OF A DARK TIME IMPRISONED IN A MADMAN'S CELLAR, SUBJECT TO UNTHINKABLE TORMENTS.
BUT THERE ARE MEMORIES STILL.
HUH... WHAT HAVE WE HERE?
NNGH...
BLOODY NECK...
MEMORIES THAT ARE PERHAPS NOT AS APPALLING, BUT WHICH CAN BE EXCRUCIATINGLY PAINFUL NONETHELESS.
MEMORIES WE WOULD CHOOSE TO FORGET WERE WE GIVEN THE CHOICE.
HM... *CIRQUE* DU ROMANI?
MEMORIES THAT COULD DESTROY US...
LADY MECHANIKA...

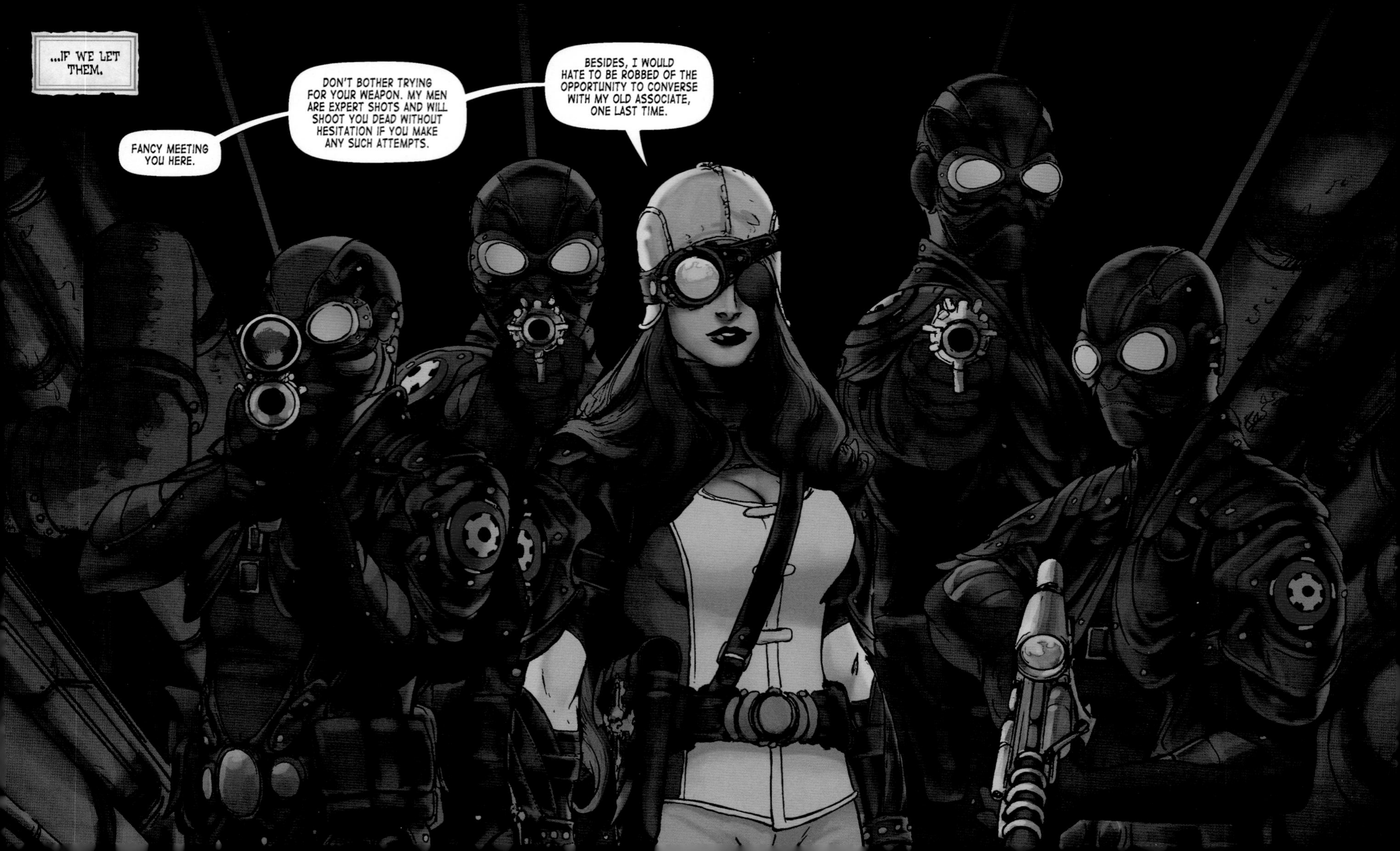
...IF WE LET THEM.
FANCY MEETING YOU HERE.
DON'T BOTHER TRYING FOR YOUR WEAPON. MY MEN ARE EXPERT SHOTS AND WILL SHOOT YOU DEAD WITHOUT HESITATION IF YOU MAKE ANY SUCH ATTEMPTS.
BESIDES, I WOULD HATE TO BE ROBBED OF THE OPPORTUNITY TO CONVERSE WITH MY OLD ASSOCIATE, ONE LAST TIME.

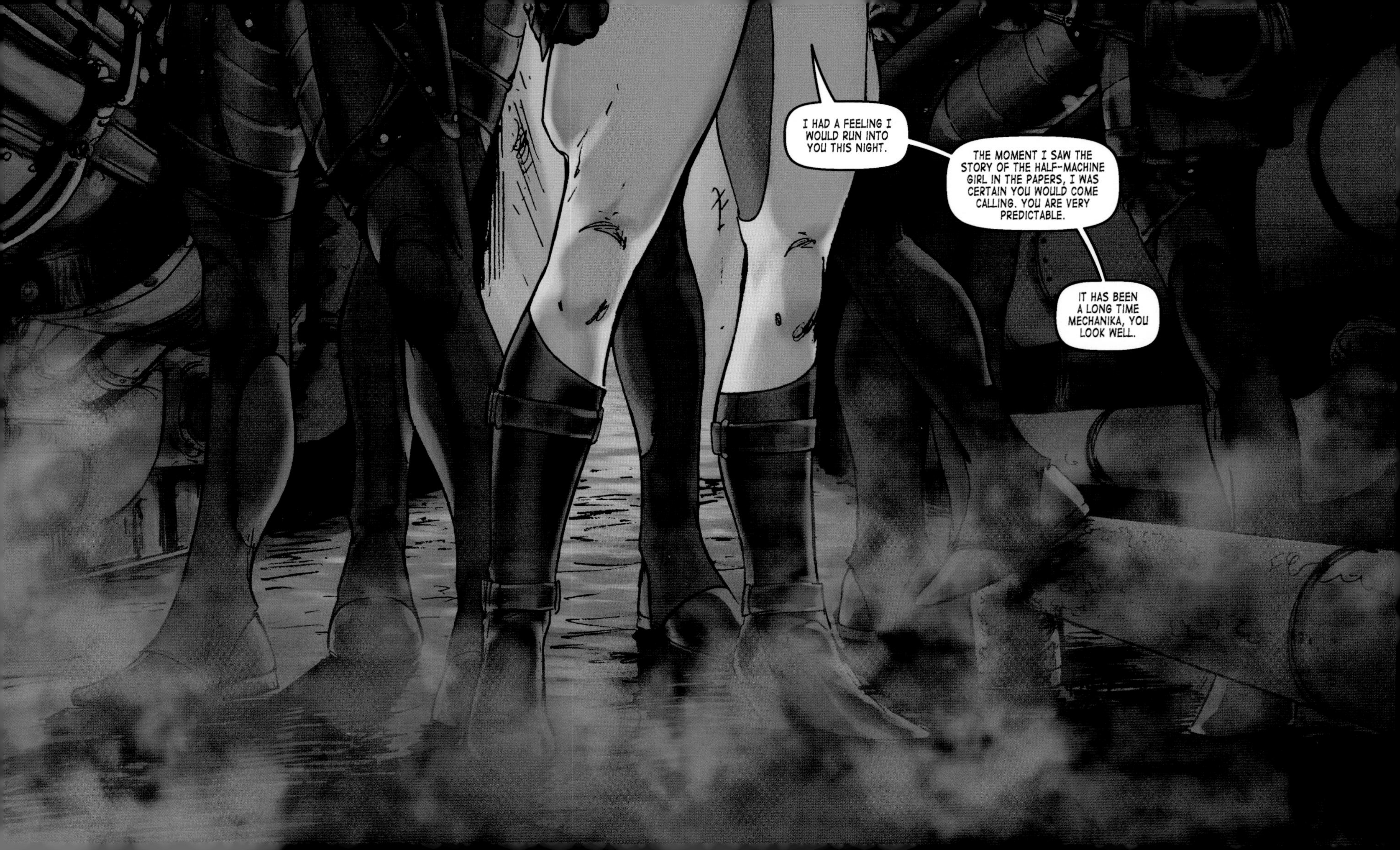
I HAD A FEELING I WOULD RUN INTO YOU THIS NIGHT.
THE MOMENT I SAW THE STORY OF THE HALF-MACHINE GIRL IN THE PAPERS, I WAS CERTAIN YOU WOULD COME CALLING. YOU ARE VERY PREDICTABLE.
IT HAS BEEN A LONG TIME MECHANIKA, YOU LOOK WELL.

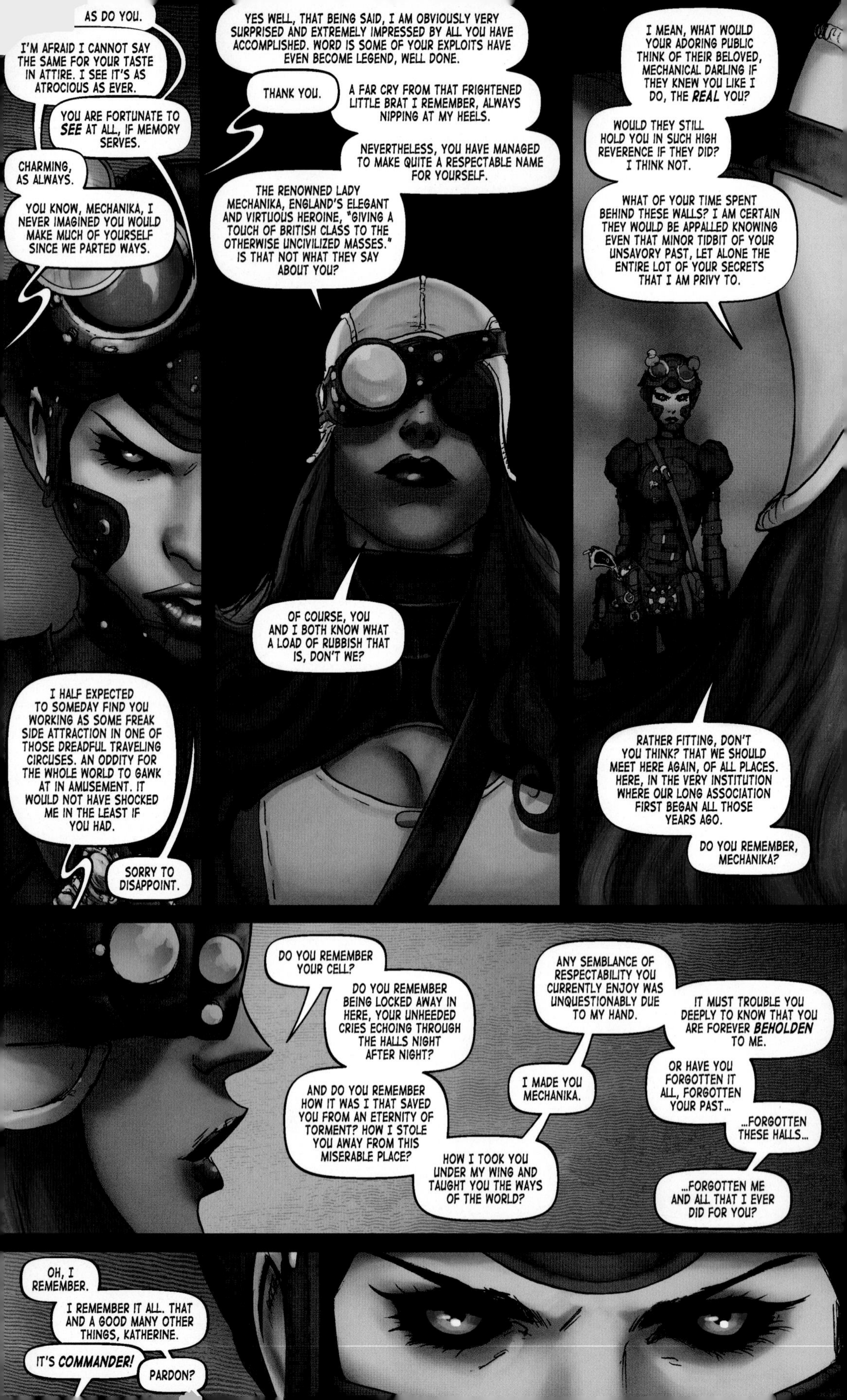
AS DO YOU.
I'M AFRAID I CANNOT SAY THE SAME FOR YOUR TASTE IN ATTIRE. I SEE IT'S AS ATROCIOUS AS EVER.
YOU ARE FORTUNATE TO SEE AT ALL, IF MEMORY SERVES.
CHARMING, AS ALWAYS.
YOU KNOW, MECHANIKA, I NEVER IMAGINED YOU WOULD MAKE MUCH OF YOURSELF SINCE WE PARTED WAYS.
YES WELL, THAT BEING SAID, I AM OBVIOUSLY VERY SURPRISED AND EXTREMELY IMPRESSED BY ALL YOU HAVE ACCOMPLISHED. WORD IS SOME OF YOUR EXPLOITS HAVE EVEN BECOME LEGEND, WELL DONE.
THANK YOU.
A FAR CRY FROM THAT FRIGHTENED LITTLE BRAT I REMEMBER, ALWAYS NIPPING AT MY HEELS.
NEVERTHELESS, YOU HAVE MANAGED TO MAKE QUITE A RESPECTABLE NAME FOR YOURSELF.
THE RENOWNED LADY MECHANIKA, ENGLAND'S ELEGANT AND VIRTUOUS HEROINE, "GIVING A TOUCH OF BRITISH CLASS TO THE OTHERWISE UNCIVILIZED MASSES." IS THAT NOT WHAT THEY SAY ABOUT YOU?
OF COURSE, YOU AND I BOTH KNOW WHAT A LOAD OF RUBBISH THAT IS, DON'T WE?
I MEAN, WHAT WOULD YOUR ADORING PUBLIC THINK OF THEIR BELOVED, MECHANICAL DARLING IF THEY KNEW YOU LIKE I DO, THE REAL YOU?
WOULD THEY STILL HOLD YOU IN SUCH HIGH REVERENCE IF THEY DID? I THINK NOT.
WHAT OF YOUR TIME SPENT BEHIND THESE WALLS? I AM CERTAIN THEY WOULD BE APPALLED KNOWING EVEN THAT MINOR TIDBIT OF YOUR UNSAVORY PAST, LET ALONE THE ENTIRE LOT OF YOUR SECRETS THAT I AM PRIVY TO.
I HALF EXPECTED TO SOMEDAY FIND YOU WORKING AS SOME FREAK SIDE ATTRACTION IN ONE OF THOSE DREADFUL TRAVELING CIRCUSES. AN ODDITY FOR THE WHOLE WORLD TO GAWK AT IN AMUSEMENT. IT WOULD NOT HAVE SHOCKED ME IN THE LEAST IF YOU HAD.
SORRY TO DISAPPOINT.
RATHER FITTING, DON'T YOU THINK? THAT WE SHOULD MEET HERE AGAIN, OF ALL PLACES. HERE, IN THE VERY INSTITUTION WHERE OUR LONG ASSOCIATION FIRST BEGAN ALL THOSE YEARS AGO.
DO YOU REMEMBER, MECHANIKA?
DO YOU REMEMBER YOUR CELL?
DO YOU REMEMBER BEING LOCKED AWAY IN HERE, YOUR UNHEEDED CRIES ECHOING THROUGH THE HALLS NIGHT AFTER NIGHT?
AND DO YOU REMEMBER HOW IT WAS I THAT SAVED YOU FROM AN ETERNITY OF TORMENT? HOW I STOLE YOU AWAY FROM THIS MISERABLE PLACE?
HOW I TOOK YOU UNDER MY WING AND TAUGHT YOU THE WAYS OF THE WORLD?
I MADE YOU MECHANIKA.
ANY SEMBLANCE OF RESPECTABILITY YOU CURRENTLY ENJOY WAS UNQUESTIONABLY DUE TO MY HAND.
IT MUST TROUBLE YOU DEEPLY TO KNOW THAT YOU ARE FOREVER BEHOLDEN TO ME.
OR HAVE YOU FORGOTTEN IT ALL, FORGOTTEN YOUR PAST...
...FORGOTTEN THESE HALLS...
...FORGOTTEN ME AND ALL THAT I EVER DID FOR YOU?
OH, I REMEMBER.
I REMEMBER IT ALL. THAT AND A GOOD MANY OTHER THINGS, KATHERINE.
IT'S COMMANDER!
PARDON?

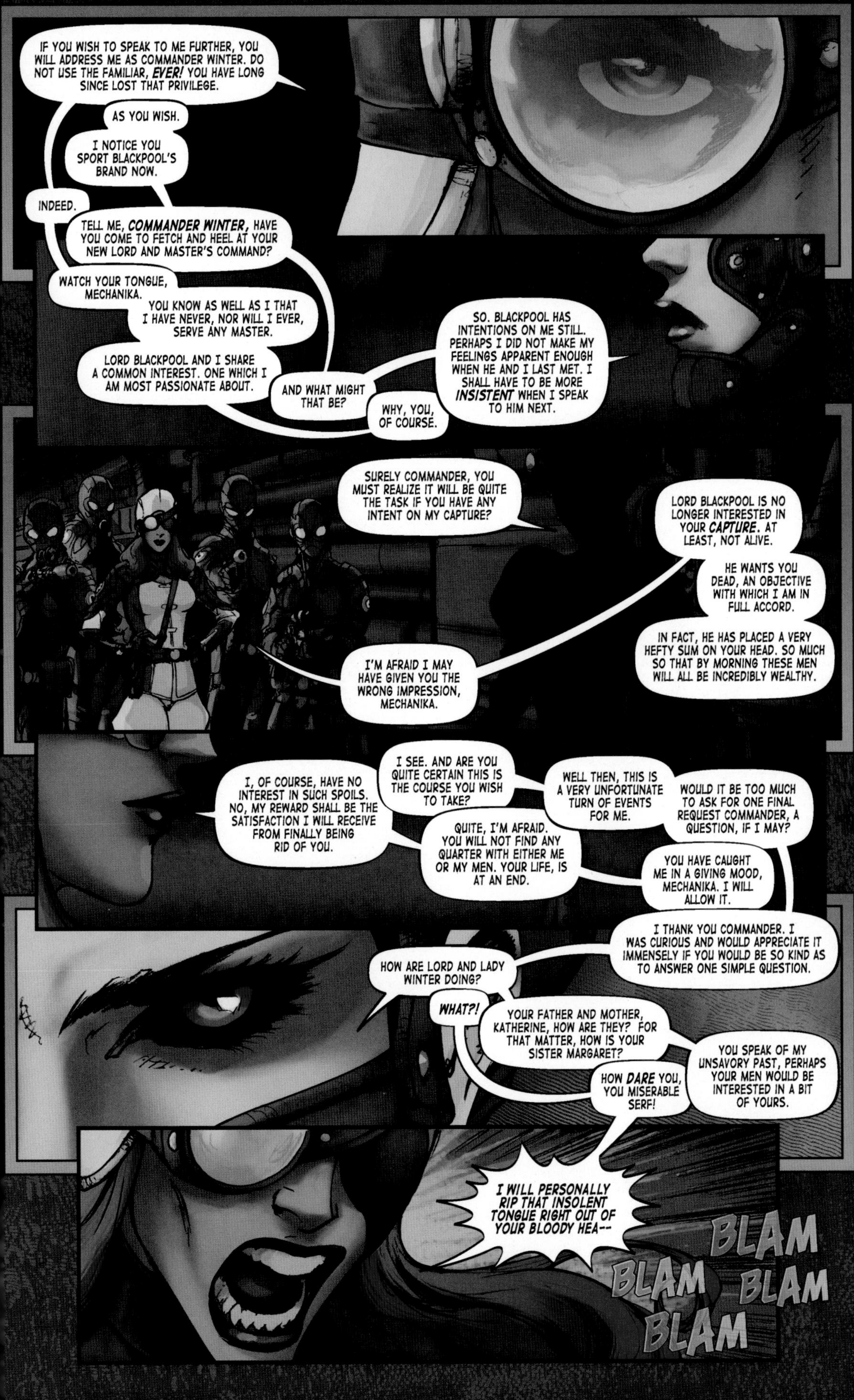
IF YOU WISH TO SPEAK TO ME FURTHER, YOU WILL ADDRESS ME AS COMMANDER WINTER. DO NOT USE THE FAMILIAR, EVER! YOU HAVE LONG SINCE LOST THAT PRIVILEGE.
AS YOU WISH.
I NOTICE YOU SPORT BLACKPOOL'S BRAND NOW.
INDEED.
TELL ME, COMMANDER WINTER, HAVE YOU COME TO FETCH AND HEEL AT YOUR NEW LORD AND MASTER'S COMMAND?
WATCH YOUR TONGUE, MECHANIKA.
YOU KNOW AS WELL AS I THAT I HAVE NEVER, NOR WILL I EVER, SERVE ANY MASTER.
LORD BLACKPOOL AND I SHARE A COMMON INTEREST. ONE WHICH I AM MOST PASSIONATE ABOUT.
AND WHAT MIGHT THAT BE?
WHY, YOU, OF COURSE.
SO. BLACKPOOL HAS INTENTIONS ON ME STILL. PERHAPS I DID NOT MAKE MY FEELINGS APPARENT ENOUGH WHEN HE AND I LAST MET. I SHALL HAVE TO BE MORE INSISTENT WHEN I SPEAK TO HIM NEXT.
SURELY COMMANDER, YOU MUST REALIZE IT WILL BE QUITE THE TASK IF YOU HAVE ANY INTENT ON MY CAPTURE?
LORD BLACKPOOL IS NO LONGER INTERESTED IN YOUR CAPTURE. AT LEAST, NOT ALIVE.
HE WANTS YOU DEAD, AN OBJECTIVE WITH WHICH I AM IN FULL ACCORD.
IN FACT, HE HAS PLACED A VERY HEFTY SUM ON YOUR HEAD. SO MUCH SO THAT BY MORNING THESE MEN WILL ALL BE INCREDIBLY WEALTHY.
I'M AFRAID I MAY HAVE GIVEN YOU THE WRONG IMPRESSION, MECHANIKA.
I, OF COURSE, HAVE NO INTEREST IN SUCH SPOILS. NO, MY REWARD SHALL BE THE SATISFACTION I WILL RECEIVE FROM FINALLY BEING RID OF YOU.
I SEE. AND ARE YOU QUITE CERTAIN THIS IS THE COURSE YOU WISH TO TAKE?
QUITE, I'M AFRAID. YOU WILL NOT FIND ANY QUARTER WITH EITHER ME OR MY MEN. YOUR LIFE, IS AT AN END.
WELL THEN, THIS IS A VERY UNFORTUNATE TURN OF EVENTS FOR ME.
WOULD IT BE TOO MUCH TO ASK FOR ONE FINAL REQUEST COMMANDER, A QUESTION, IF I MAY?
YOU HAVE CAUGHT ME IN A GIVING MOOD, MECHANIKA. I WILL ALLOW IT.
I THANK YOU COMMANDER. I WAS CURIOUS AND WOULD APPRECIATE IT IMMENSELY IF YOU WOULD BE SO KIND AS TO ANSWER ONE SIMPLE QUESTION.
HOW ARE LORD AND LADY WINTER DOING?
WHAT?!
YOUR FATHER AND MOTHER, KATHERINE, HOW ARE THEY? FOR THAT MATTER, HOW IS YOUR SISTER MARGARET?
YOU SPEAK OF MY UNSAVORY PAST, PERHAPS YOUR MEN WOULD BE INTERESTED IN A BIT OF YOURS.
HOW DARE YOU, YOU MISERABLE SERF!
I WILL PERSONALLY RIP THAT INSOLENT TONGUE RIGHT OUT OF YOUR BLOODY HEA--
BLAM
BLAM
BLAM
BLAM

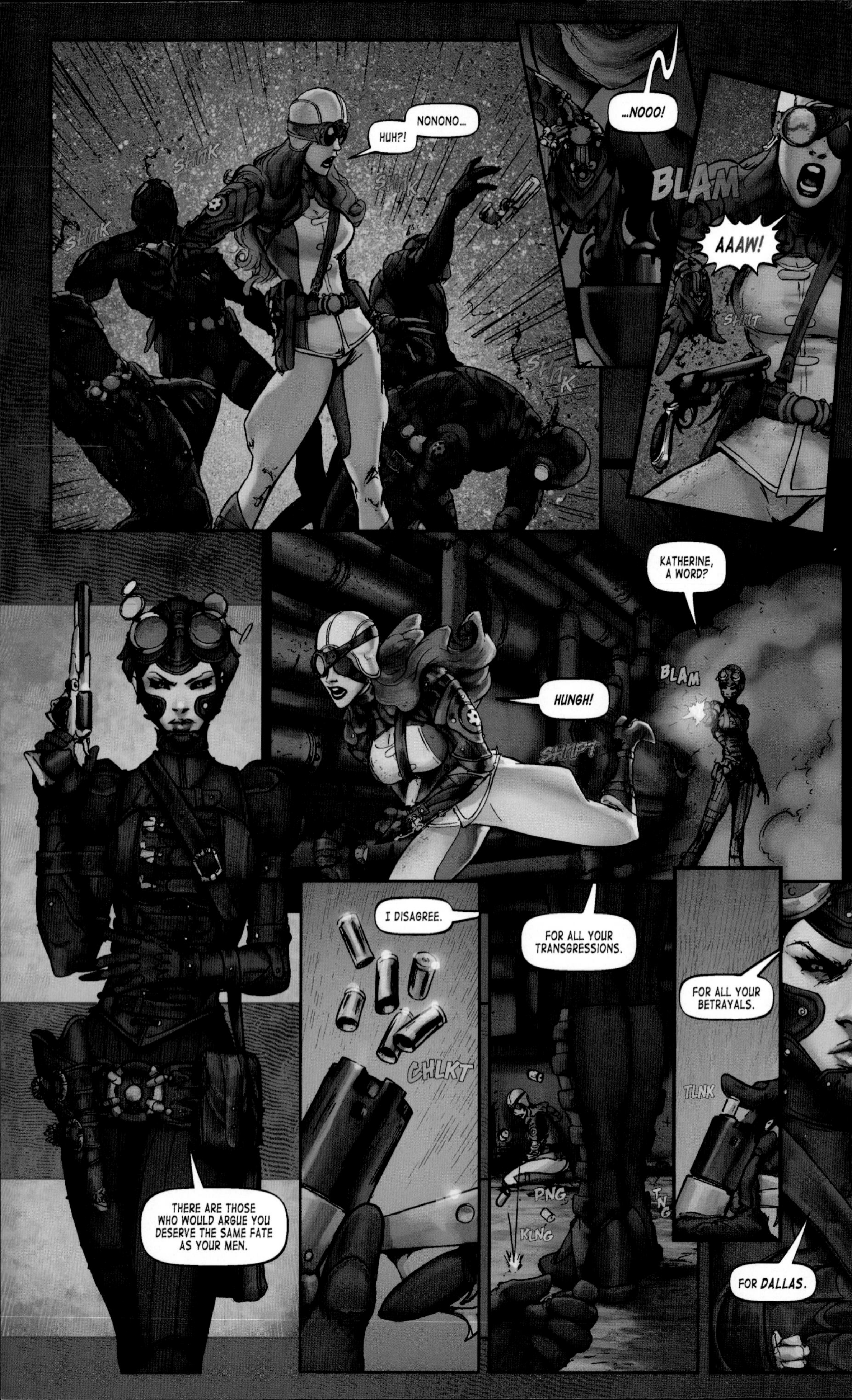
HUH?!
NONONO...
...NOOO!
BLAM
AAAW!
KATHERINE, A WORD?
BLAM
HUNGH!
THERE ARE THOSE WHO WOULD ARGUE YOU DESERVE THE SAME FATE AS YOUR MEN.
I DISAGREE.
CHLKT
FOR ALL YOUR TRANSGRESSIONS.
PNG
KLNG
TNG
FOR ALL YOUR BETRAYALS.
TLNK
FOR DALLAS.

YOU DESERVE A FATE FAR WORSE THAN DEATH.
OH SHUT UP **SHUT UP!** JUST SHOOT ME... ≶HNG≶ BE DONE WITH IT! RID ME OF YOUR INCESSANT DRONE.
I WOULD LOVE NOTHING MORE THAN TO OBLIGE YOU, KATHERINE. HOWEVER...
...I **DO** REMEMBER MY TIME IN THE MINISTRY. I **WAS** TRAPPED HERE, TORMENTED DAILY, NO CHANCE OF ESCAPE. BUT THEN YOU CAME, RELEASED ME FROM THAT HELL.
YOU WERE MY SAVIOR. MY ONLY FRIEND, MY SISTER, THE CLOSEST THING TO FAMILY I HAD EVER KNOWN.
YES, YES... *NGH*... AND YOU WERE NOTHING MORE THAN A WRETCHED URCHIN I REGRET EVER TAKING PITY ON.
I SHOULD HAVE LEFT YOU TO ROT IN YOUR HOLE!
I WAS BLIND TO THE PERSON YOU REALLY ARE, KATHERINE. I BELIEVED YOUR LIES. BUT YOU ARE RIGHT, I **AM** INDEBTED TO YOU. YOU **DID** SAVE ME FROM THESE HALLS.
YOU GAVE ME A LIFE, NOW IN RETURN I SPARE YOU YOURS. A LIFE FOR A LIFE. I AM INDEBTED TO YOU NO MORE. MY DEBT IS PAID IN FULL.
YOU, HOWEVER--
DEAD!
THEY'RE ALL DEAD! ALL OF THEM, THE ENTIRE SQUADRON...
CLICK
WHAT THE DEVIL ≶HNG≶ ARE YOU GOING ON ABOUT?
DEVIL! IT WAS THE DEVIL, LUCIFER HIMSELF! IT MUST HAVE BEEN! NO MAN COULD HAVE DONE WHAT HE DID... HE... HE KILLED ...HE KILLED THEM ALL!
TROOPER! CONTROL YOURSELF! ≶HNG≶ WHAT ARE YOU BLABBERING ABOUT?

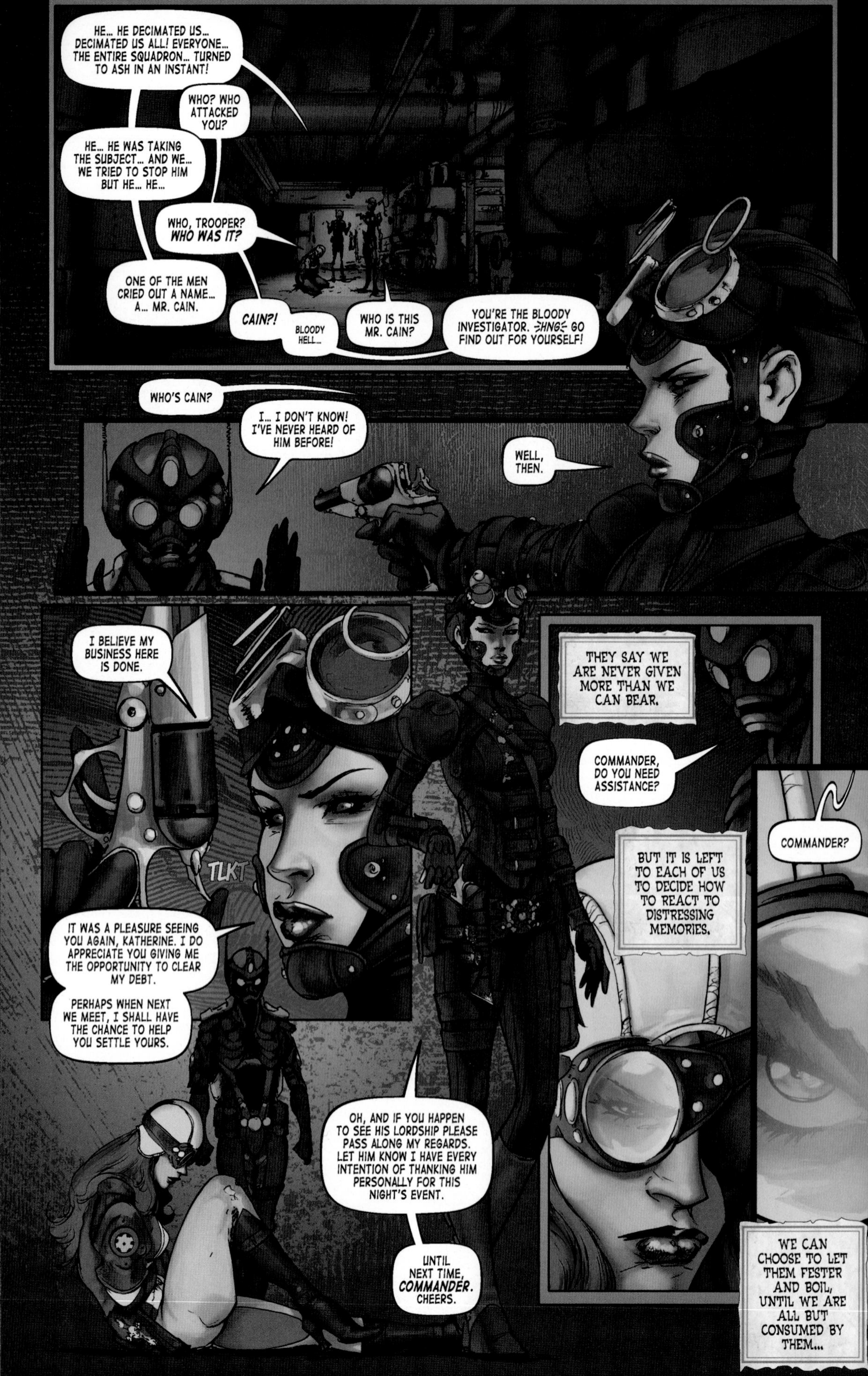
HE... HE DECIMATED US... DECIMATED US ALL! EVERYONE... THE ENTIRE SQUADRON... TURNED TO ASH IN AN INSTANT!
WHO? WHO ATTACKED YOU?
HE... HE WAS TAKING THE SUBJECT... AND WE... WE TRIED TO STOP HIM BUT HE... HE...
WHO, TROOPER? *WHO WAS IT?*
ONE OF THE MEN CRIED OUT A NAME... A... MR. CAIN.
CAIN?!
BLOODY HELL...
WHO IS THIS MR. CAIN?
YOU'RE THE BLOODY INVESTIGATOR. *HNG* GO FIND OUT FOR YOURSELF!
WHO'S CAIN?
I... I DON'T KNOW! I'VE NEVER HEARD OF HIM BEFORE!
WELL, THEN.
I BELIEVE MY BUSINESS HERE IS DONE.
TLKT
IT WAS A PLEASURE SEEING YOU AGAIN, KATHERINE. I DO APPRECIATE YOU GIVING ME THE OPPORTUNITY TO CLEAR MY DEBT.
PERHAPS WHEN NEXT WE MEET, I SHALL HAVE THE CHANCE TO HELP YOU SETTLE YOURS.
OH, AND IF YOU HAPPEN TO SEE HIS LORDSHIP PLEASE PASS ALONG MY REGARDS. LET HIM KNOW I HAVE EVERY INTENTION OF THANKING HIM PERSONALLY FOR THIS NIGHT'S EVENT.
UNTIL NEXT TIME, **COMMANDER.** CHEERS.
THEY SAY WE ARE NEVER GIVEN MORE THAN WE CAN BEAR.
COMMANDER, DO YOU NEED ASSISTANCE?
BUT IT IS LEFT TO EACH OF US TO DECIDE HOW TO REACT TO DISTRESSING MEMORIES.
COMMANDER?
WE CAN CHOOSE TO LET THEM FESTER AND BOIL, UNTIL WE ARE ALL BUT CONSUMED BY THEM...

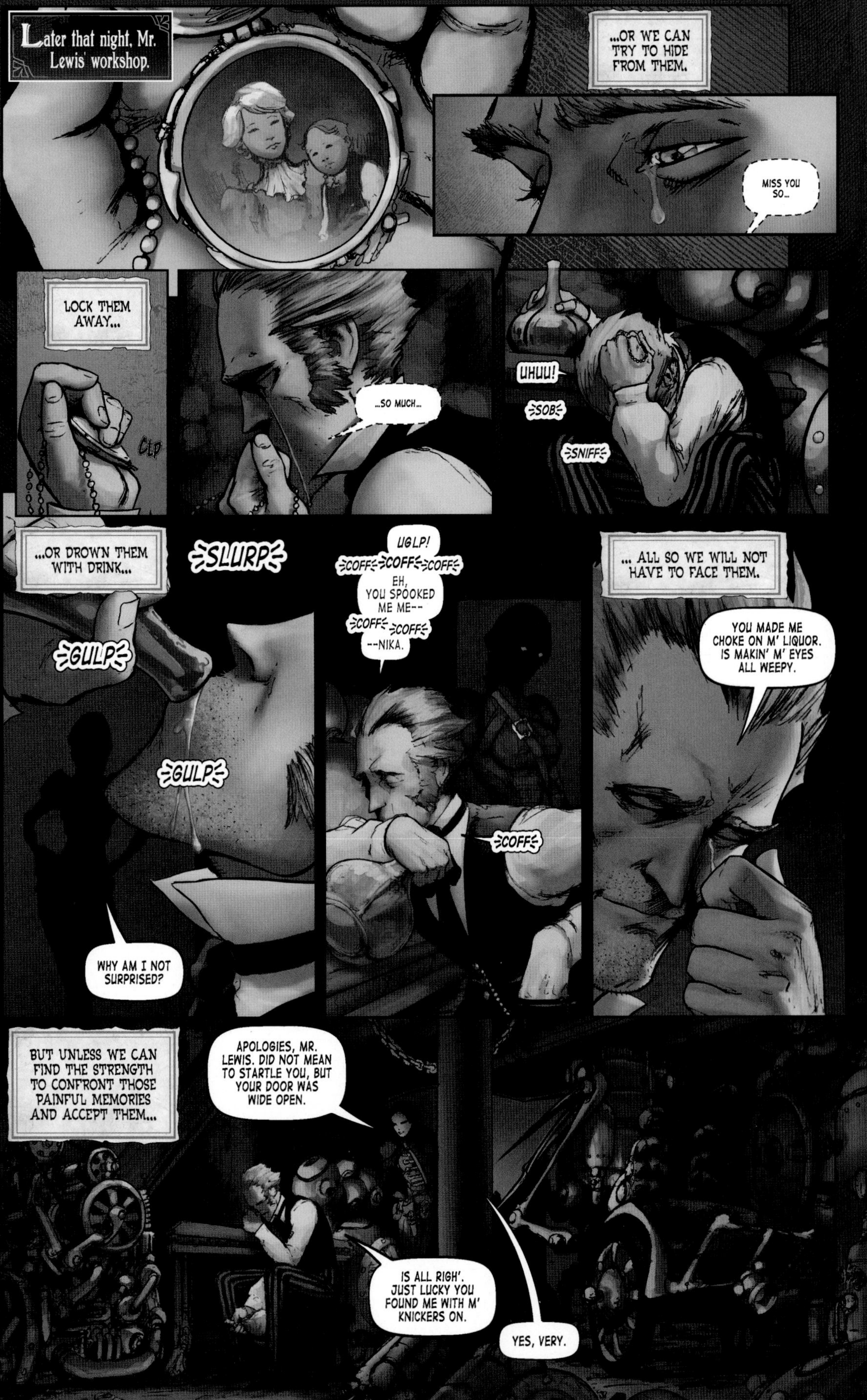
Later that night, Mr. Lewis' workshop.
...OR WE CAN TRY TO HIDE FROM THEM.
MISS YOU SO...
LOCK THEM AWAY...
CLIP
...SO MUCH...
UHUU!
SOB
SNIFF
...OR DROWN THEM WITH DRINK...
SLURP
GULP
GULP
WHY AM I NOT SURPRISED?
UGLP!
COFF COFF COFF
EH, YOU SPOOKED ME ME--
COFF COFF
--NIKA.
COFF
... ALL SO WE WILL NOT HAVE TO FACE THEM.
YOU MADE ME CHOKE ON M' LIQUOR. IS MAKIN' M' EYES ALL WEEPY.
BUT UNLESS WE CAN FIND THE STRENGTH TO CONFRONT THOSE PAINFUL MEMORIES AND ACCEPT THEM...
APOLOGIES, MR. LEWIS. DID NOT MEAN TO STARTLE YOU, BUT YOUR DOOR WAS WIDE OPEN.
IS ALL RIGH'. JUST LUCKY YOU FOUND ME WITH M' KNICKERS ON.
YES, VERY.

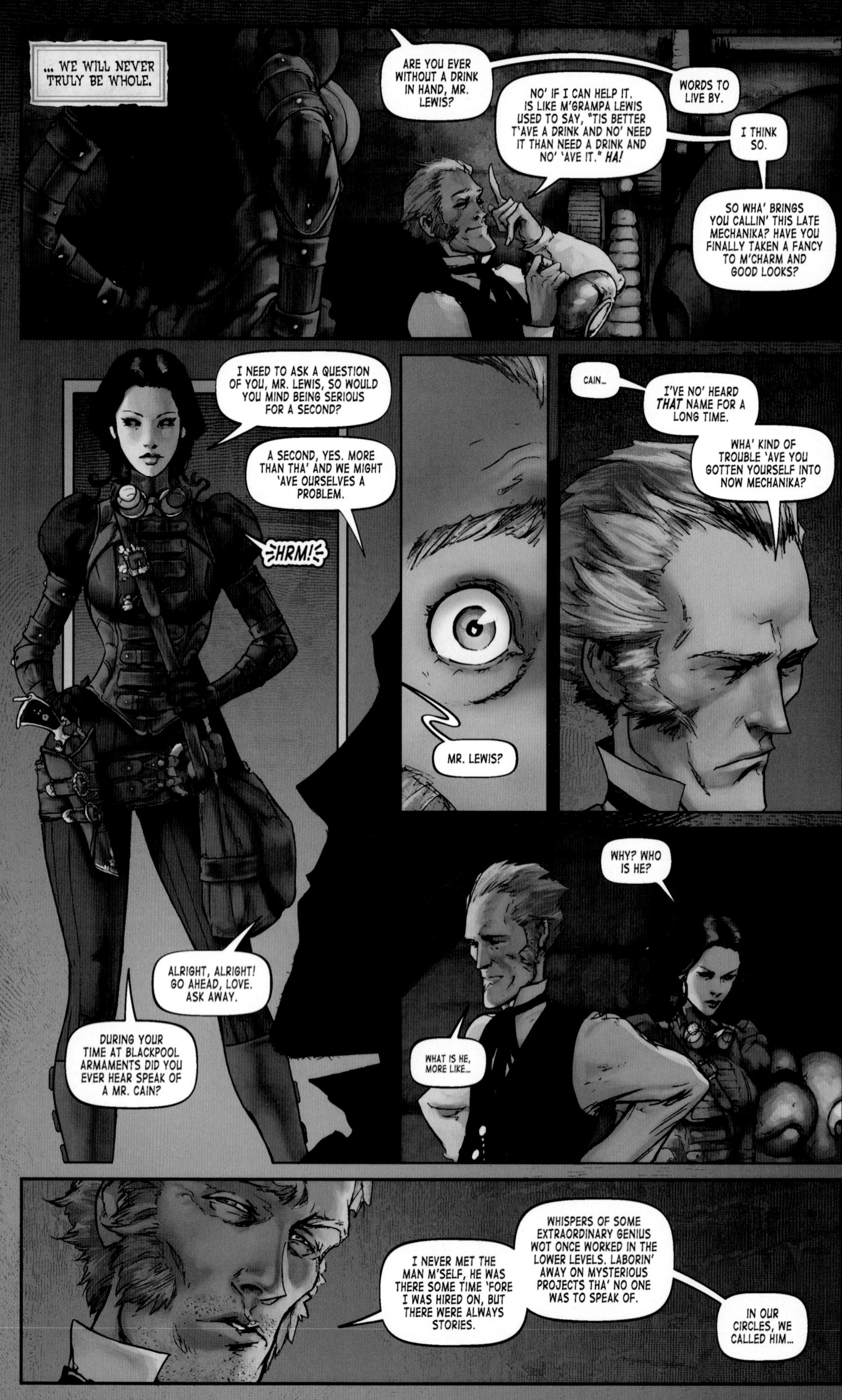

... WE WILL NEVER TRULY BE WHOLE.
ARE YOU EVER WITHOUT A DRINK IN HAND, MR. LEWIS?
NO' IF I CAN HELP IT. IS LIKE M'GRAMPA LEWIS USED TO SAY, "TIS BETTER T'AVE A DRINK AND NO' NEED IT THAN NEED A DRINK AND NO' 'AVE IT." HA!
WORDS TO LIVE BY.
I THINK SO.
SO WHA' BRINGS YOU CALLIN' THIS LATE MECHANIKA? HAVE YOU FINALLY TAKEN A FANCY TO M'CHARM AND GOOD LOOKS?
I NEED TO ASK A QUESTION OF YOU, MR. LEWIS, SO WOULD YOU MIND BEING SERIOUS FOR A SECOND?
A SECOND, YES. MORE THAN THA' AND WE MIGHT 'AVE OURSELVES A PROBLEM.
HRM!
ALRIGHT, ALRIGHT! GO AHEAD, LOVE. ASK AWAY.
DURING YOUR TIME AT BLACKPOOL ARMAMENTS DID YOU EVER HEAR SPEAK OF A MR. CAIN?
MR. LEWIS?
CAIN...
I'VE NO' HEARD THAT NAME FOR A LONG TIME.
WHA' KIND OF TROUBLE 'AVE YOU GOTTEN YOURSELF INTO NOW MECHANIKA?
WHY? WHO IS HE?
WHAT IS HE, MORE LIKE...
I NEVER MET THE MAN M'SELF, HE WAS THERE SOME TIME 'FORE I WAS HIRED ON, BUT THERE WERE ALWAYS STORIES.
WHISPERS OF SOME EXTRAORDINARY GENIUS WOT ONCE WORKED IN THE LOWER LEVELS. LABORIN' AWAY ON MYSTERIOUS PROJECTS THA' NO ONE WAS TO SPEAK OF.
IN OUR CIRCLES, WE CALLED HIM...

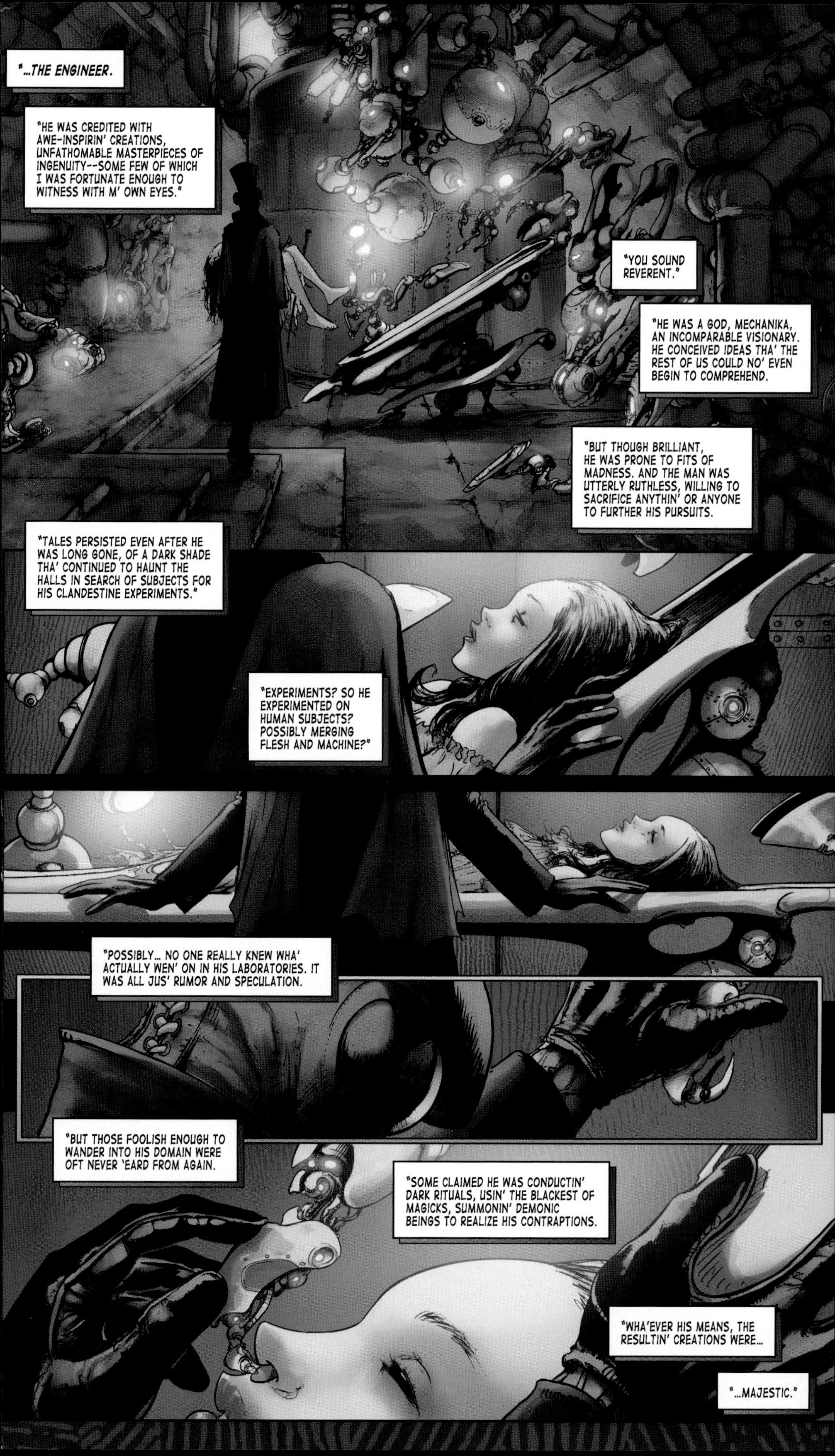
"...THE ENGINEER.
"HE WAS CREDITED WITH AWE-INSPIRIN' CREATIONS, UNFATHOMABLE MASTERPIECES OF INGENUITY--SOME FEW OF WHICH I WAS FORTUNATE ENOUGH TO WITNESS WITH M' OWN EYES."
"YOU SOUND REVERENT."
"HE WAS A GOD, MECHANIKA, AN INCOMPARABLE VISIONARY. HE CONCEIVED IDEAS THA' THE REST OF US COULD NO' EVEN BEGIN TO COMPREHEND.
"BUT THOUGH BRILLIANT, HE WAS PRONE TO FITS OF MADNESS. AND THE MAN WAS UTTERLY RUTHLESS, WILLING TO SACRIFICE ANYTHIN' OR ANYONE TO FURTHER HIS PURSUITS.
"TALES PERSISTED EVEN AFTER HE WAS LONG GONE, OF A DARK SHADE THA' CONTINUED TO HAUNT THE HALLS IN SEARCH OF SUBJECTS FOR HIS CLANDESTINE EXPERIMENTS."
"EXPERIMENTS? SO HE EXPERIMENTED ON HUMAN SUBJECTS? POSSIBLY MERGING FLESH AND MACHINE?"
"POSSIBLY... NO ONE REALLY KNEW WHA' ACTUALLY WEN' ON IN HIS LABORATORIES. IT WAS ALL JUS' RUMOR AND SPECULATION.
"BUT THOSE FOOLISH ENOUGH TO WANDER INTO HIS DOMAIN WERE OFT NEVER 'EARD FROM AGAIN.
"SOME CLAIMED HE WAS CONDUCTIN' DARK RITUALS, USIN' THE BLACKEST OF MAGICKS, SUMMONIN' DEMONIC BEINGS TO REALIZE HIS CONTRAPTIONS.
"WHA'EVER HIS MEANS, THE RESULTIN' CREATIONS WERE...
"...MAJESTIC."

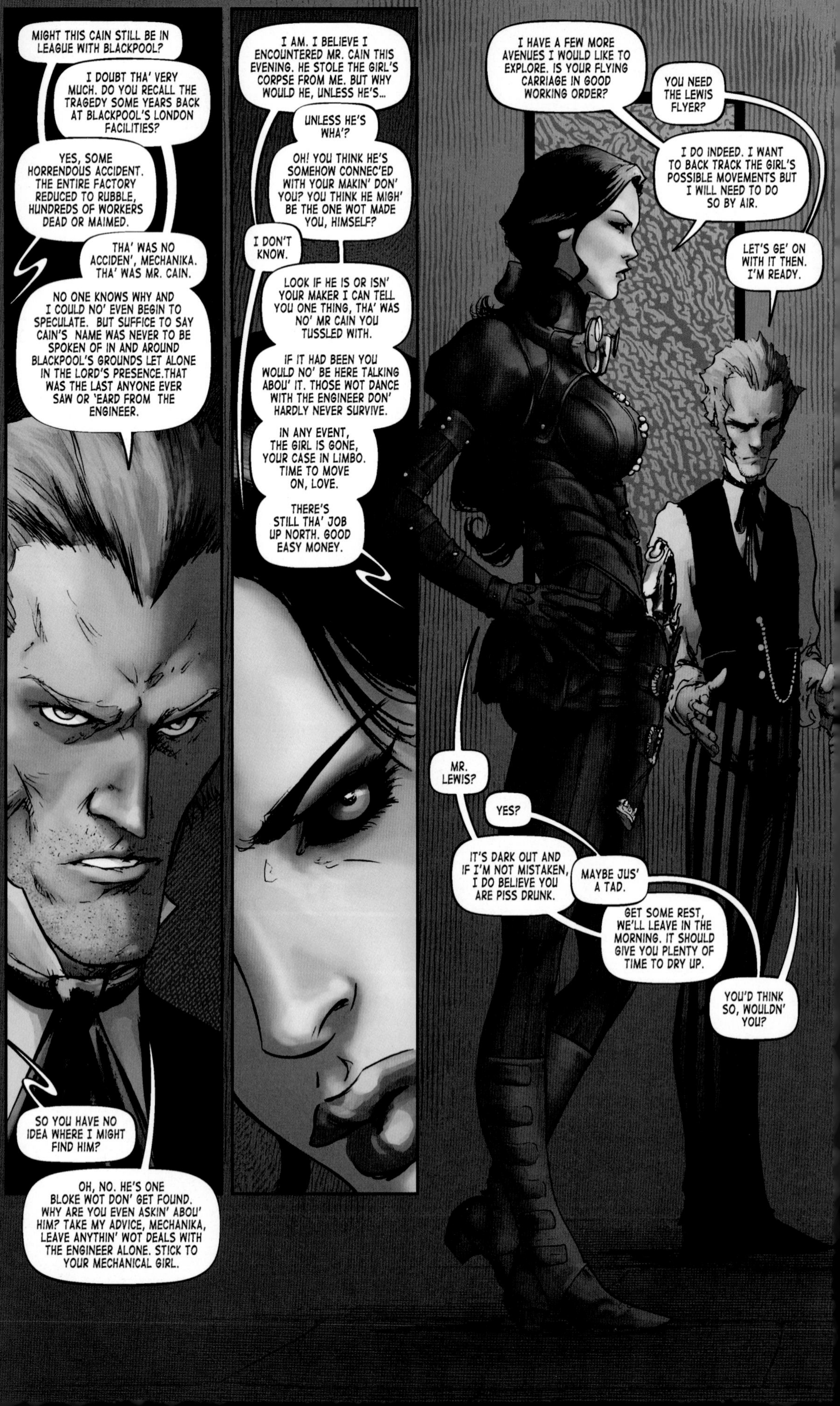
MIGHT THIS CAIN STILL BE IN LEAGUE WITH BLACKPOOL?
I DOUBT THA' VERY MUCH. DO YOU RECALL THE TRAGEDY SOME YEARS BACK AT BLACKPOOL'S LONDON FACILITIES?
YES, SOME HORRENDOUS ACCIDENT. THE ENTIRE FACTORY REDUCED TO RUBBLE, HUNDREDS OF WORKERS DEAD OR MAIMED.
THA' WAS NO ACCIDEN', MECHANIKA. THA' WAS MR. CAIN.
NO ONE KNOWS WHY AND I COULD NO' EVEN BEGIN TO SPECULATE. BUT SUFFICE TO SAY CAIN'S NAME WAS NEVER TO BE SPOKEN OF IN AND AROUND BLACKPOOL'S GROUNDS LET ALONE IN THE LORD'S PRESENCE.THAT WAS THE LAST ANYONE EVER SAW OR 'EARD FROM THE ENGINEER.
SO YOU HAVE NO IDEA WHERE I MIGHT FIND HIM?
OH, NO. HE'S ONE BLOKE WOT DON' GET FOUND. WHY ARE YOU EVEN ASKIN' ABOU' HIM? TAKE MY ADVICE, MECHANIKA, LEAVE ANYTHIN' WOT DEALS WITH THE ENGINEER ALONE. STICK TO YOUR MECHANICAL GIRL.
I AM. I BELIEVE I ENCOUNTERED MR. CAIN THIS EVENING. HE STOLE THE GIRL'S CORPSE FROM ME. BUT WHY WOULD HE, UNLESS HE'S...
UNLESS HE'S WHA'?
OH! YOU THINK HE'S SOMEHOW CONNEC'ED WITH YOUR MAKIN' DON' YOU? YOU THINK HE MIGH' BE THE ONE WOT MADE YOU, HIMSELF?
I DON'T KNOW.
LOOK IF HE IS OR ISN' YOUR MAKER I CAN TELL YOU ONE THING, THA' WAS NO' MR CAIN YOU TUSSLED WITH.
IF IT HAD BEEN YOU WOULD NO' BE HERE TALKING ABOU' IT. THOSE WOT DANCE WITH THE ENGINEER DON' HARDLY NEVER SURVIVE.
IN ANY EVENT, THE GIRL IS GONE, YOUR CASE IN LIMBO. TIME TO MOVE ON, LOVE.
THERE'S STILL THA' JOB UP NORTH. GOOD EASY MONEY.
I HAVE A FEW MORE AVENUES I WOULD LIKE TO EXPLORE. IS YOUR FLYING CARRIAGE IN GOOD WORKING ORDER?
YOU NEED THE LEWIS FLYER?
I DO INDEED. I WANT TO BACK TRACK THE GIRL'S POSSIBLE MOVEMENTS BUT I WILL NEED TO DO SO BY AIR.
LET'S GE' ON WITH IT THEN. I'M READY.
MR. LEWIS?
YES?
IT'S DARK OUT AND IF I'M NOT MISTAKEN, I DO BELIEVE YOU ARE PISS DRUNK.
MAYBE JUS' A TAD.
GET SOME REST, WE'LL LEAVE IN THE MORNING. IT SHOULD GIVE YOU PLENTY OF TIME TO DRY UP.
YOU'D THINK SO, WOULDN' YOU?

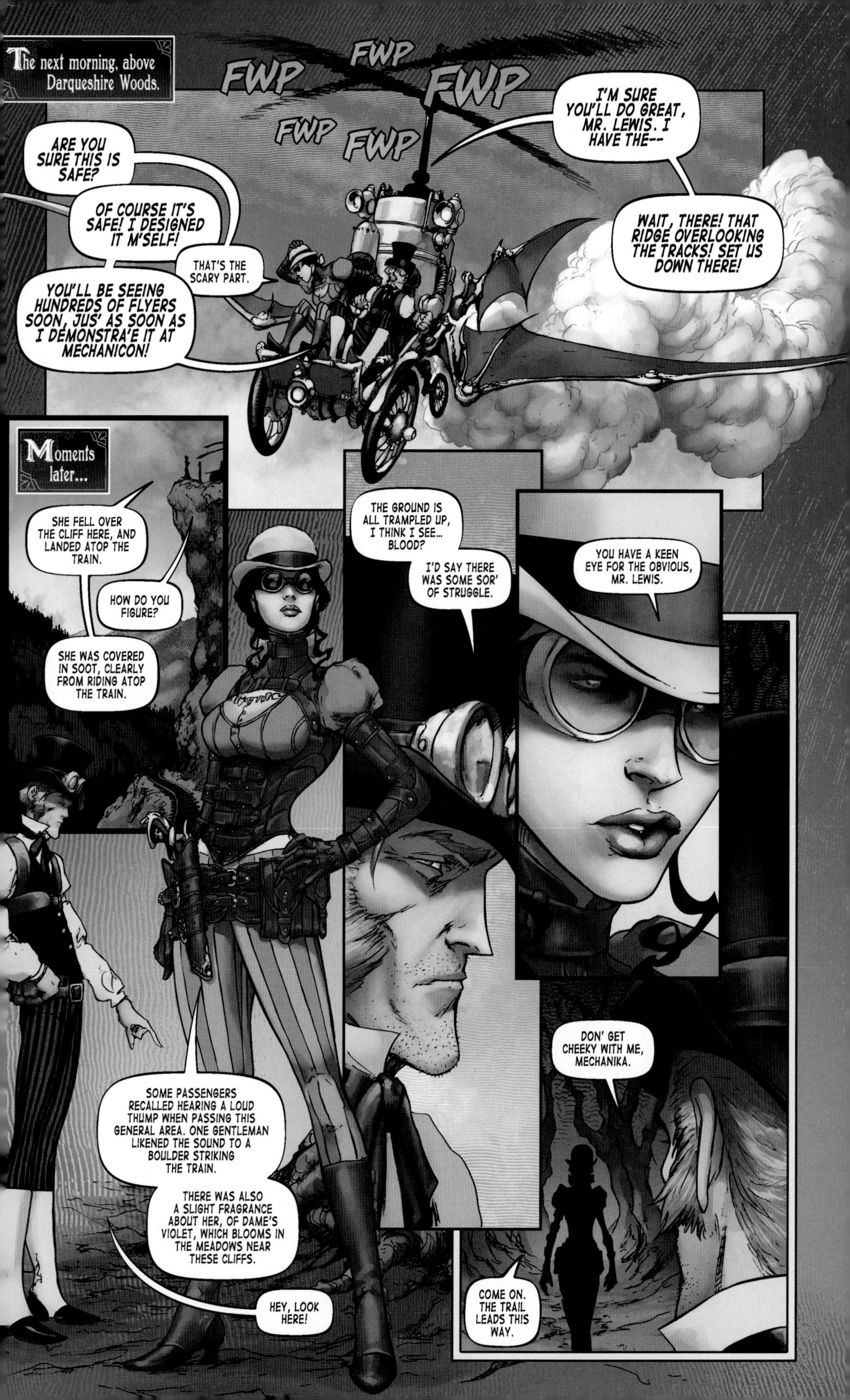

The next morning, above Darqueshire Woods.
FWP FWP FWP FWP FWP
ARE YOU SURE THIS IS SAFE?
OF COURSE IT'S SAFE! I DESIGNED IT M'SELF!
THAT'S THE SCARY PART.
YOU'LL BE SEEING HUNDREDS OF FLYERS SOON, JUS' AS SOON AS I DEMONSTRA'E IT AT MECHANICON!
I'M SURE YOU'LL DO GREAT, MR. LEWIS. I HAVE THE--
WAIT, THERE! THAT RIDGE OVERLOOKING THE TRACKS! SET US DOWN THERE!
Moments later...
SHE FELL OVER THE CLIFF HERE, AND LANDED ATOP THE TRAIN.
HOW DO YOU FIGURE?
SHE WAS COVERED IN SOOT, CLEARLY FROM RIDING ATOP THE TRAIN.
SOME PASSENGERS RECALLED HEARING A LOUD THUMP WHEN PASSING THIS GENERAL AREA. ONE GENTLEMAN LIKENED THE SOUND TO A BOULDER STRIKING THE TRAIN.
THERE WAS ALSO A SLIGHT FRAGRANCE ABOUT HER, OF DAME'S VIOLET, WHICH BLOOMS IN THE MEADOWS NEAR THESE CLIFFS.
HEY, LOOK HERE!
THE GROUND IS ALL TRAMPLED UP, I THINK I SEE... BLOOD?
I'D SAY THERE WAS SOME SOR' OF STRUGGLE.
YOU HAVE A KEEN EYE FOR THE OBVIOUS, MR. LEWIS.
DON' GET CHEEKY WITH ME, MECHANIKA.
COME ON. THE TRAIL LEADS THIS WAY.

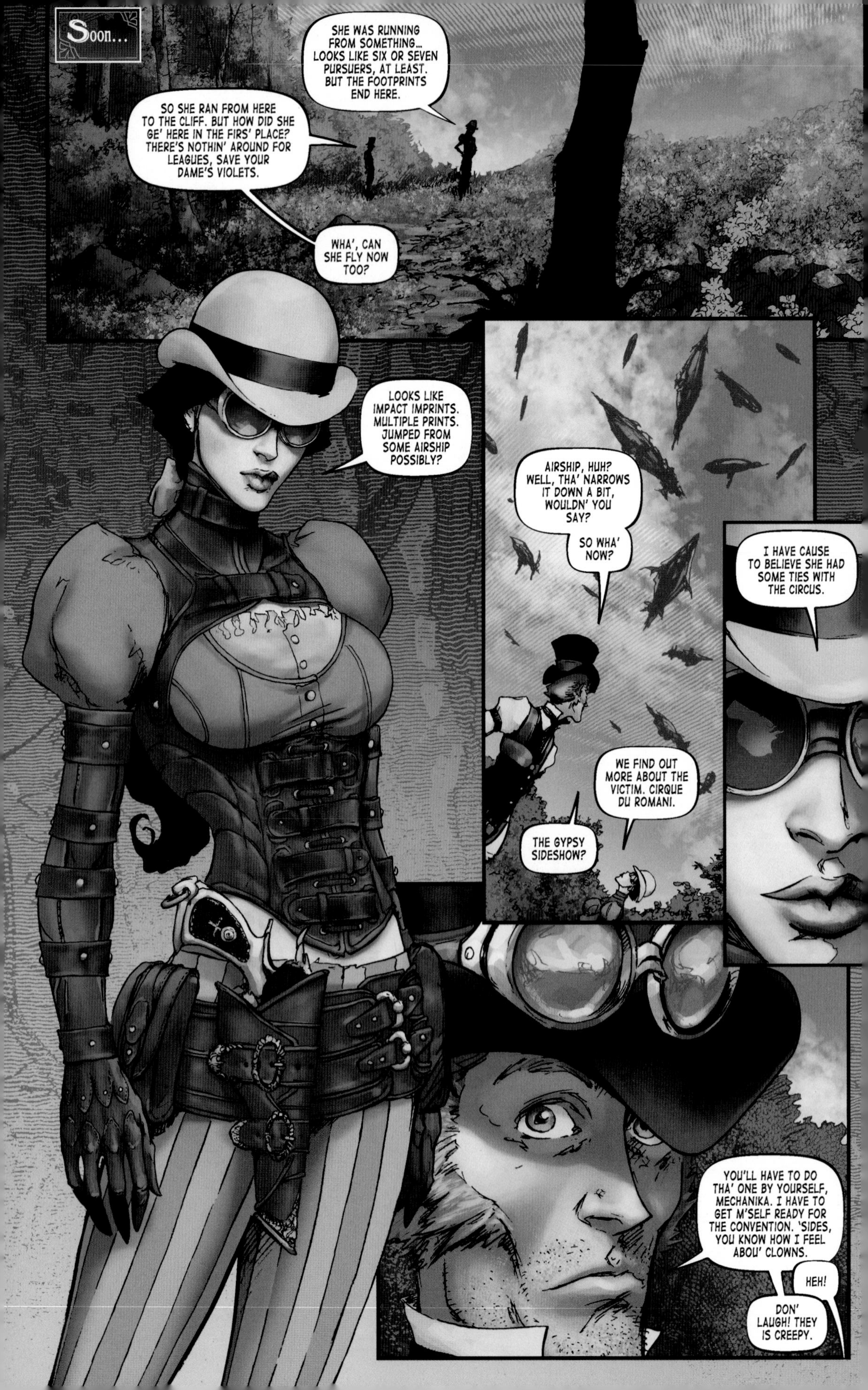
Soon...
SHE WAS RUNNING FROM SOMETHING... LOOKS LIKE SIX OR SEVEN PURSUERS, AT LEAST. BUT THE FOOTPRINTS END HERE.
SO SHE RAN FROM HERE TO THE CLIFF. BUT HOW DID SHE GE' HERE IN THE FIRS' PLACE? THERE'S NOTHIN' AROUND FOR LEAGUES, SAVE YOUR DAME'S VIOLETS.
WHA', CAN SHE FLY NOW TOO?
LOOKS LIKE IMPACT IMPRINTS. MULTIPLE PRINTS. JUMPED FROM SOME AIRSHIP POSSIBLY?
AIRSHIP, HUH? WELL, THA' NARROWS IT DOWN A BIT, WOULDN' YOU SAY?
SO WHA' NOW?
WE FIND OUT MORE ABOUT THE VICTIM. CIRQUE DU ROMANI.
THE GYPSY SIDESHOW?
I HAVE CAUSE TO BELIEVE SHE HAD SOME TIES WITH THE CIRCUS.
YOU'LL HAVE TO DO THA' ONE BY YOURSELF, MECHANIKA. I HAVE TO GET M'SELF READY FOR THE CONVENTION. 'SIDES, YOU KNOW HOW I FEEL ABOU' CLOWNS.
HEH!
DON' LAUGH! THEY IS CREEPY.

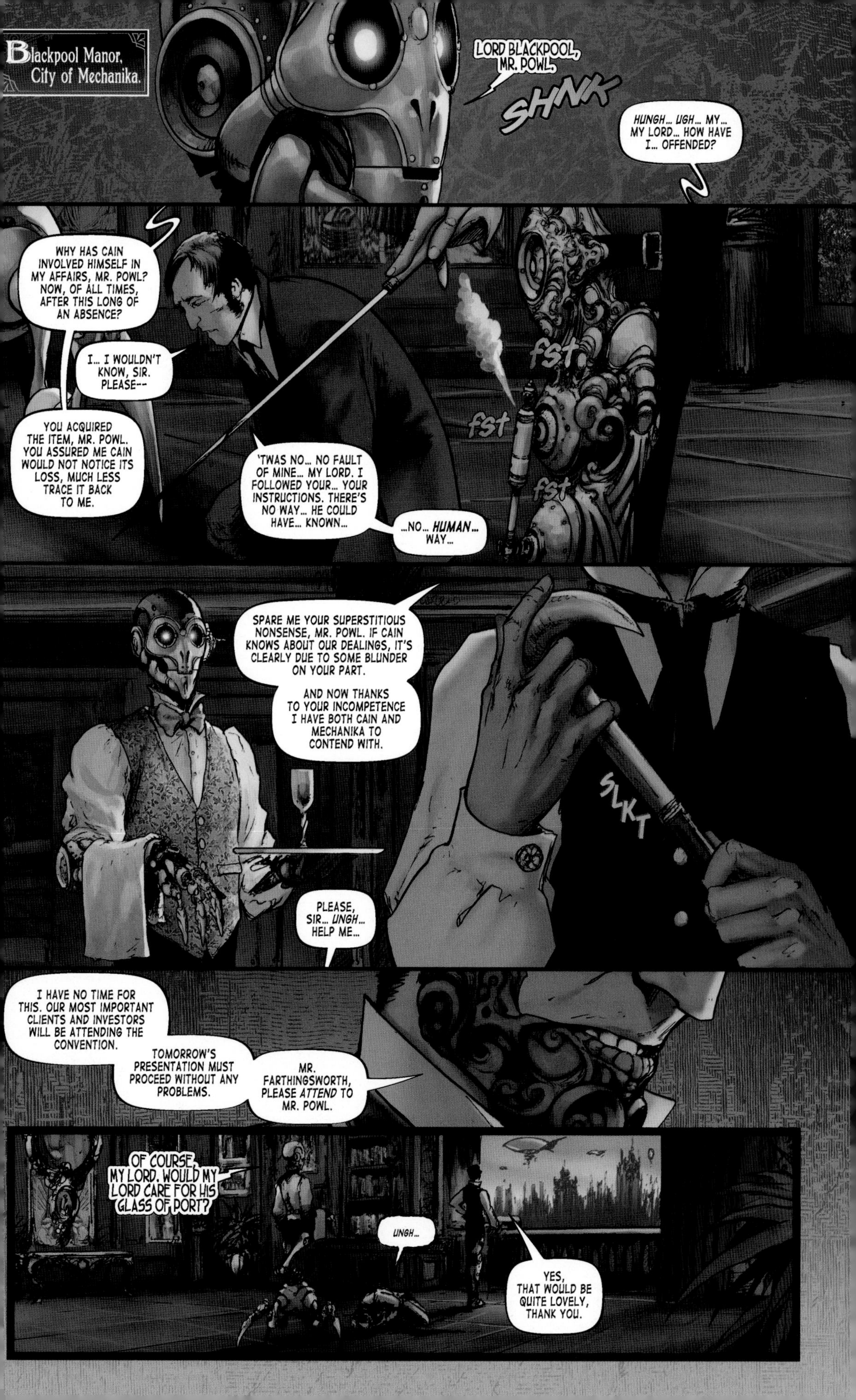

Blackpool Manor, City of Mechanika.
LORD BLACKPOOL, MR. POWL.
SHNK
HUNGH... UGH... MY... MY LORD... HOW HAVE I... OFFENDED?
WHY HAS CAIN INVOLVED HIMSELF IN MY AFFAIRS, MR. POWL? NOW, OF ALL TIMES, AFTER THIS LONG OF AN ABSENCE?
I... I WOULDN'T KNOW, SIR. PLEASE--
fst
fst
YOU ACQUIRED THE ITEM, MR. POWL. YOU ASSURED ME CAIN WOULD NOT NOTICE ITS LOSS, MUCH LESS TRACE IT BACK TO ME.
'TWAS NO... NO FAULT OF MINE... MY LORD. I FOLLOWED YOUR... YOUR INSTRUCTIONS. THERE'S NO WAY... HE COULD HAVE... KNOWN...
fst
...NO... HUMAN... WAY...
SPARE ME YOUR SUPERSTITIOUS NONSENSE, MR. POWL. IF CAIN KNOWS ABOUT OUR DEALINGS, IT'S CLEARLY DUE TO SOME BLUNDER ON YOUR PART.
AND NOW THANKS TO YOUR INCOMPETENCE I HAVE BOTH CAIN AND MECHANIKA TO CONTEND WITH.
SLKT
PLEASE, SIR... UNGH... HELP ME...
I HAVE NO TIME FOR THIS. OUR MOST IMPORTANT CLIENTS AND INVESTORS WILL BE ATTENDING THE CONVENTION.
TOMORROW'S PRESENTATION MUST PROCEED WITHOUT ANY PROBLEMS.
MR. FARTHINGSWORTH, PLEASE ATTEND TO MR. POWL.
OF COURSE, MY LORD. WOULD MY LORD CARE FOR HIS GLASS OF PORT?
UNGH...
YES, THAT WOULD BE QUITE LOVELY, THANK YOU.

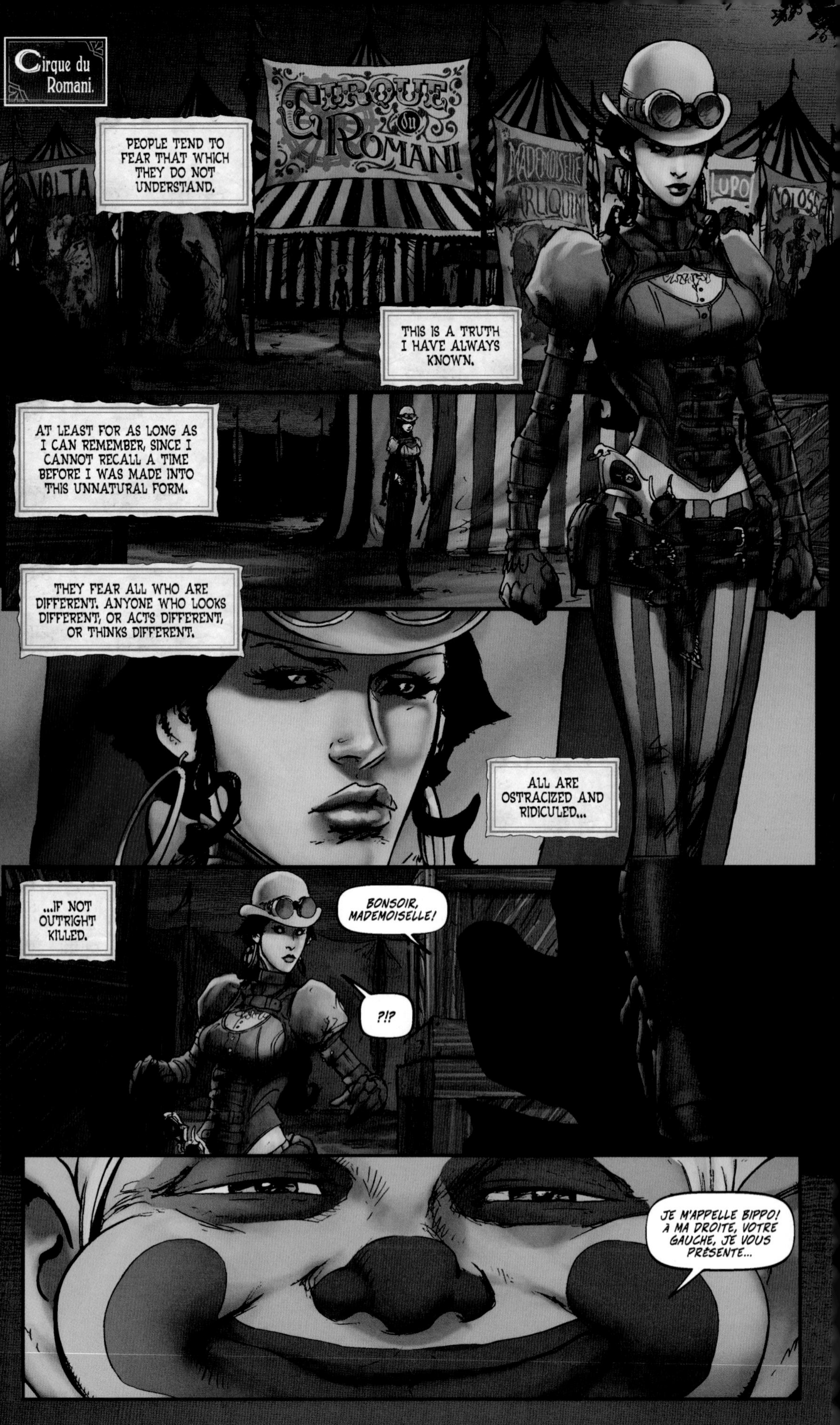
Cirque du Romani.
CIRQUE DU ROMANI
VOLTA
MADEMOISELLE ARLEQUIN
LUPO
COLOSSE
PEOPLE TEND TO FEAR THAT WHICH THEY DO NOT UNDERSTAND.
THIS IS A TRUTH I HAVE ALWAYS KNOWN.
AT LEAST FOR AS LONG AS I CAN REMEMBER, SINCE I CANNOT RECALL A TIME BEFORE I WAS MADE INTO THIS UNNATURAL FORM.
THEY FEAR ALL WHO ARE DIFFERENT. ANYONE WHO LOOKS DIFFERENT, OR ACTS DIFFERENT, OR THINKS DIFFERENT.
ALL ARE OSTRACIZED AND RIDICULED...
...IF NOT OUTRIGHT KILLED.
BONSOIR, MADEMOISELLE!
?!?
JE M'APPELLE BIPPO! À MA DROITE, VOTRE GAUCHE, JE VOUS PRÉSENTE...

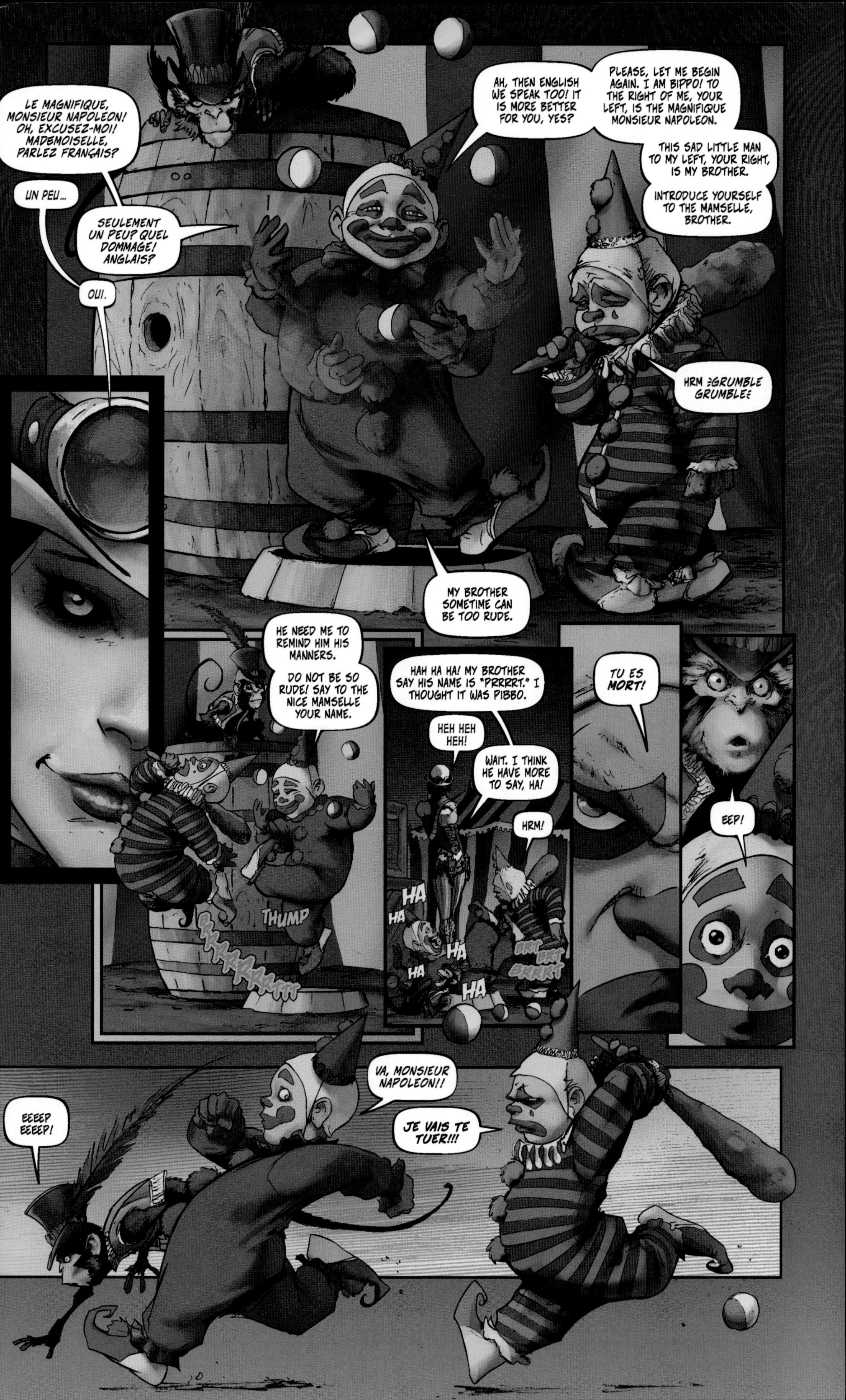
LE MAGNIFIQUE, MONSIEUR NAPOLEON! OH, EXCUSEZ-MOI! MADEMOISELLE, PARLEZ FRANÇAIS?
UN PEU...
SEULEMENT UN PEU? QUEL DOMMAGE! ANGLAIS?
OUI.
AH, THEN ENGLISH WE SPEAK TOO! IT IS MORE BETTER FOR YOU, YES?
PLEASE, LET ME BEGIN AGAIN. I AM BIPPO! TO THE RIGHT OF ME, YOUR LEFT, IS THE MAGNIFIQUE MONSIEUR NAPOLEON.
THIS SAD LITTLE MAN TO MY LEFT, YOUR RIGHT, IS MY BROTHER.
INTRODUCE YOURSELF TO THE MAMSELLE, BROTHER.
HRM =GRUMBLE GRUMBLE=
MY BROTHER SOMETIME CAN BE TOO RUDE.
HE NEED ME TO REMIND HIM HIS MANNERS.
DO NOT BE SO RUDE! SAY TO THE NICE MAMSELLE YOUR NAME.
THUMP
HAH HA HA! MY BROTHER SAY HIS NAME IS "PRRRRT." I THOUGHT IT WAS PIBBO.
HEH HEH HEH!
WAIT. I THINK HE HAVE MORE TO SAY, HA!
HRM!
HA
HA
HA
HA
HA
TU ES MORT!
EEP!
EEEEP EEEEP!
VA, MONSIEUR NAPOLEON!!
JE VAIS TE TUER!!!

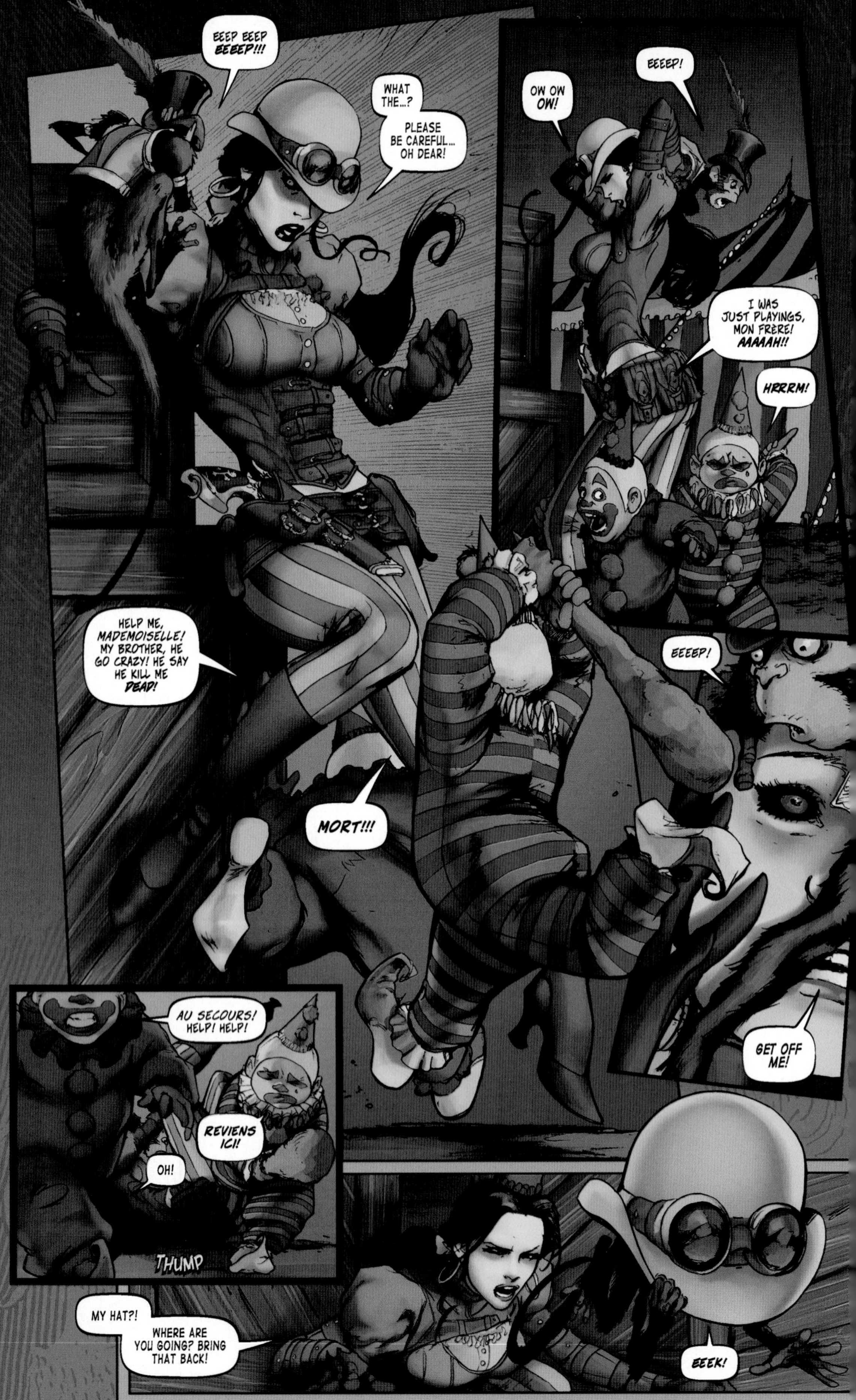
EEEP EEEP EEEEP!!!
WHAT THE...?
PLEASE BE CAREFUL... OH DEAR!
OW OW OW!
EEEEP!
I WAS JUST PLAYINGS, MON FRÈRE! AAAAAH!!
HRRRM!
HELP ME, MADEMOISELLE! MY BROTHER, HE GO CRAZY! HE SAY HE KILL ME DEAD!
EEEEP!
MORT!!!
GET OFF ME!
AU SECOURS! HELP! HELP!
REVIENS ICI!
OH!
THUMP
MY HAT?!
WHERE ARE YOU GOING? BRING THAT BACK!
EEEK!

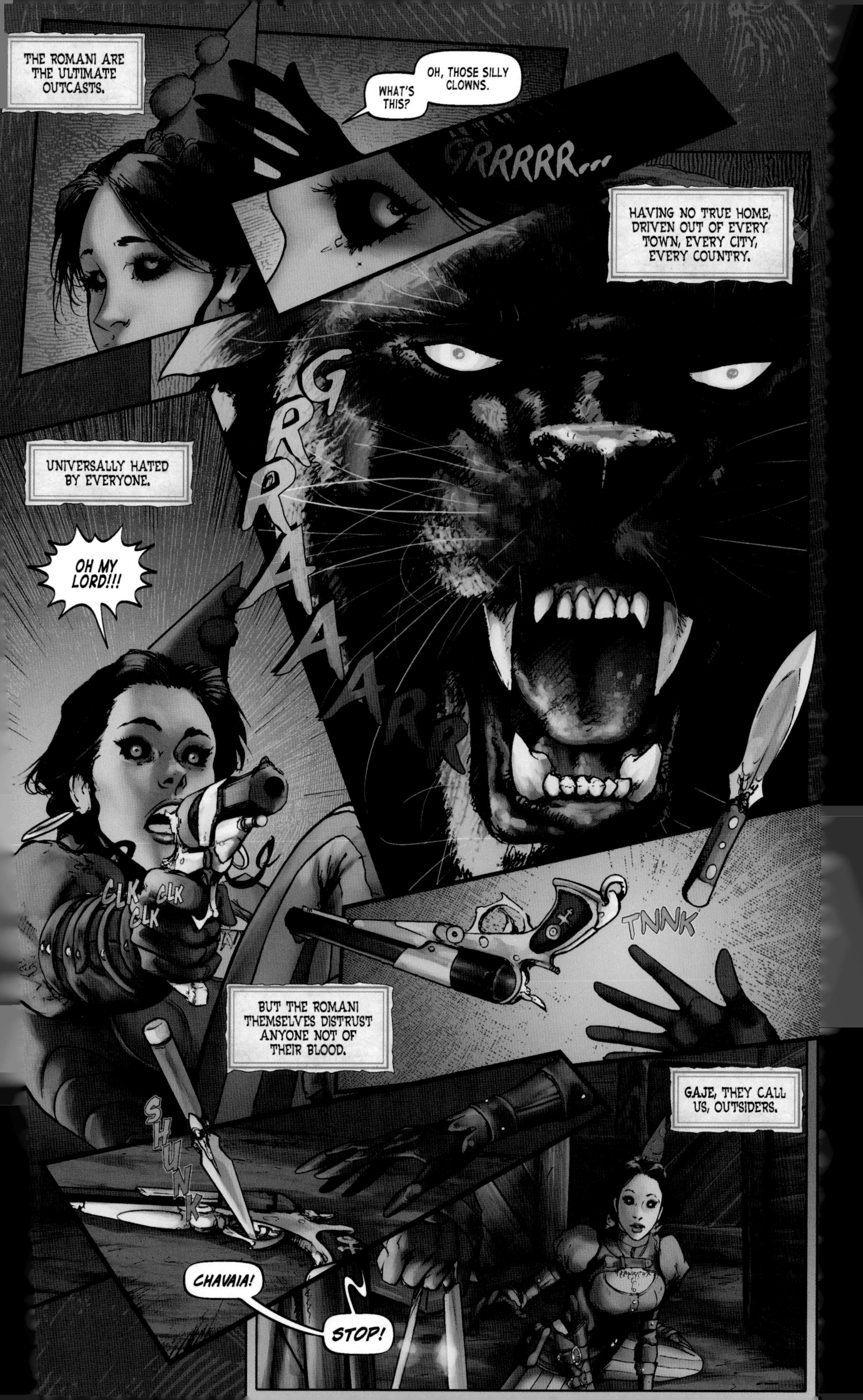
THE ROMANI ARE THE ULTIMATE OUTCASTS.
WHAT'S THIS?
OH, THOSE SILLY CLOWNS.
GRRRRR...
HAVING NO TRUE HOME, DRIVEN OUT OF EVERY TOWN, EVERY CITY, EVERY COUNTRY.
GRRAAAARR
UNIVERSALLY HATED BY EVERYONE.
OH MY LORD!!!
CLK CLK CLK
TNNK
BUT THE ROMANI THEMSELVES DISTRUST ANYONE NOT OF THEIR BLOOD.
GAJE, THEY CALL US, OUTSIDERS.
SHUNK
CHAVAIA!
STOP!

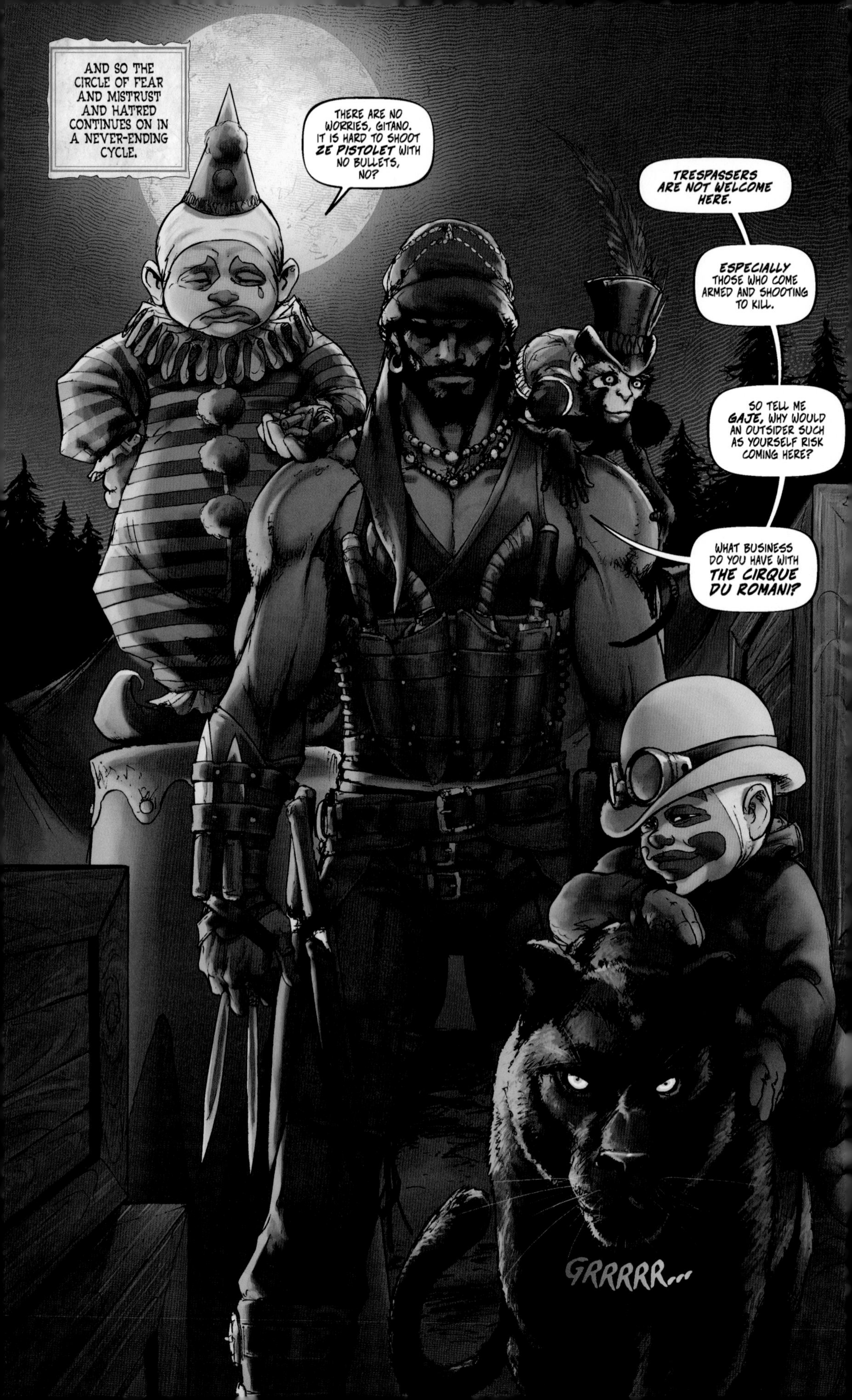

AND SO THE CIRCLE OF FEAR AND MISTRUST AND HATRED CONTINUES ON IN A NEVER-ENDING CYCLE.
THERE ARE NO WORRIES, GITANO. IT IS HARD TO SHOOT ZE PISTOLET WITH NO BULLETS, NO?
TRESPASSERS ARE NOT WELCOME HERE.
ESPECIALLY THOSE WHO COME ARMED AND SHOOTING TO KILL.
SO TELL ME GAJE, WHY WOULD AN OUTSIDER SUCH AS YOURSELF RISK COMING HERE?
WHAT BUSINESS DO YOU HAVE WITH THE CIRQUE DU ROMANI?
GRRRRR...

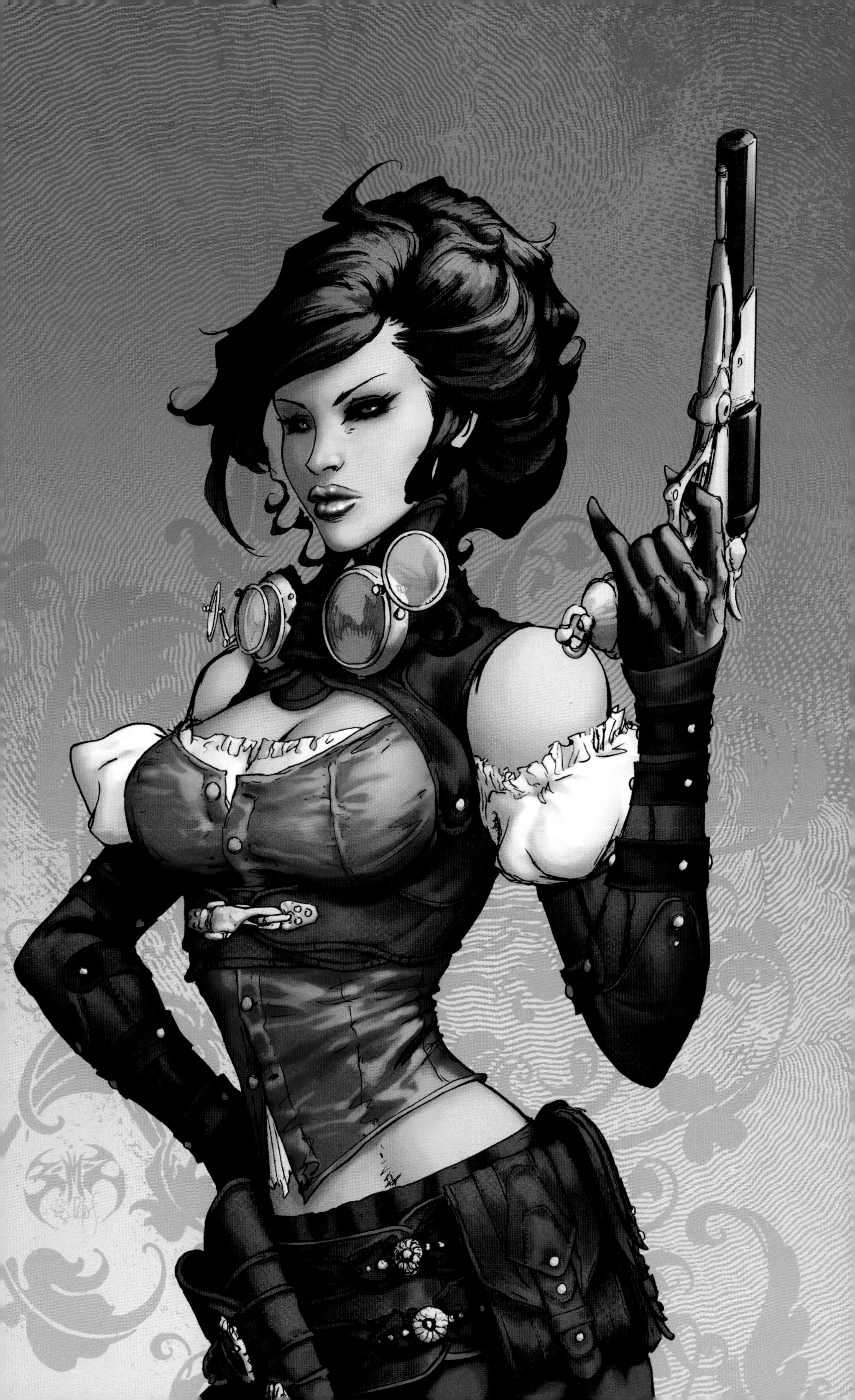

Chapter Three

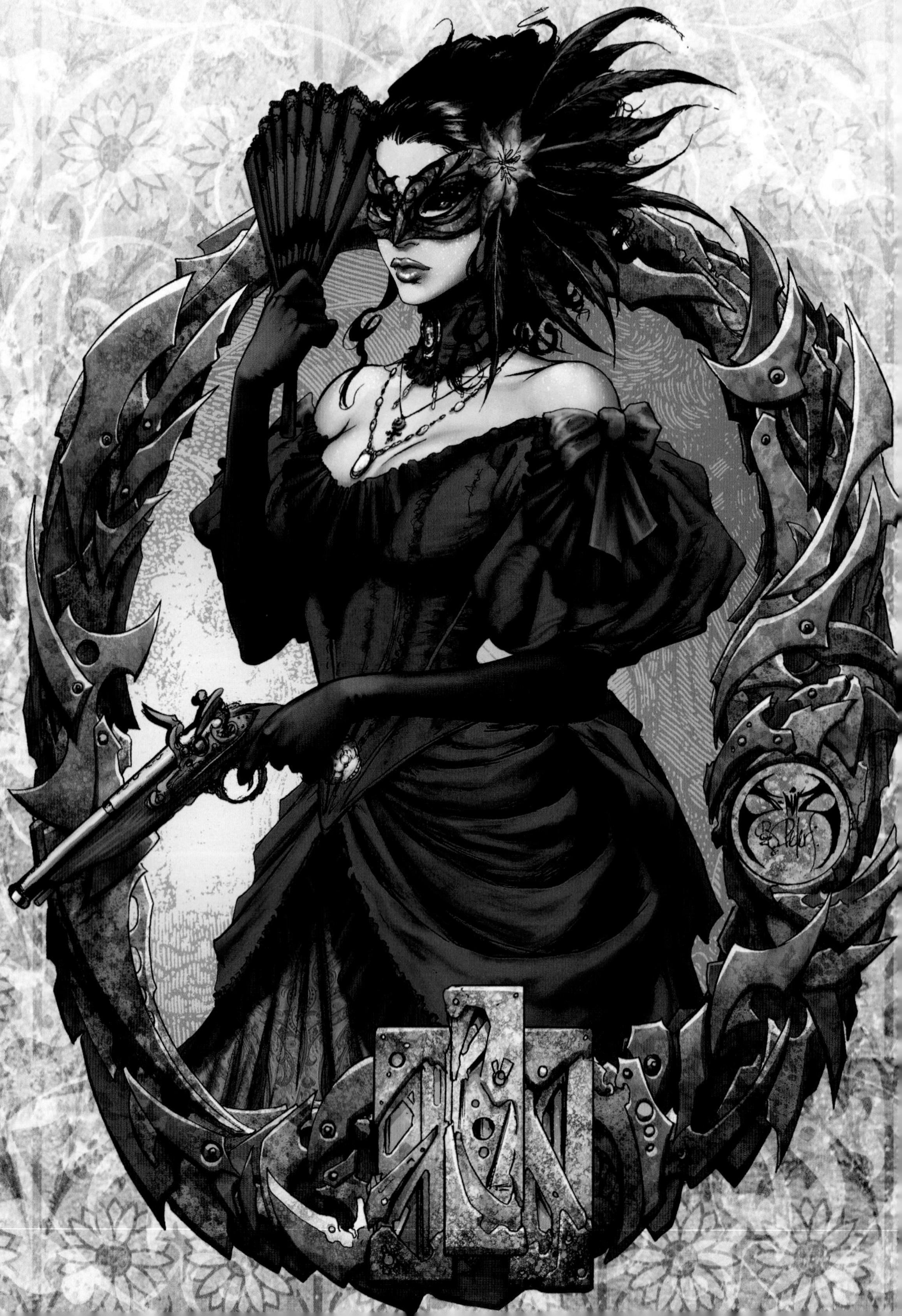

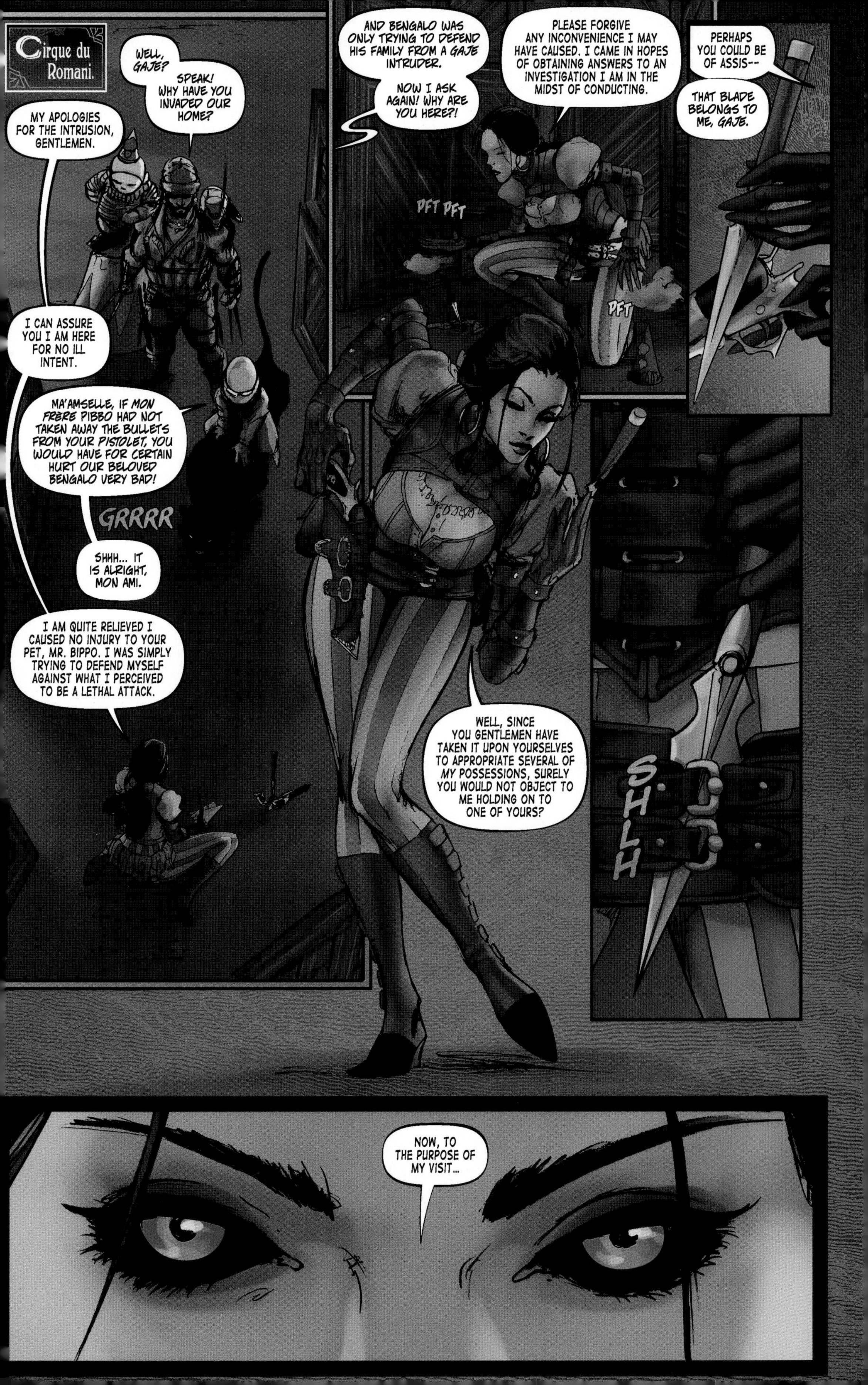
Cirque du Romani.
WELL, GAJE?
SPEAK! WHY HAVE YOU INVADED OUR HOME?
MY APOLOGIES FOR THE INTRUSION, GENTLEMEN.
AND BENGALO WAS ONLY TRYING TO DEFEND HIS FAMILY FROM A GAJE INTRUDER.
NOW I ASK AGAIN! WHY ARE YOU HERE?!
PLEASE FORGIVE ANY INCONVENIENCE I MAY HAVE CAUSED. I CAME IN HOPES OF OBTAINING ANSWERS TO AN INVESTIGATION I AM IN THE MIDST OF CONDUCTING.
PFT PFT
PFT
PERHAPS YOU COULD BE OF ASSIS--
THAT BLADE BELONGS TO ME, GAJE.
I CAN ASSURE YOU I AM HERE FOR NO ILL INTENT.
MA'AMSELLE, IF MON FRÈRE PIBBO HAD NOT TAKEN AWAY THE BULLETS FROM YOUR PISTOLET, YOU WOULD HAVE FOR CERTAIN HURT OUR BELOVED BENGALO VERY BAD!
GRRRR
SHHH... IT IS ALRIGHT, MON AMI.
I AM QUITE RELIEVED I CAUSED NO INJURY TO YOUR PET, MR. BIPPO. I WAS SIMPLY TRYING TO DEFEND MYSELF AGAINST WHAT I PERCEIVED TO BE A LETHAL ATTACK.
WELL, SINCE YOU GENTLEMEN HAVE TAKEN IT UPON YOURSELVES TO APPROPRIATE SEVERAL OF MY POSSESSIONS, SURELY YOU WOULD NOT OBJECT TO ME HOLDING ON TO ONE OF YOURS?
SHLH
NOW, TO THE PURPOSE OF MY VISIT...

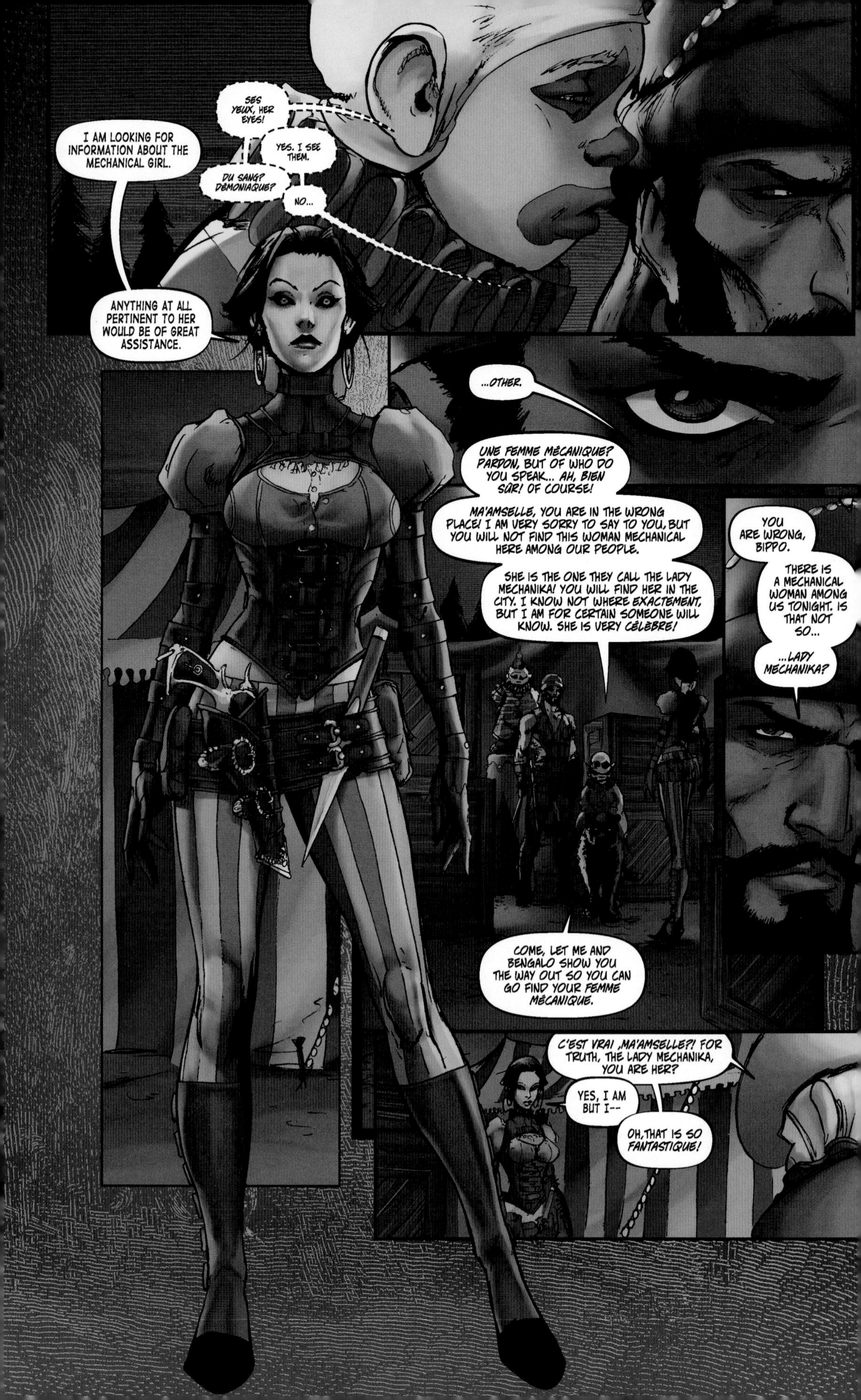
I AM LOOKING FOR INFORMATION ABOUT THE MECHANICAL GIRL.
SES YEUX, HER EYES!
YES. I SEE THEM.
DU SANG? DÉMONIAQUE?
NO...
ANYTHING AT ALL PERTINENT TO HER WOULD BE OF GREAT ASSISTANCE.
...OTHER.
UNE FEMME MÉCANIQUE? PARDON, BUT OF WHO DO YOU SPEAK... AH, BIEN SÛR! OF COURSE!
MA'AMSELLE, YOU ARE IN THE WRONG PLACE! I AM VERY SORRY TO SAY TO YOU, BUT YOU WILL NOT FIND THIS WOMAN MECHANICAL HERE AMONG OUR PEOPLE.
SHE IS THE ONE THEY CALL THE LADY MECHANIKA! YOU WILL FIND HER IN THE CITY. I KNOW NOT WHERE EXACTEMENT, BUT I AM FOR CERTAIN SOMEONE WILL KNOW. SHE IS VERY CÉLÈBRE!
COME, LET ME AND BENGALO SHOW YOU THE WAY OUT SO YOU CAN GO FIND YOUR FEMME MÉCANIQUE.
YOU ARE WRONG, BIPPO.
THERE IS A MECHANICAL WOMAN AMONG US TONIGHT. IS THAT NOT SO...
...LADY MECHANIKA?
C'EST VRAI ,MA'AMSELLE?! FOR TRUTH, THE LADY MECHANIKA, YOU ARE HER?
YES, I AM BUT I--
OH,THAT IS SO FANTASTIQUE!

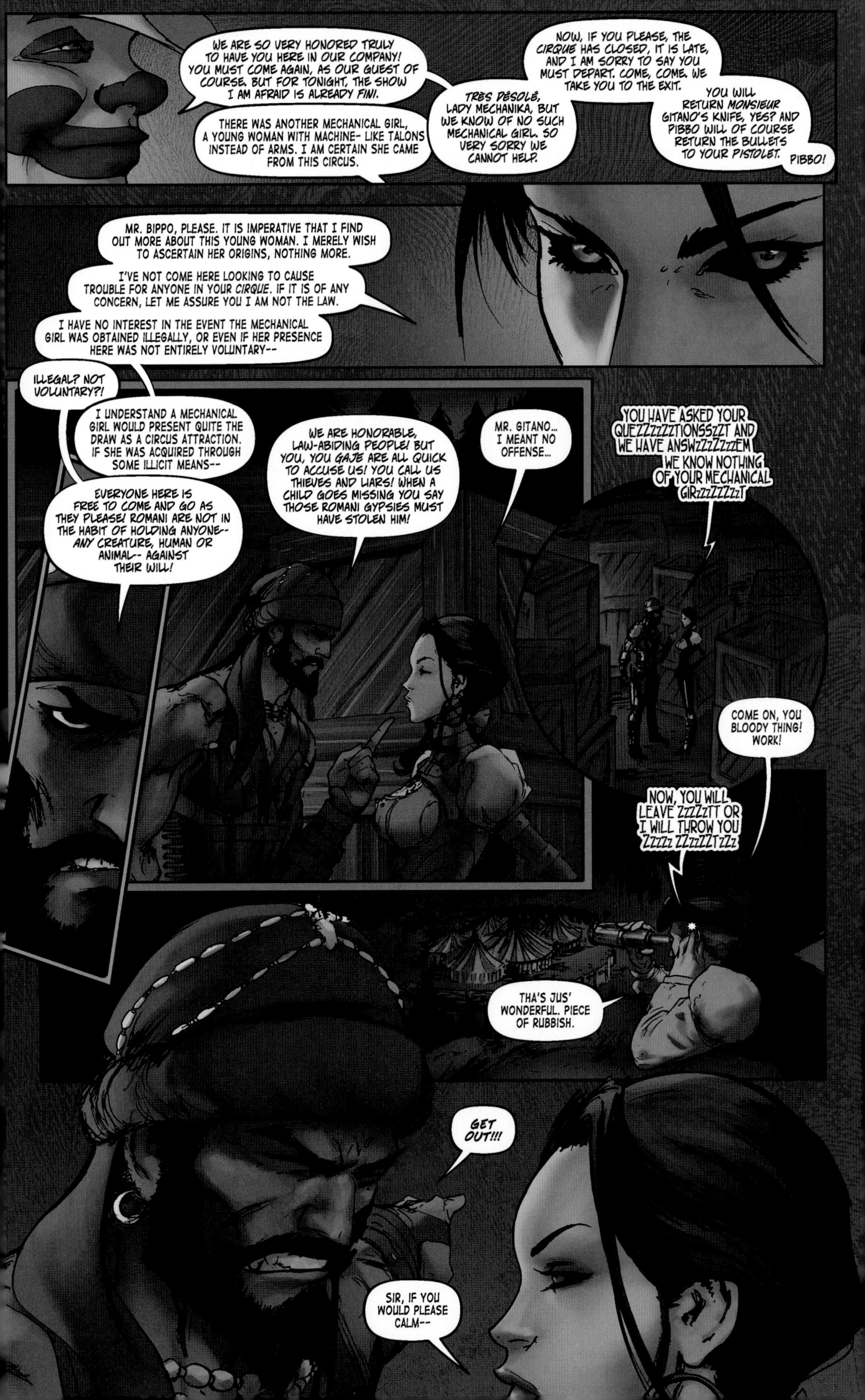

WE ARE SO VERY HONORED TRULY TO HAVE YOU HERE IN OUR COMPANY! YOU MUST COME AGAIN, AS OUR GUEST OF COURSE. BUT FOR TONIGHT, THE SHOW I AM AFRAID IS ALREADY FINI.
THERE WAS ANOTHER MECHANICAL GIRL, A YOUNG WOMAN WITH MACHINE- LIKE TALONS INSTEAD OF ARMS. I AM CERTAIN SHE CAME FROM THIS CIRCUS.
TRÈS DÉSOLÉ, LADY MECHANIKA, BUT WE KNOW OF NO SUCH MECHANICAL GIRL. SO VERY SORRY WE CANNOT HELP.
NOW, IF YOU PLEASE, THE CIRQUE HAS CLOSED, IT IS LATE, AND I AM SORRY TO SAY YOU MUST DEPART. COME, COME. WE TAKE YOU TO THE EXIT.
YOU WILL RETURN MONSIEUR GITANO'S KNIFE, YES? AND PIBBO WILL OF COURSE RETURN THE BULLETS TO YOUR PISTOLET.
PIBBO!
MR. BIPPO, PLEASE. IT IS IMPERATIVE THAT I FIND OUT MORE ABOUT THIS YOUNG WOMAN. I MERELY WISH TO ASCERTAIN HER ORIGINS, NOTHING MORE.
I'VE NOT COME HERE LOOKING TO CAUSE TROUBLE FOR ANYONE IN YOUR CIRQUE. IF IT IS OF ANY CONCERN, LET ME ASSURE YOU I AM NOT THE LAW.
I HAVE NO INTEREST IN THE EVENT THE MECHANICAL GIRL WAS OBTAINED ILLEGALLY, OR EVEN IF HER PRESENCE HERE WAS NOT ENTIRELY VOLUNTARY--
ILLEGAL? NOT VOLUNTARY?!
I UNDERSTAND A MECHANICAL GIRL WOULD PRESENT QUITE THE DRAW AS A CIRCUS ATTRACTION. IF SHE WAS ACQUIRED THROUGH SOME ILLICIT MEANS--
EVERYONE HERE IS FREE TO COME AND GO AS THEY PLEASE! ROMANI ARE NOT IN THE HABIT OF HOLDING ANYONE-- ANY CREATURE, HUMAN OR ANIMAL-- AGAINST THEIR WILL!
WE ARE HONORABLE, LAW-ABIDING PEOPLE! BUT YOU, YOU GAJE ARE ALL QUICK TO ACCUSE US! YOU CALL US THIEVES AND LIARS! WHEN A CHILD GOES MISSING YOU SAY THOSE ROMANI GYPSIES MUST HAVE STOLEN HIM!
MR. GITANO... I MEANT NO OFFENSE...
YOU HAVE ASKED YOUR QUEZZZzzzzTIONSSzZT AND WE HAVE ANSWzZzZzzzEM WE KNOW NOTHING OF YOUR MECHANICAL GIRzzzZZZZzT
COME ON, YOU BLOODY THING! WORK!
NOW, YOU WILL LEAVE ZzZZzTT OR I WILL THROW YOU ZzZZz ZZzzZZTzZz
THA'S JUS' WONDERFUL. PIECE OF RUBBISH.
GET OUT!!!
SIR, IF YOU WOULD PLEASE CALM--

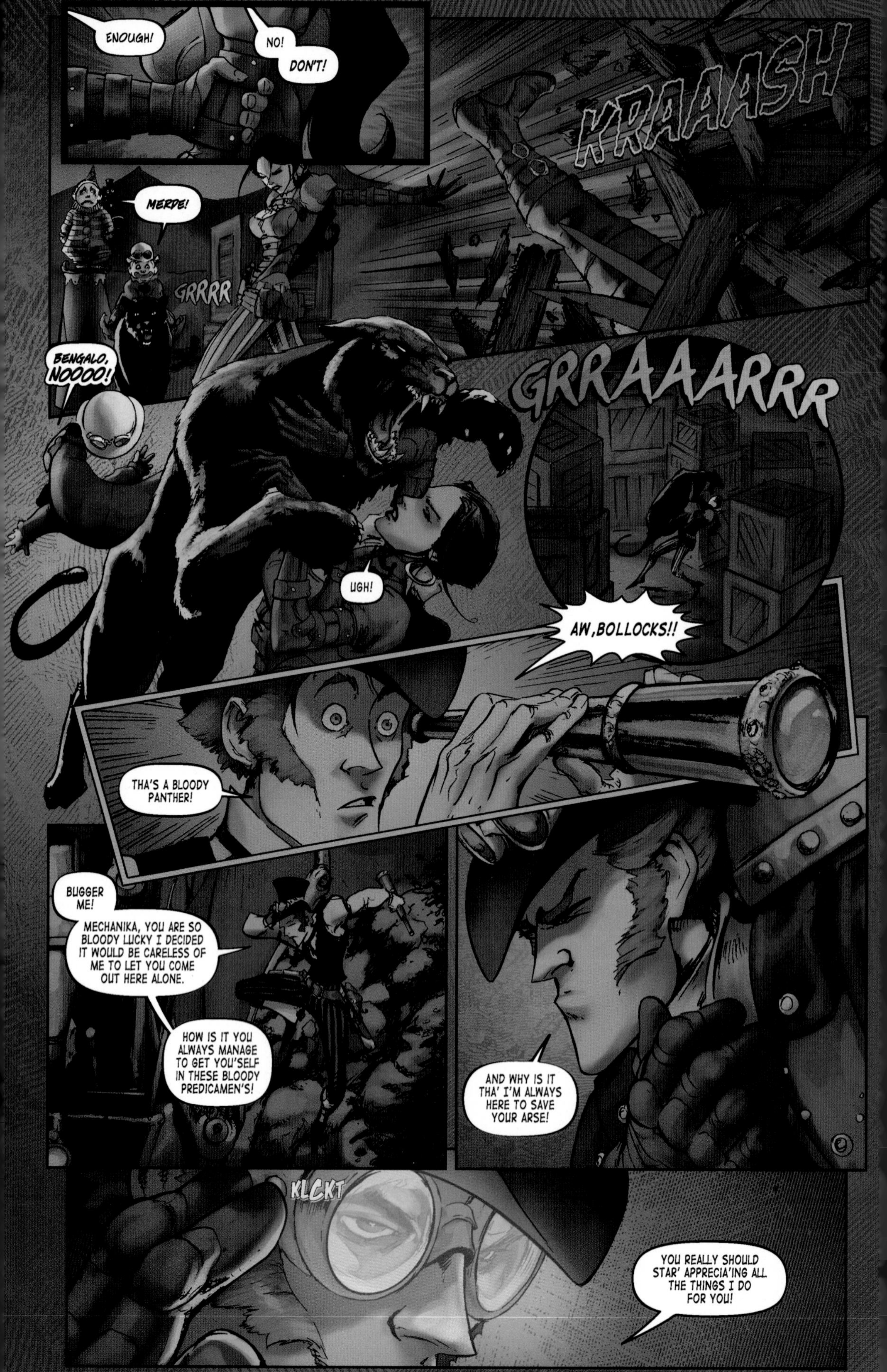
ENOUGH!
NO!
DON'T!
KRAAASH
MERDE!
GRRRR
BENGALO, NOOOO!
GRRAAARRR
UGH!
AW, BOLLOCKS!!
THA'S A BLOODY PANTHER!
BUGGER ME!
MECHANIKA, YOU ARE SO BLOODY LUCKY I DECIDED IT WOULD BE CARELESS OF ME TO LET YOU COME OUT HERE ALONE.
HOW IS IT YOU ALWAYS MANAGE TO GET YOU'SELF IN THESE BLOODY PREDICAMEN'S!
AND WHY IS IT THA' I'M ALWAYS HERE TO SAVE YOUR ARSE!
KLCKT
YOU REALLY SHOULD STAR' APPRECIA'ING ALL THE THINGS I DO FOR YOU!

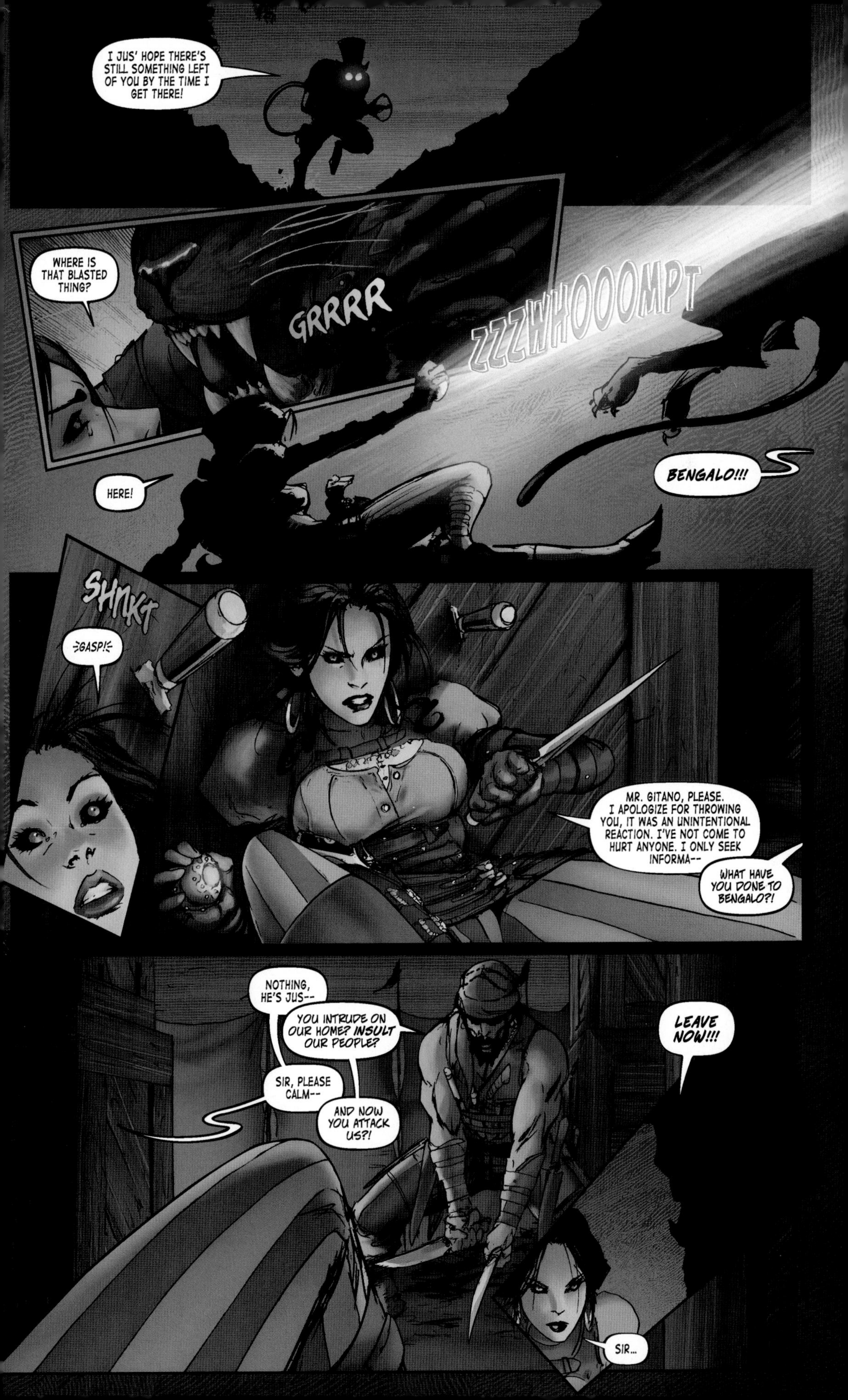
I JUS' HOPE THERE'S STILL SOMETHING LEFT OF YOU BY THE TIME I GET THERE!
WHERE IS THAT BLASTED THING?
GRRRR
ZZZWHOOOMPT
HERE!
BENGALO!!!
SHNKT
GASP!
MR. GITANO, PLEASE. I APOLOGIZE FOR THROWING YOU, IT WAS AN UNINTENTIONAL REACTION. I'VE NOT COME TO HURT ANYONE. I ONLY SEEK INFORMA--
WHAT HAVE YOU DONE TO BENGALO?!
NOTHING, HE'S JUS--
YOU INTRUDE ON OUR HOME? INSULT OUR PEOPLE?
SIR, PLEASE CALM--
AND NOW YOU ATTACK US?!
LEAVE NOW!!!
SIR...

PLEASE, HEAR ME OUT...
GET OUT NOW!!!
I DON'T WISH TO FIGHT YOU!
PTHMK
WHAK
WILL YOU PLEASE...
HNG!
...LISTEN!
HUNGH!
TMWP
BENGALO IS FINE, I PROMISE YOU! HE IS SIMPLY STUNNED, NOTHING MORE. HE SHOULD BE UP AND ABOUT IN A MATTER OF MOMENTS.
AS I'VE STATED, I AM HERE FOR INFORMATION ON THE MECHANICAL GIRL, THAT IS ALL.
AND WE HAVE STATED WE KNOW NOTHING OF ANY MECHANICAL GIRL!
YOU WILL FORGIVE ME IF I AM NOT FULLY CONVINCED BY YOUR PROTESTATIONS OF INNOCENCE. CLEARLY YOU ARE HIDING SOMETHING. YOU HAVE BEEN FAR TOO EAGER FOR ME TO DEPART.
YOU BREAK IN AND ATTACK US IN OUR OWN HOME! OF COURSE WE WANT YOU TO LEAVE!
AGAIN, I APOLOGIZE. I INTENDED NO HARM TO YOU OR YOUR CAT, MR. GITANO. YOU, ON THE OTHER HAND, WOULD HAVE KILLED ME IF YOUR KNIFE HAD NOT MISSED.
MY BLADES NEVER... MISS.
STOP.

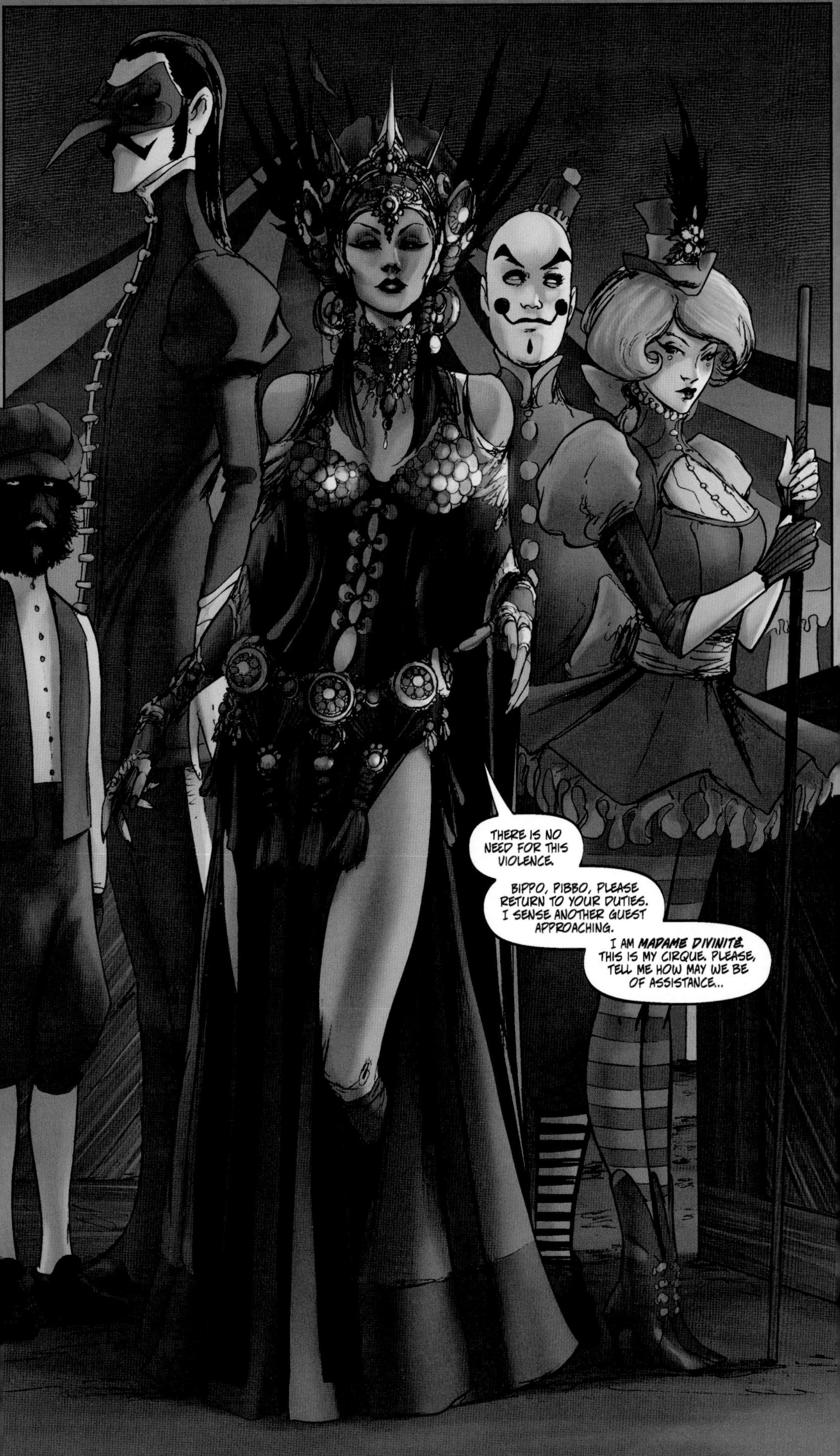
THERE IS NO NEED FOR THIS VIOLENCE.
BIPPO, PIBBO, PLEASE RETURN TO YOUR DUTIES. I SENSE ANOTHER GUEST APPROACHING.
I AM MADAME DIVINITÉ. THIS IS MY CIRQUE. PLEASE, TELL ME HOW MAY WE BE OF ASSISTANCE...

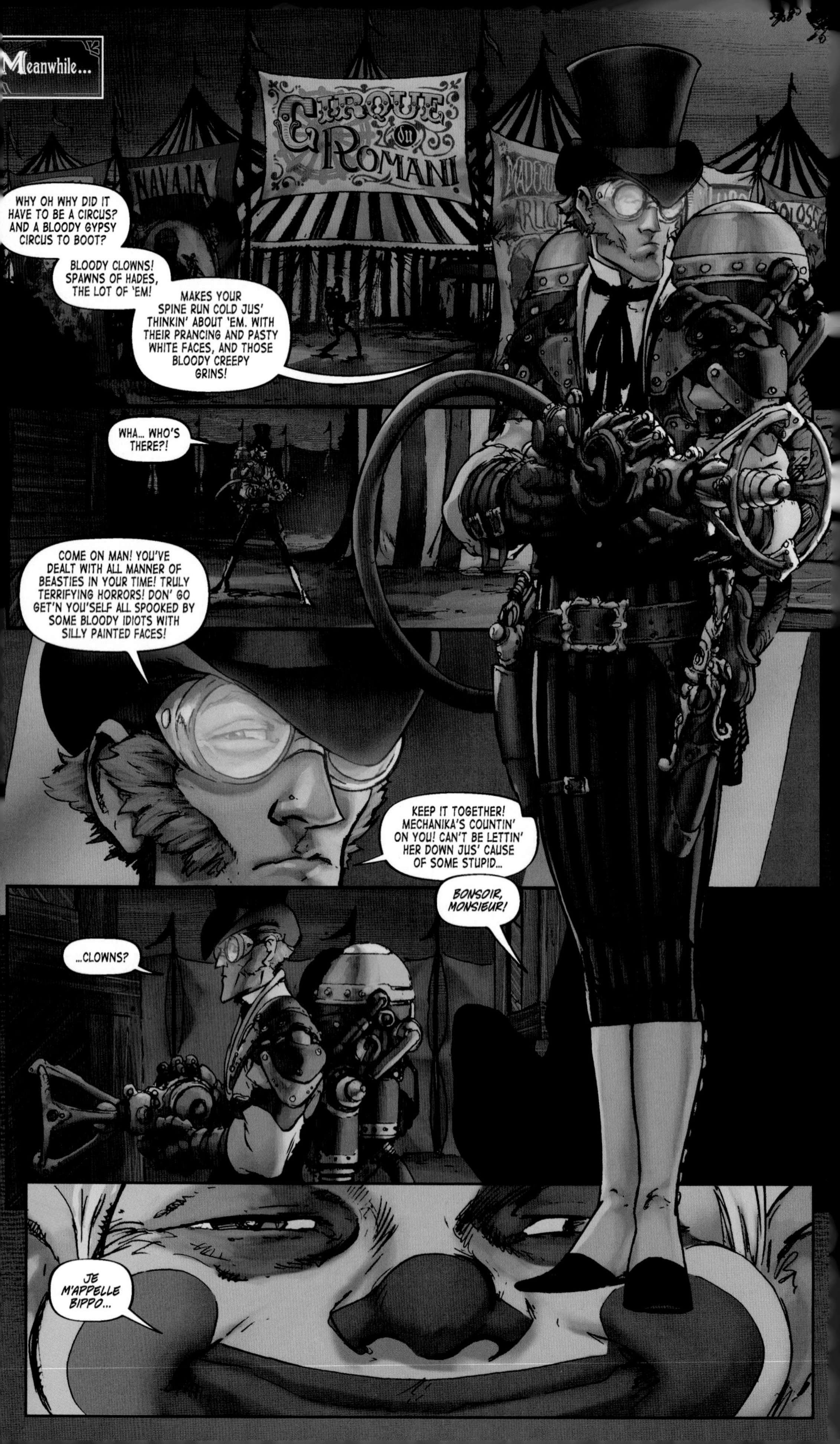
Meanwhile...
CIRQUE ON ROMANI!
WHY OH WHY DID IT HAVE TO BE A CIRCUS? AND A BLOODY GYPSY CIRCUS TO BOOT?
BLOODY CLOWNS! SPAWNS OF HADES, THE LOT OF 'EM!
MAKES YOUR SPINE RUN COLD JUS' THINKIN' ABOUT 'EM. WITH THEIR PRANCING AND PASTY WHITE FACES, AND THOSE BLOODY CREEPY GRINS!
WHA... WHO'S THERE?!
COME ON MAN! YOU'VE DEALT WITH ALL MANNER OF BEASTIES IN YOUR TIME! TRULY TERRIFYING HORRORS! DON' GO GET'N YOU'SELF ALL SPOOKED BY SOME BLOODY IDIOTS WITH SILLY PAINTED FACES!
KEEP IT TOGETHER! MECHANIKA'S COUNTIN' ON YOU! CAN'T BE LETTIN' HER DOWN JUS' CAUSE OF SOME STUPID...
BONSOIR, MONSIEUR!
...CLOWNS?
JE M'APPELLE BIPPO...

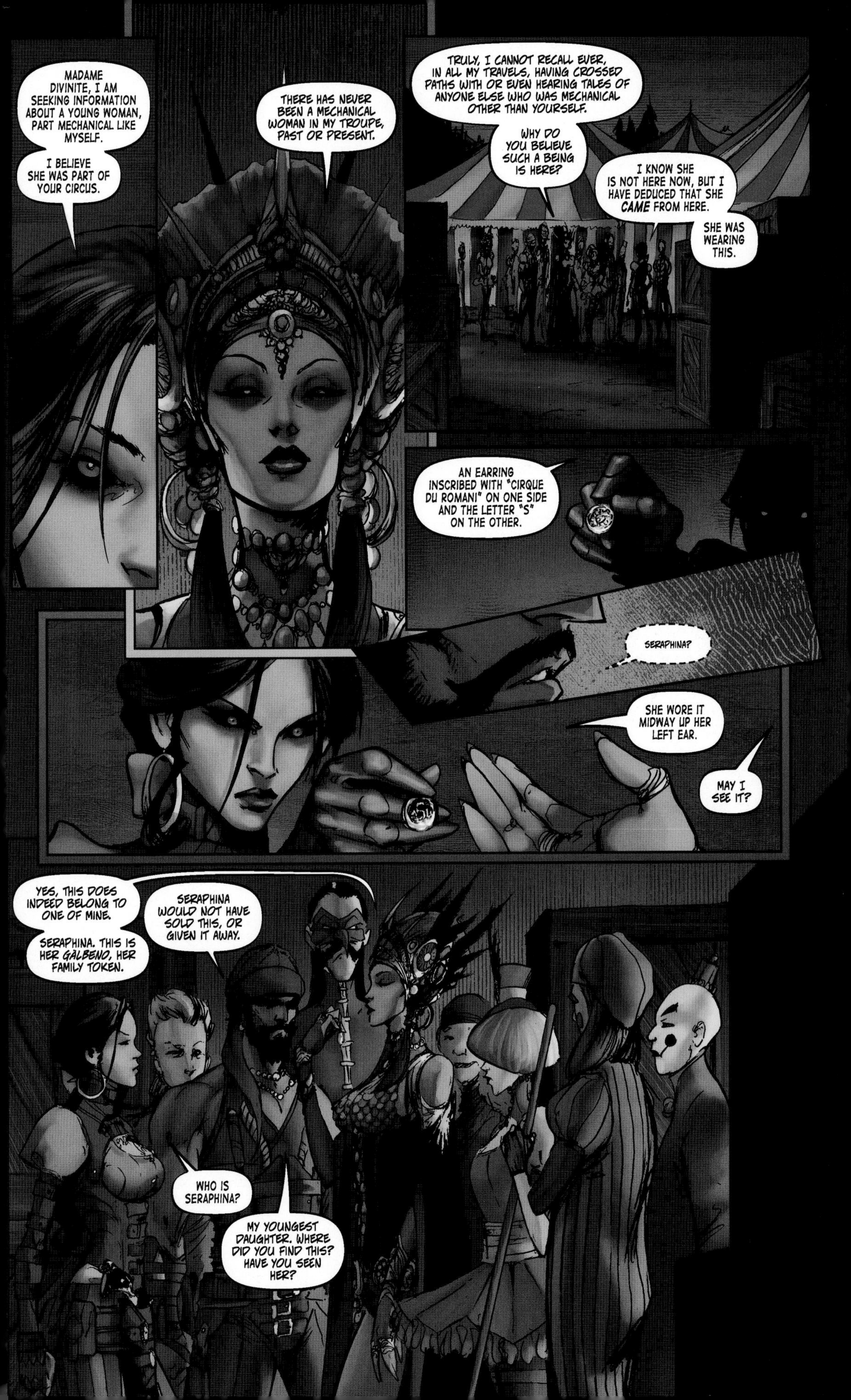

MADAME DIVINITE, I AM SEEKING INFORMATION ABOUT A YOUNG WOMAN, PART MECHANICAL LIKE MYSELF.
I BELIEVE SHE WAS PART OF YOUR CIRCUS.
THERE HAS NEVER BEEN A MECHANICAL WOMAN IN MY TROUPE, PAST OR PRESENT.
TRULY, I CANNOT RECALL EVER, IN ALL MY TRAVELS, HAVING CROSSED PATHS WITH OR EVEN HEARING TALES OF ANYONE ELSE WHO WAS MECHANICAL OTHER THAN YOURSELF.
WHY DO YOU BELIEVE SUCH A BEING IS HERE?
I KNOW SHE IS NOT HERE NOW, BUT I HAVE DEDUCED THAT SHE CAME FROM HERE.
SHE WAS WEARING THIS.
AN EARRING INSCRIBED WITH "CIRQUE DU ROMANI" ON ONE SIDE AND THE LETTER "S" ON THE OTHER.
SERAPHINA?
SHE WORE IT MIDWAY UP HER LEFT EAR.
MAY I SEE IT?
YES, THIS DOES INDEED BELONG TO ONE OF MINE.
SERAPHINA. THIS IS HER GALBENO, HER FAMILY TOKEN.
SERAPHINA WOULD NOT HAVE SOLD THIS, OR GIVEN IT AWAY.
WHO IS SERAPHINA?
MY YOUNGEST DAUGHTER. WHERE DID YOU FIND THIS? HAVE YOU SEEN HER?

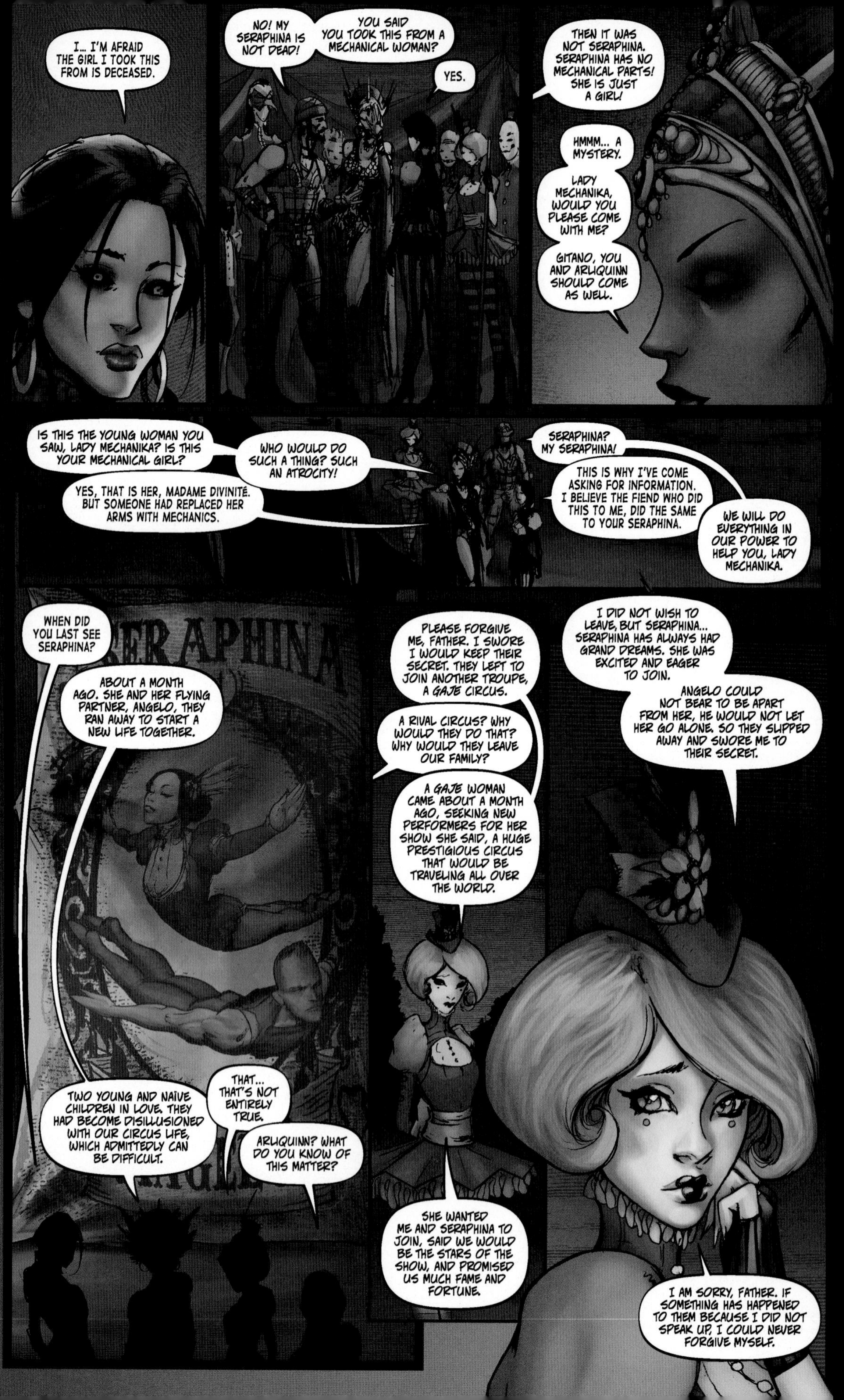
I... I'M AFRAID THE GIRL I TOOK THIS FROM IS DECEASED.
NO! MY SERAPHINA IS NOT DEAD!
YOU SAID YOU TOOK THIS FROM A MECHANICAL WOMAN?
YES.
THEN IT WAS NOT SERAPHINA. SERAPHINA HAS NO MECHANICAL PARTS! SHE IS JUST A GIRL!
HMMM... A MYSTERY.
LADY MECHANIKA, WOULD YOU PLEASE COME WITH ME?
GITANO, YOU AND ARLIQUINN SHOULD COME AS WELL.
IS THIS THE YOUNG WOMAN YOU SAW, LADY MECHANIKA? IS THIS YOUR MECHANICAL GIRL?
YES, THAT IS HER, MADAME DIVINITÉ. BUT SOMEONE HAD REPLACED HER ARMS WITH MECHANICS.
WHO WOULD DO SUCH A THING? SUCH AN ATROCITY!
SERAPHINA? MY SERAPHINA!
THIS IS WHY I'VE COME ASKING FOR INFORMATION. I BELIEVE THE FIEND WHO DID THIS TO ME, DID THE SAME TO YOUR SERAPHINA.
WE WILL DO EVERYTHING IN OUR POWER TO HELP YOU, LADY MECHANIKA.
WHEN DID YOU LAST SEE SERAPHINA?
SERAPHINA
ABOUT A MONTH AGO. SHE AND HER FLYING PARTNER, ANGELO, THEY RAN AWAY TO START A NEW LIFE TOGETHER.
TWO YOUNG AND NAIVE CHILDREN IN LOVE. THEY HAD BECOME DISILLUSIONED WITH OUR CIRCUS LIFE, WHICH ADMITTEDLY CAN BE DIFFICULT.
THAT... THAT'S NOT ENTIRELY TRUE.
ARLIQUINN? WHAT DO YOU KNOW OF THIS MATTER?
PLEASE FORGIVE ME, FATHER. I SWORE I WOULD KEEP THEIR SECRET. THEY LEFT TO JOIN ANOTHER TROUPE, A GAJE CIRCUS.
A RIVAL CIRCUS? WHY WOULD THEY DO THAT? WHY WOULD THEY LEAVE OUR FAMILY?
A GAJE WOMAN CAME ABOUT A MONTH AGO, SEEKING NEW PERFORMERS FOR HER SHOW SHE SAID, A HUGE PRESTIGIOUS CIRCUS THAT WOULD BE TRAVELING ALL OVER THE WORLD.
SHE WANTED ME AND SERAPHINA TO JOIN, SAID WE WOULD BE THE STARS OF THE SHOW, AND PROMISED US MUCH FAME AND FORTUNE.
I DID NOT WISH TO LEAVE, BUT SERAPHINA... SERAPHINA HAS ALWAYS HAD GRAND DREAMS. SHE WAS EXCITED AND EAGER TO JOIN.
ANGELO COULD NOT BEAR TO BE APART FROM HER, HE WOULD NOT LET HER GO ALONE. SO THEY SLIPPED AWAY AND SWORE ME TO THEIR SECRET.
I AM SORRY, FATHER. IF SOMETHING HAS HAPPENED TO THEM BECAUSE I DID NOT SPEAK UP, I COULD NEVER FORGIVE MYSELF.

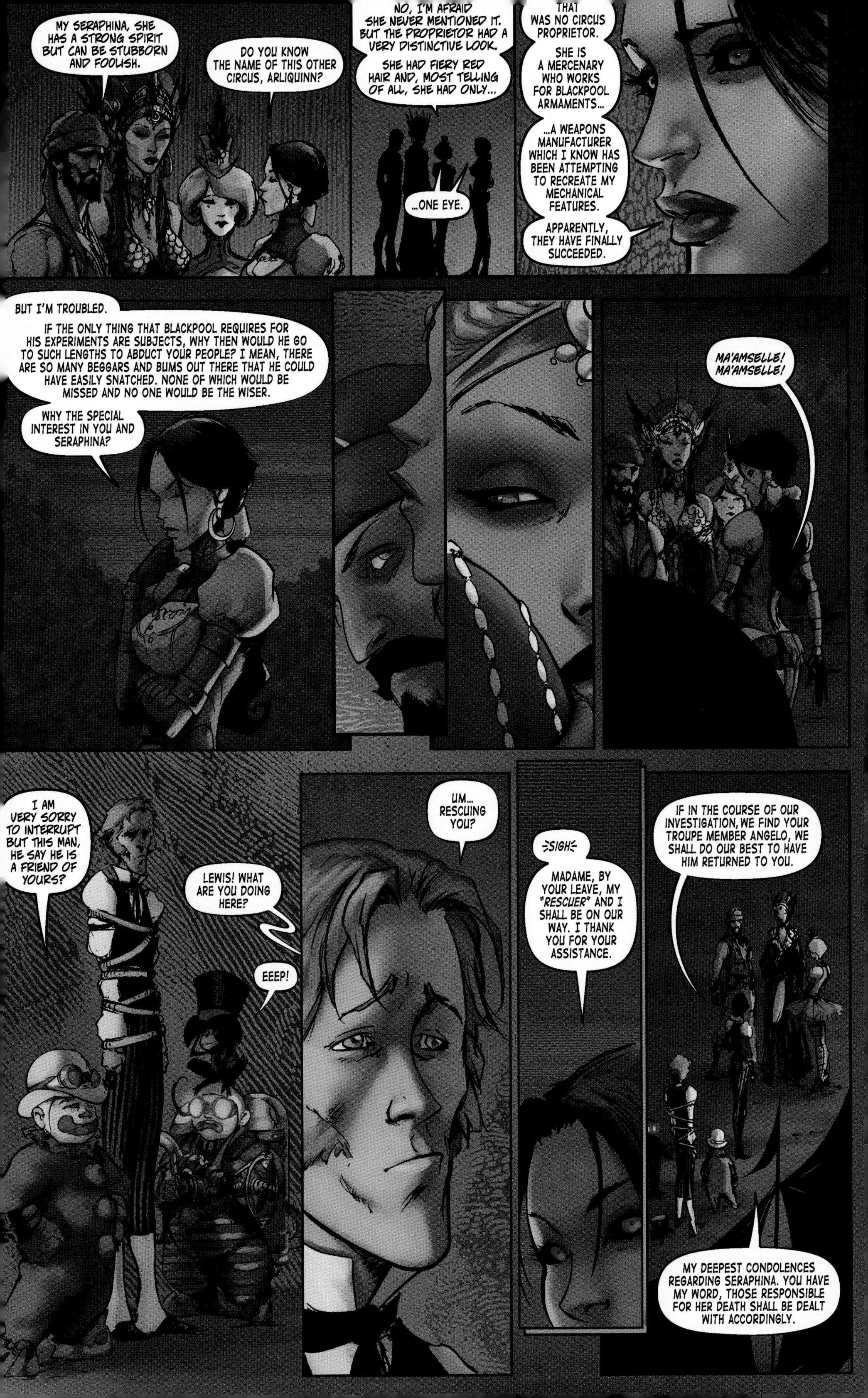
MY SERAPHINA, SHE HAS A STRONG SPIRIT BUT CAN BE STUBBORN AND FOOLISH.
DO YOU KNOW THE NAME OF THIS OTHER CIRCUS, ARLIQUINN?
NO, I'M AFRAID SHE NEVER MENTIONED IT. BUT THE PROPRIETOR HAD A VERY DISTINCTIVE LOOK.
SHE HAD FIERY RED HAIR AND, MOST TELLING OF ALL, SHE HAD ONLY...
...ONE EYE.
THAT WAS NO CIRCUS PROPRIETOR.
SHE IS A MERCENARY WHO WORKS FOR BLACKPOOL ARMAMENTS...
...A WEAPONS MANUFACTURER WHICH I KNOW HAS BEEN ATTEMPTING TO RECREATE MY MECHANICAL FEATURES.
APPARENTLY, THEY HAVE FINALLY SUCCEEDED.
BUT I'M TROUBLED.
IF THE ONLY THING THAT BLACKPOOL REQUIRES FOR HIS EXPERIMENTS ARE SUBJECTS, WHY THEN WOULD HE GO TO SUCH LENGTHS TO ABDUCT YOUR PEOPLE? I MEAN, THERE ARE SO MANY BEGGARS AND BUMS OUT THERE THAT HE COULD HAVE EASILY SNATCHED. NONE OF WHICH WOULD BE MISSED AND NO ONE WOULD BE THE WISER.
WHY THE SPECIAL INTEREST IN YOU AND SERAPHINA?
MA'AMSELLE! MA'AMSELLE!
I AM VERY SORRY TO INTERRUPT BUT THIS MAN, HE SAY HE IS A FRIEND OF YOURS?
LEWIS! WHAT ARE YOU DOING HERE?
EEEP!
UM... RESCUING YOU?
SIGH
MADAME, BY YOUR LEAVE, MY "RESCUER" AND I SHALL BE ON OUR WAY. I THANK YOU FOR YOUR ASSISTANCE.
IF IN THE COURSE OF OUR INVESTIGATION, WE FIND YOUR TROUPE MEMBER ANGELO, WE SHALL DO OUR BEST TO HAVE HIM RETURNED TO YOU.
MY DEEPEST CONDOLENCES REGARDING SERAPHINA. YOU HAVE MY WORD, THOSE RESPONSIBLE FOR HER DEATH SHALL BE DEALT WITH ACCORDINGLY.

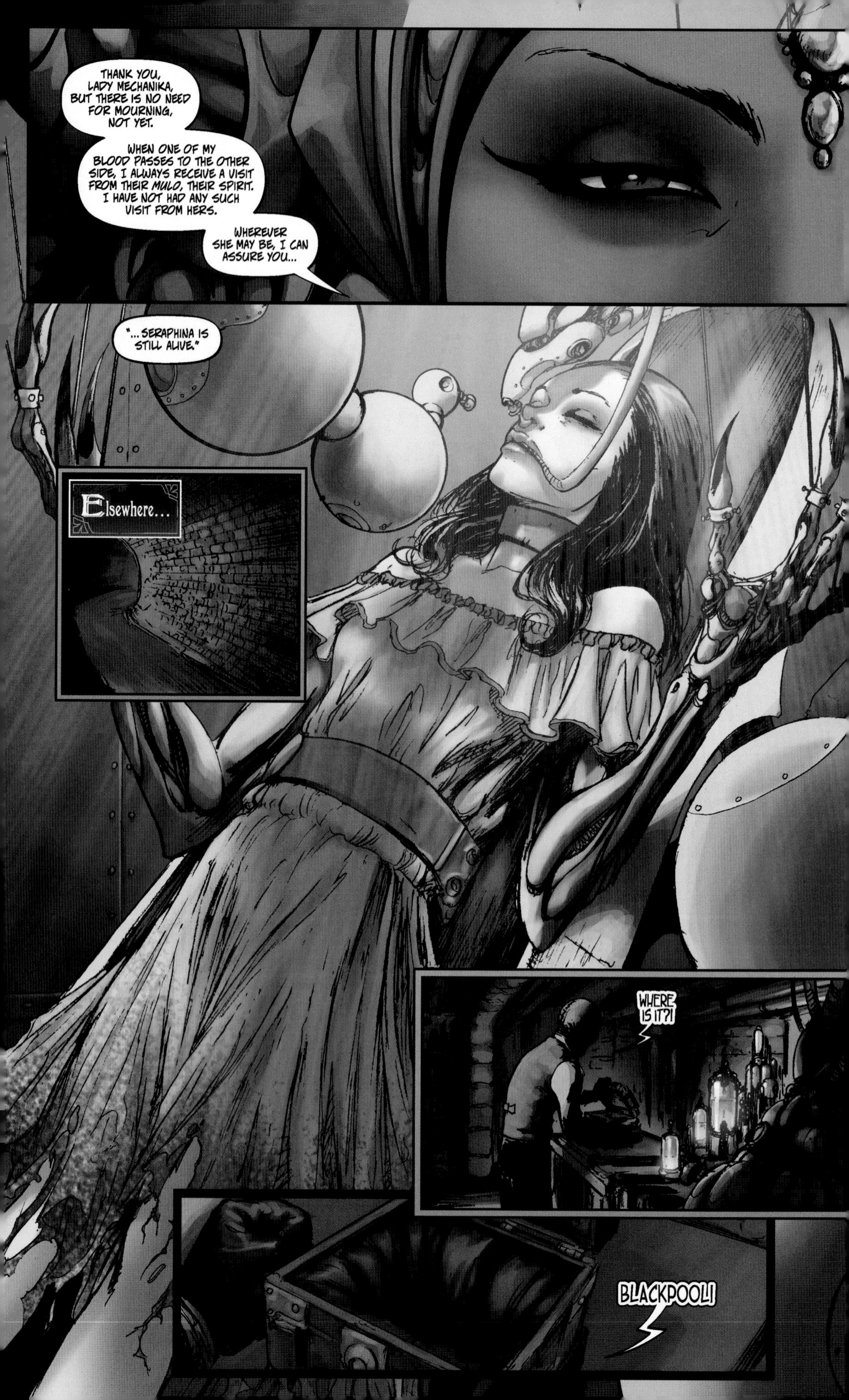
THANK YOU, LADY MECHANIKA, BUT THERE IS NO NEED FOR MOURNING, NOT YET.
WHEN ONE OF MY BLOOD PASSES TO THE OTHER SIDE, I ALWAYS RECEIVE A VISIT FROM THEIR *MULO*, THEIR SPIRIT. I HAVE NOT HAD ANY SUCH VISIT FROM HERS.
WHEREVER SHE MAY BE, I CAN ASSURE YOU...
"...SERAPHINA IS STILL ALIVE."
Elsewhere...
WHERE IS IT?!
BLACKPOOL!

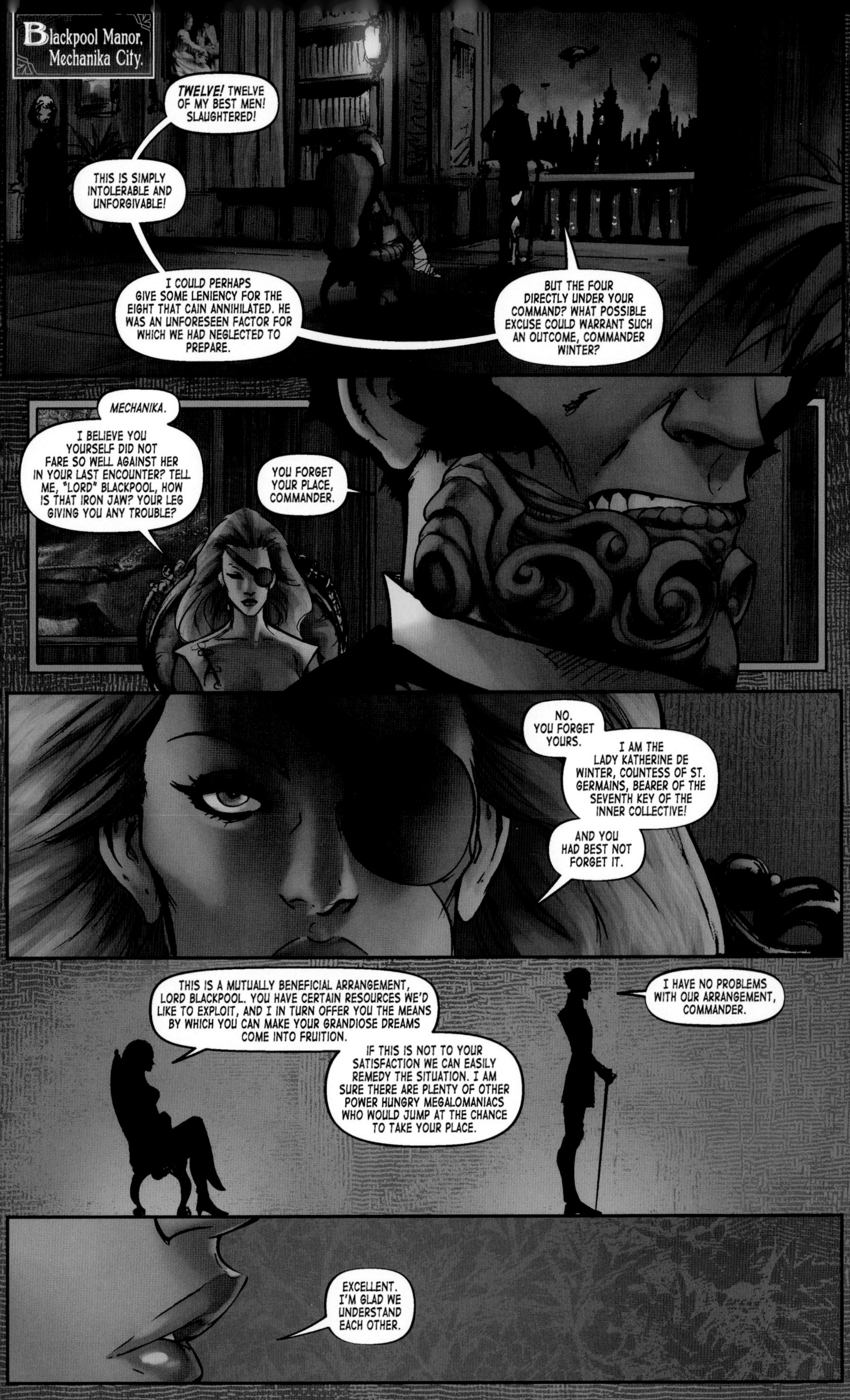
Blackpool Manor,
Mechanika City.
TWELVE! TWELVE OF MY BEST MEN! SLAUGHTERED!
THIS IS SIMPLY INTOLERABLE AND UNFORGIVABLE!
I COULD PERHAPS GIVE SOME LENIENCY FOR THE EIGHT THAT CAIN ANNIHILATED. HE WAS AN UNFORESEEN FACTOR FOR WHICH WE HAD NEGLECTED TO PREPARE.
BUT THE FOUR DIRECTLY UNDER YOUR COMMAND? WHAT POSSIBLE EXCUSE COULD WARRANT SUCH AN OUTCOME, COMMANDER WINTER?
MECHANIKA.
I BELIEVE YOU YOURSELF DID NOT FARE SO WELL AGAINST HER IN YOUR LAST ENCOUNTER? TELL ME, "LORD" BLACKPOOL, HOW IS THAT IRON JAW? YOUR LEG GIVING YOU ANY TROUBLE?
YOU FORGET YOUR PLACE, COMMANDER.
NO. YOU FORGET YOURS.
I AM THE LADY KATHERINE DE WINTER, COUNTESS OF ST. GERMAINS, BEARER OF THE SEVENTH KEY OF THE INNER COLLECTIVE!
AND YOU HAD BEST NOT FORGET IT.
THIS IS A MUTUALLY BENEFICIAL ARRANGEMENT, LORD BLACKPOOL. YOU HAVE CERTAIN RESOURCES WE'D LIKE TO EXPLOIT, AND I IN TURN OFFER YOU THE MEANS BY WHICH YOU CAN MAKE YOUR GRANDIOSE DREAMS COME INTO FRUITION.
IF THIS IS NOT TO YOUR SATISFACTION WE CAN EASILY REMEDY THE SITUATION. I AM SURE THERE ARE PLENTY OF OTHER POWER HUNGRY MEGALOMANIACS WHO WOULD JUMP AT THE CHANCE TO TAKE YOUR PLACE.
I HAVE NO PROBLEMS WITH OUR ARRANGEMENT, COMMANDER.
EXCELLENT. I'M GLAD WE UNDERSTAND EACH OTHER.

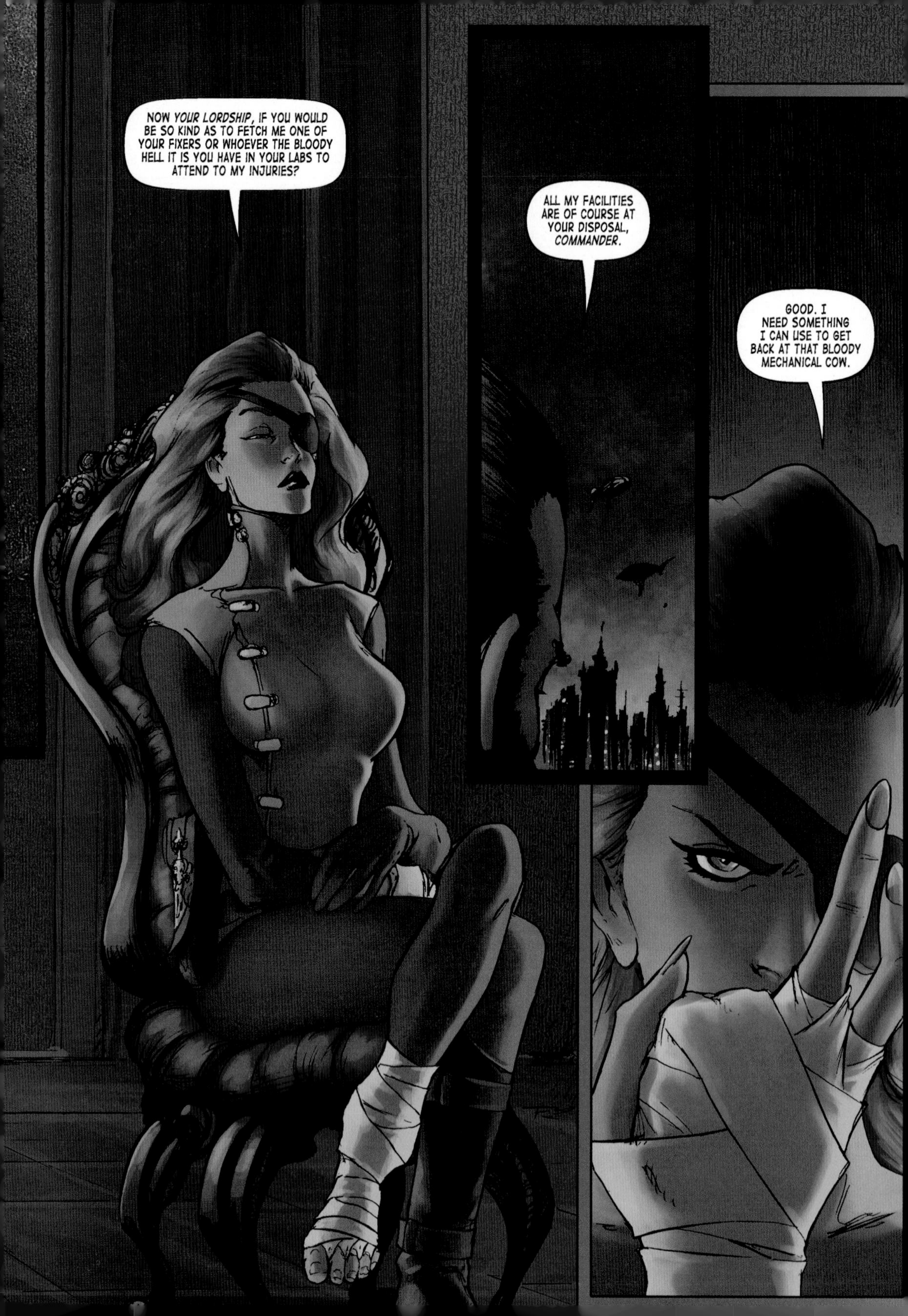
NOW *YOUR LORDSHIP*, IF YOU WOULD BE SO KIND AS TO FETCH ME ONE OF YOUR FIXERS OR WHOEVER THE BLOODY HELL IT IS YOU HAVE IN YOUR LABS TO ATTEND TO MY INJURIES?
ALL MY FACILITIES ARE OF COURSE AT YOUR DISPOSAL, *COMMANDER*.
GOOD. I NEED SOMETHING I CAN USE TO GET BACK AT THAT BLOODY MECHANICAL COW.

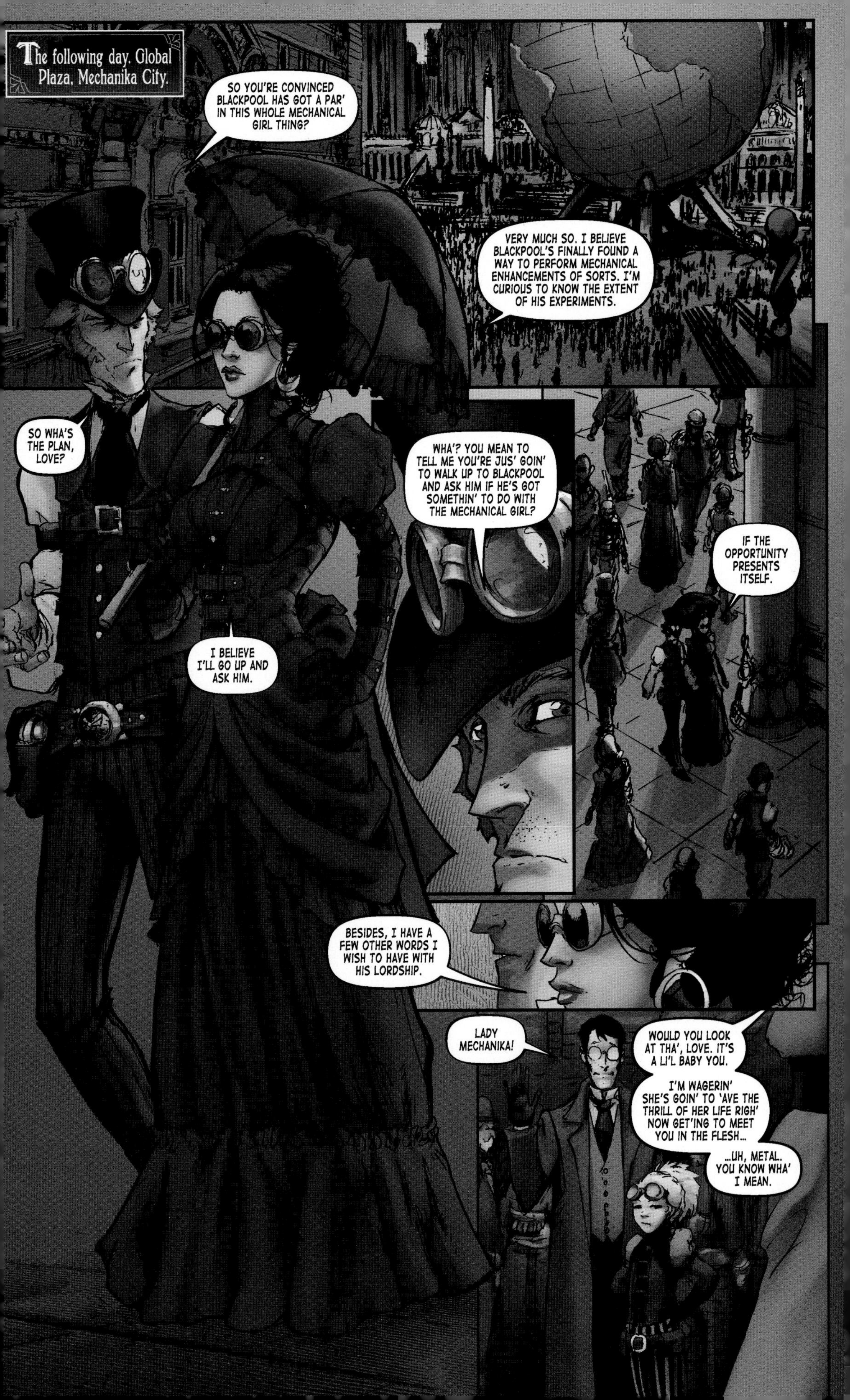
The following day. Global Plaza, Mechanika City.
SO YOU'RE CONVINCED BLACKPOOL HAS GOT A PAR' IN THIS WHOLE MECHANICAL GIRL THING?
VERY MUCH SO. I BELIEVE BLACKPOOL'S FINALLY FOUND A WAY TO PERFORM MECHANICAL ENHANCEMENTS OF SORTS. I'M CURIOUS TO KNOW THE EXTENT OF HIS EXPERIMENTS.
SO WHA'S THE PLAN, LOVE?
I BELIEVE I'LL GO UP AND ASK HIM.
WHA'? YOU MEAN TO TELL ME YOU'RE JUS' GOIN' TO WALK UP TO BLACKPOOL AND ASK HIM IF HE'S GOT SOMETHIN' TO DO WITH THE MECHANICAL GIRL?
IF THE OPPORTUNITY PRESENTS ITSELF.
BESIDES, I HAVE A FEW OTHER WORDS I WISH TO HAVE WITH HIS LORDSHIP.
LADY MECHANIKA!
WOULD YOU LOOK AT THA', LOVE. IT'S A LI'L BABY YOU.
I'M WAGERIN' SHE'S GOIN' TO 'AVE THE THRILL OF HER LIFE RIGH' NOW GET'ING TO MEET YOU IN THE FLESH...
...UH, METAL. YOU KNOW WHA' I MEAN.

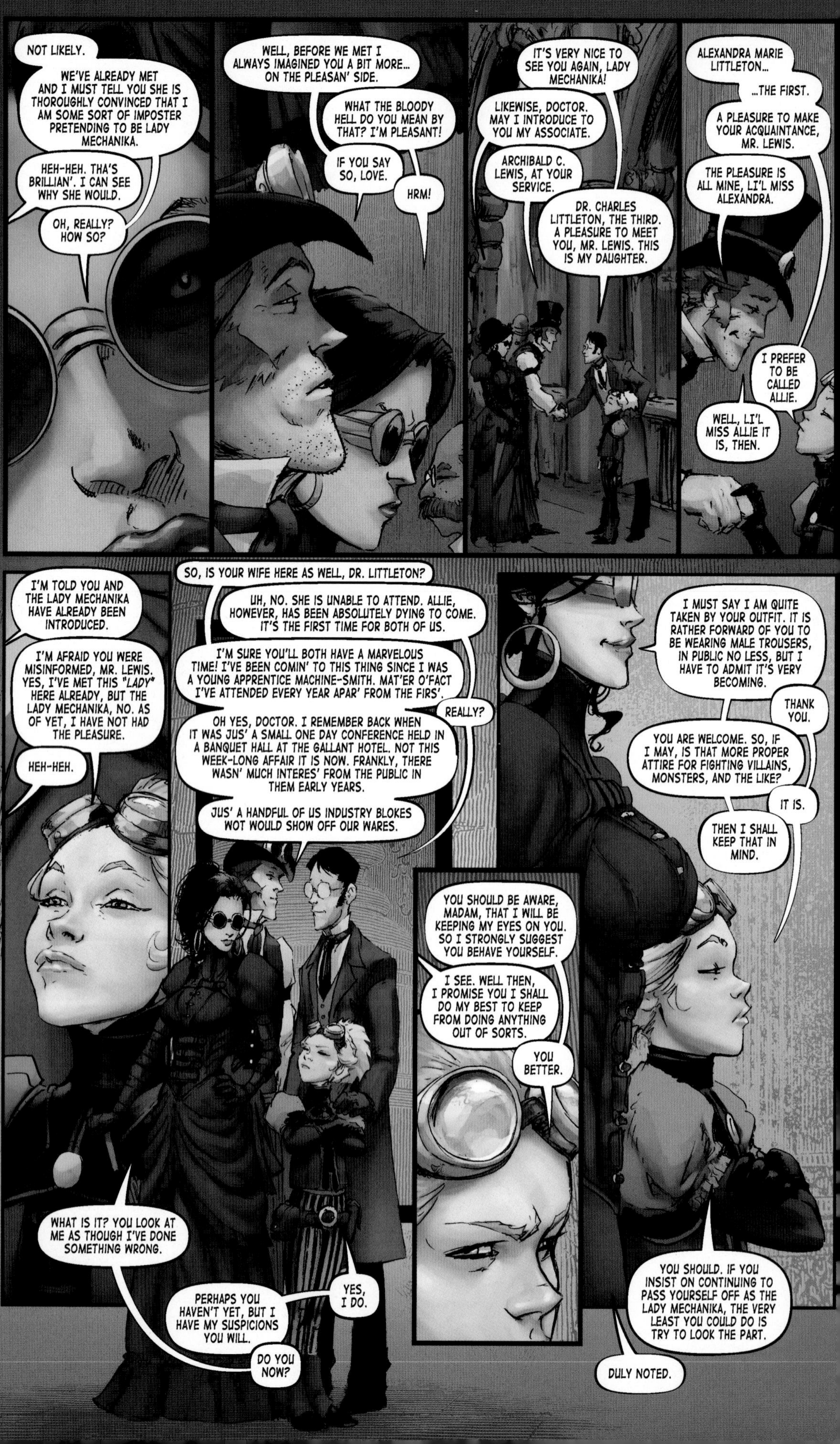
NOT LIKELY.
WE'VE ALREADY MET AND I MUST TELL YOU SHE IS THOROUGHLY CONVINCED THAT I AM SOME SORT OF IMPOSTER PRETENDING TO BE LADY MECHANIKA.
HEH-HEH. THA'S BRILLIAN'. I CAN SEE WHY SHE WOULD.
OH, REALLY? HOW SO?
WELL, BEFORE WE MET I ALWAYS IMAGINED YOU A BIT MORE... ON THE PLEASAN' SIDE.
WHAT THE BLOODY HELL DO YOU MEAN BY THAT? I'M PLEASANT!
IF YOU SAY SO, LOVE.
HRM!
IT'S VERY NICE TO SEE YOU AGAIN, LADY MECHANIKA!
LIKEWISE, DOCTOR. MAY I INTRODUCE TO YOU MY ASSOCIATE.
ARCHIBALD C. LEWIS, AT YOUR SERVICE.
DR. CHARLES LITTLETON, THE THIRD. A PLEASURE TO MEET YOU, MR. LEWIS. THIS IS MY DAUGHTER.
ALEXANDRA MARIE LITTLETON...
...THE FIRST.
A PLEASURE TO MAKE YOUR ACQUAINTANCE, MR. LEWIS.
THE PLEASURE IS ALL MINE, LI'L MISS ALEXANDRA.
I PREFER TO BE CALLED ALLIE.
WELL, LI'L MISS ALLIE IT IS, THEN.
I'M TOLD YOU AND THE LADY MECHANIKA HAVE ALREADY BEEN INTRODUCED.
I'M AFRAID YOU WERE MISINFORMED, MR. LEWIS. YES, I'VE MET THIS *"LADY"* HERE ALREADY, BUT THE LADY MECHANIKA, NO. AS OF YET, I HAVE NOT HAD THE PLEASURE.
HEH-HEH.
WHAT IS IT? YOU LOOK AT ME AS THOUGH I'VE DONE SOMETHING WRONG.
YES, I DO.
PERHAPS YOU HAVEN'T YET, BUT I HAVE MY SUSPICIONS YOU WILL.
DO YOU NOW?
SO, IS YOUR WIFE HERE AS WELL, DR. LITTLETON?
UH, NO. SHE IS UNABLE TO ATTEND. ALLIE, HOWEVER, HAS BEEN ABSOLUTELY DYING TO COME. IT'S THE FIRST TIME FOR BOTH OF US.
I'M SURE YOU'LL BOTH HAVE A MARVELOUS TIME! I'VE BEEN COMIN' TO THIS THING SINCE I WAS A YOUNG APPRENTICE MACHINE-SMITH. MAT'ER O'FACT I'VE ATTENDED EVERY YEAR APAR' FROM THE FIRS'.
REALLY?
OH YES, DOCTOR. I REMEMBER BACK WHEN IT WAS JUS' A SMALL ONE DAY CONFERENCE HELD IN A BANQUET HALL AT THE GALLANT HOTEL. NOT THIS WEEK-LONG AFFAIR IT IS NOW. FRANKLY, THERE WASN' MUCH INTERES' FROM THE PUBLIC IN THEM EARLY YEARS.
JUS' A HANDFUL OF US INDUSTRY BLOKES WOT WOULD SHOW OFF OUR WARES.
I MUST SAY I AM QUITE TAKEN BY YOUR OUTFIT. IT IS RATHER FORWARD OF YOU TO BE WEARING MALE TROUSERS, IN PUBLIC NO LESS, BUT I HAVE TO ADMIT IT'S VERY BECOMING.
THANK YOU.
YOU ARE WELCOME. SO, IF I MAY, IS THAT MORE PROPER ATTIRE FOR FIGHTING VILLAINS, MONSTERS, AND THE LIKE?
IT IS.
THEN I SHALL KEEP THAT IN MIND.
YOU SHOULD BE AWARE, MADAM, THAT I WILL BE KEEPING MY EYES ON YOU. SO I STRONGLY SUGGEST YOU BEHAVE YOURSELF.
I SEE. WELL THEN, I PROMISE YOU I SHALL DO MY BEST TO KEEP FROM DOING ANYTHING OUT OF SORTS.
YOU BETTER.
YOU SHOULD. IF YOU INSIST ON CONTINUING TO PASS YOURSELF OFF AS THE LADY MECHANIKA, THE VERY LEAST YOU COULD DO IS TRY TO LOOK THE PART.
DULY NOTED.

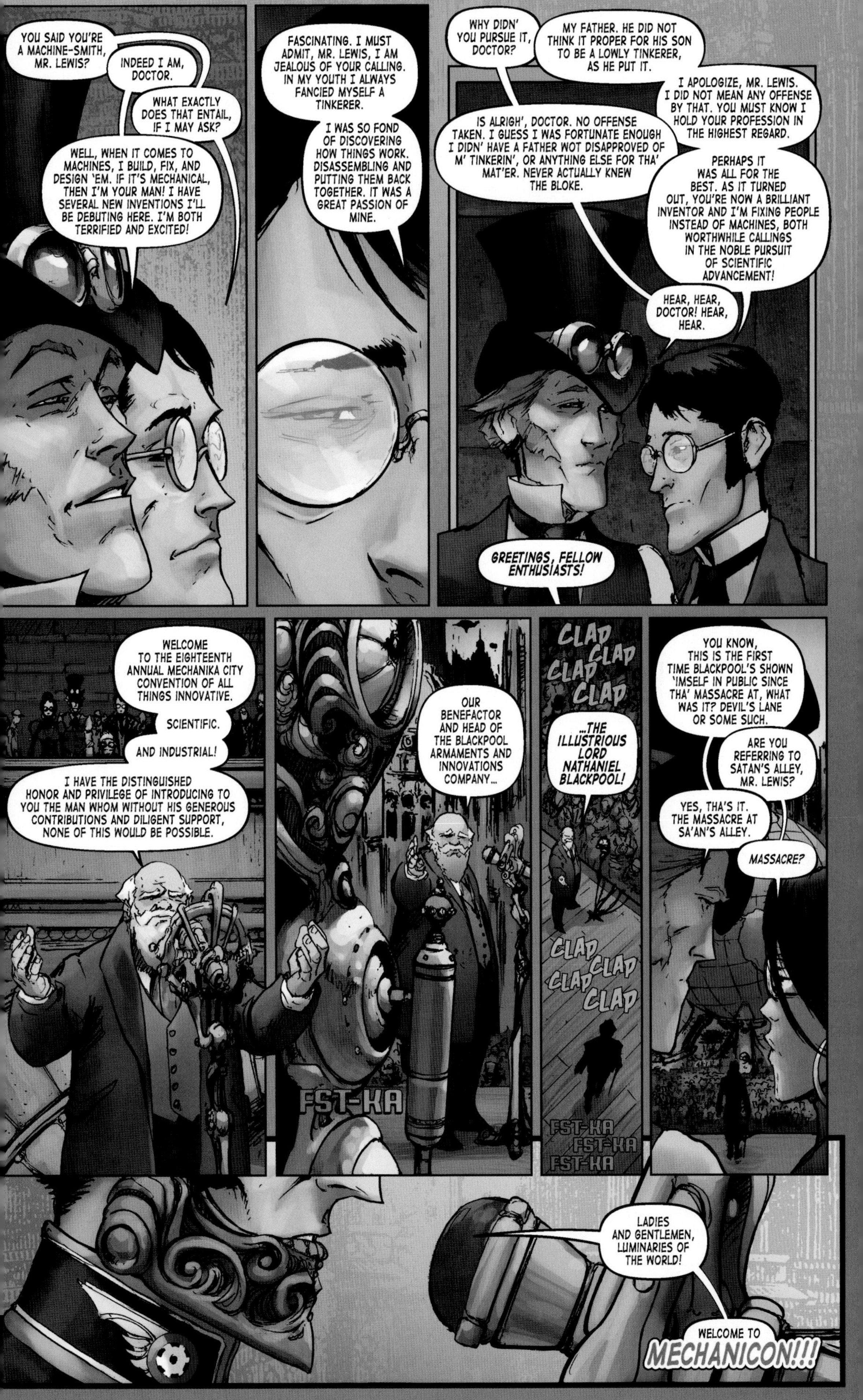
YOU SAID YOU'RE A MACHINE-SMITH, MR. LEWIS?
INDEED I AM, DOCTOR.
WHAT EXACTLY DOES THAT ENTAIL, IF I MAY ASK?
WELL, WHEN IT COMES TO MACHINES, I BUILD, FIX, AND DESIGN 'EM. IF IT'S MECHANICAL, THEN I'M YOUR MAN! I HAVE SEVERAL NEW INVENTIONS I'LL BE DEBUTING HERE. I'M BOTH TERRIFIED AND EXCITED!
FASCINATING. I MUST ADMIT, MR. LEWIS, I AM JEALOUS OF YOUR CALLING. IN MY YOUTH I ALWAYS FANCIED MYSELF A TINKERER.
I WAS SO FOND OF DISCOVERING HOW THINGS WORK. DISASSEMBLING AND PUTTING THEM BACK TOGETHER. IT WAS A GREAT PASSION OF MINE.
WHY DIDN' YOU PURSUE IT, DOCTOR?
MY FATHER. HE DID NOT THINK IT PROPER FOR HIS SON TO BE A LOWLY TINKERER, AS HE PUT IT.
IS ALRIGH', DOCTOR. NO OFFENSE TAKEN. I GUESS I WAS FORTUNATE ENOUGH I DIDN' HAVE A FATHER WOT DISAPPROVED OF M' TINKERIN', OR ANYTHING ELSE FOR THA' MAT'ER. NEVER ACTUALLY KNEW THE BLOKE.
I APOLOGIZE, MR. LEWIS. I DID NOT MEAN ANY OFFENSE BY THAT. YOU MUST KNOW I HOLD YOUR PROFESSION IN THE HIGHEST REGARD.
PERHAPS IT WAS ALL FOR THE BEST. AS IT TURNED OUT, YOU'RE NOW A BRILLIANT INVENTOR AND I'M FIXING PEOPLE INSTEAD OF MACHINES, BOTH WORTHWHILE CALLINGS IN THE NOBLE PURSUIT OF SCIENTIFIC ADVANCEMENT!
HEAR, HEAR, DOCTOR! HEAR, HEAR.
GREETINGS, FELLOW ENTHUSIASTS!
WELCOME TO THE EIGHTEENTH ANNUAL MECHANIKA CITY CONVENTION OF ALL THINGS INNOVATIVE.
SCIENTIFIC.
AND INDUSTRIAL!
I HAVE THE DISTINGUISHED HONOR AND PRIVILEGE OF INTRODUCING TO YOU THE MAN WHOM WITHOUT HIS GENEROUS CONTRIBUTIONS AND DILIGENT SUPPORT, NONE OF THIS WOULD BE POSSIBLE.
OUR BENEFACTOR AND HEAD OF THE BLACKPOOL ARMAMENTS AND INNOVATIONS COMPANY...
FST-KA
CLAP CLAP CLAP CLAP CLAP
...THE ILLUSTRIOUS LORD NATHANIEL BLACKPOOL!
CLAP CLAP CLAP CLAP CLAP
FST-KA FST-KA FST-KA
YOU KNOW, THIS IS THE FIRST TIME BLACKPOOL'S SHOWN 'IMSELF IN PUBLIC SINCE THA' MASSACRE AT, WHAT WAS IT? DEVIL'S LANE OR SOME SUCH.
ARE YOU REFERRING TO SATAN'S ALLEY, MR. LEWIS?
YES, THA'S IT. THE MASSACRE AT SA'AN'S ALLEY.
MASSACRE?
LADIES AND GENTLEMEN, LUMINARIES OF THE WORLD!
WELCOME TO MECHANICON!!!

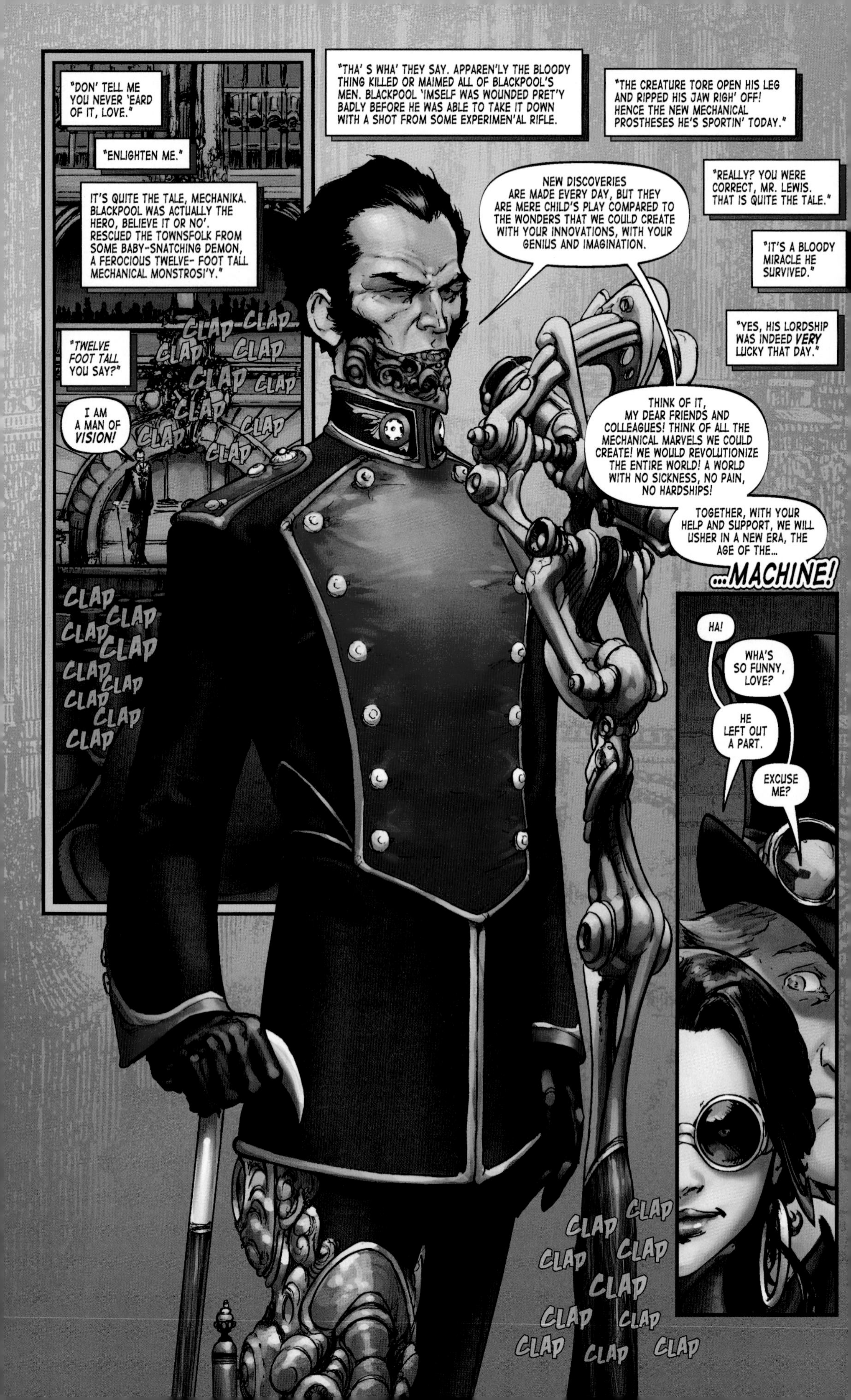

"DON' TELL ME YOU NEVER 'EARD OF IT, LOVE."
"ENLIGHTEN ME."
IT'S QUITE THE TALE, MECHANIKA. BLACKPOOL WAS ACTUALLY THE HERO, BELIEVE IT OR NO'. RESCUED THE TOWNSFOLK FROM SOME BABY-SNATCHING DEMON, A FEROCIOUS TWELVE- FOOT TALL MECHANICAL MONSTROSI'Y."
"TWELVE FOOT TALL YOU SAY?"
I AM A MAN OF VISION!
CLAP CLAP CLAP CLAP CLAP CLAP CLAP CLAP CLAP CLAP
"THA' S WHA' THEY SAY. APPAREN'LY THE BLOODY THING KILLED OR MAIMED ALL OF BLACKPOOL'S MEN. BLACKPOOL 'IMSELF WAS WOUNDED PRET'Y BADLY BEFORE HE WAS ABLE TO TAKE IT DOWN WITH A SHOT FROM SOME EXPERIMEN'AL RIFLE.
"THE CREATURE TORE OPEN HIS LEG AND RIPPED HIS JAW RIGH' OFF! HENCE THE NEW MECHANICAL PROSTHESES HE'S SPORTIN' TODAY."
NEW DISCOVERIES ARE MADE EVERY DAY, BUT THEY ARE MERE CHILD'S PLAY COMPARED TO THE WONDERS THAT WE COULD CREATE WITH YOUR INNOVATIONS, WITH YOUR GENIUS AND IMAGINATION.
"REALLY? YOU WERE CORRECT, MR. LEWIS. THAT IS QUITE THE TALE."
"IT'S A BLOODY MIRACLE HE SURVIVED."
"YES, HIS LORDSHIP WAS INDEED VERY LUCKY THAT DAY."
THINK OF IT, MY DEAR FRIENDS AND COLLEAGUES! THINK OF ALL THE MECHANICAL MARVELS WE COULD CREATE! WE WOULD REVOLUTIONIZE THE ENTIRE WORLD! A WORLD WITH NO SICKNESS, NO PAIN, NO HARDSHIPS!
TOGETHER, WITH YOUR HELP AND SUPPORT, WE WILL USHER IN A NEW ERA, THE AGE OF THE...
...MACHINE!
CLAP CLAP CLAP CLAP CLAP CLAP CLAP CLAP CLAP
HA!
WHA'S SO FUNNY, LOVE?
HE LEFT OUT A PART.
EXCUSE ME?
CLAP CLAP CLAP CLAP CLAP CLAP CLAP CLAP CLAP CLAP

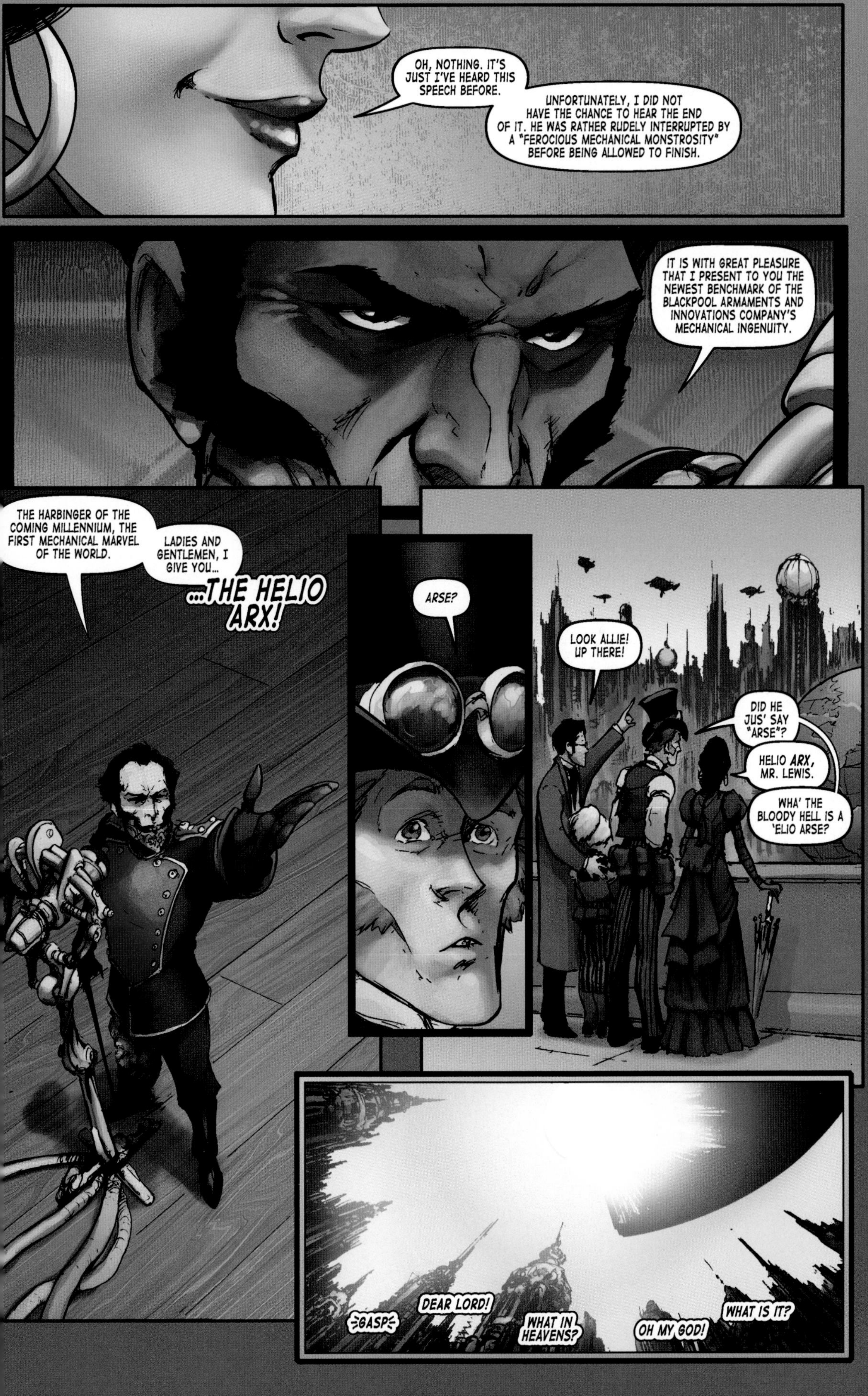
OH, NOTHING. IT'S JUST I'VE HEARD THIS SPEECH BEFORE.
UNFORTUNATELY, I DID NOT HAVE THE CHANCE TO HEAR THE END OF IT. HE WAS RATHER RUDELY INTERRUPTED BY A "FEROCIOUS MECHANICAL MONSTROSITY" BEFORE BEING ALLOWED TO FINISH.
IT IS WITH GREAT PLEASURE THAT I PRESENT TO YOU THE NEWEST BENCHMARK OF THE BLACKPOOL ARMAMENTS AND INNOVATIONS COMPANY'S MECHANICAL INGENUITY.
THE HARBINGER OF THE COMING MILLENNIUM, THE FIRST MECHANICAL MARVEL OF THE WORLD.
LADIES AND GENTLEMEN, I GIVE YOU...
...THE HELIO ARX!
ARSE?
LOOK ALLIE! UP THERE!
DID HE JUS' SAY "ARSE"?
HELIO ARX, MR. LEWIS.
WHA' THE BLOODY HELL IS A 'ELIO ARSE?
GASP
DEAR LORD!
WHAT IN HEAVENS?
OH MY GOD!
WHAT IS IT?

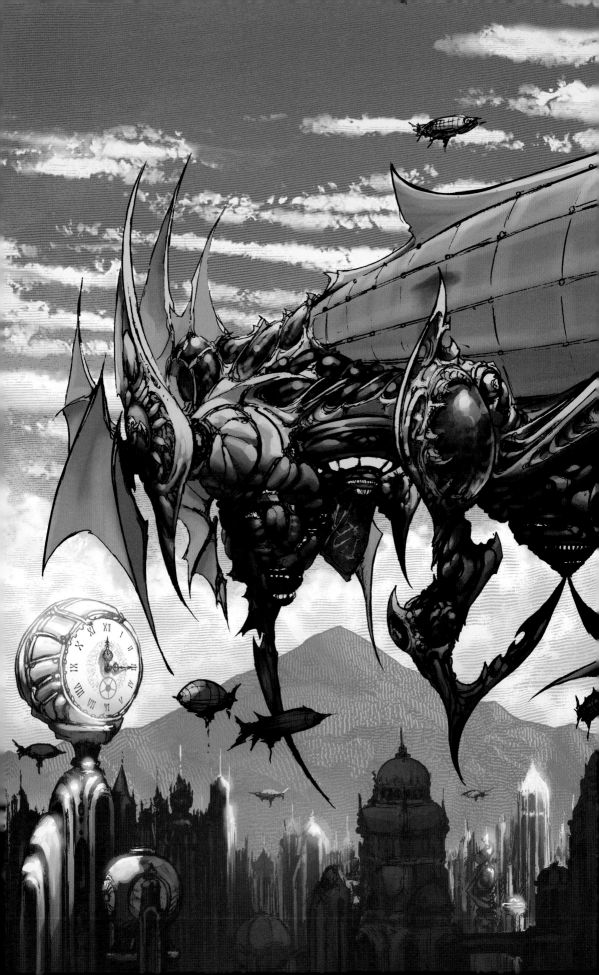

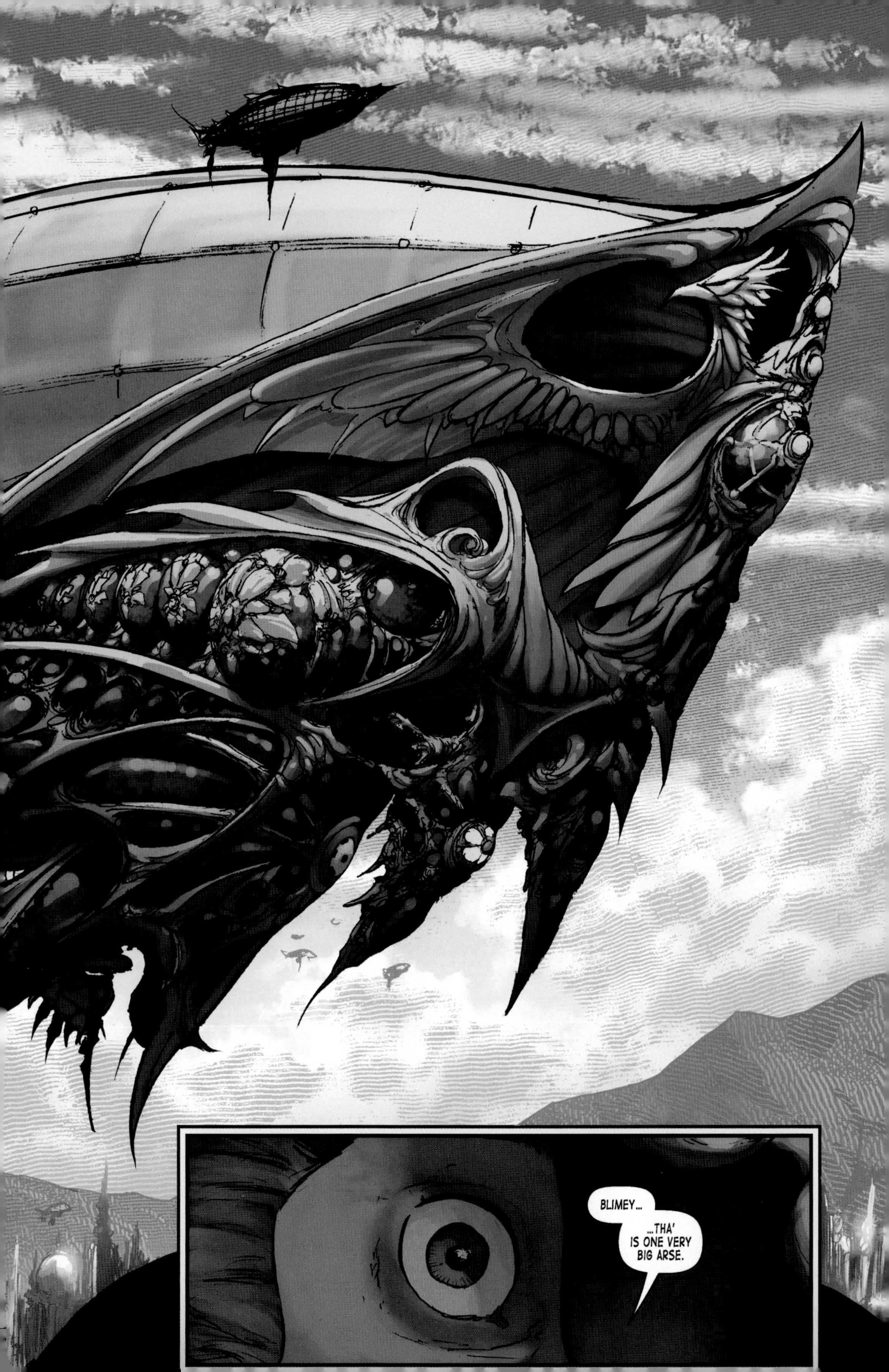
BLIMEY...
...THA' IS ONE VERY BIG ARSE.

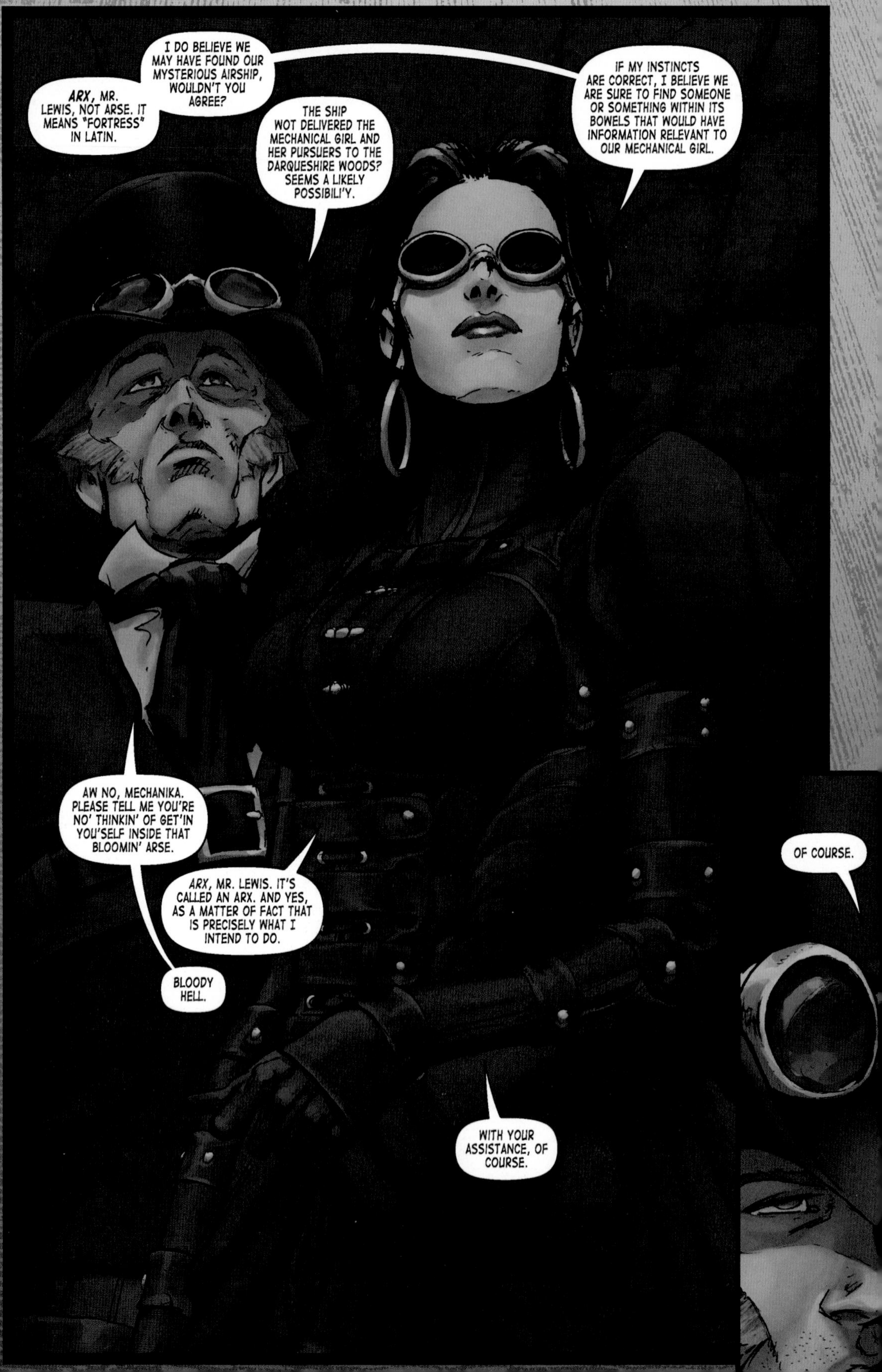
I DO BELIEVE WE MAY HAVE FOUND OUR MYSTERIOUS AIRSHIP, WOULDN'T YOU AGREE?
IF MY INSTINCTS ARE CORRECT, I BELIEVE WE ARE SURE TO FIND SOMEONE OR SOMETHING WITHIN ITS BOWELS THAT WOULD HAVE INFORMATION RELEVANT TO OUR MECHANICAL GIRL.
THE SHIP WOT DELIVERED THE MECHANICAL GIRL AND HER PURSUERS TO THE DARQUESHIRE WOODS? SEEMS A LIKELY POSSIBILI'Y.
ARX, MR. LEWIS, NOT ARSE. IT MEANS "FORTRESS" IN LATIN.
AW NO, MECHANIKA. PLEASE TELL ME YOU'RE NO' THINKIN' OF GET'IN YOU'SELF INSIDE THAT BLOOMIN' ARSE.
ARX, MR. LEWIS. IT'S CALLED AN ARX. AND YES, AS A MATTER OF FACT THAT IS PRECISELY WHAT I INTEND TO DO.
BLOODY HELL.
WITH YOUR ASSISTANCE, OF COURSE.
OF COURSE.

Chapter Four

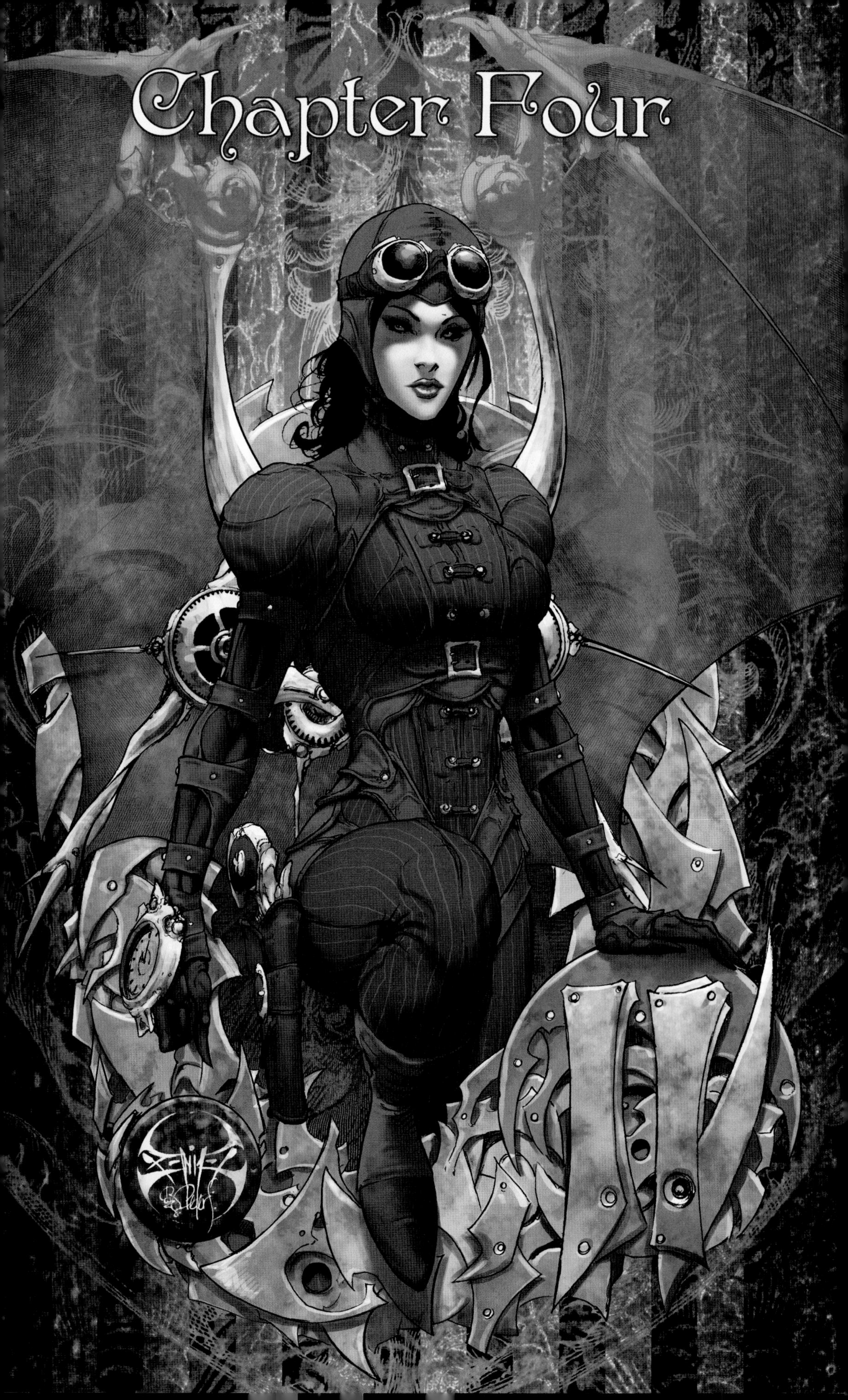

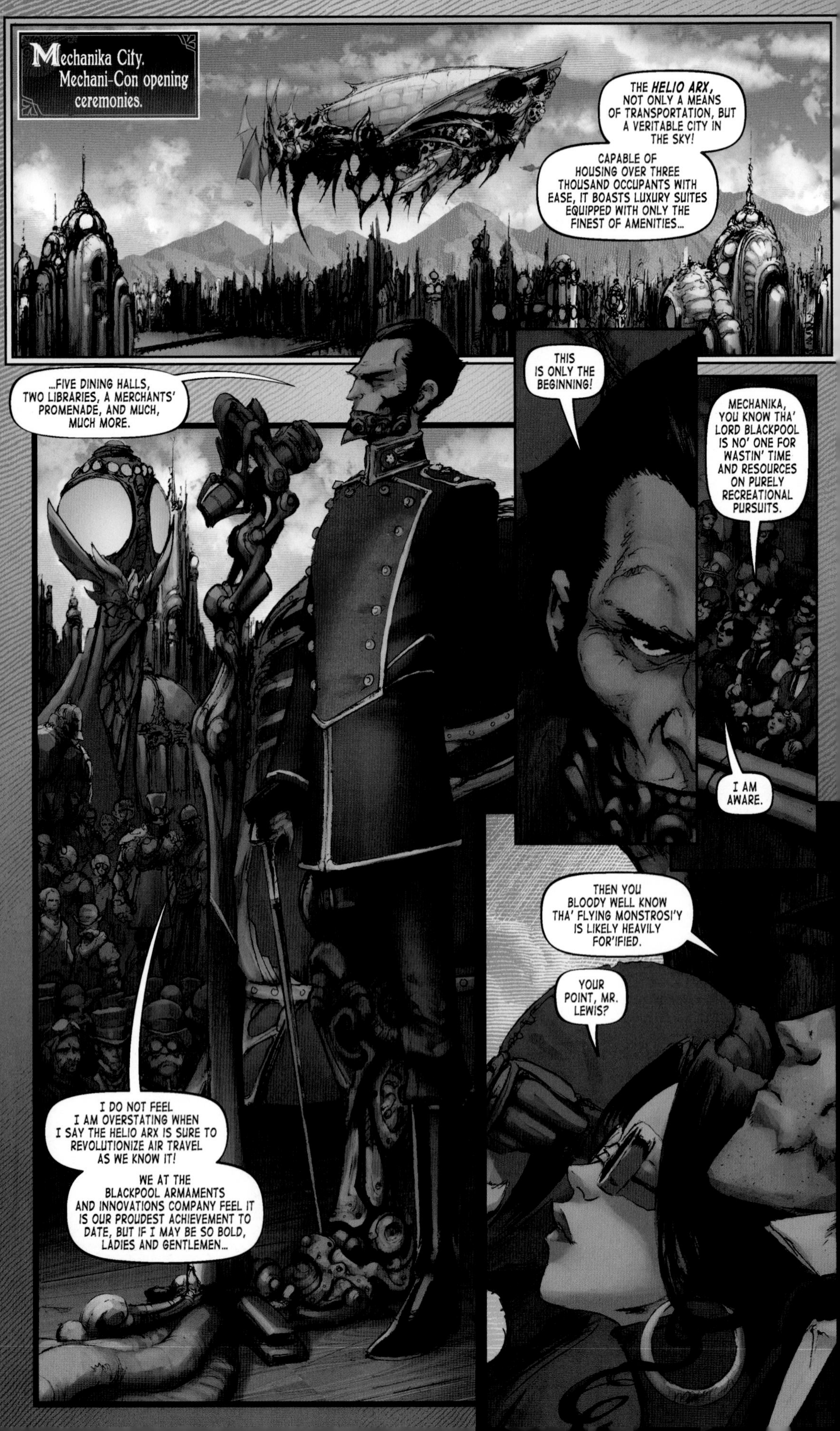
Mechanika City. Mechani-Con opening ceremonies.
THE HELIO ARX, NOT ONLY A MEANS OF TRANSPORTATION, BUT A VERITABLE CITY IN THE SKY!
CAPABLE OF HOUSING OVER THREE THOUSAND OCCUPANTS WITH EASE, IT BOASTS LUXURY SUITES EQUIPPED WITH ONLY THE FINEST OF AMENITIES...
...FIVE DINING HALLS, TWO LIBRARIES, A MERCHANTS' PROMENADE, AND MUCH, MUCH MORE.
I DO NOT FEEL I AM OVERSTATING WHEN I SAY THE HELIO ARX IS SURE TO REVOLUTIONIZE AIR TRAVEL AS WE KNOW IT!
WE AT THE BLACKPOOL ARMAMENTS AND INNOVATIONS COMPANY FEEL IT IS OUR PROUDEST ACHIEVEMENT TO DATE, BUT IF I MAY BE SO BOLD, LADIES AND GENTLEMEN...
THIS IS ONLY THE BEGINNING!
MECHANIKA, YOU KNOW THA' LORD BLACKPOOL IS NO' ONE FOR WASTIN' TIME AND RESOURCES ON PURELY RECREATIONAL PURSUITS.
I AM AWARE.
THEN YOU BLOODY WELL KNOW THA' FLYING MONSTROSI'Y IS LIKELY HEAVILY FOR'IFIED.
YOUR POINT, MR. LEWIS?

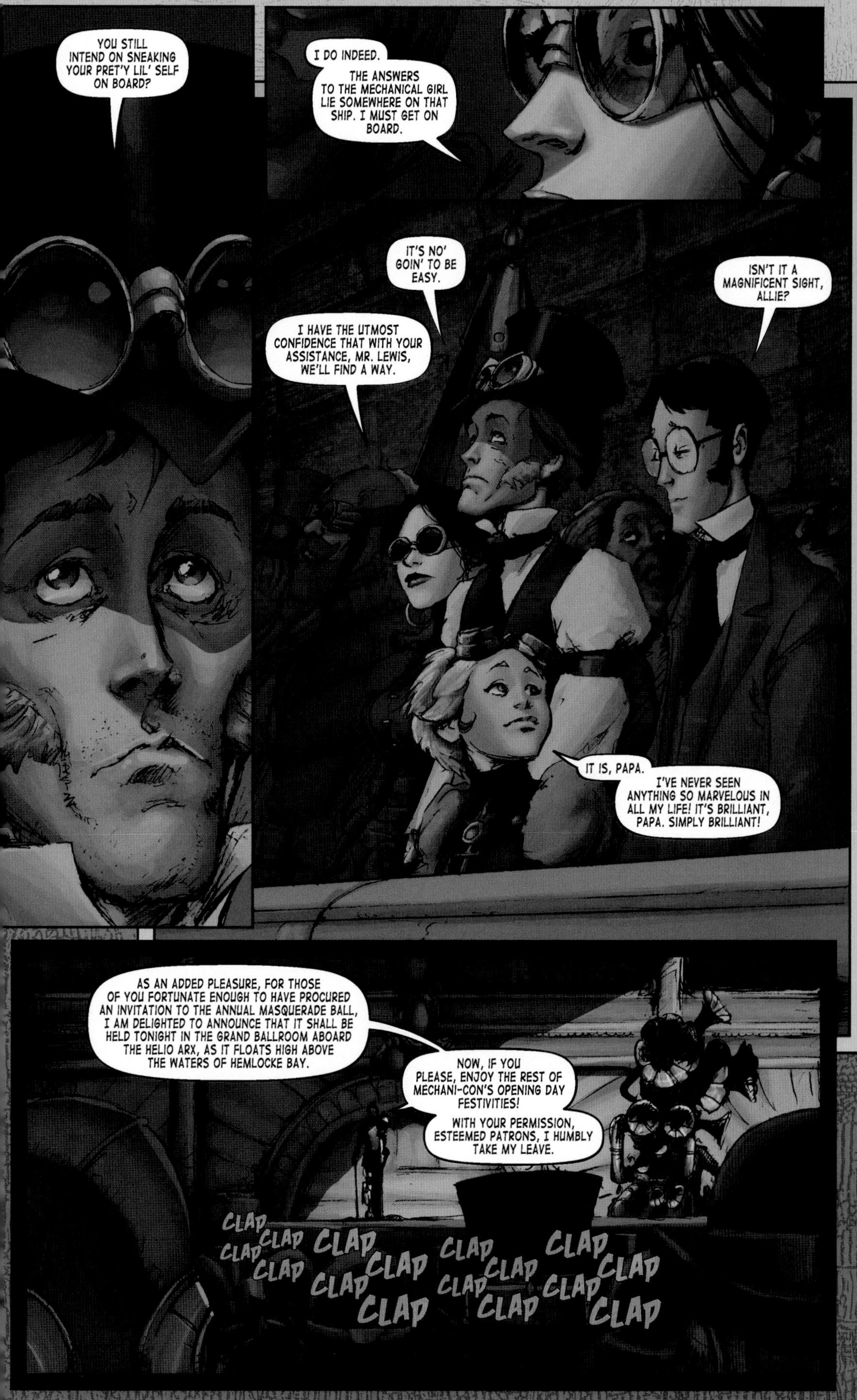
YOU STILL INTEND ON SNEAKING YOUR PRET'Y LIL' SELF ON BOARD?
I DO INDEED.
THE ANSWERS TO THE MECHANICAL GIRL LIE SOMEWHERE ON THAT SHIP. I MUST GET ON BOARD.
IT'S NO' GOIN' TO BE EASY.
I HAVE THE UTMOST CONFIDENCE THAT WITH YOUR ASSISTANCE, MR. LEWIS, WE'LL FIND A WAY.
ISN'T IT A MAGNIFICENT SIGHT, ALLIE?
IT IS, PAPA.
I'VE NEVER SEEN ANYTHING SO MARVELOUS IN ALL MY LIFE! IT'S BRILLIANT, PAPA. SIMPLY BRILLIANT!
AS AN ADDED PLEASURE, FOR THOSE OF YOU FORTUNATE ENOUGH TO HAVE PROCURED AN INVITATION TO THE ANNUAL MASQUERADE BALL, I AM DELIGHTED TO ANNOUNCE THAT IT SHALL BE HELD TONIGHT IN THE GRAND BALLROOM ABOARD THE HELIO ARX, AS IT FLOATS HIGH ABOVE THE WATERS OF HEMLOCKE BAY.
NOW, IF YOU PLEASE, ENJOY THE REST OF MECHANI-CON'S OPENING DAY FESTIVITIES!
WITH YOUR PERMISSION, ESTEEMED PATRONS, I HUMBLY TAKE MY LEAVE.
CLAP CLAP CLAP CLAP CLAP CLAP CLAP CLAP CLAP CLAP CLAP CLAP CLAP CLAP CLAP CLAP CLAP CLAP

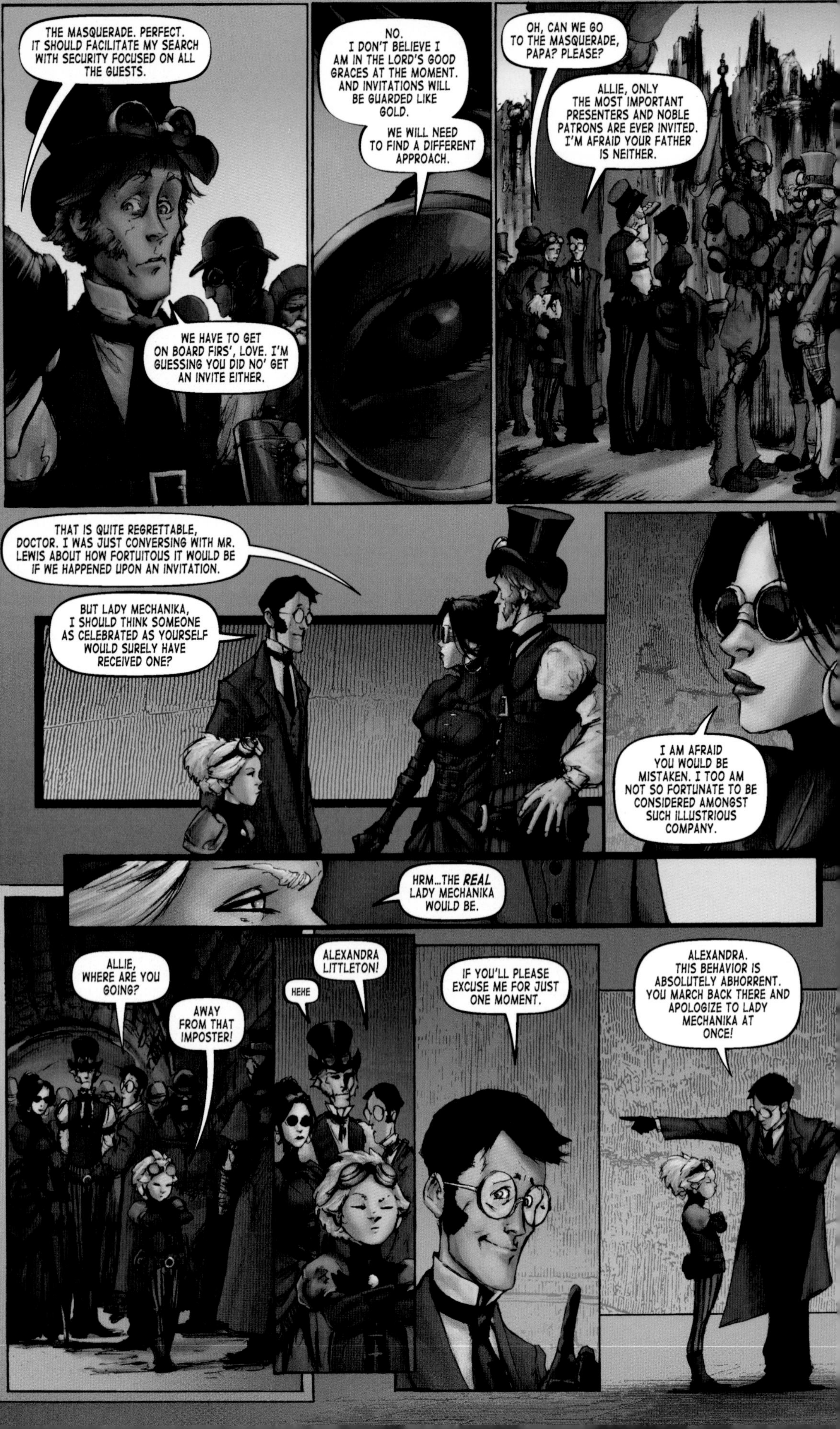
THE MASQUERADE. PERFECT. IT SHOULD FACILITATE MY SEARCH WITH SECURITY FOCUSED ON ALL THE GUESTS.
WE HAVE TO GET ON BOARD FIRS', LOVE. I'M GUESSING YOU DID NO' GET AN INVITE EITHER.
NO. I DON'T BELIEVE I AM IN THE LORD'S GOOD GRACES AT THE MOMENT. AND INVITATIONS WILL BE GUARDED LIKE GOLD.
WE WILL NEED TO FIND A DIFFERENT APPROACH.
OH, CAN WE GO TO THE MASQUERADE, PAPA? PLEASE?
ALLIE, ONLY THE MOST IMPORTANT PRESENTERS AND NOBLE PATRONS ARE EVER INVITED. I'M AFRAID YOUR FATHER IS NEITHER.
THAT IS QUITE REGRETTABLE, DOCTOR. I WAS JUST CONVERSING WITH MR. LEWIS ABOUT HOW FORTUITOUS IT WOULD BE IF WE HAPPENED UPON AN INVITATION.
BUT LADY MECHANIKA, I SHOULD THINK SOMEONE AS CELEBRATED AS YOURSELF WOULD SURELY HAVE RECEIVED ONE?
I AM AFRAID YOU WOULD BE MISTAKEN. I TOO AM NOT SO FORTUNATE TO BE CONSIDERED AMONGST SUCH ILLUSTRIOUS COMPANY.
HRM...THE *REAL* LADY MECHANIKA WOULD BE.
ALLIE, WHERE ARE YOU GOING?
AWAY FROM THAT IMPOSTER!
ALEXANDRA LITTLETON!
HEHE
IF YOU'LL PLEASE EXCUSE ME FOR JUST ONE MOMENT.
ALEXANDRA. THIS BEHAVIOR IS ABSOLUTELY ABHORRENT. YOU MARCH BACK THERE AND APOLOGIZE TO LADY MECHANIKA AT ONCE!

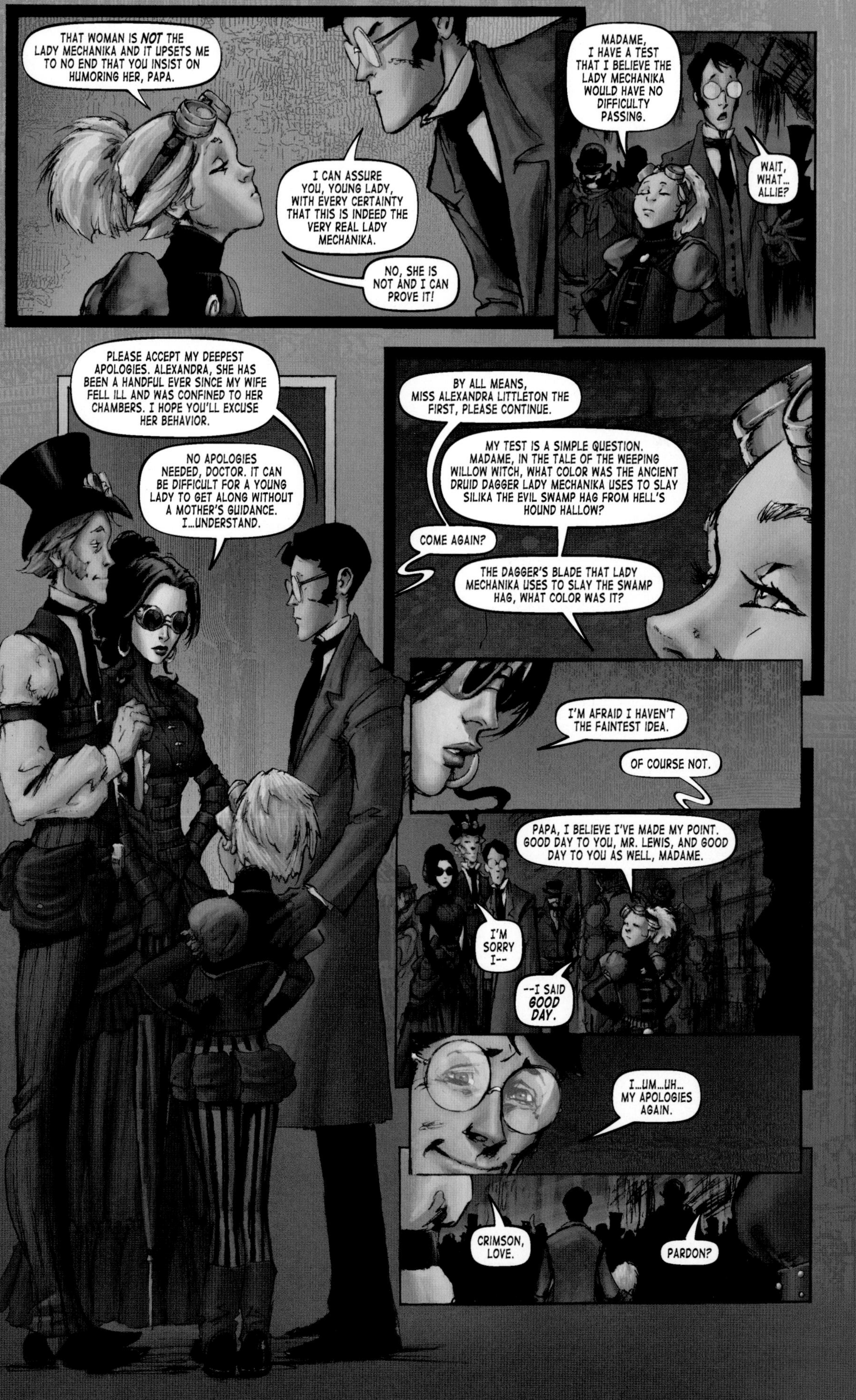
THAT WOMAN IS NOT THE LADY MECHANIKA AND IT UPSETS ME TO NO END THAT YOU INSIST ON HUMORING HER, PAPA.
I CAN ASSURE YOU, YOUNG LADY, WITH EVERY CERTAINTY THAT THIS IS INDEED THE VERY REAL LADY MECHANIKA.
NO, SHE IS NOT AND I CAN PROVE IT!
MADAME, I HAVE A TEST THAT I BELIEVE THE LADY MECHANIKA WOULD HAVE NO DIFFICULTY PASSING.
WAIT, WHAT... ALLIE?
PLEASE ACCEPT MY DEEPEST APOLOGIES. ALEXANDRA, SHE HAS BEEN A HANDFUL EVER SINCE MY WIFE FELL ILL AND WAS CONFINED TO HER CHAMBERS. I HOPE YOU'LL EXCUSE HER BEHAVIOR.
NO APOLOGIES NEEDED, DOCTOR. IT CAN BE DIFFICULT FOR A YOUNG LADY TO GET ALONG WITHOUT A MOTHER'S GUIDANCE. I...UNDERSTAND.
BY ALL MEANS, MISS ALEXANDRA LITTLETON THE FIRST, PLEASE CONTINUE.
MY TEST IS A SIMPLE QUESTION. MADAME, IN THE TALE OF THE WEEPING WILLOW WITCH, WHAT COLOR WAS THE ANCIENT DRUID DAGGER LADY MECHANIKA USES TO SLAY SILIKA THE EVIL SWAMP HAG FROM HELL'S HOUND HALLOW?
COME AGAIN?
THE DAGGER'S BLADE THAT LADY MECHANIKA USES TO SLAY THE SWAMP HAG, WHAT COLOR WAS IT?
I'M AFRAID I HAVEN'T THE FAINTEST IDEA.
OF COURSE NOT.
PAPA, I BELIEVE I'VE MADE MY POINT. GOOD DAY TO YOU, MR. LEWIS, AND GOOD DAY TO YOU AS WELL, MADAME.
I'M SORRY I--
--I SAID GOOD DAY.
I...UM...UH... MY APOLOGIES AGAIN.
CRIMSON, LOVE.
PARDON?

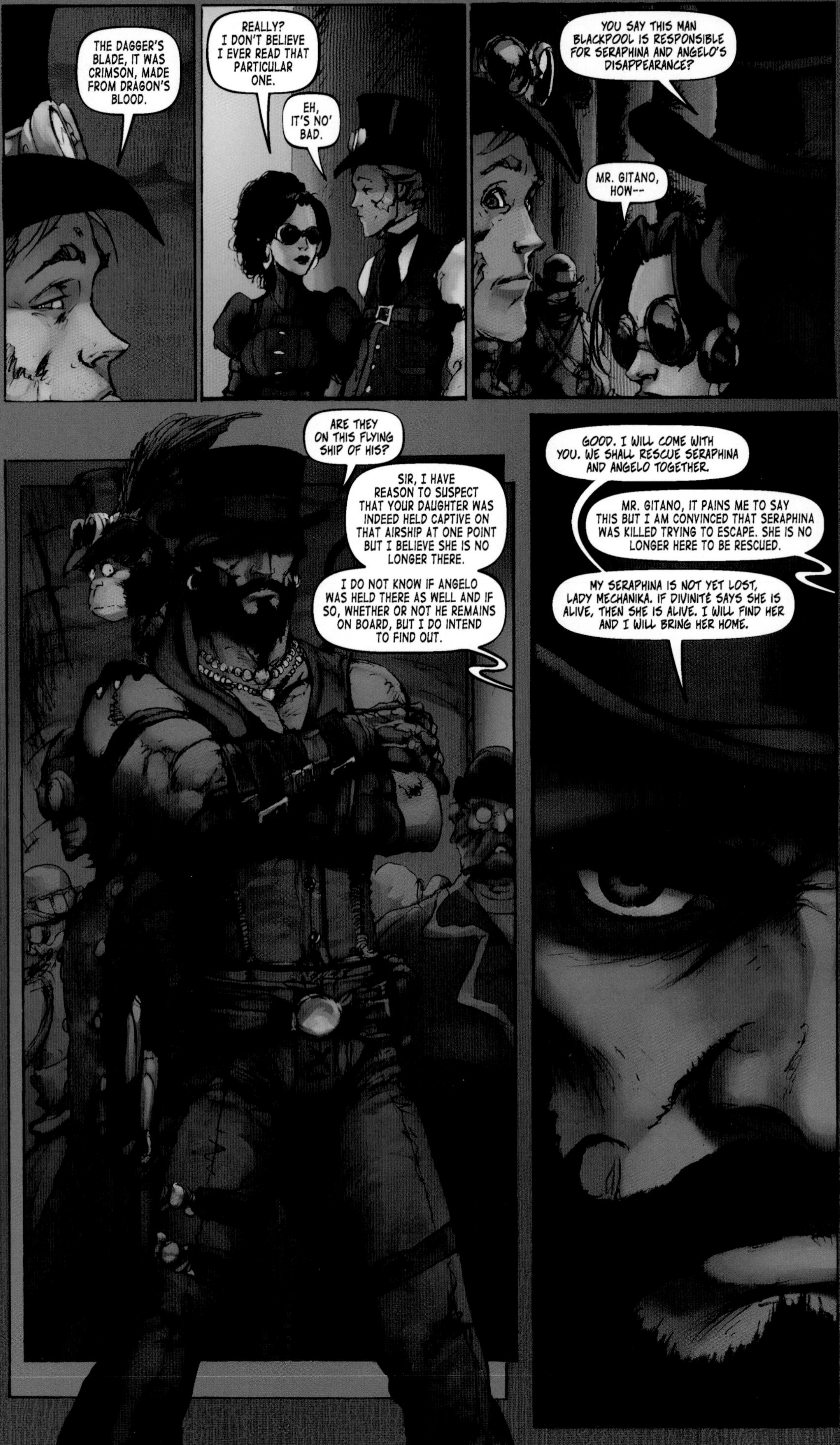

THE DAGGER'S BLADE, IT WAS CRIMSON, MADE FROM DRAGON'S BLOOD.
REALLY? I DON'T BELIEVE I EVER READ THAT PARTICULAR ONE.
EH, IT'S NO' BAD.
YOU SAY THIS MAN BLACKPOOL IS RESPONSIBLE FOR SERAPHINA AND ANGELO'S DISAPPEARANCE?
MR. GITANO, HOW--
ARE THEY ON THIS FLYING SHIP OF HIS?
SIR, I HAVE REASON TO SUSPECT THAT YOUR DAUGHTER WAS INDEED HELD CAPTIVE ON THAT AIRSHIP AT ONE POINT BUT I BELIEVE SHE IS NO LONGER THERE.
I DO NOT KNOW IF ANGELO WAS HELD THERE AS WELL AND IF SO, WHETHER OR NOT HE REMAINS ON BOARD, BUT I DO INTEND TO FIND OUT.
GOOD. I WILL COME WITH YOU. WE SHALL RESCUE SERAPHINA AND ANGELO TOGETHER.
MR. GITANO, IT PAINS ME TO SAY THIS BUT I AM CONVINCED THAT SERAPHINA WAS KILLED TRYING TO ESCAPE. SHE IS NO LONGER HERE TO BE RESCUED.
MY SERAPHINA IS NOT YET LOST, LADY MECHANIKA. IF DIVINITÉ SAYS SHE IS ALIVE, THEN SHE IS ALIVE. I WILL FIND HER AND I WILL BRING HER HOME.

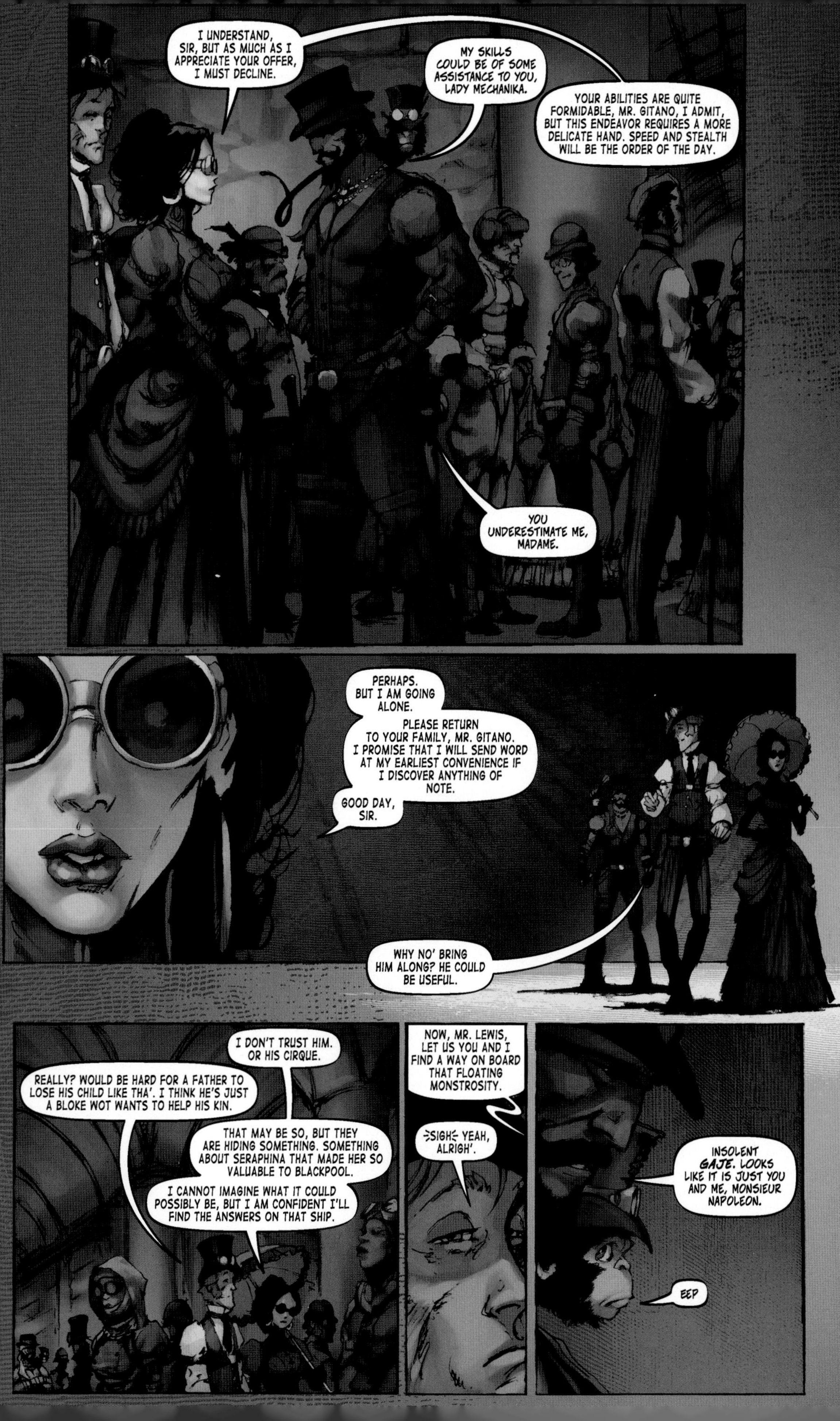
I UNDERSTAND, SIR, BUT AS MUCH AS I APPRECIATE YOUR OFFER, I MUST DECLINE.
MY SKILLS COULD BE OF SOME ASSISTANCE TO YOU, LADY MECHANIKA.
YOUR ABILITIES ARE QUITE FORMIDABLE, MR. GITANO, I ADMIT, BUT THIS ENDEAVOR REQUIRES A MORE DELICATE HAND. SPEED AND STEALTH WILL BE THE ORDER OF THE DAY.
YOU UNDERESTIMATE ME, MADAME.
PERHAPS. BUT I AM GOING ALONE.
PLEASE RETURN TO YOUR FAMILY, MR. GITANO. I PROMISE THAT I WILL SEND WORD AT MY EARLIEST CONVENIENCE IF I DISCOVER ANYTHING OF NOTE.
GOOD DAY, SIR.
WHY NO' BRING HIM ALONG? HE COULD BE USEFUL.
I DON'T TRUST HIM. OR HIS CIRQUE.
REALLY? WOULD BE HARD FOR A FATHER TO LOSE HIS CHILD LIKE THA'. I THINK HE'S JUST A BLOKE WOT WANTS TO HELP HIS KIN.
THAT MAY BE SO, BUT THEY ARE HIDING SOMETHING. SOMETHING ABOUT SERAPHINA THAT MADE HER SO VALUABLE TO BLACKPOOL.
I CANNOT IMAGINE WHAT IT COULD POSSIBLY BE, BUT I AM CONFIDENT I'LL FIND THE ANSWERS ON THAT SHIP.
NOW, MR. LEWIS, LET US YOU AND I FIND A WAY ON BOARD THAT FLOATING MONSTROSITY.
≈SIGH≈ YEAH, ALRIGH'.
INSOLENT GAJE. LOOKS LIKE IT IS JUST YOU AND ME, MONSIEUR NAPOLEON.
EEP

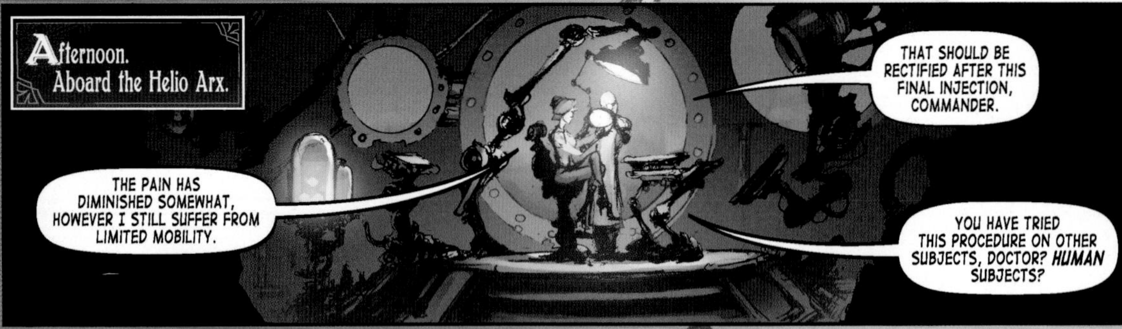
Afternoon.
Aboard the Helio Arx.
THE PAIN HAS DIMINISHED SOMEWHAT, HOWEVER I STILL SUFFER FROM LIMITED MOBILITY.
THAT SHOULD BE RECTIFIED AFTER THIS FINAL INJECTION, COMMANDER.
YOU HAVE TRIED THIS PROCEDURE ON OTHER SUBJECTS, DOCTOR? HUMAN SUBJECTS?

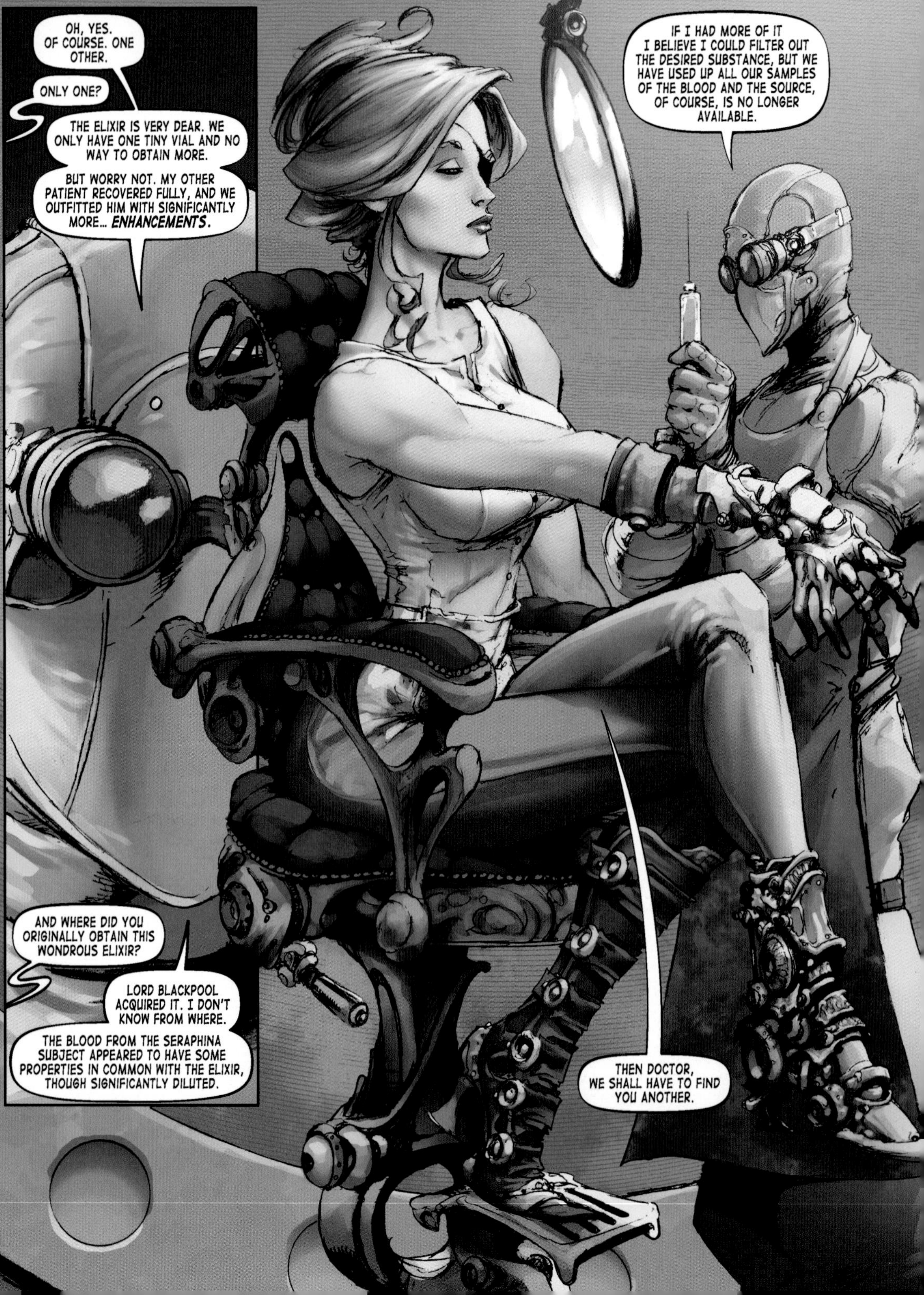
OH, YES. OF COURSE. ONE OTHER.
ONLY ONE?
THE ELIXIR IS VERY DEAR. WE ONLY HAVE ONE TINY VIAL AND NO WAY TO OBTAIN MORE.
BUT WORRY NOT. MY OTHER PATIENT RECOVERED FULLY, AND WE OUTFITTED HIM WITH SIGNIFICANTLY MORE... ENHANCEMENTS.
IF I HAD MORE OF IT I BELIEVE I COULD FILTER OUT THE DESIRED SUBSTANCE, BUT WE HAVE USED UP ALL OUR SAMPLES OF THE BLOOD AND THE SOURCE, OF COURSE, IS NO LONGER AVAILABLE.
AND WHERE DID YOU ORIGINALLY OBTAIN THIS WONDROUS ELIXIR?
LORD BLACKPOOL ACQUIRED IT. I DON'T KNOW FROM WHERE.
THE BLOOD FROM THE SERAPHINA SUBJECT APPEARED TO HAVE SOME PROPERTIES IN COMMON WITH THE ELIXIR, THOUGH SIGNIFICANTLY DILUTED.
THEN DOCTOR, WE SHALL HAVE TO FIND YOU ANOTHER.

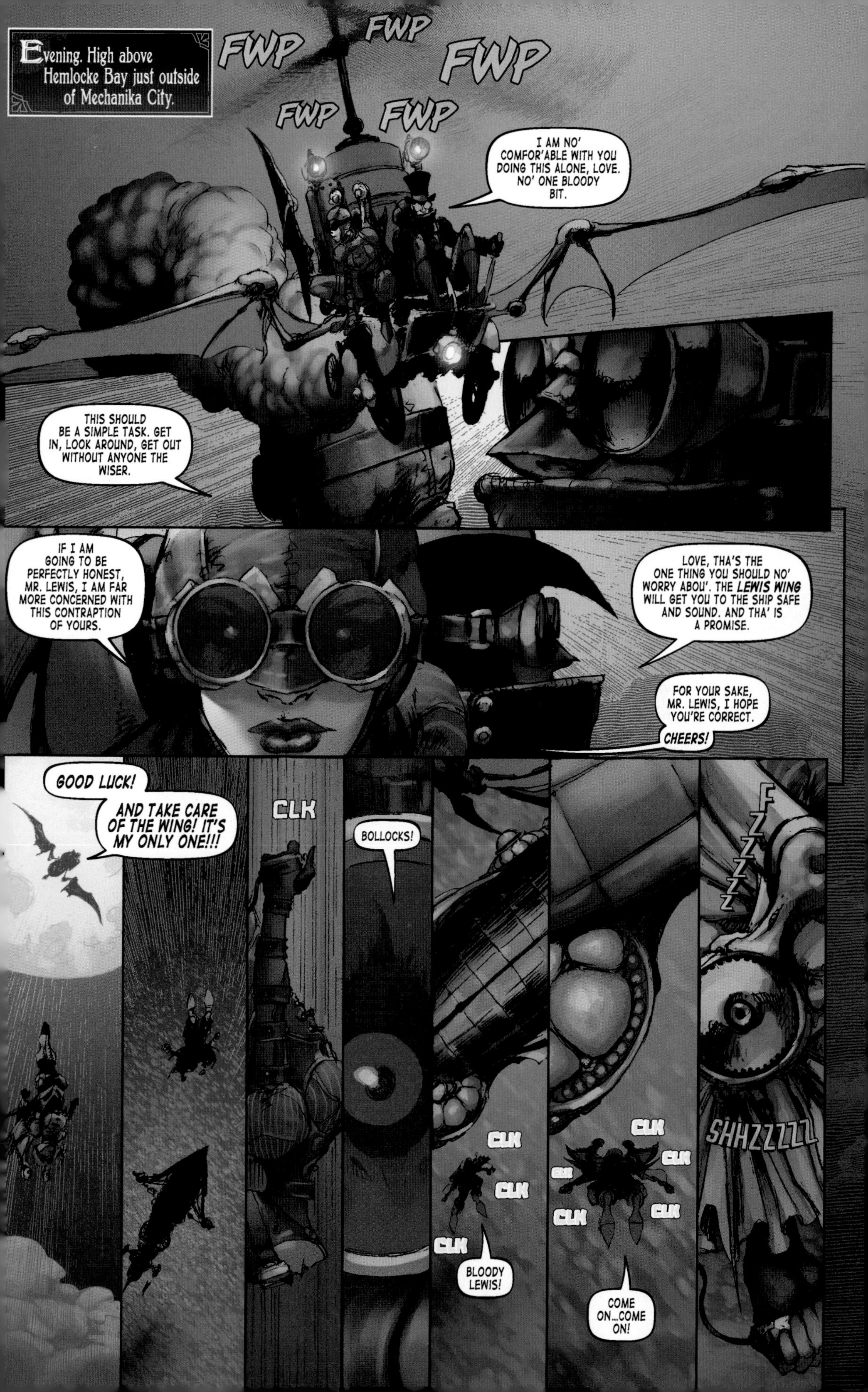
Evening. High above Hemlocke Bay just outside of Mechanika City.
FWP
FWP
FWP
FWP
FWP
I AM NO' COMFOR'ABLE WITH YOU DOING THIS ALONE, LOVE. NO' ONE BLOODY BIT.
THIS SHOULD BE A SIMPLE TASK. GET IN, LOOK AROUND, GET OUT WITHOUT ANYONE THE WISER.
IF I AM GOING TO BE PERFECTLY HONEST, MR. LEWIS, I AM FAR MORE CONCERNED WITH THIS CONTRAPTION OF YOURS.
LOVE, THA'S THE ONE THING YOU SHOULD NO' WORRY ABOU'. THE LEWIS WING WILL GET YOU TO THE SHIP SAFE AND SOUND. AND THA' IS A PROMISE.
FOR YOUR SAKE, MR. LEWIS, I HOPE YOU'RE CORRECT.
CHEERS!
GOOD LUCK!
AND TAKE CARE OF THE WING! IT'S MY ONLY ONE!!!
CLK
BOLLOCKS!
CLK
CLK
CLK
BLOODY LEWIS!
CLK
CLK
CLK
CLK
CLK
COME ON...COME ON!
FZZZZZ
SHHZZZZZ

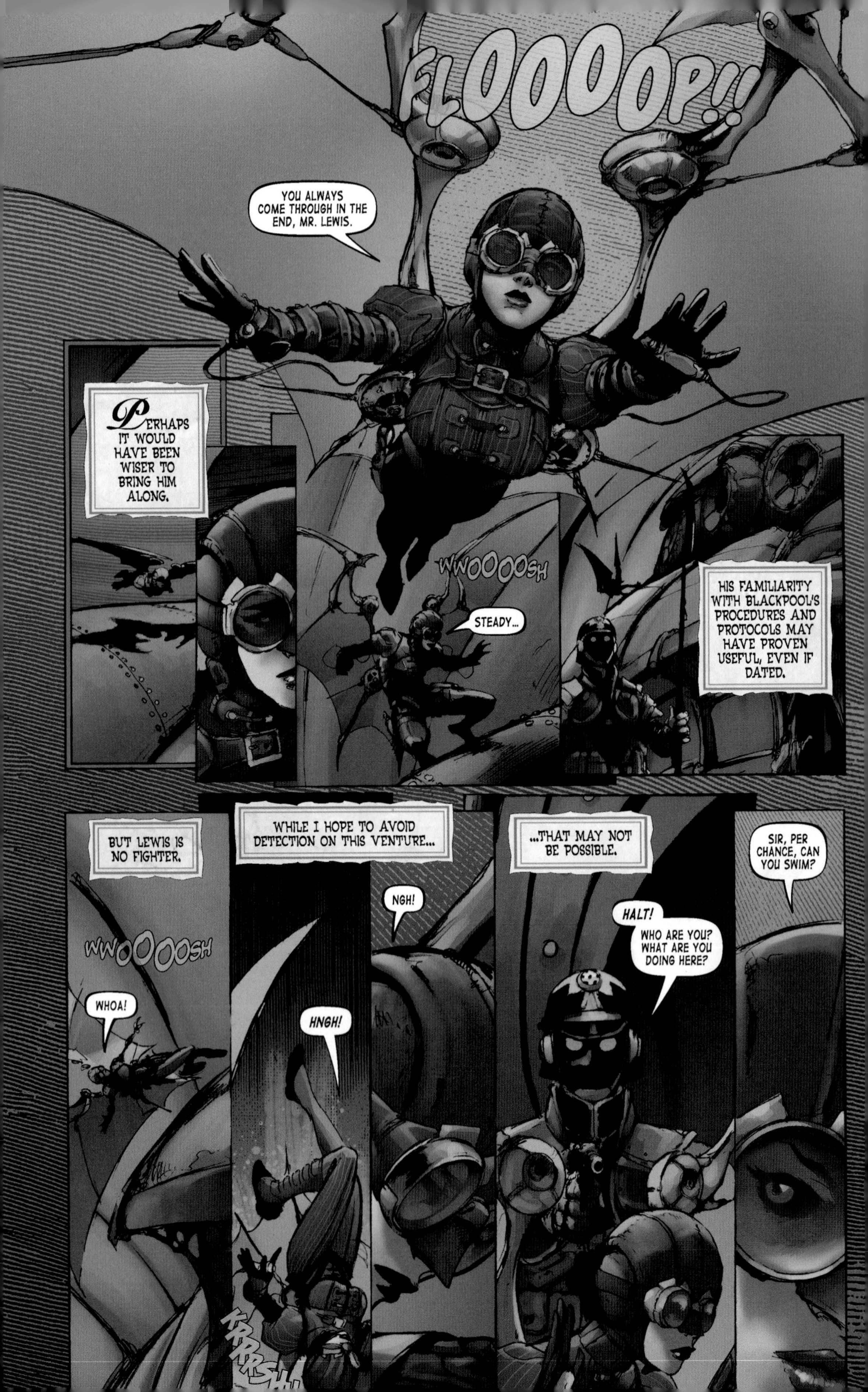
FLOOOOP!!
YOU ALWAYS COME THROUGH IN THE END, MR. LEWIS.
PERHAPS IT WOULD HAVE BEEN WISER TO BRING HIM ALONG.
WWOOOOSH
STEADY...
HIS FAMILIARITY WITH BLACKPOOL'S PROCEDURES AND PROTOCOLS MAY HAVE PROVEN USEFUL, EVEN IF DATED.
BUT LEWIS IS NO FIGHTER.
WWOOOOSH
WHOA!
WHILE I HOPE TO AVOID DETECTION ON THIS VENTURE...
HNGH!
KRRRSH!!
NGH!
...THAT MAY NOT BE POSSIBLE.
HALT!
WHO ARE YOU? WHAT ARE YOU DOING HERE?
SIR, PER CHANCE, CAN YOU SWIM?

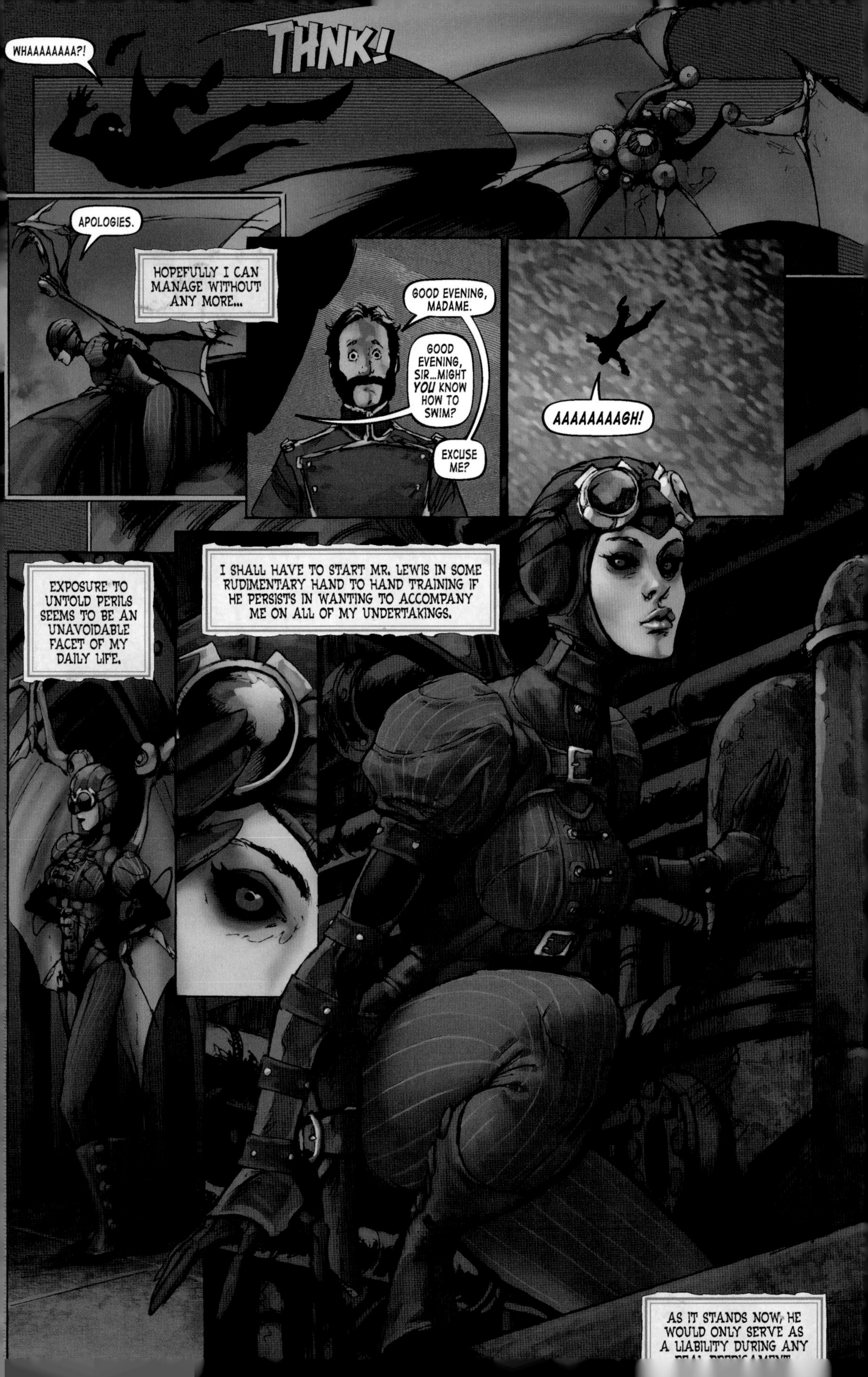

WHAAAAAAAAA?!
THNK!
APOLOGIES.
HOPEFULLY I CAN MANAGE WITHOUT ANY MORE...
GOOD EVENING, MADAME.
GOOD EVENING, SIR...MIGHT YOU KNOW HOW TO SWIM?
EXCUSE ME?
AAAAAAAAGH!
EXPOSURE TO UNTOLD PERILS SEEMS TO BE AN UNAVOIDABLE FACET OF MY DAILY LIFE.
I SHALL HAVE TO START MR. LEWIS IN SOME RUDIMENTARY HAND TO HAND TRAINING IF HE PERSISTS IN WANTING TO ACCOMPANY ME ON ALL OF MY UNDERTAKINGS.
AS IT STANDS NOW, HE WOULD ONLY SERVE AS A LIABILITY DURING ANY

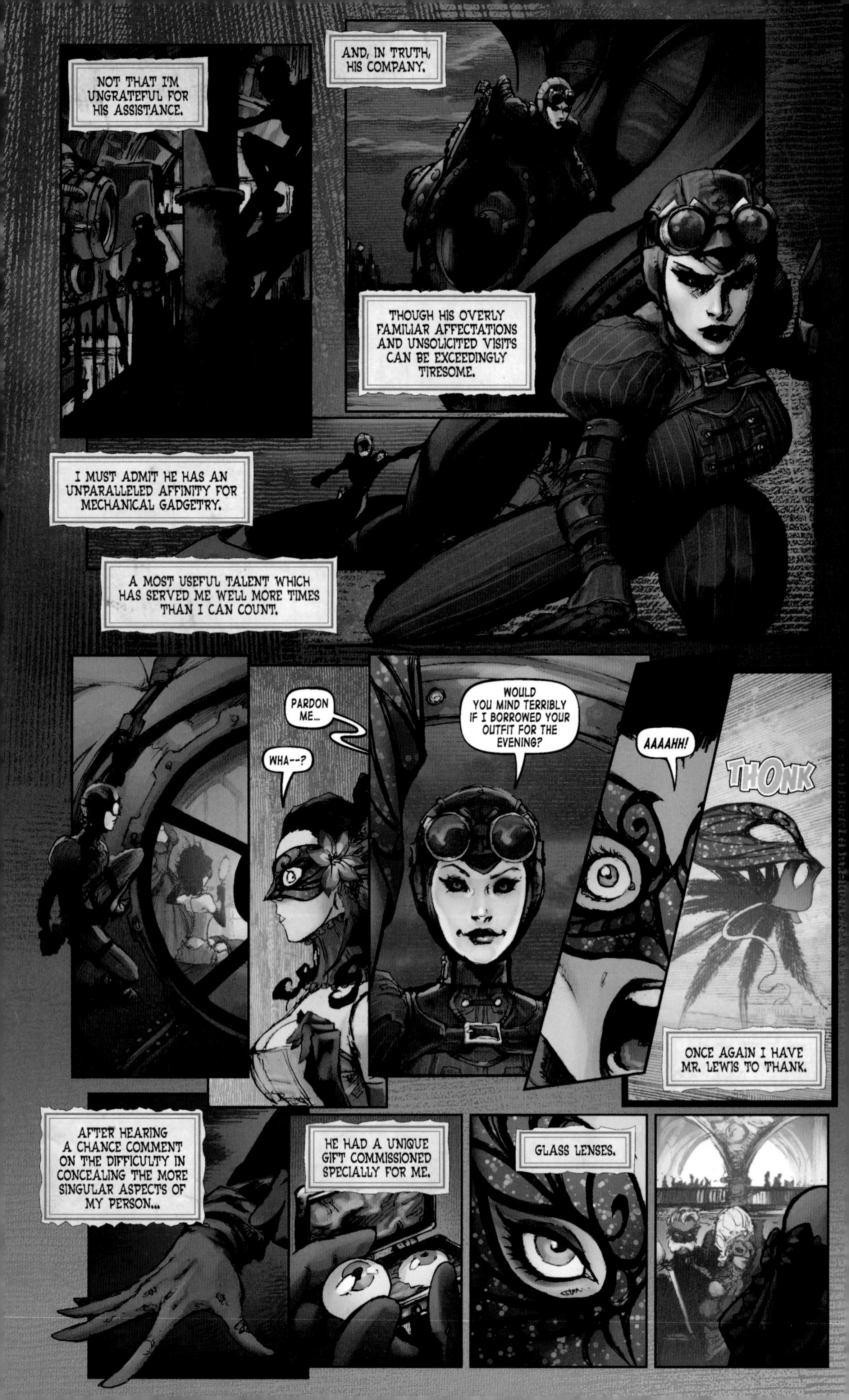
NOT THAT I'M UNGRATEFUL FOR HIS ASSISTANCE.
AND, IN TRUTH, HIS COMPANY.
THOUGH HIS OVERLY FAMILIAR AFFECTATIONS AND UNSOLICITED VISITS CAN BE EXCEEDINGLY TIRESOME.
I MUST ADMIT HE HAS AN UNPARALLELED AFFINITY FOR MECHANICAL GADGETRY.
A MOST USEFUL TALENT WHICH HAS SERVED ME WELL MORE TIMES THAN I CAN COUNT.
PARDON ME...
WHA--?
WOULD YOU MIND TERRIBLY IF I BORROWED YOUR OUTFIT FOR THE EVENING?
AAAAHH!
THONK
ONCE AGAIN I HAVE MR. LEWIS TO THANK.
AFTER HEARING A CHANCE COMMENT ON THE DIFFICULTY IN CONCEALING THE MORE SINGULAR ASPECTS OF MY PERSON...
HE HAD A UNIQUE GIFT COMMISSIONED SPECIALLY FOR ME.
GLASS LENSES.

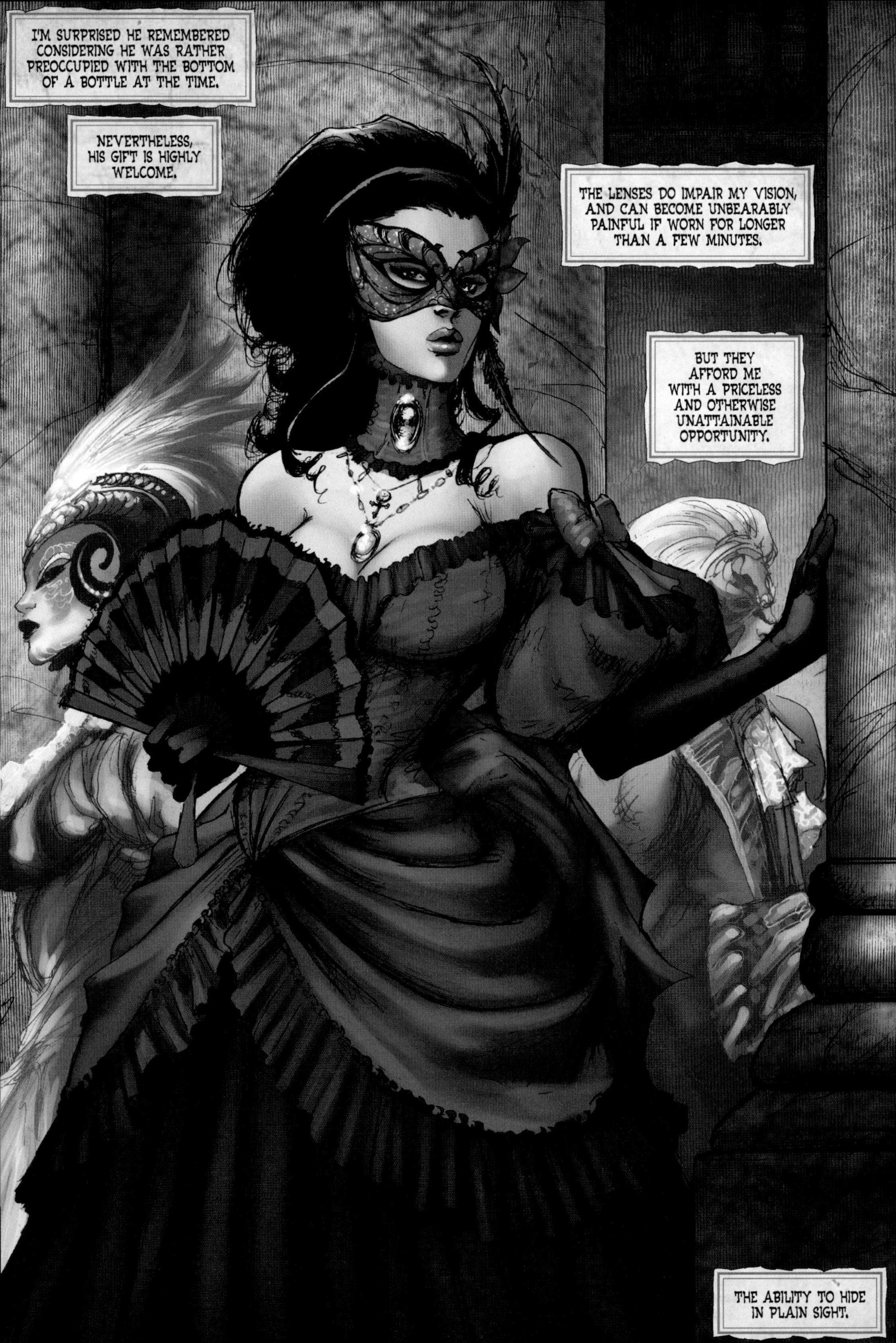
I'M SURPRISED HE REMEMBERED CONSIDERING HE WAS RATHER PREOCCUPIED WITH THE BOTTOM OF A BOTTLE AT THE TIME.
NEVERTHELESS, HIS GIFT IS HIGHLY WELCOME.
THE LENSES DO IMPAIR MY VISION, AND CAN BECOME UNBEARABLY PAINFUL IF WORN FOR LONGER THAN A FEW MINUTES.
BUT THEY AFFORD ME WITH A PRICELESS AND OTHERWISE UNATTAINABLE OPPORTUNITY.
THE ABILITY TO HIDE IN PLAIN SIGHT.

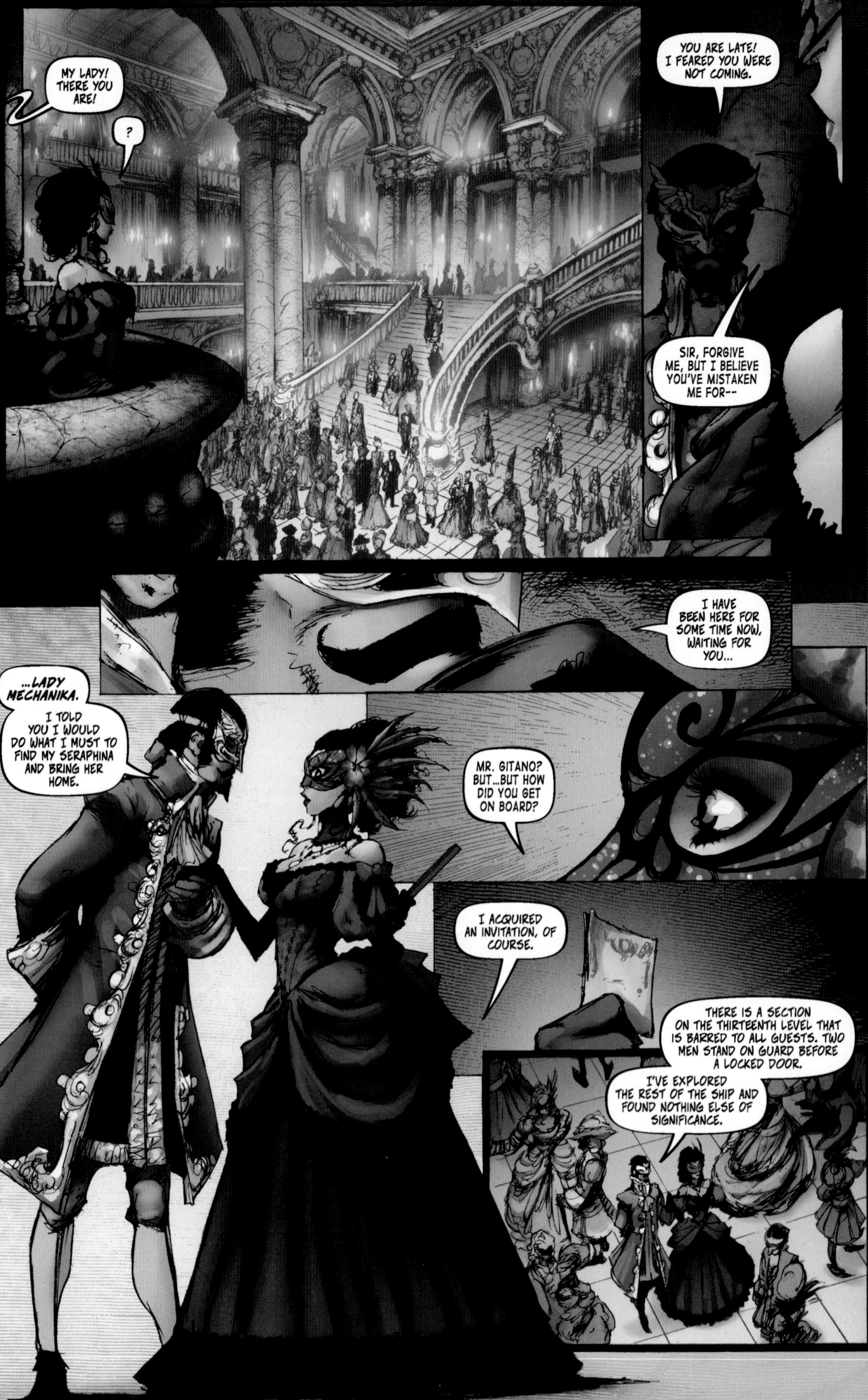
MY LADY! THERE YOU ARE!
?
YOU ARE LATE! I FEARED YOU WERE NOT COMING.
SIR, FORGIVE ME, BUT I BELIEVE YOU'VE MISTAKEN ME FOR--
I HAVE BEEN HERE FOR SOME TIME NOW, WAITING FOR YOU...
...LADY MECHANIKA.
I TOLD YOU I WOULD DO WHAT I MUST TO FIND MY SERAPHINA AND BRING HER HOME.
MR. GITANO? BUT...BUT HOW DID YOU GET ON BOARD?
I ACQUIRED AN INVITATION, OF COURSE.
THERE IS A SECTION ON THE THIRTEENTH LEVEL THAT IS BARRED TO ALL GUESTS. TWO MEN STAND ON GUARD BEFORE A LOCKED DOOR.
I'VE EXPLORED THE REST OF THE SHIP AND FOUND NOTHING ELSE OF SIGNIFICANCE.

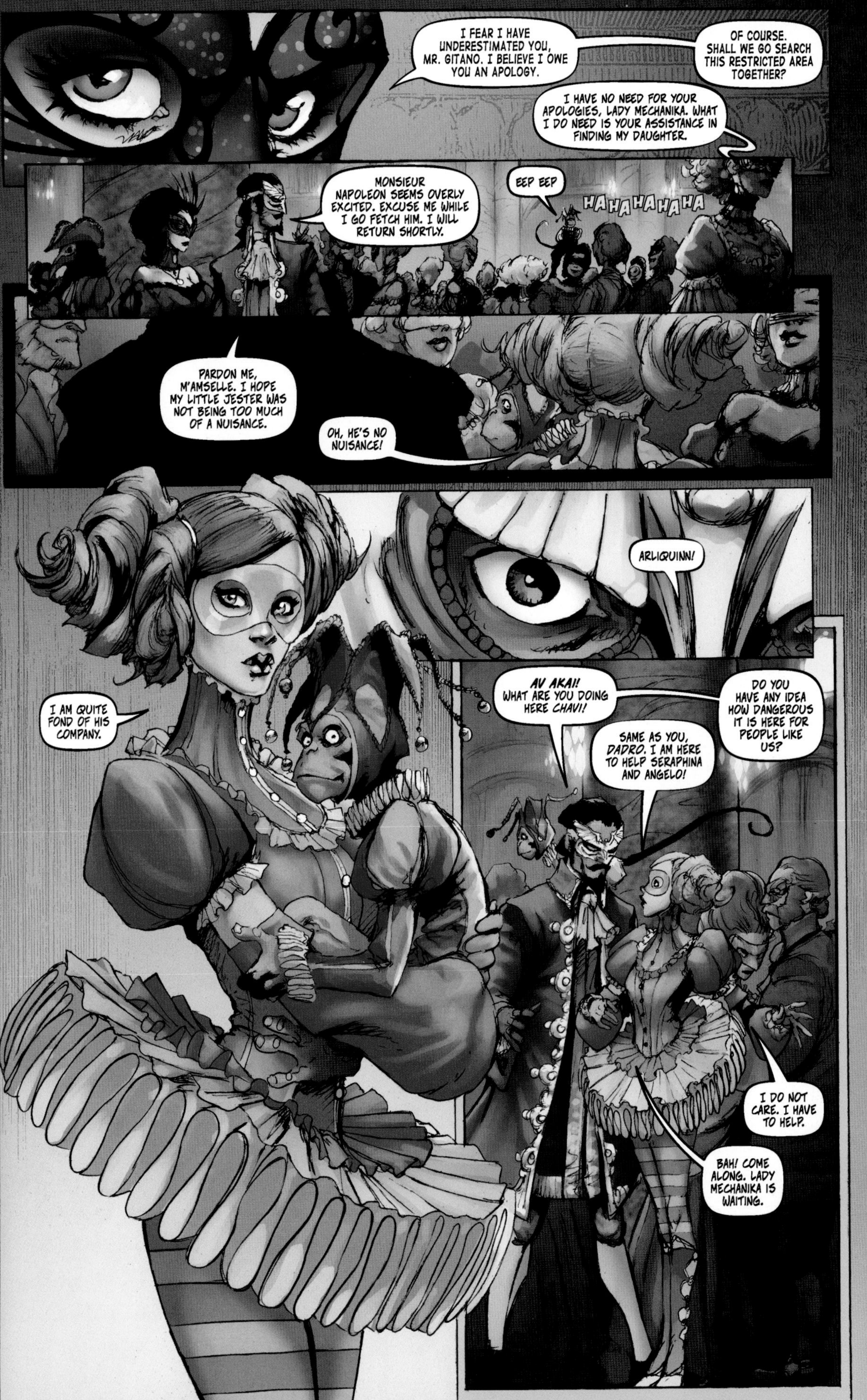
I FEAR I HAVE UNDERESTIMATED YOU, MR. GITANO. I BELIEVE I OWE YOU AN APOLOGY.
I HAVE NO NEED FOR YOUR APOLOGIES, LADY MECHANIKA. WHAT I DO NEED IS YOUR ASSISTANCE IN FINDING MY DAUGHTER.
OF COURSE. SHALL WE GO SEARCH THIS RESTRICTED AREA TOGETHER?
MONSIEUR NAPOLEON SEEMS OVERLY EXCITED. EXCUSE ME WHILE I GO FETCH HIM. I WILL RETURN SHORTLY.
EEP EEP
HAHAHAHAHAHA
PARDON ME, M'AMSELLE. I HOPE MY LITTLE JESTER WAS NOT BEING TOO MUCH OF A NUISANCE.
OH, HE'S NO NUISANCE!
I AM QUITE FOND OF HIS COMPANY.
ARLIQUINN!
AV AKAI! WHAT ARE YOU DOING HERE CHAVI!
DO YOU HAVE ANY IDEA HOW DANGEROUS IT IS HERE FOR PEOPLE LIKE US?
SAME AS YOU, DADRO. I AM HERE TO HELP SERAPHINA AND ANGELO!
I DO NOT CARE. I HAVE TO HELP.
BAH! COME ALONG. LADY MECHANIKA IS WAITING.

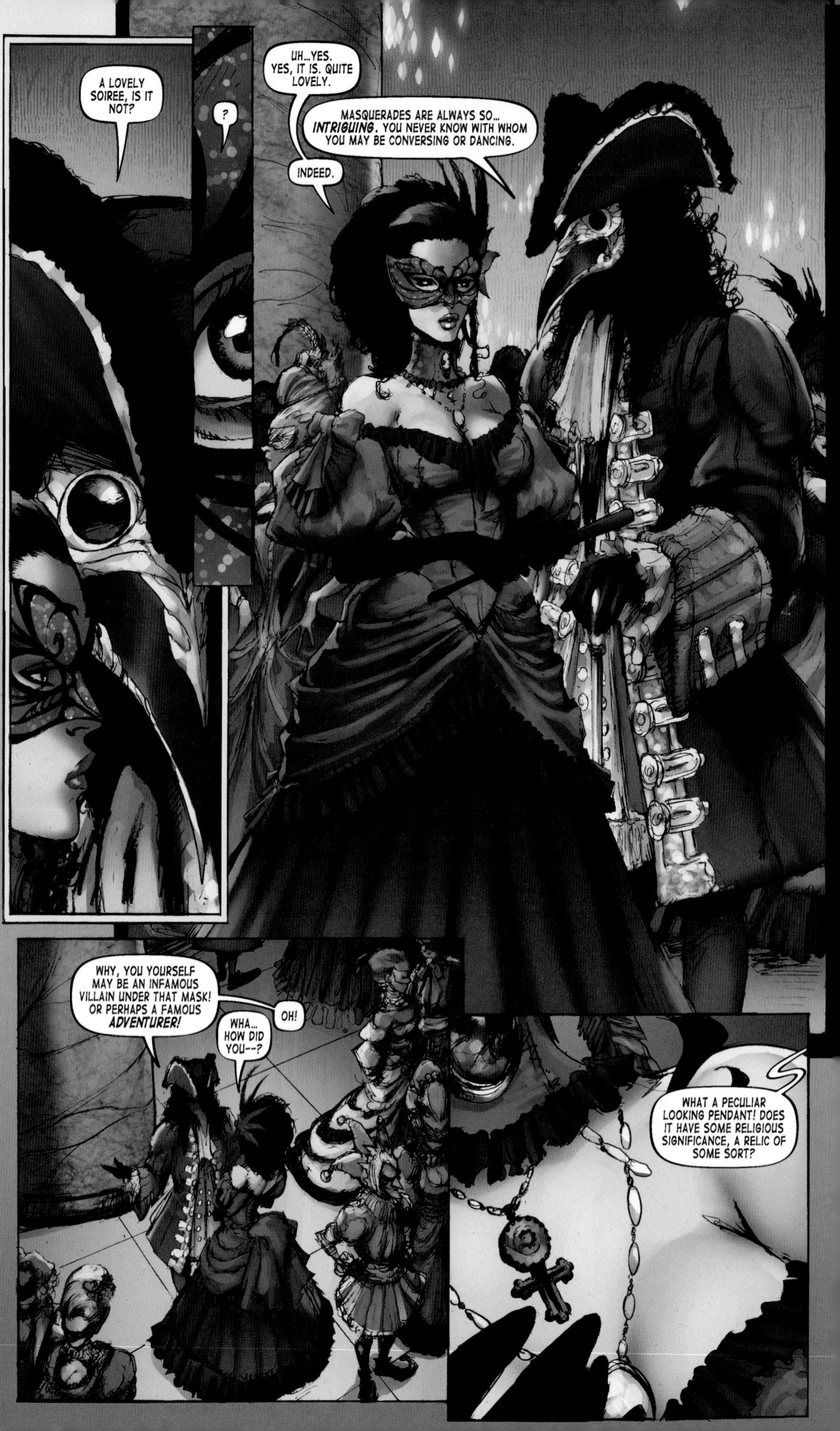
A LOVELY SOIREE, IS IT NOT?
?
UH...YES. YES, IT IS. QUITE LOVELY.
MASQUERADES ARE ALWAYS SO... INTRIGUING. YOU NEVER KNOW WITH WHOM YOU MAY BE CONVERSING OR DANCING.
INDEED.
WHY, YOU YOURSELF MAY BE AN INFAMOUS VILLAIN UNDER THAT MASK! OR PERHAPS A FAMOUS ADVENTURER!
OH!
WHA... HOW DID YOU--?
WHAT A PECULIAR LOOKING PENDANT! DOES IT HAVE SOME RELIGIOUS SIGNIFICANCE, A RELIC OF SOME SORT?

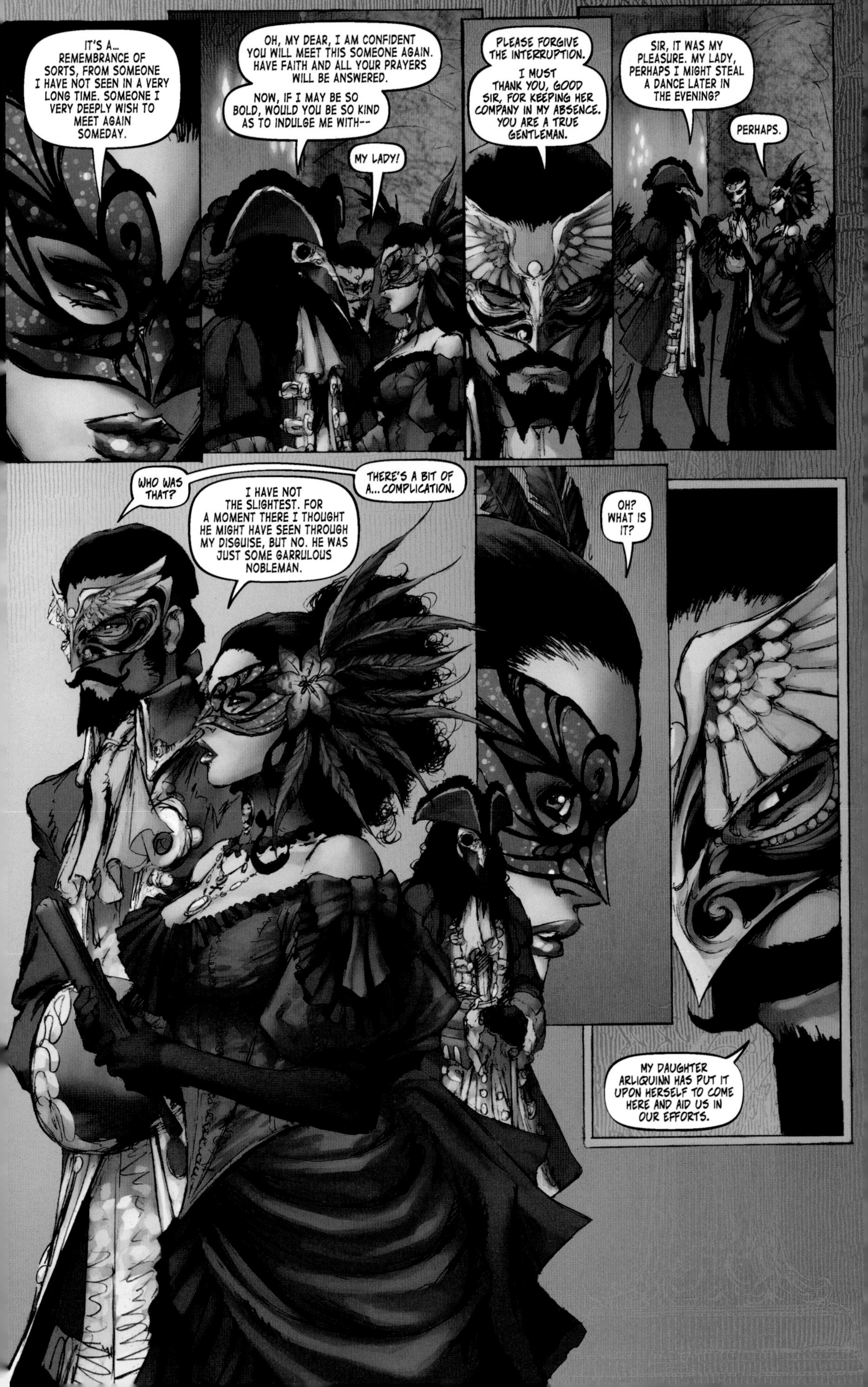
IT'S A... REMEMBRANCE OF SORTS, FROM SOMEONE I HAVE NOT SEEN IN A VERY LONG TIME. SOMEONE I VERY DEEPLY WISH TO MEET AGAIN SOMEDAY.
OH, MY DEAR, I AM CONFIDENT YOU WILL MEET THIS SOMEONE AGAIN. HAVE FAITH AND ALL YOUR PRAYERS WILL BE ANSWERED.
NOW, IF I MAY BE SO BOLD, WOULD YOU BE SO KIND AS TO INDULGE ME WITH--
MY LADY!
PLEASE FORGIVE THE INTERRUPTION.
I MUST THANK YOU, GOOD SIR, FOR KEEPING HER COMPANY IN MY ABSENCE. YOU ARE A TRUE GENTLEMAN.
SIR, IT WAS MY PLEASURE. MY LADY, PERHAPS I MIGHT STEAL A DANCE LATER IN THE EVENING?
PERHAPS.
WHO WAS THAT?
I HAVE NOT THE SLIGHTEST. FOR A MOMENT THERE I THOUGHT HE MIGHT HAVE SEEN THROUGH MY DISGUISE, BUT NO. HE WAS JUST SOME GARRULOUS NOBLEMAN.
THERE'S A BIT OF A...COMPLICATION.
OH? WHAT IS IT?
MY DAUGHTER ARLIQUINN HAS PUT IT UPON HERSELF TO COME HERE AND AID US IN OUR EFFORTS.

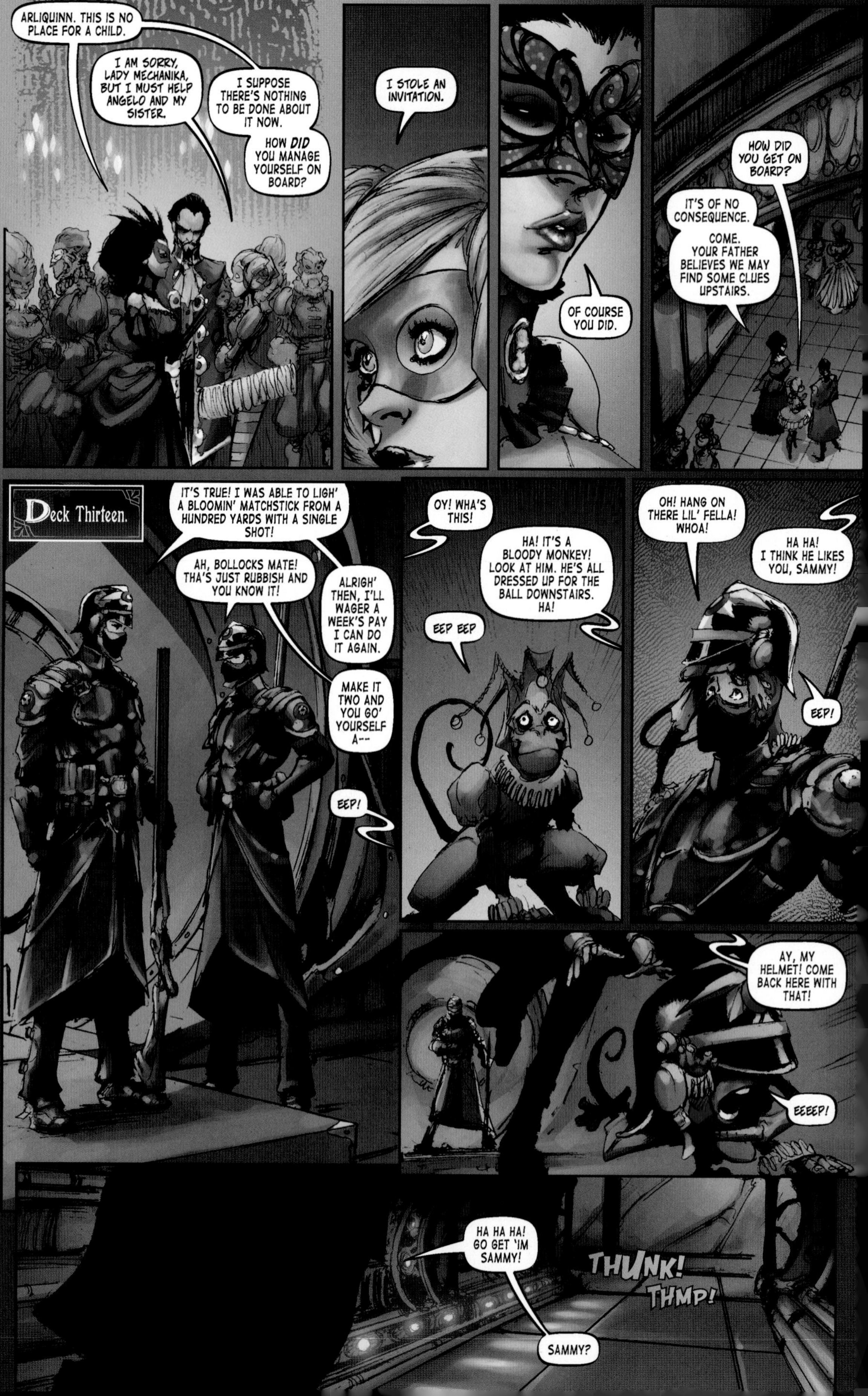
ARLIQUINN. THIS IS NO PLACE FOR A CHILD.
I AM SORRY, LADY MECHANIKA, BUT I MUST HELP ANGELO AND MY SISTER.
I SUPPOSE THERE'S NOTHING TO BE DONE ABOUT IT NOW.
HOW DID YOU MANAGE YOURSELF ON BOARD?
I STOLE AN INVITATION.
OF COURSE YOU DID.
HOW DID YOU GET ON BOARD?
IT'S OF NO CONSEQUENCE.
COME. YOUR FATHER BELIEVES WE MAY FIND SOME CLUES UPSTAIRS.
Deck Thirteen.
IT'S TRUE! I WAS ABLE TO LIGH' A BLOOMIN' MATCHSTICK FROM A HUNDRED YARDS WITH A SINGLE SHOT!
AH, BOLLOCKS MATE! THA'S JUST RUBBISH AND YOU KNOW IT!
ALRIGH' THEN, I'LL WAGER A WEEK'S PAY I CAN DO IT AGAIN.
MAKE IT TWO AND YOU GO' YOURSELF A--
EEP!
OY! WHA'S THIS!
HA! IT'S A BLOODY MONKEY! LOOK AT HIM. HE'S ALL DRESSED UP FOR THE BALL DOWNSTAIRS. HA!
EEP EEP
OH! HANG ON THERE LIL' FELLA! WHOA!
HA HA! I THINK HE LIKES YOU, SAMMY!
EEP!
AY, MY HELMET! COME BACK HERE WITH THAT!
EEEEP!
HA HA HA! GO GET 'IM SAMMY!
THUNK!
THMP!
SAMMY?

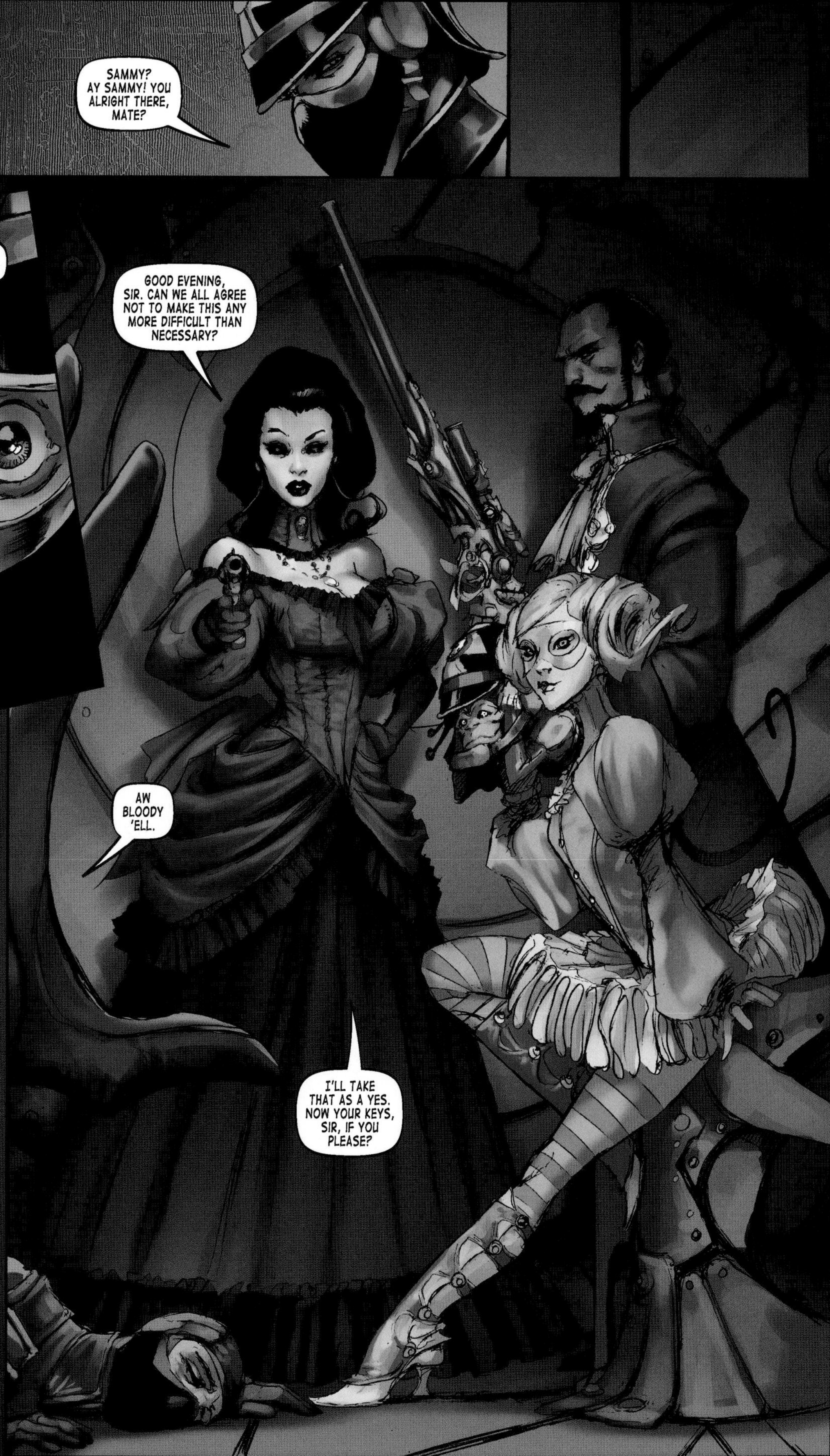
SAMMY? AY SAMMY! YOU ALRIGHT THERE, MATE?
GOOD EVENING, SIR. CAN WE ALL AGREE NOT TO MAKE THIS ANY MORE DIFFICULT THAN NECESSARY?
AW BLOODY 'ELL.
I'LL TAKE THAT AS A YES. NOW YOUR KEYS, SIR, IF YOU PLEASE?

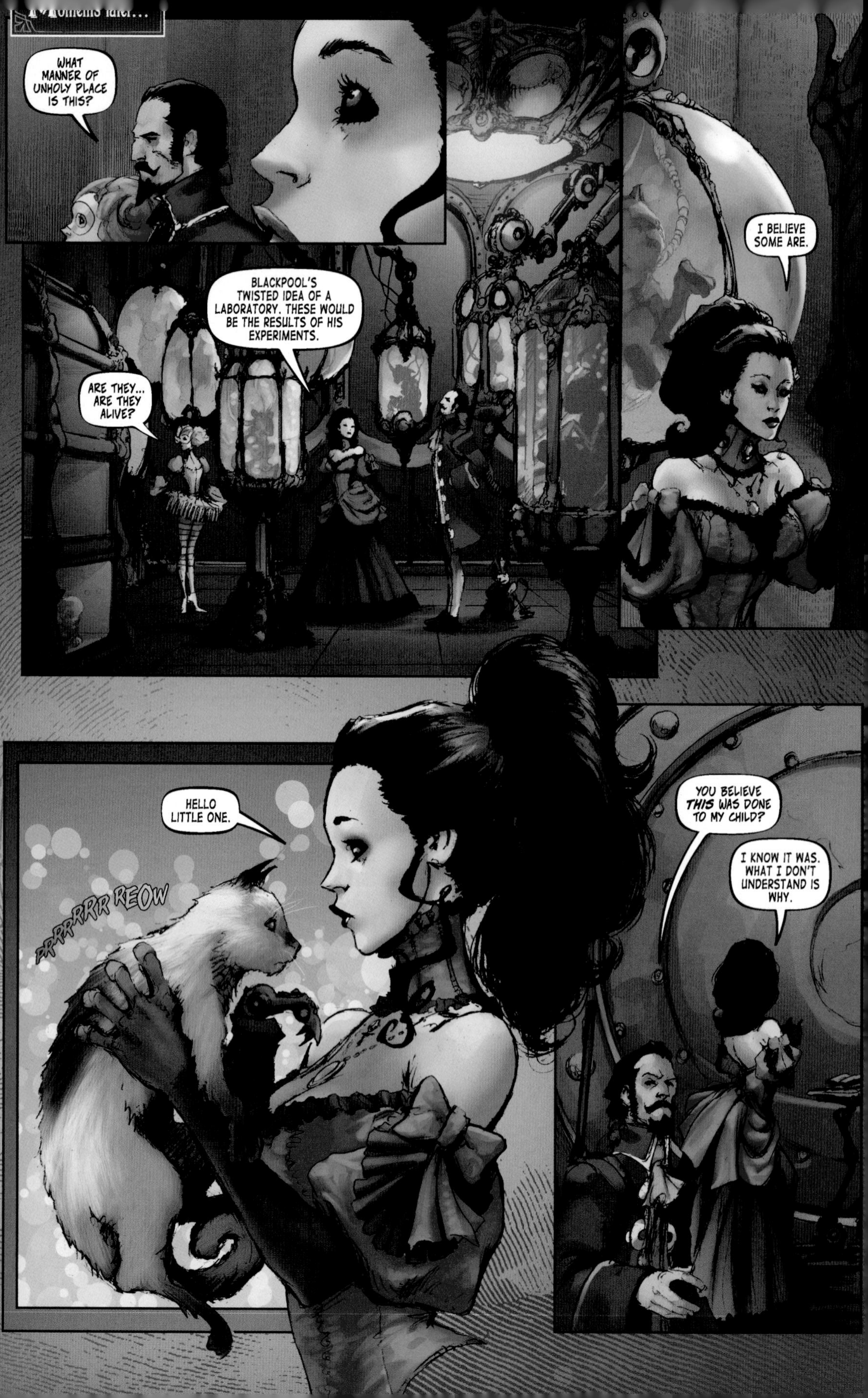
WHAT MANNER OF UNHOLY PLACE IS THIS?
BLACKPOOL'S TWISTED IDEA OF A LABORATORY. THESE WOULD BE THE RESULTS OF HIS EXPERIMENTS.
ARE THEY... ARE THEY ALIVE?
I BELIEVE SOME ARE.
HELLO LITTLE ONE.
PRRRRRR REOW
YOU BELIEVE *THIS* WAS DONE TO MY CHILD?
I KNOW IT WAS. WHAT I DON'T UNDERSTAND IS WHY.

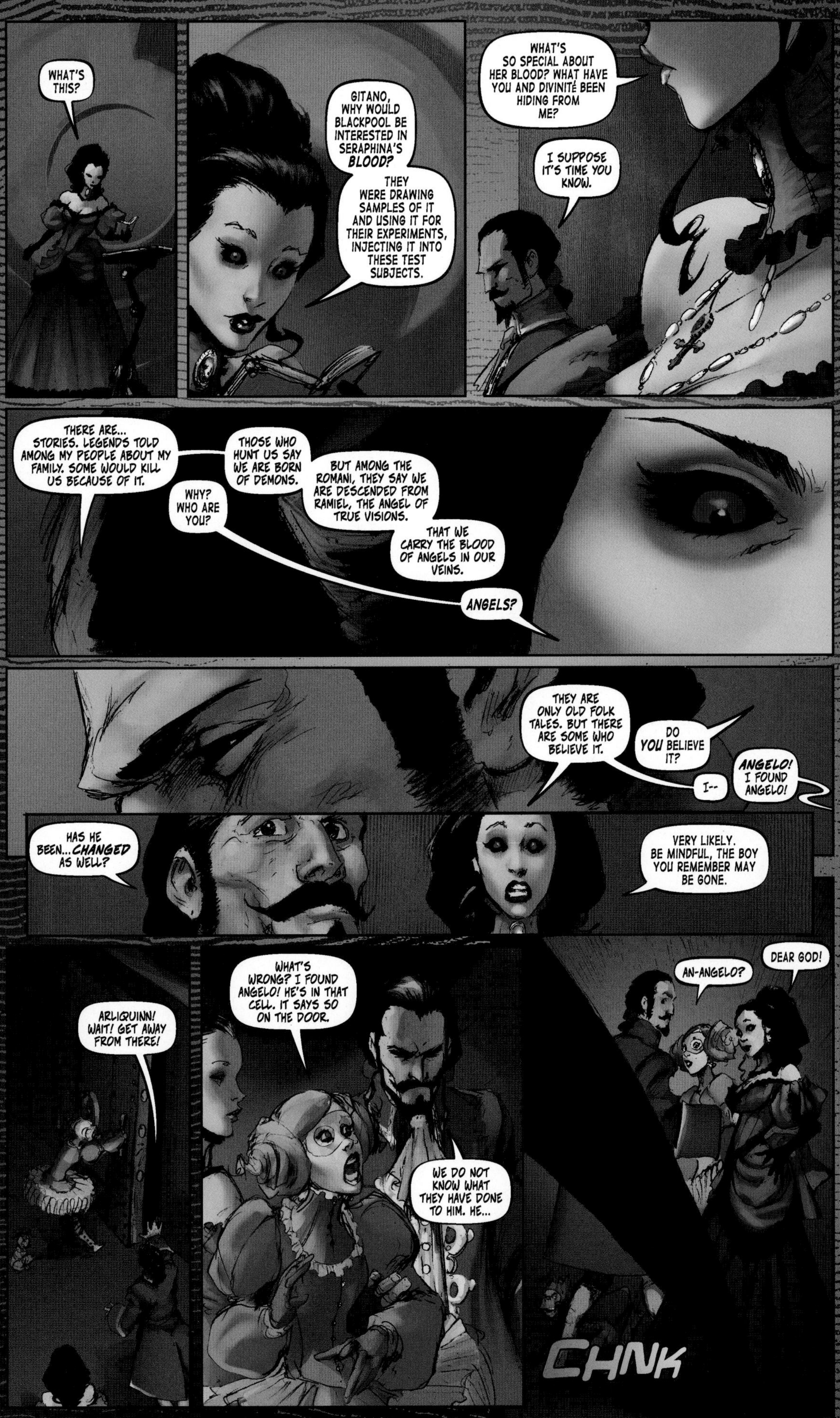
WHAT'S THIS?
GITANO, WHY WOULD BLACKPOOL BE INTERESTED IN SERAPHINA'S BLOOD?
THEY WERE DRAWING SAMPLES OF IT AND USING IT FOR THEIR EXPERIMENTS, INJECTING IT INTO THESE TEST SUBJECTS.
WHAT'S SO SPECIAL ABOUT HER BLOOD? WHAT HAVE YOU AND DIVINITÉ BEEN HIDING FROM ME?
I SUPPOSE IT'S TIME YOU KNOW.
THERE ARE... STORIES. LEGENDS TOLD AMONG MY PEOPLE ABOUT MY FAMILY. SOME WOULD KILL US BECAUSE OF IT.
WHY? WHO ARE YOU?
THOSE WHO HUNT US SAY WE ARE BORN OF DEMONS.
BUT AMONG THE ROMANI, THEY SAY WE ARE DESCENDED FROM RAMIEL, THE ANGEL OF TRUE VISIONS.
THAT WE CARRY THE BLOOD OF ANGELS IN OUR VEINS.
ANGELS?
THEY ARE ONLY OLD FOLK TALES. BUT THERE ARE SOME WHO BELIEVE IT.
DO YOU BELIEVE IT?
I--
ANGELO! I FOUND ANGELO!
HAS HE BEEN...CHANGED AS WELL?
VERY LIKELY. BE MINDFUL, THE BOY YOU REMEMBER MAY BE GONE.
ARLIQUINN! WAIT! GET AWAY FROM THERE!
WHAT'S WRONG? I FOUND ANGELO! HE'S IN THAT CELL. IT SAYS SO ON THE DOOR.
WE DO NOT KNOW WHAT THEY HAVE DONE TO HIM. HE...
AN-ANGELO?
DEAR GOD!
CHNK

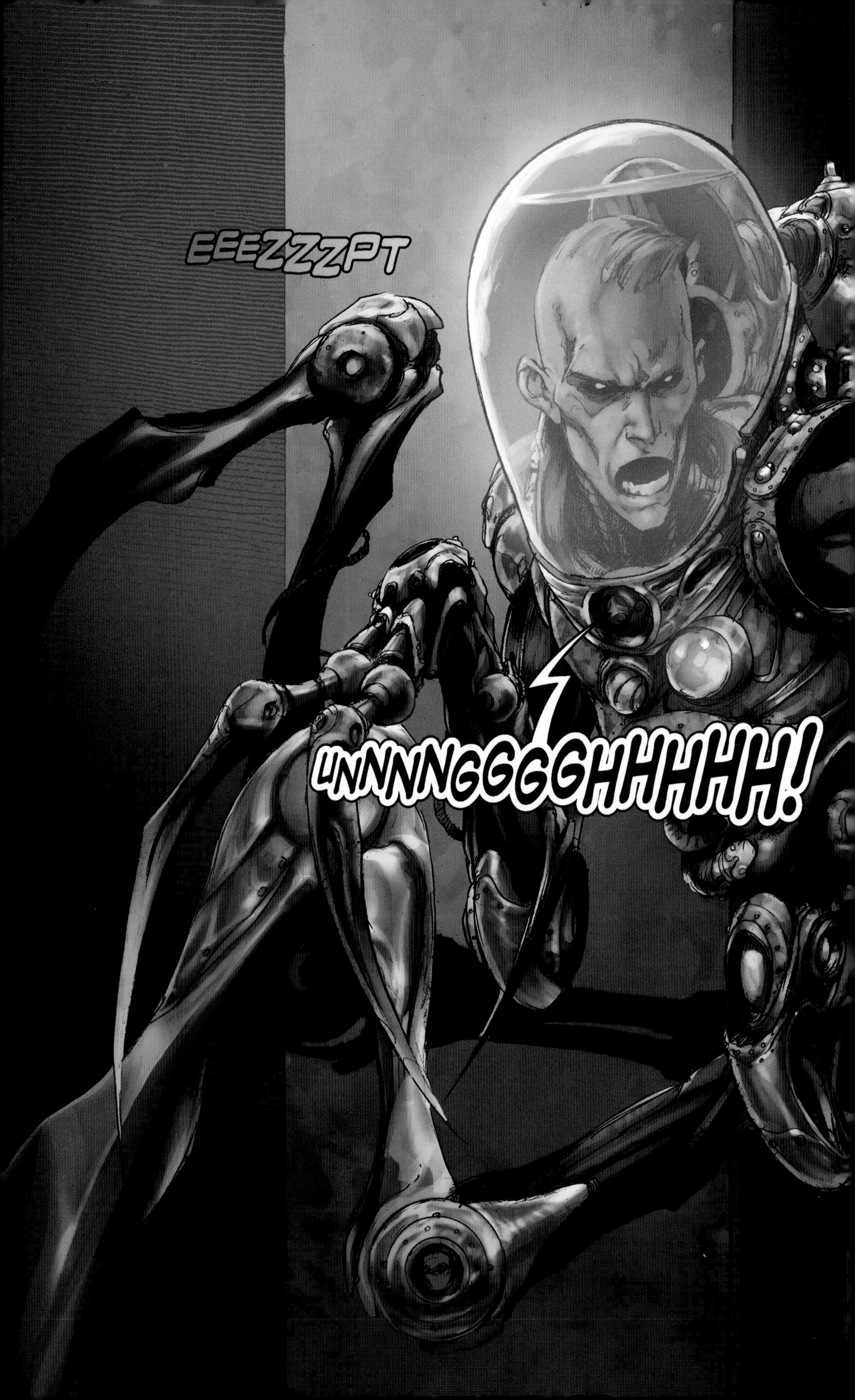
EEEZZZPT
UNNNNGGGGHHHHHH!

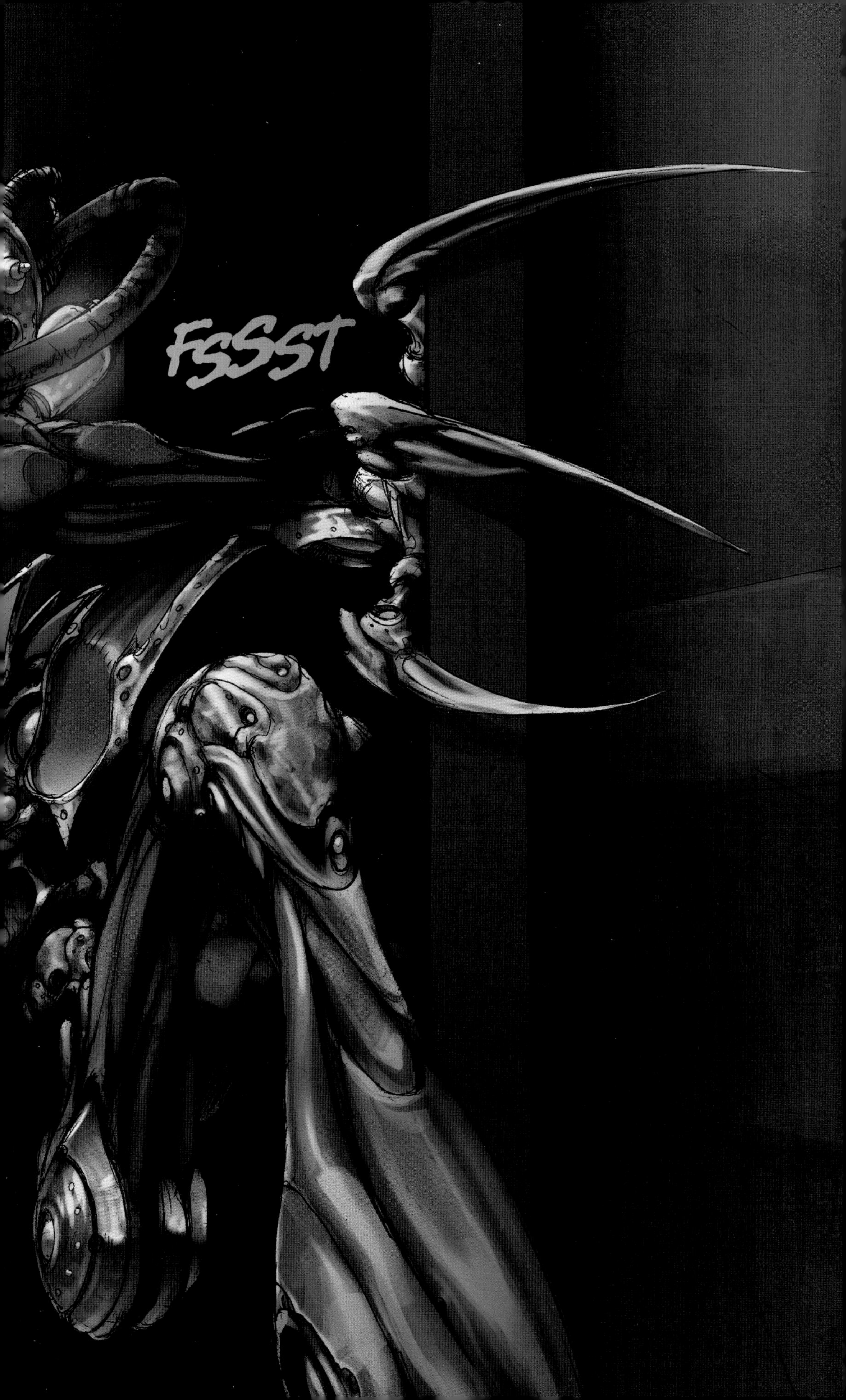
FSSST

Chapter Five

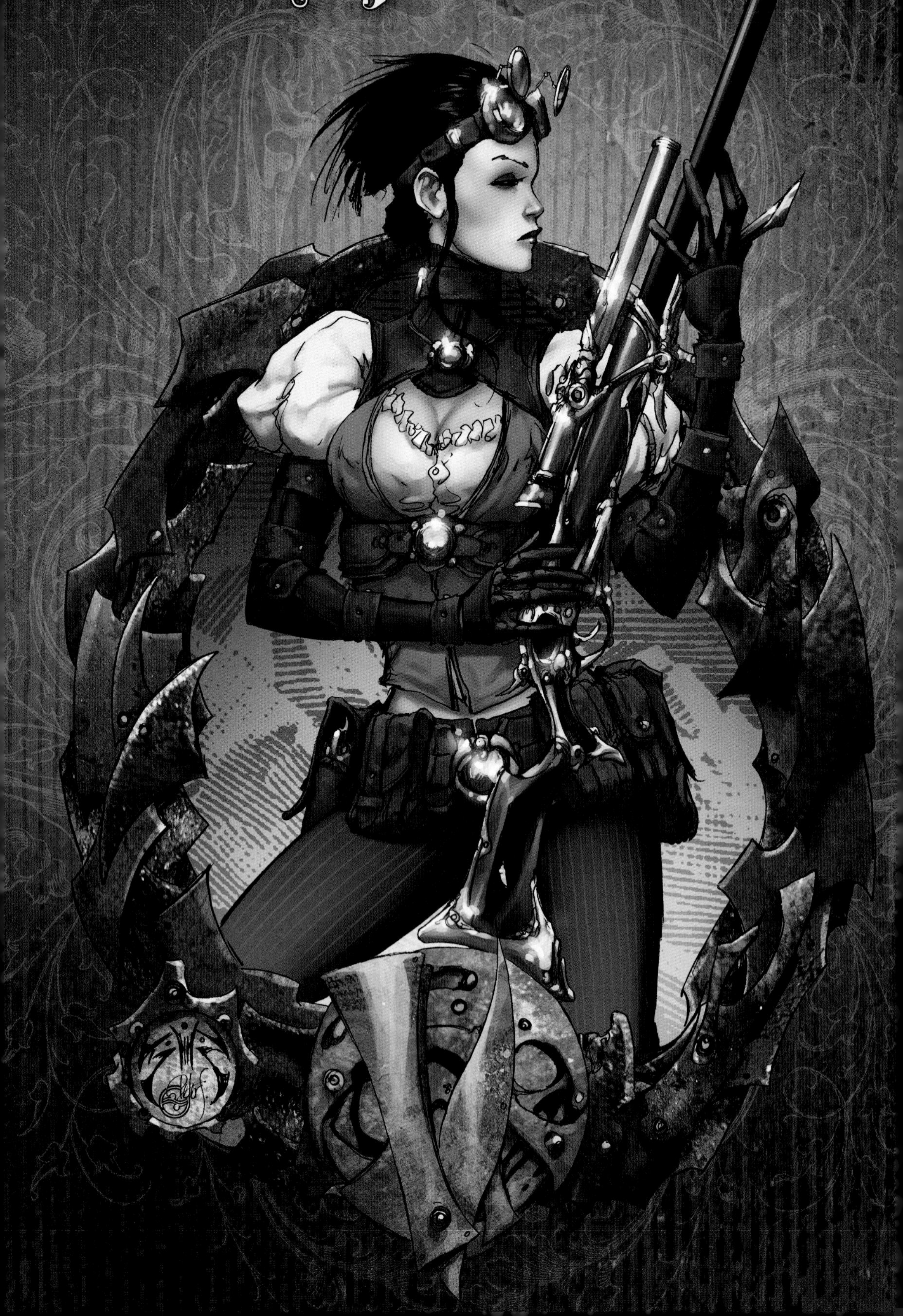

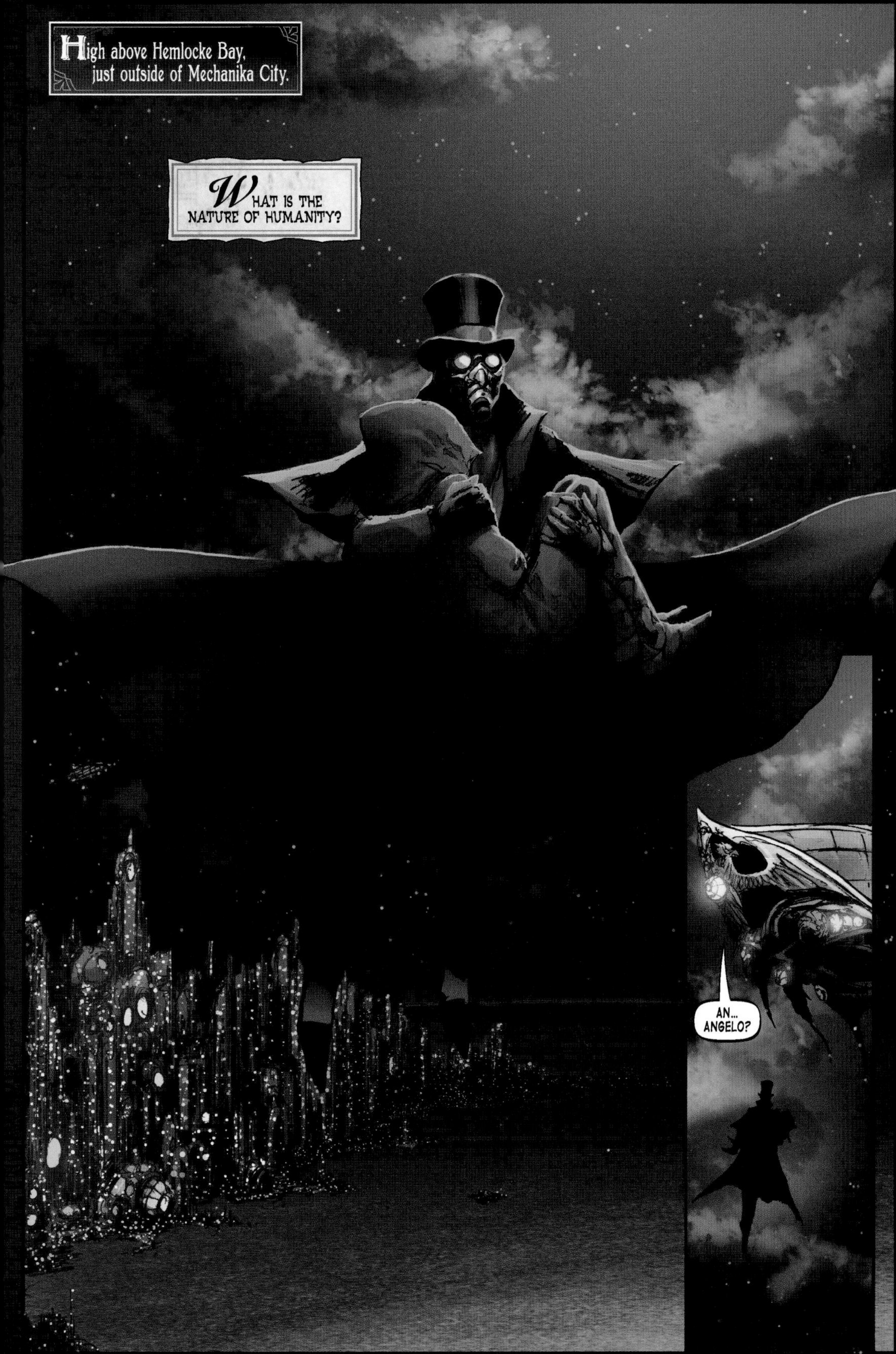
High above Hemlocke Bay, just outside of Mechanika City.
WHAT IS THE NATURE OF HUMANITY?
AN... ANGELO?

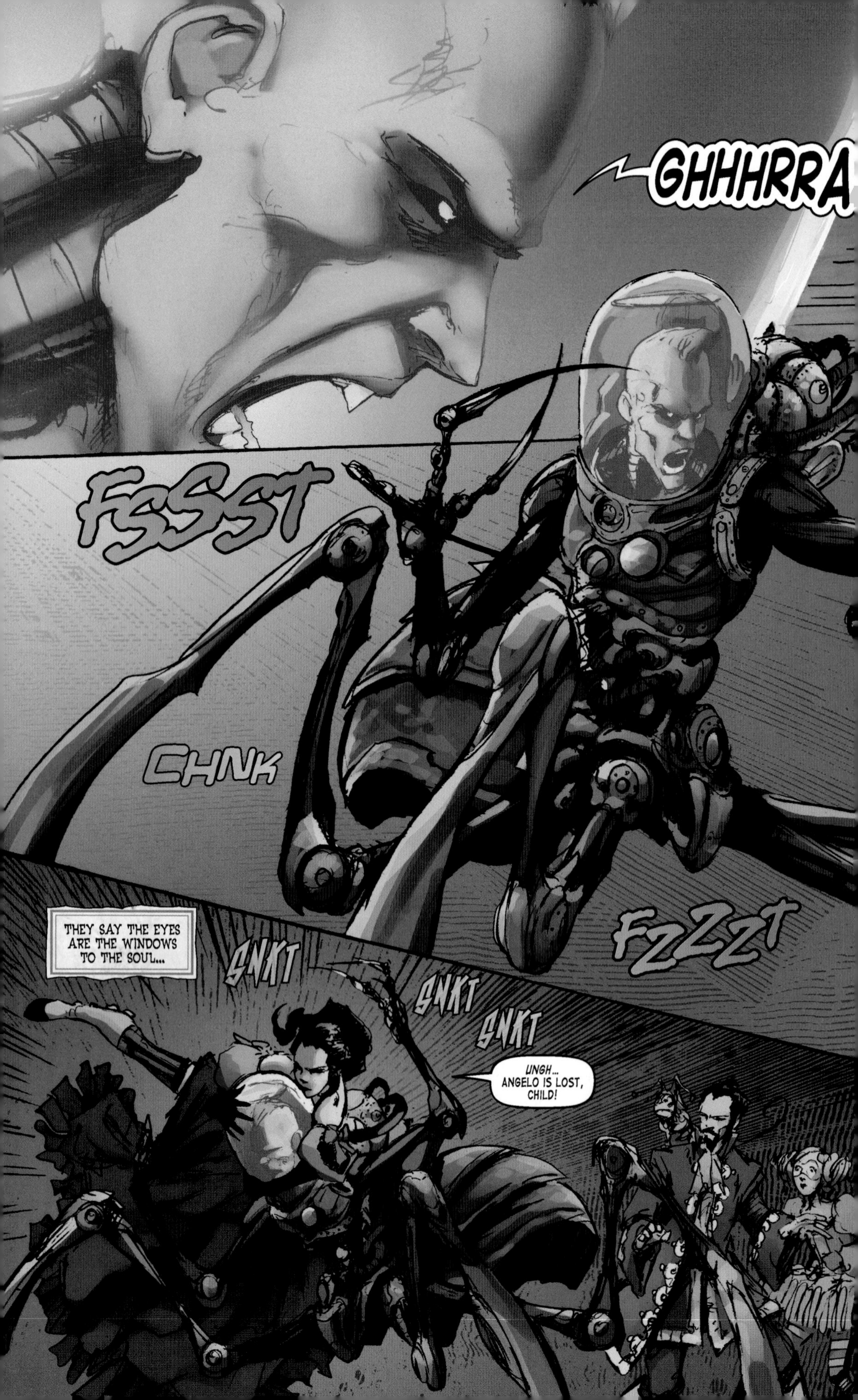
GHHHRRA
FSSST
CHNK
FZZZT
THEY SAY THE EYES ARE THE WINDOWS TO THE SOUL...
SNKT
SNKT
SNKT
UNGH... ANGELO IS LOST, CHILD!

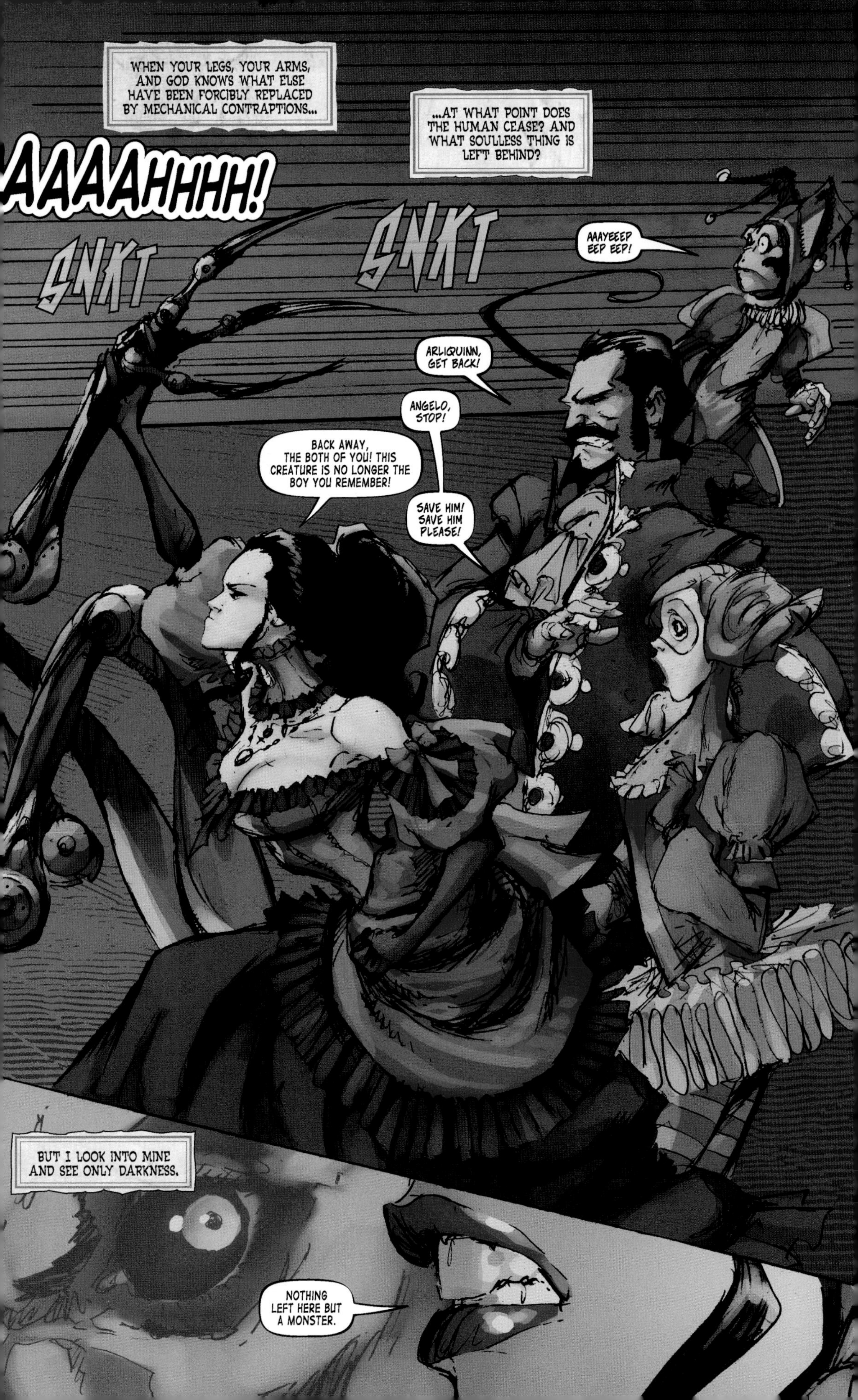
WHEN YOUR LEGS, YOUR ARMS, AND GOD KNOWS WHAT ELSE HAVE BEEN FORCIBLY REPLACED BY MECHANICAL CONTRAPTIONS...
...AT WHAT POINT DOES THE HUMAN CEASE? AND WHAT SOULLESS THING IS LEFT BEHIND?
AAAAHHHH!
SNKT
SNKT
AAAYEEEP EEP EEP!
ARLIQUINN, GET BACK!
ANGELO, STOP!
BACK AWAY, THE BOTH OF YOU! THIS CREATURE IS NO LONGER THE BOY YOU REMEMBER!
SAVE HIM! SAVE HIM PLEASE!
BUT I LOOK INTO MINE AND SEE ONLY DARKNESS.
NOTHING LEFT HERE BUT A MONSTER.

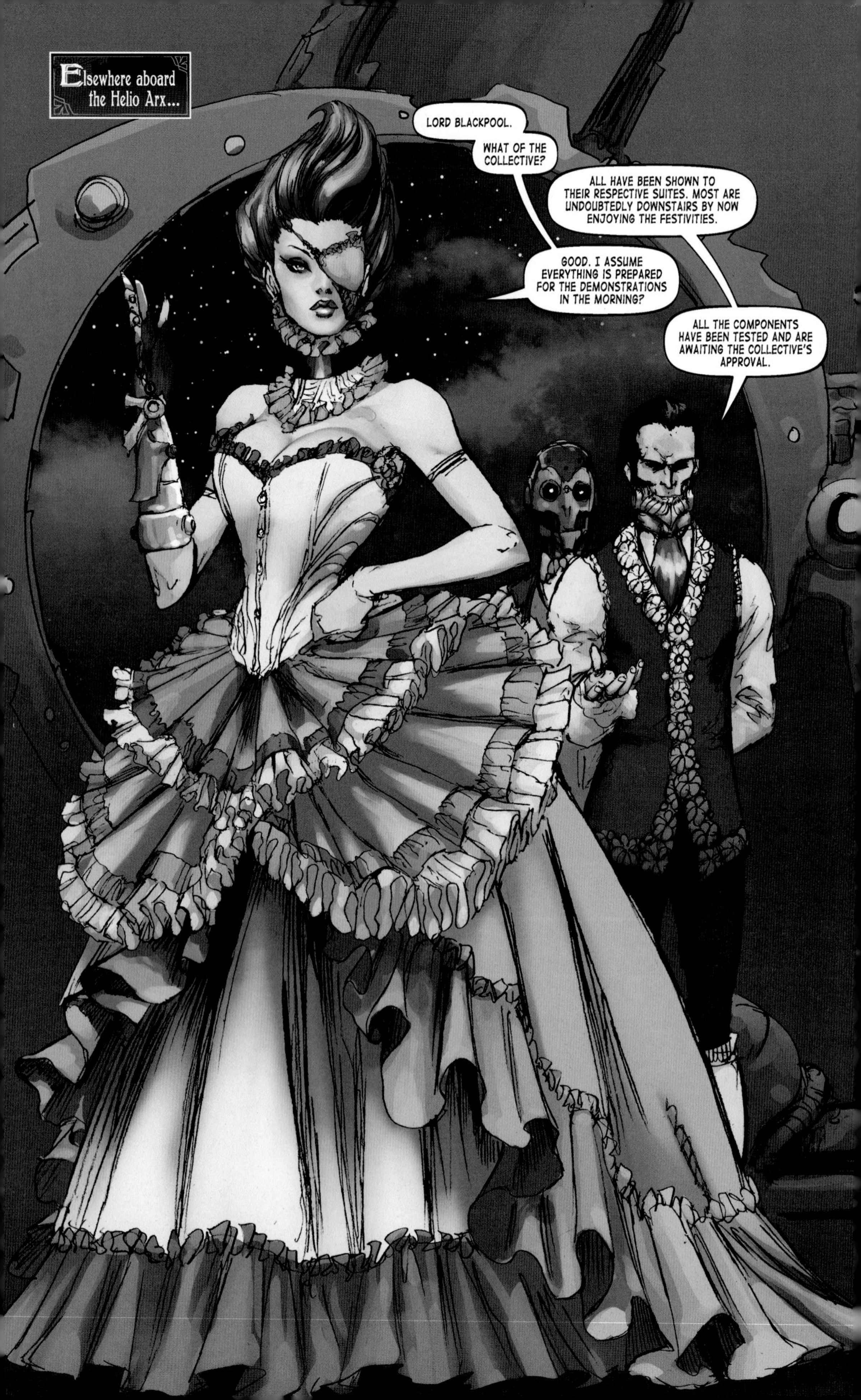

Elsewhere aboard the Helio Arx...
LORD BLACKPOOL.
WHAT OF THE COLLECTIVE?
ALL HAVE BEEN SHOWN TO THEIR RESPECTIVE SUITES. MOST ARE UNDOUBTEDLY DOWNSTAIRS BY NOW ENJOYING THE FESTIVITIES.
GOOD. I ASSUME EVERYTHING IS PREPARED FOR THE DEMONSTRATIONS IN THE MORNING?
ALL THE COMPONENTS HAVE BEEN TESTED AND ARE AWAITING THE COLLECTIVE'S APPROVAL.

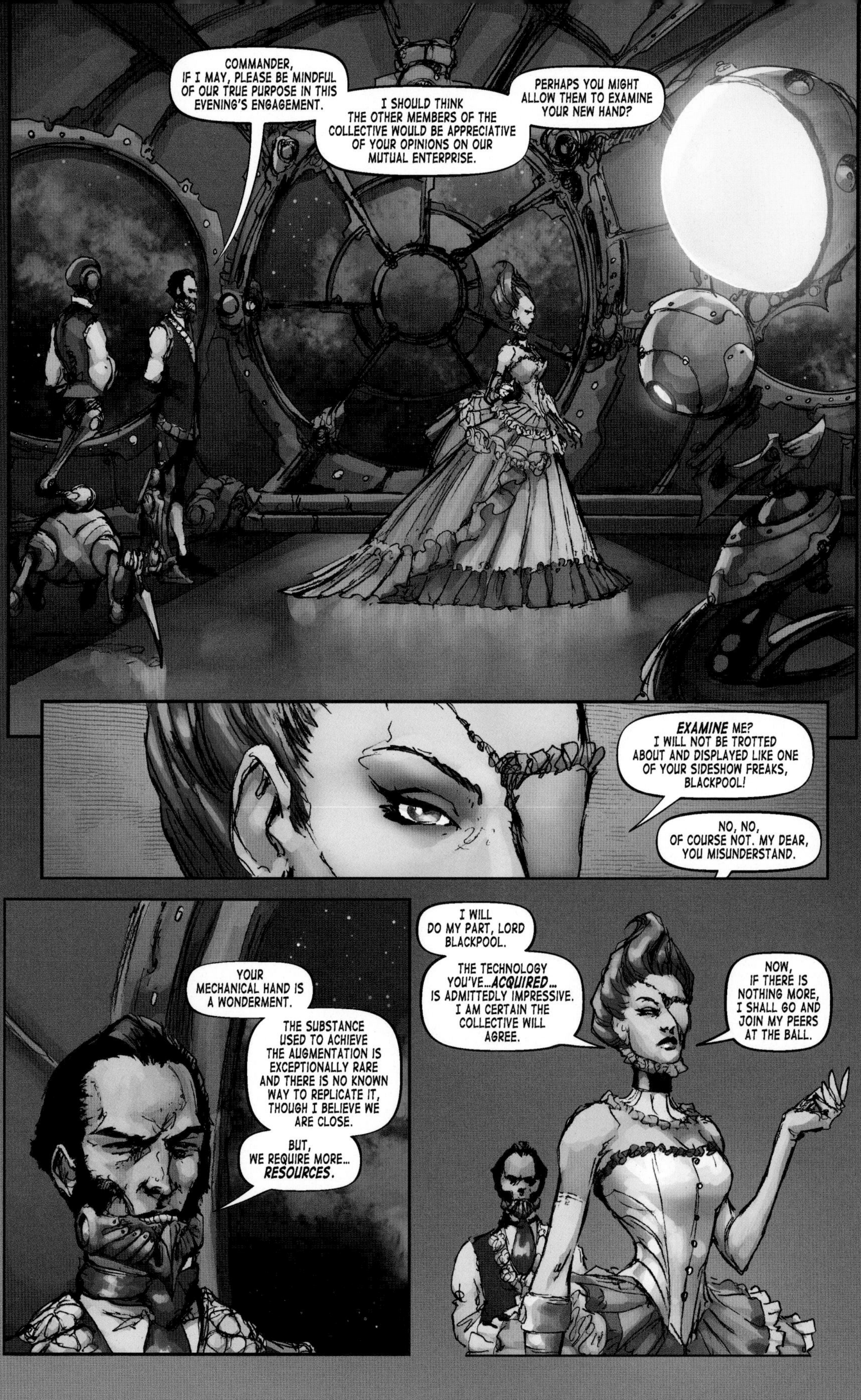
COMMANDER, IF I MAY, PLEASE BE MINDFUL OF OUR TRUE PURPOSE IN THIS EVENING'S ENGAGEMENT.
I SHOULD THINK THE OTHER MEMBERS OF THE COLLECTIVE WOULD BE APPRECIATIVE OF YOUR OPINIONS ON OUR MUTUAL ENTERPRISE.
PERHAPS YOU MIGHT ALLOW THEM TO EXAMINE YOUR NEW HAND?
EXAMINE ME? I WILL NOT BE TROTTED ABOUT AND DISPLAYED LIKE ONE OF YOUR SIDESHOW FREAKS, BLACKPOOL!
NO, NO, OF COURSE NOT. MY DEAR, YOU MISUNDERSTAND.
YOUR MECHANICAL HAND IS A WONDERMENT.
THE SUBSTANCE USED TO ACHIEVE THE AUGMENTATION IS EXCEPTIONALLY RARE AND THERE IS NO KNOWN WAY TO REPLICATE IT, THOUGH I BELIEVE WE ARE CLOSE.
BUT, WE REQUIRE MORE... RESOURCES.
I WILL DO MY PART, LORD BLACKPOOL.
THE TECHNOLOGY YOU'VE...ACQUIRED... IS ADMITTEDLY IMPRESSIVE. I AM CERTAIN THE COLLECTIVE WILL AGREE.
NOW, IF THERE IS NOTHING MORE, I SHALL GO AND JOIN MY PEERS AT THE BALL.

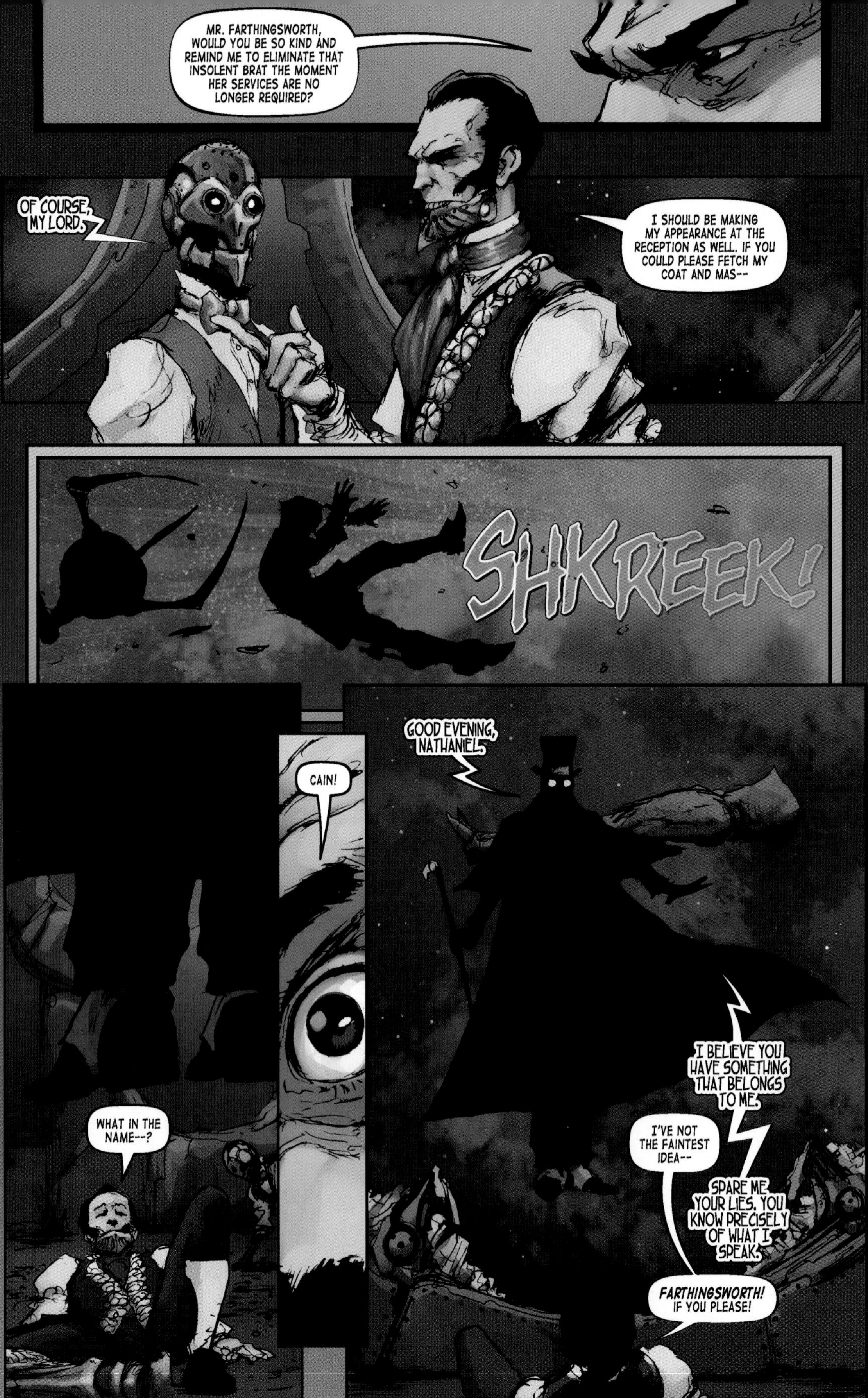
MR. FARTHINGSWORTH, WOULD YOU BE SO KIND AND REMIND ME TO ELIMINATE THAT INSOLENT BRAT THE MOMENT HER SERVICES ARE NO LONGER REQUIRED?
OF COURSE, MY LORD.
I SHOULD BE MAKING MY APPEARANCE AT THE RECEPTION AS WELL. IF YOU COULD PLEASE FETCH MY COAT AND MAS--
SHKREEK!
WHAT IN THE NAME--?
CAIN!
GOOD EVENING, NATHANIEL.
I BELIEVE YOU HAVE SOMETHING THAT BELONGS TO ME.
I'VE NOT THE FAINTEST IDEA--
SPARE ME YOUR LIES. YOU KNOW PRECISELY OF WHAT I SPEAK.
FARTHINGSWORTH! IF YOU PLEASE!

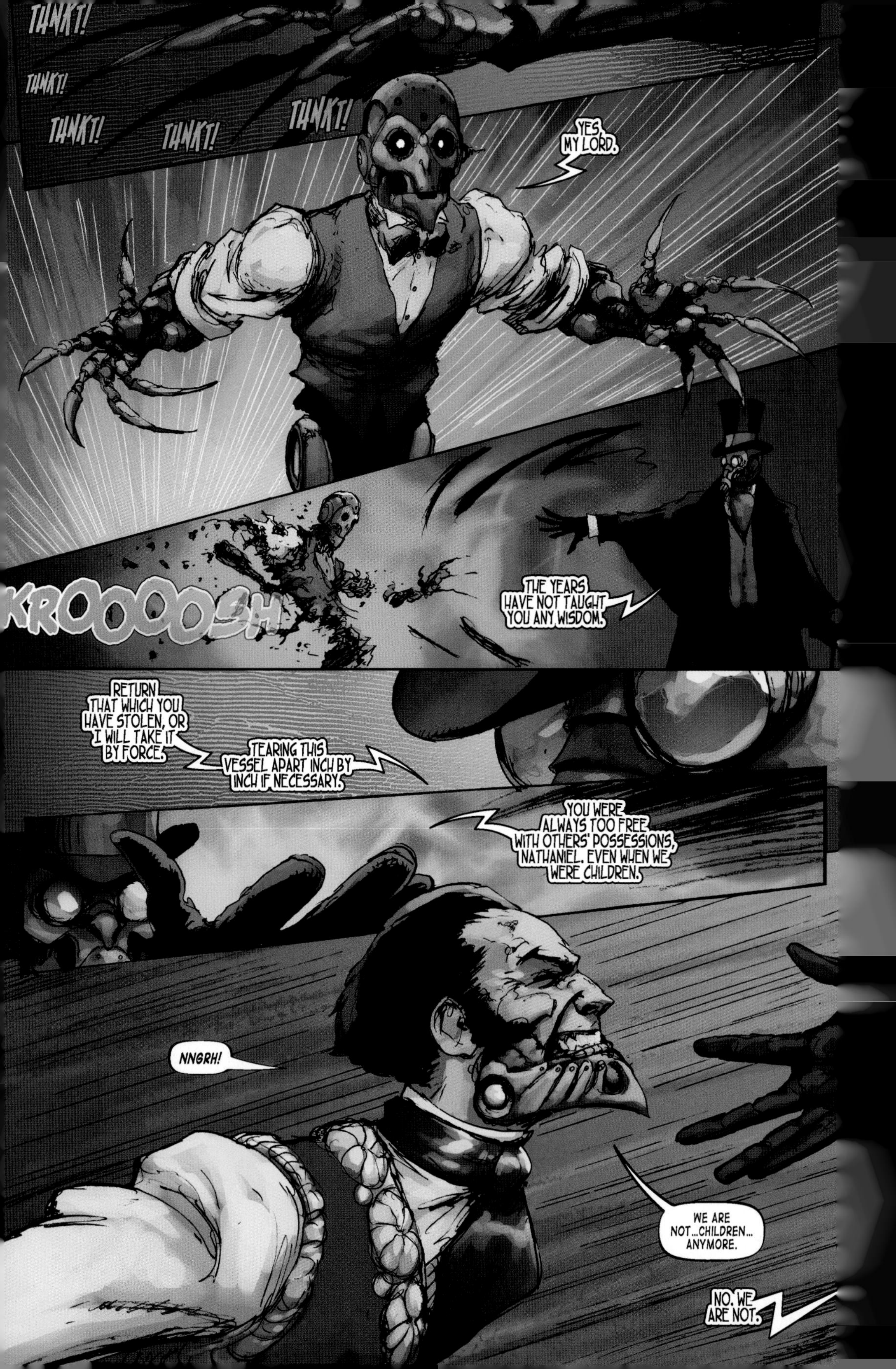
THNKT!
THNKT!
THNKT!
THNKT!
THNKT!
YES, MY LORD.
KROOOOOSH
THE YEARS HAVE NOT TAUGHT YOU ANY WISDOM.
RETURN THAT WHICH YOU HAVE STOLEN, OR I WILL TAKE IT BY FORCE.
TEARING THIS VESSEL APART INCH BY INCH IF NECESSARY.
YOU WERE ALWAYS TOO FREE WITH OTHERS' POSSESSIONS, NATHANIEL. EVEN WHEN WE WERE CHILDREN.
NNGRH!
WE ARE NOT...CHILDREN... ANYMORE.
NO. WE ARE NOT.

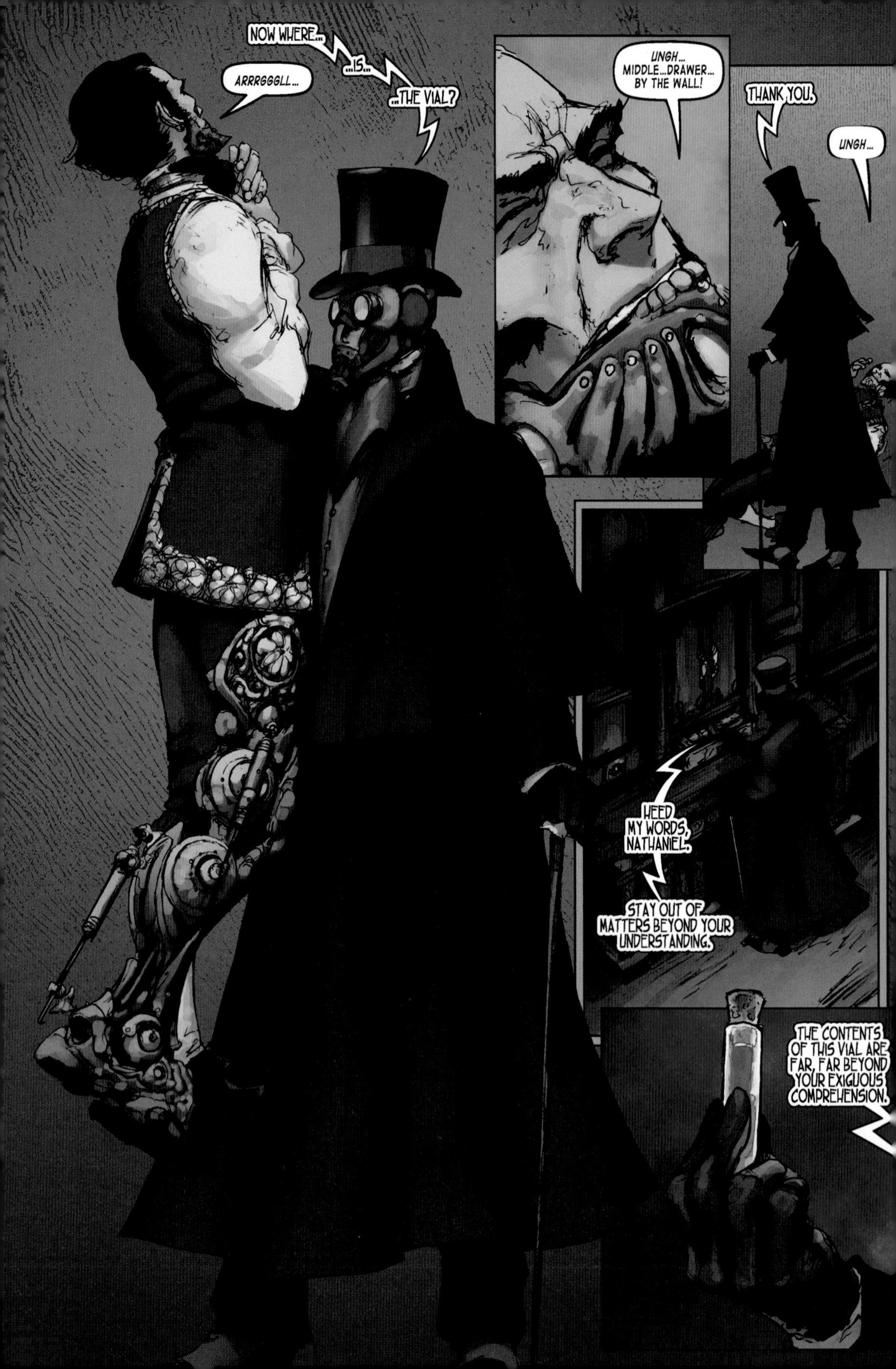

ARRRGGGLL...
NOW WHERE...
...IS...
...THE VIAL?
UNGH... MIDDLE...DRAWER... BY THE WALL!
THANK YOU.
UNGH...
HEED MY WORDS, NATHANIEL.
STAY OUT OF MATTERS BEYOND YOUR UNDERSTANDING.
THE CONTENTS OF THIS VIAL ARE FAR, FAR BEYOND YOUR EXIGUOUS COMPREHENSION.

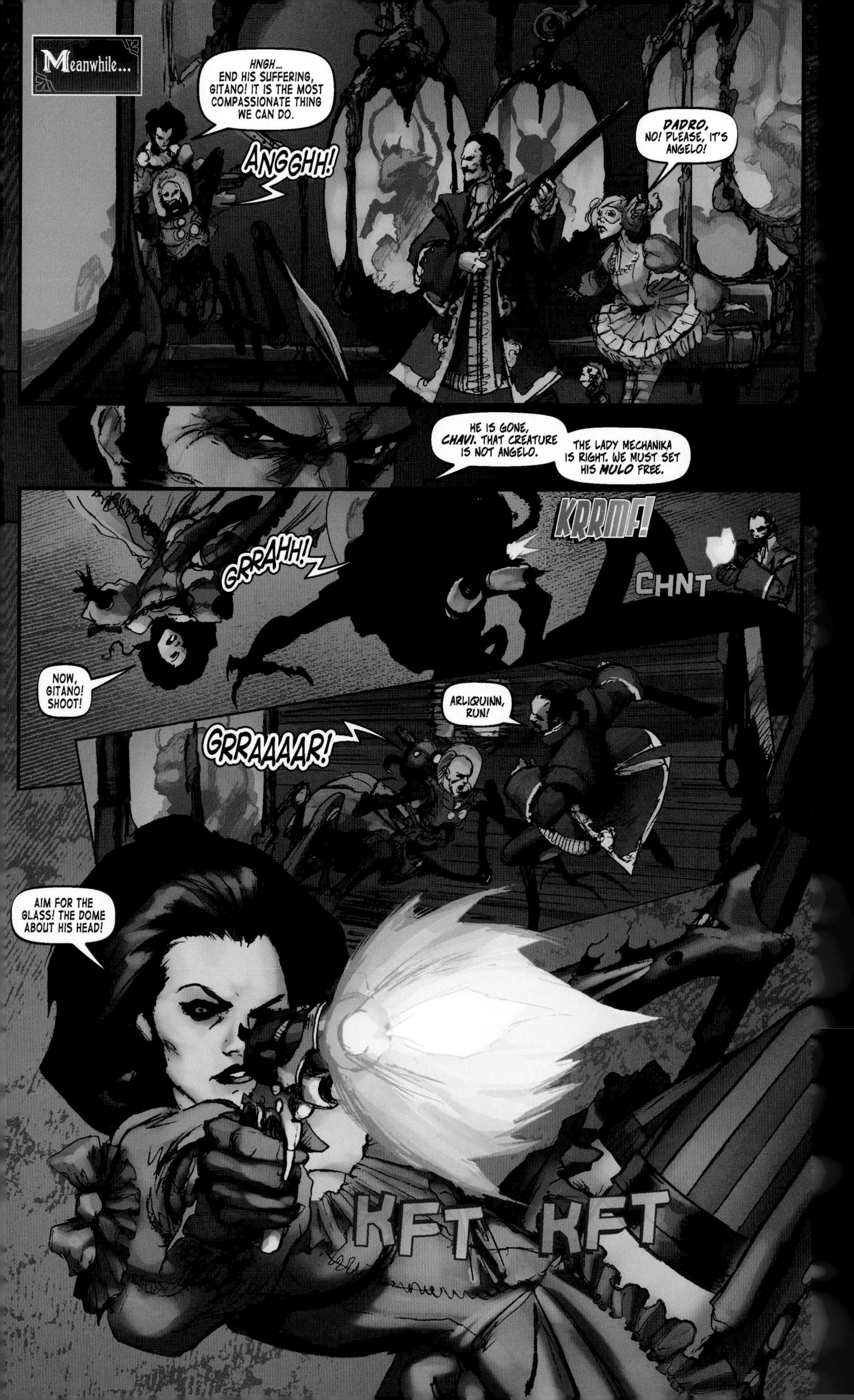
Meanwhile...
HNGH... END HIS SUFFERING, GITANO! IT IS THE MOST COMPASSIONATE THING WE CAN DO.
ANGGHH!
DADRO, NO! PLEASE, IT'S ANGELO!
HE IS GONE, CHAVI. THAT CREATURE IS NOT ANGELO.
THE LADY MECHANIKA IS RIGHT. WE MUST SET HIS MULO FREE.
GRRAHH!
KRRMF!
CHNT
NOW, GITANO! SHOOT!
ARLIQUINN, RUN!
GRRAAAAR!
AIM FOR THE GLASS! THE DOME ABOUT HIS HEAD!
KFT KFT

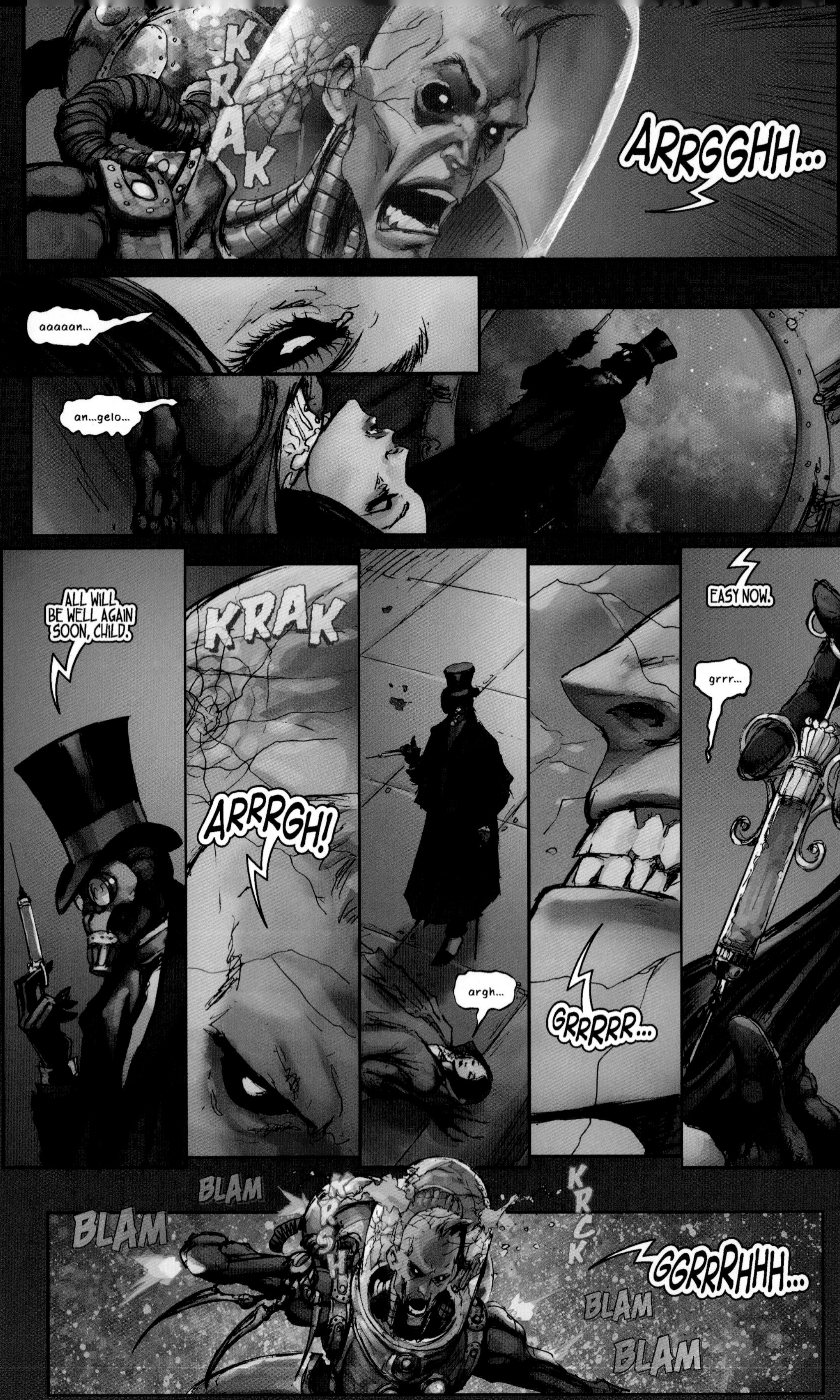
KRAK
ARRGGHH...
aaaaan...
an...gelo...
ALL WILL BE WELL AGAIN SOON, CHILD.
KRAK
ARRRGH!
argh...
GRRRRR...
EASY NOW.
grrr...
BLAM
KRSH
KRCK
BLAM
GGRRRHHH...
BLAM
BLAM

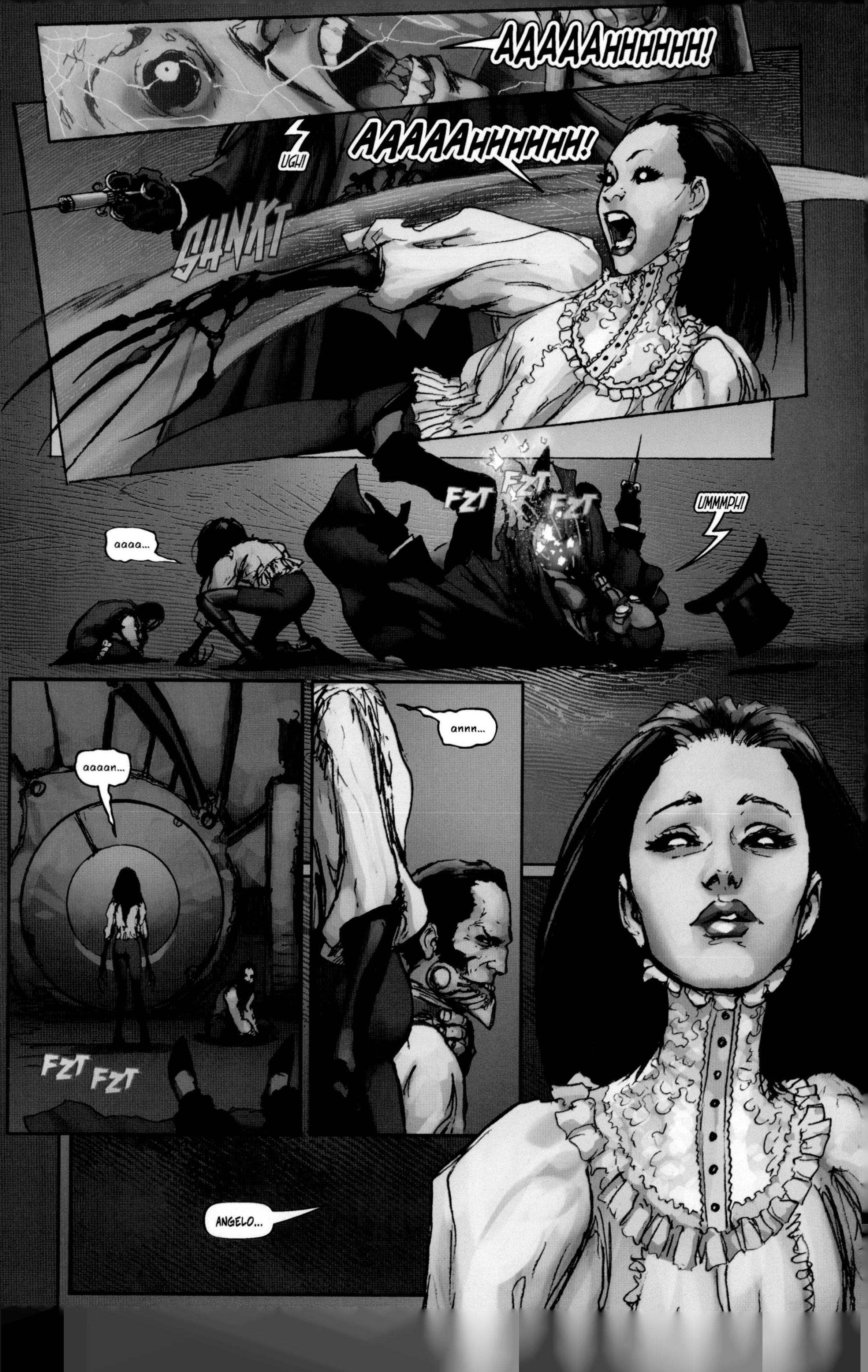
AAAAAHHHHHH!
UGH!
AAAAAHHHHHH!
SHNKT
FZT
FZT
FZT
UMMMPH!
aaaa...
aaaan...
FZT FZT
annn...
ANGELO...

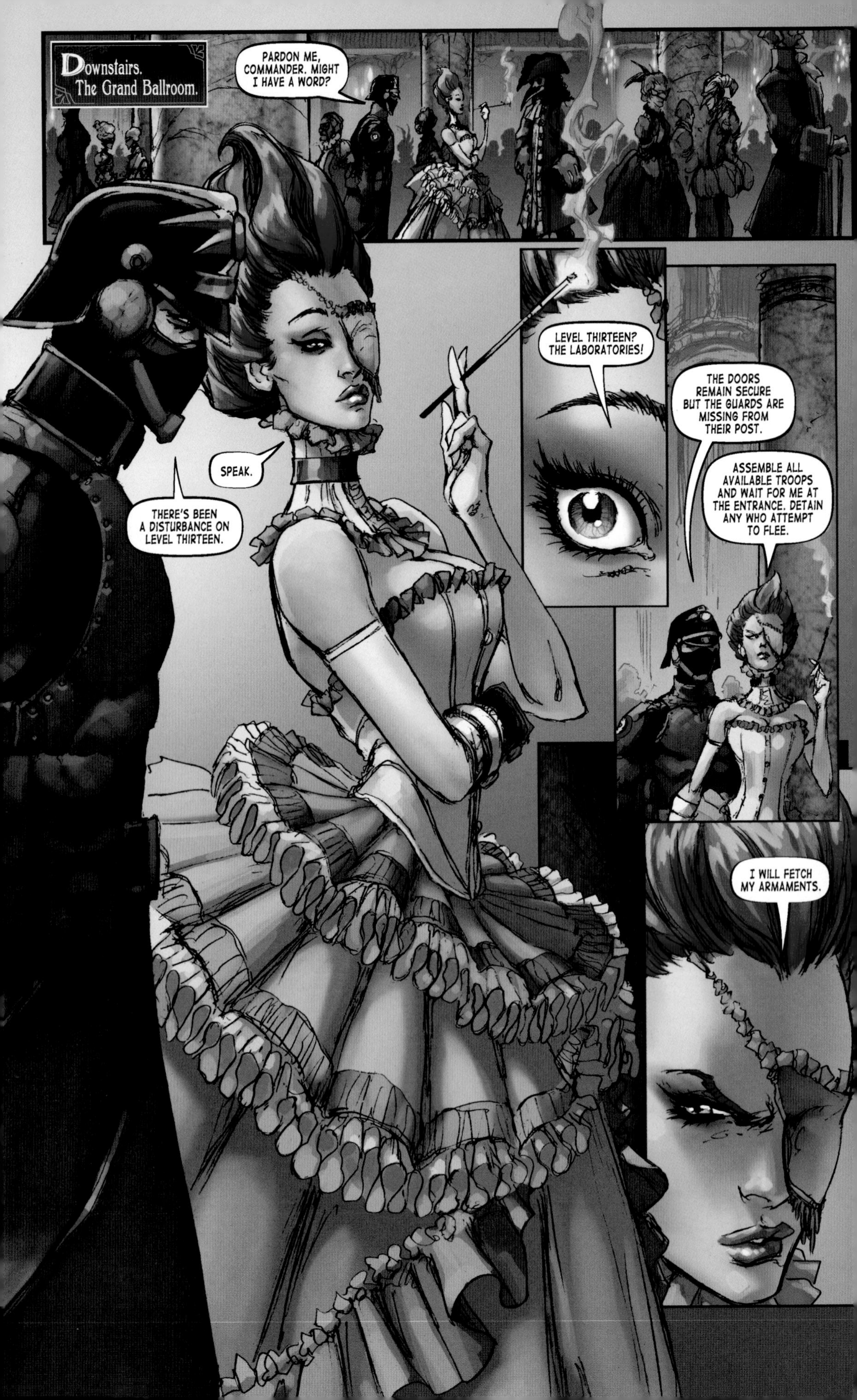
Downstairs. The Grand Ballroom.
PARDON ME, COMMANDER. MIGHT I HAVE A WORD?
SPEAK.
THERE'S BEEN A DISTURBANCE ON LEVEL THIRTEEN.
LEVEL THIRTEEN? THE LABORATORIES!
THE DOORS REMAIN SECURE BUT THE GUARDS ARE MISSING FROM THEIR POST.
ASSEMBLE ALL AVAILABLE TROOPS AND WAIT FOR ME AT THE ENTRANCE. DETAIN ANY WHO ATTEMPT TO FLEE.
I WILL FETCH MY ARMAMENTS.

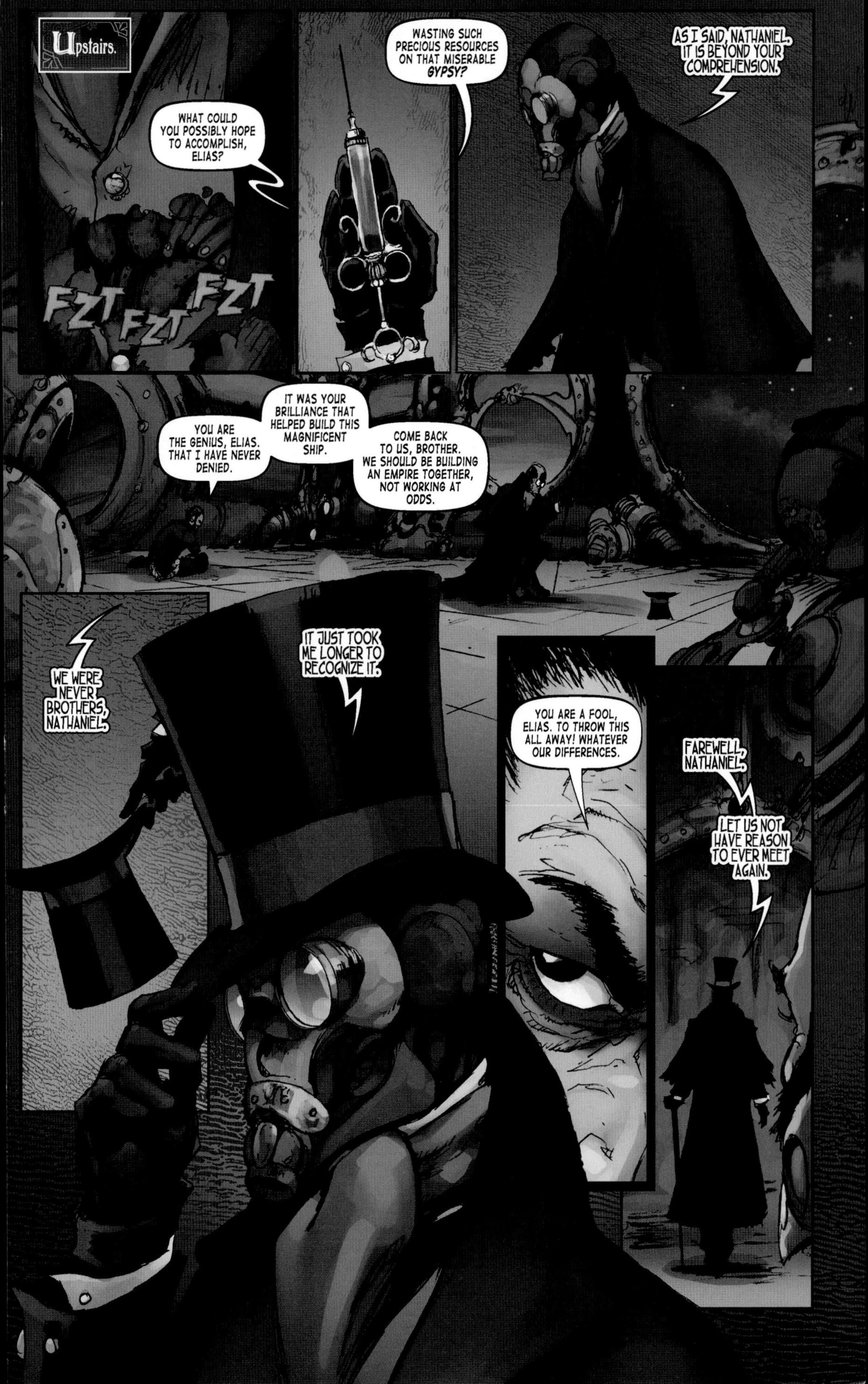

Upstairs.
WHAT COULD YOU POSSIBLY HOPE TO ACCOMPLISH, ELIAS?
FZT FZT FZT
WASTING SUCH PRECIOUS RESOURCES ON THAT MISERABLE GYPSY?
AS I SAID, NATHANIEL. IT IS BEYOND YOUR COMPREHENSION.
YOU ARE THE GENIUS, ELIAS. THAT I HAVE NEVER DENIED.
IT WAS YOUR BRILLIANCE THAT HELPED BUILD THIS MAGNIFICENT SHIP.
COME BACK TO US, BROTHER. WE SHOULD BE BUILDING AN EMPIRE TOGETHER, NOT WORKING AT ODDS.
WE WERE NEVER BROTHERS, NATHANIEL.
IT JUST TOOK ME LONGER TO RECOGNIZE IT.
YOU ARE A FOOL, ELIAS. TO THROW THIS ALL AWAY! WHATEVER OUR DIFFERENCES.
FAREWELL, NATHANIEL.
LET US NOT HAVE REASON TO EVER MEET AGAIN.

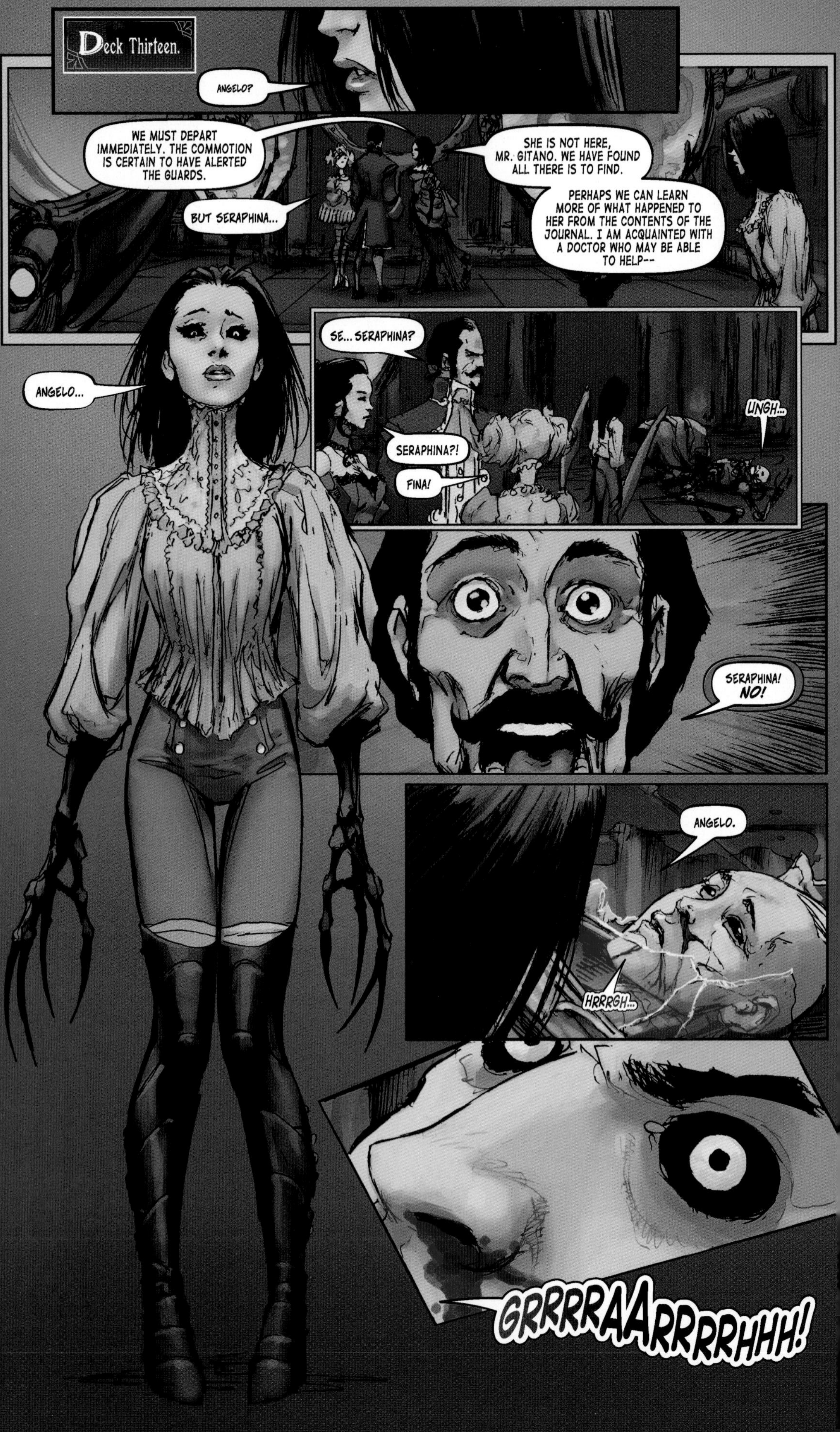
Deck Thirteen.
ANGELO?
WE MUST DEPART IMMEDIATELY. THE COMMOTION IS CERTAIN TO HAVE ALERTED THE GUARDS.
BUT SERAPHINA...
SHE IS NOT HERE, MR. GITANO. WE HAVE FOUND ALL THERE IS TO FIND.
PERHAPS WE CAN LEARN MORE OF WHAT HAPPENED TO HER FROM THE CONTENTS OF THE JOURNAL. I AM ACQUAINTED WITH A DOCTOR WHO MAY BE ABLE TO HELP--
ANGELO...
SE... SERAPHINA?
SERAPHINA?!
FINA!
UNGH...
SERAPHINA! NO!
ANGELO.
HRRRGH...
GRRRRAARRRRHHH!

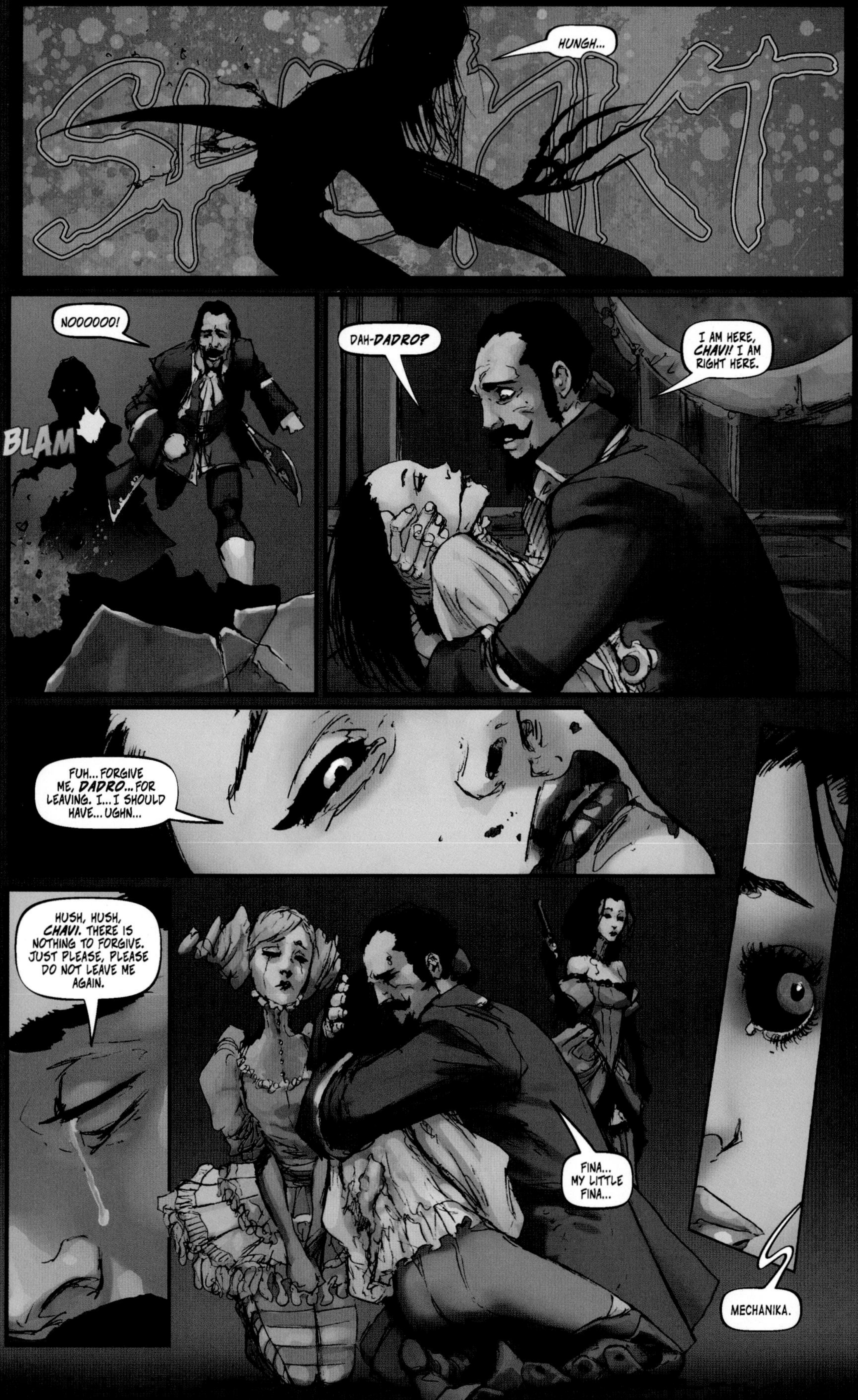
HUNGH...
SHHHUKT
NOOOOOO!
BLAM
DAH-DADRO?
I AM HERE, CHAVI! I AM RIGHT HERE.
FUH...FORGIVE ME, DADRO...FOR LEAVING. I...I SHOULD HAVE...UGHN...
HUSH, HUSH, CHAVI. THERE IS NOTHING TO FORGIVE. JUST PLEASE, PLEASE DO NOT LEAVE ME AGAIN.
FINA... MY LITTLE FINA...
MECHANIKA.

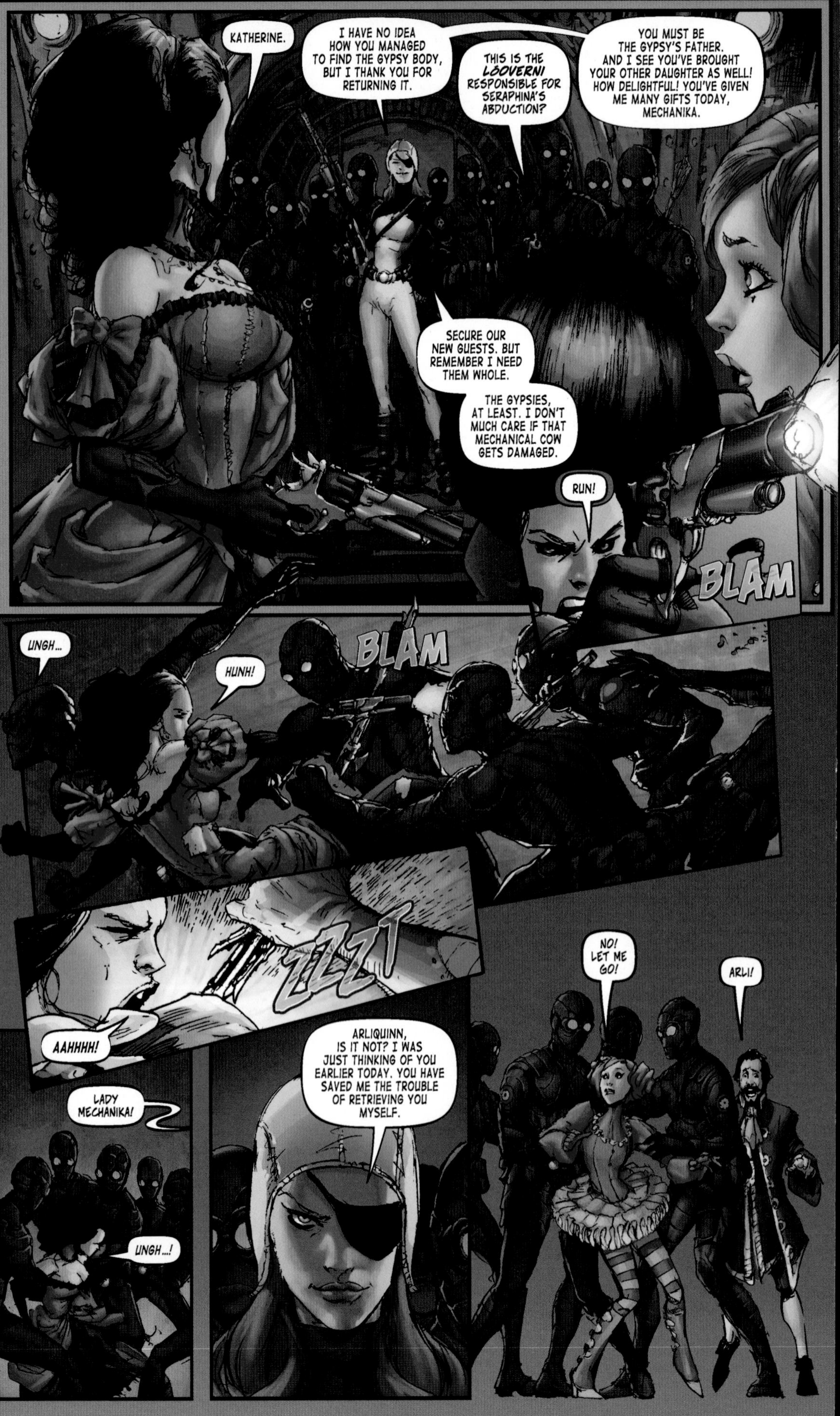
KATHERINE.
I HAVE NO IDEA HOW YOU MANAGED TO FIND THE GYPSY BODY, BUT I THANK YOU FOR RETURNING IT.
THIS IS THE *LOOVERNI* RESPONSIBLE FOR SERAPHINA'S ABDUCTION?
YOU MUST BE THE GYPSY'S FATHER. AND I SEE YOU'VE BROUGHT YOUR OTHER DAUGHTER AS WELL! HOW DELIGHTFUL! YOU'VE GIVEN ME MANY GIFTS TODAY, MECHANIKA.
SECURE OUR NEW GUESTS. BUT REMEMBER I NEED THEM WHOLE.
THE GYPSIES, AT LEAST. I DON'T MUCH CARE IF THAT MECHANICAL COW GETS DAMAGED.
RUN!
BLAM
UNGH...
HUNH!
BLAM
ZZZT
AAHHHH!
LADY MECHANIKA!
UNGH...!
ARLIQUINN, IS IT NOT? I WAS JUST THINKING OF YOU EARLIER TODAY. YOU HAVE SAVED ME THE TROUBLE OF RETRIEVING YOU MYSELF.
NO! LET ME GO!
ARLI!

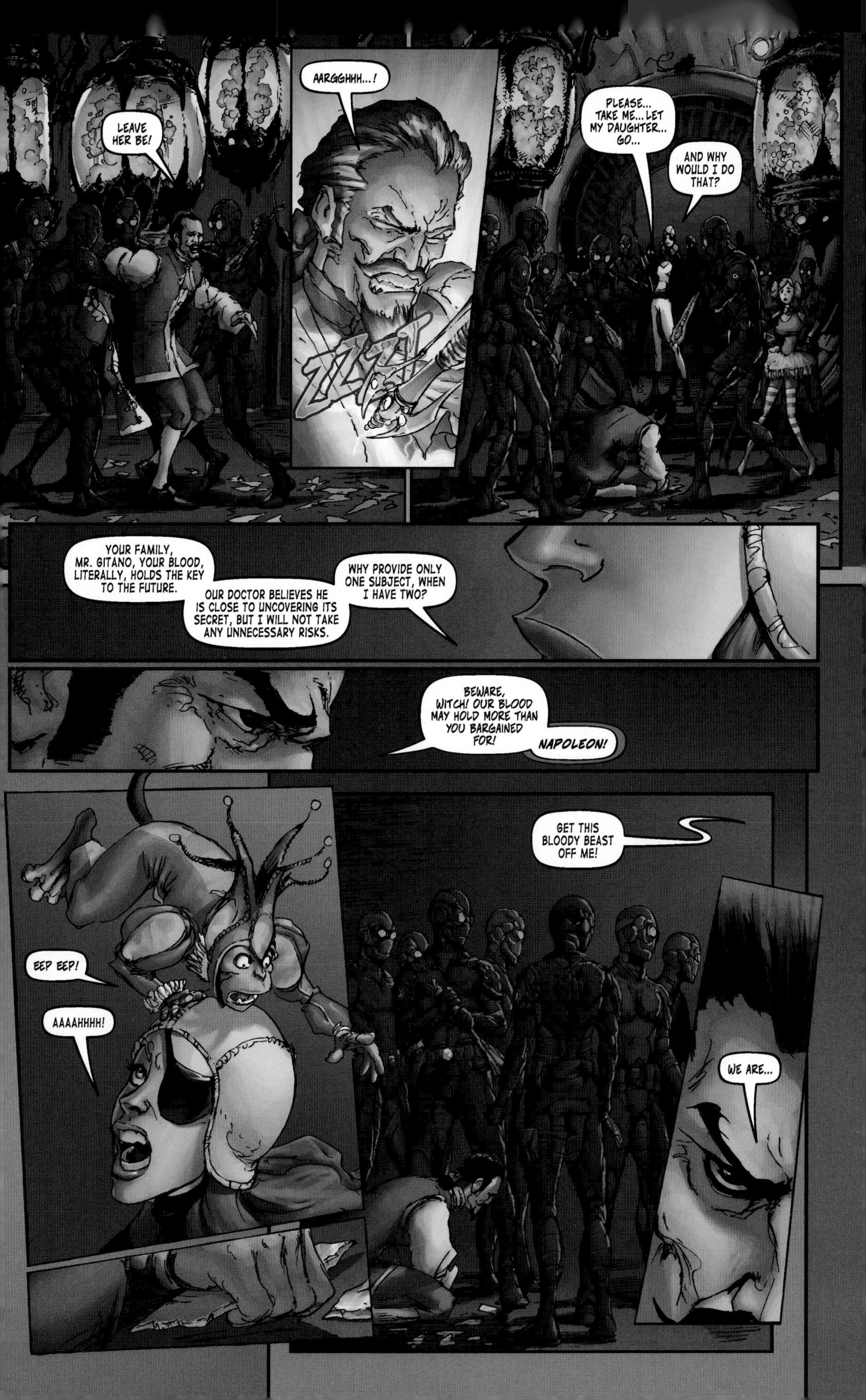
LEAVE HER BE!
AARGGHHH...!
ZZZAT
PLEASE... TAKE ME... LET MY DAUGHTER... GO...
AND WHY WOULD I DO THAT?
YOUR FAMILY, MR. GITANO, YOUR BLOOD, LITERALLY, HOLDS THE KEY TO THE FUTURE.
OUR DOCTOR BELIEVES HE IS CLOSE TO UNCOVERING ITS SECRET, BUT I WILL NOT TAKE ANY UNNECESSARY RISKS.
WHY PROVIDE ONLY ONE SUBJECT, WHEN I HAVE TWO?
BEWARE, WITCH! OUR BLOOD MAY HOLD MORE THAN YOU BARGAINED FOR!
NAPOLEON!
EEP EEP!
AAAAHHHH!
GET THIS BLOODY BEAST OFF ME!
WE ARE...

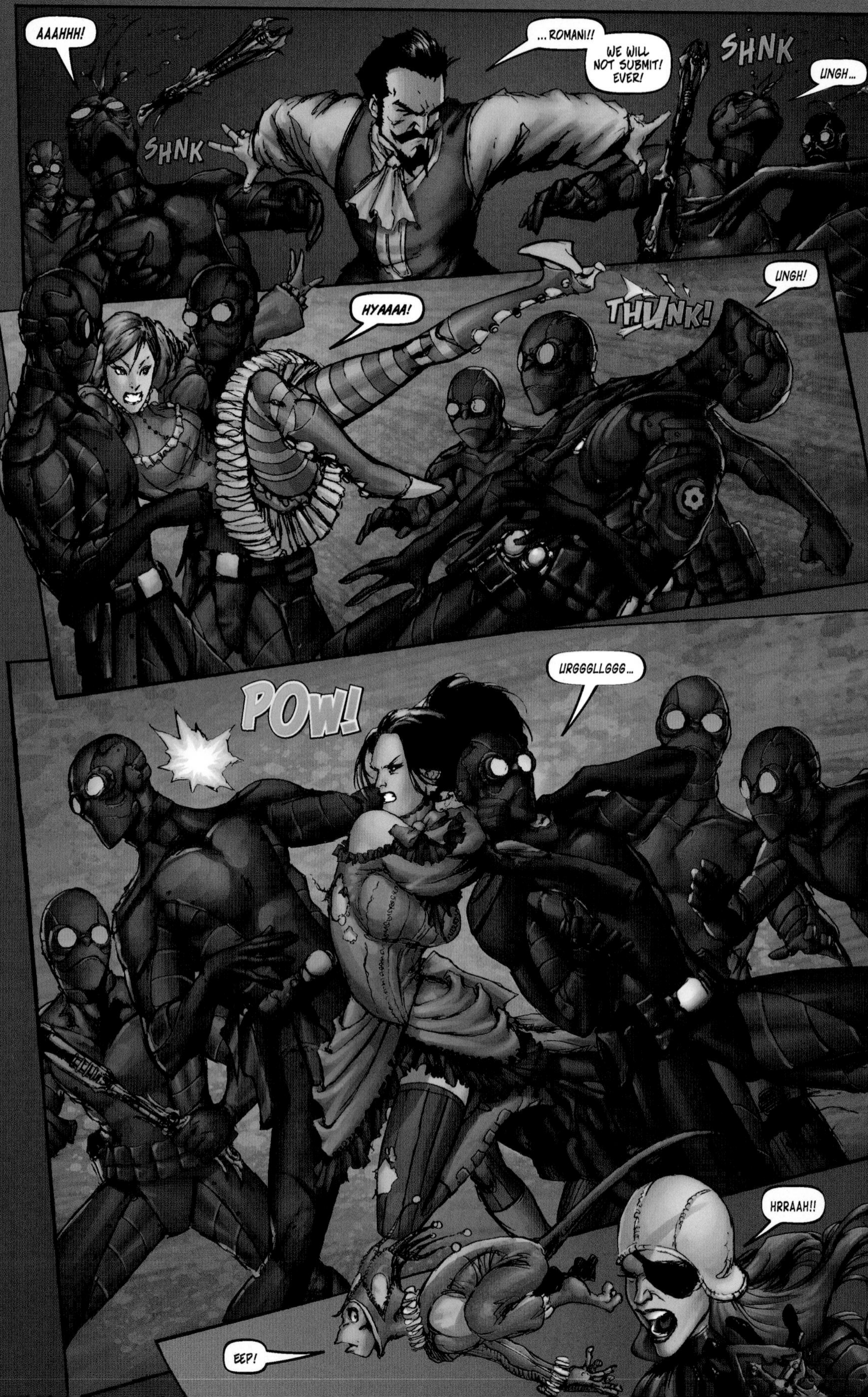
AAAHHH!
SHNK
...ROMANI!!
WE WILL NOT SUBMIT! EVER!
SHNK
UNGH...
HYAAAA!
THUNK!
UNGH!
POW!
URGGGLLGGG...
HRRAAH!!
EEP!

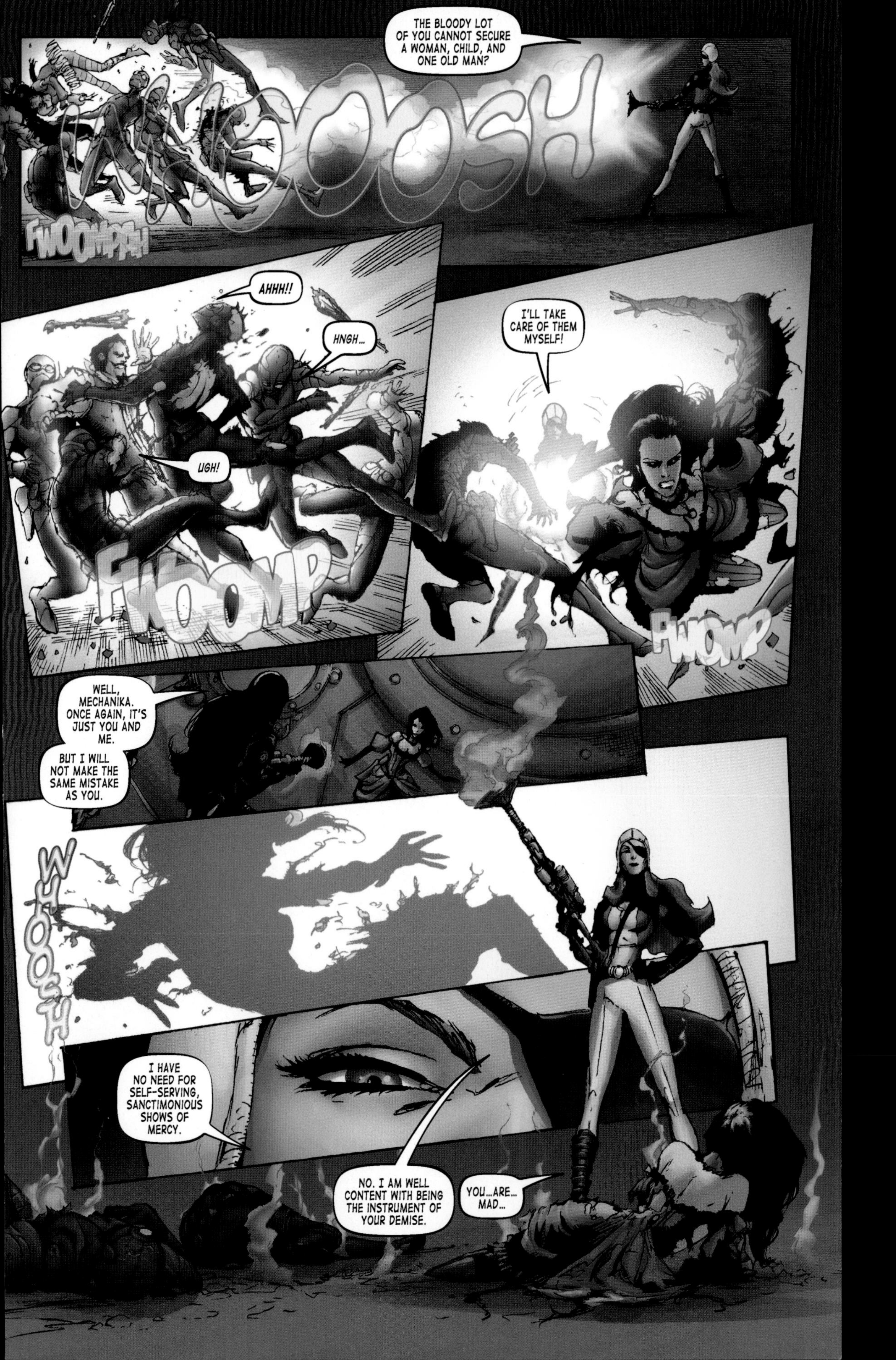
THE BLOODY LOT OF YOU CANNOT SECURE A WOMAN, CHILD, AND ONE OLD MAN?
WOOOSH
FWOOMPAH
AHHH!!
HNGH...
UGH!
FWOOMP
I'LL TAKE CARE OF THEM MYSELF!
PWOMP
WELL, MECHANIKA. ONCE AGAIN, IT'S JUST YOU AND ME.
BUT I WILL NOT MAKE THE SAME MISTAKE AS YOU.
WHOOOSH
I HAVE NO NEED FOR SELF-SERVING, SANCTIMONIOUS SHOWS OF MERCY.
NO. I AM WELL CONTENT WITH BEING THE INSTRUMENT OF YOUR DEMISE.
YOU...ARE... MAD...

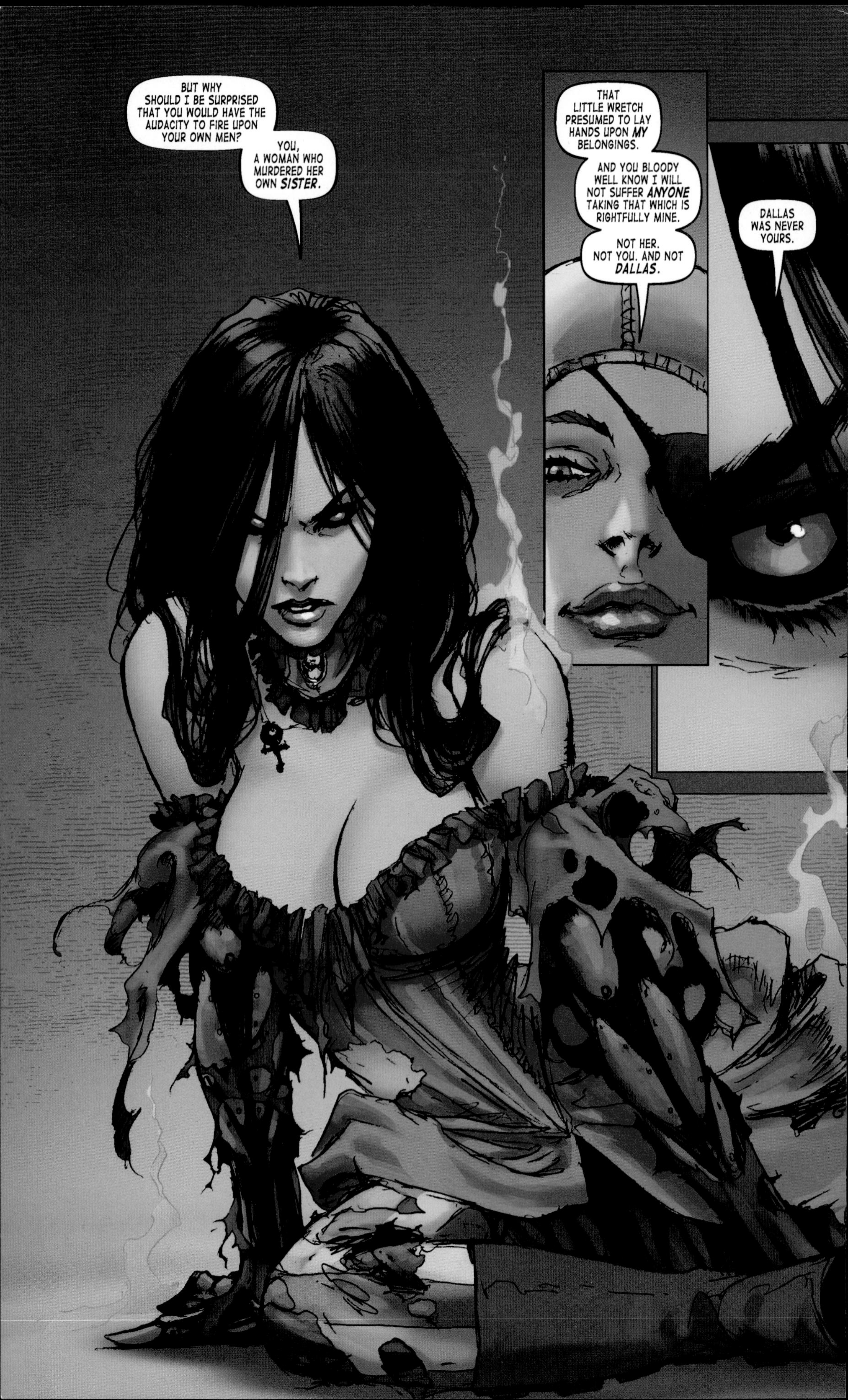
BUT WHY SHOULD I BE SURPRISED THAT YOU WOULD HAVE THE AUDACITY TO FIRE UPON YOUR OWN MEN?
YOU, A WOMAN WHO MURDERED HER OWN SISTER.
THAT LITTLE WRETCH PRESUMED TO LAY HANDS UPON MY BELONGINGS.
AND YOU BLOODY WELL KNOW I WILL NOT SUFFER ANYONE TAKING THAT WHICH IS RIGHTFULLY MINE.
NOT HER. NOT YOU. AND NOT DALLAS.
DALLAS WAS NEVER YOURS.

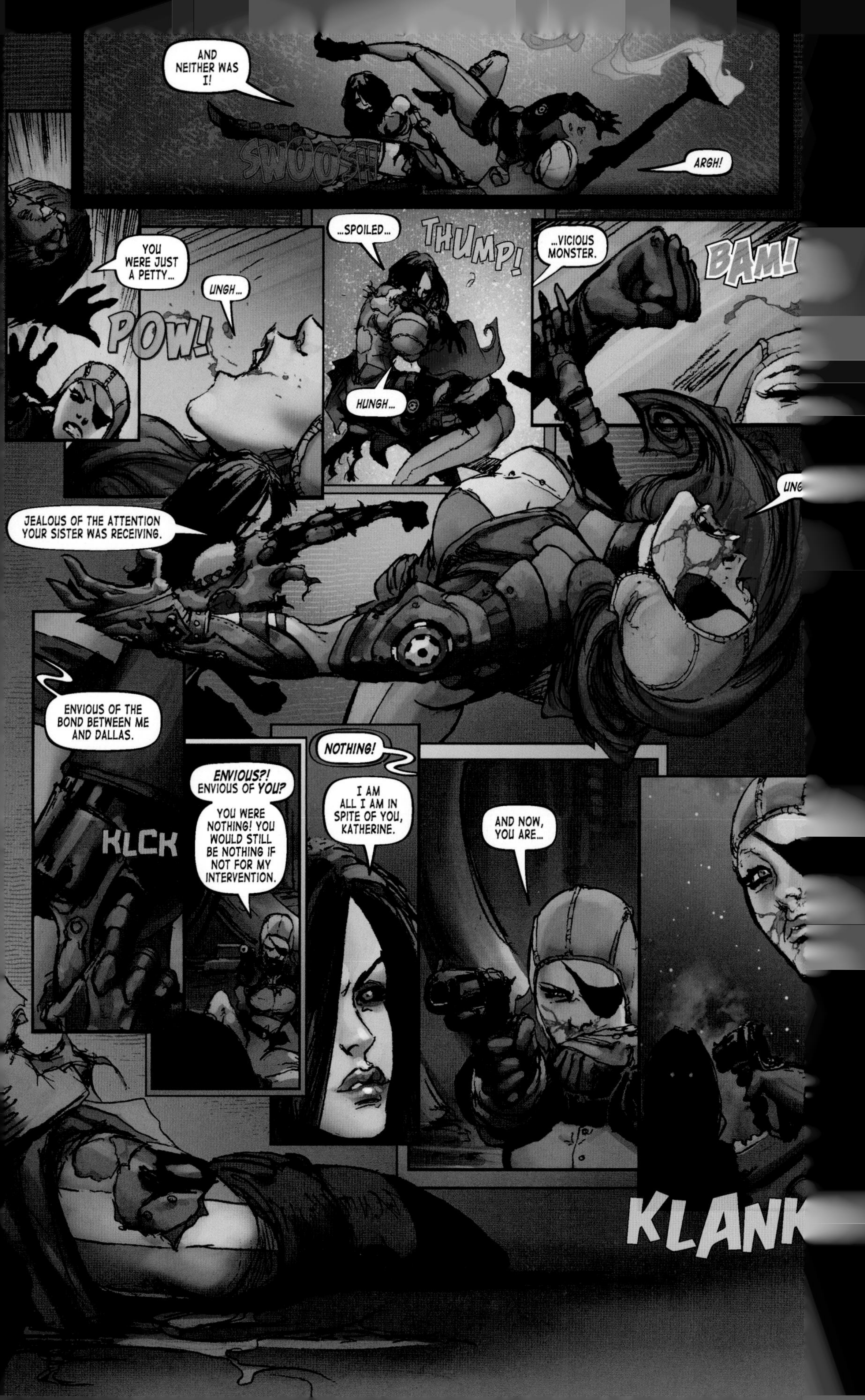
AND NEITHER WAS I!
SWOOSH
ARGH!
YOU WERE JUST A PETTY...
UNGH...
POW!
...SPOILED...
THUMP!
HUNGH...
...VICIOUS MONSTER.
BAM!
UNG
JEALOUS OF THE ATTENTION YOUR SISTER WAS RECEIVING.
ENVIOUS OF THE BOND BETWEEN ME AND DALLAS.
KLCK
ENVIOUS?! ENVIOUS OF YOU?
YOU WERE NOTHING! YOU WOULD STILL BE NOTHING IF NOT FOR MY INTERVENTION.
NOTHING!
I AM ALL I AM IN SPITE OF YOU, KATHERINE.
AND NOW, YOU ARE...
KLANK

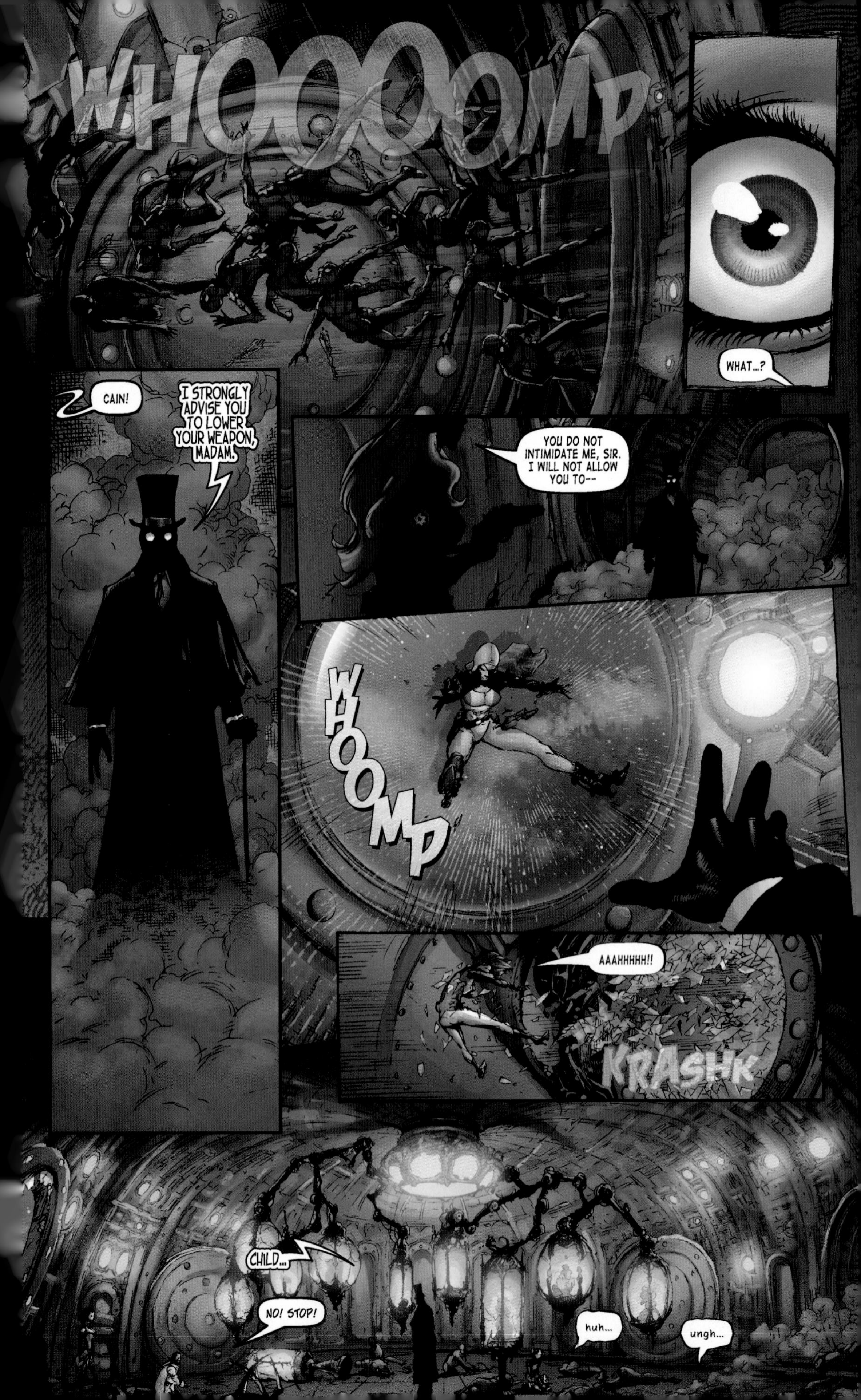
WHOOOOOMP
WHAT...?
CAIN!
I STRONGLY ADVISE YOU TO LOWER YOUR WEAPON, MADAM.
YOU DO NOT INTIMIDATE ME, SIR. I WILL NOT ALLOW YOU TO--
WHOOMP
AAAHHHHH!!
KRASHK
CHILD...
NO! STOP!
huh...
ungh...

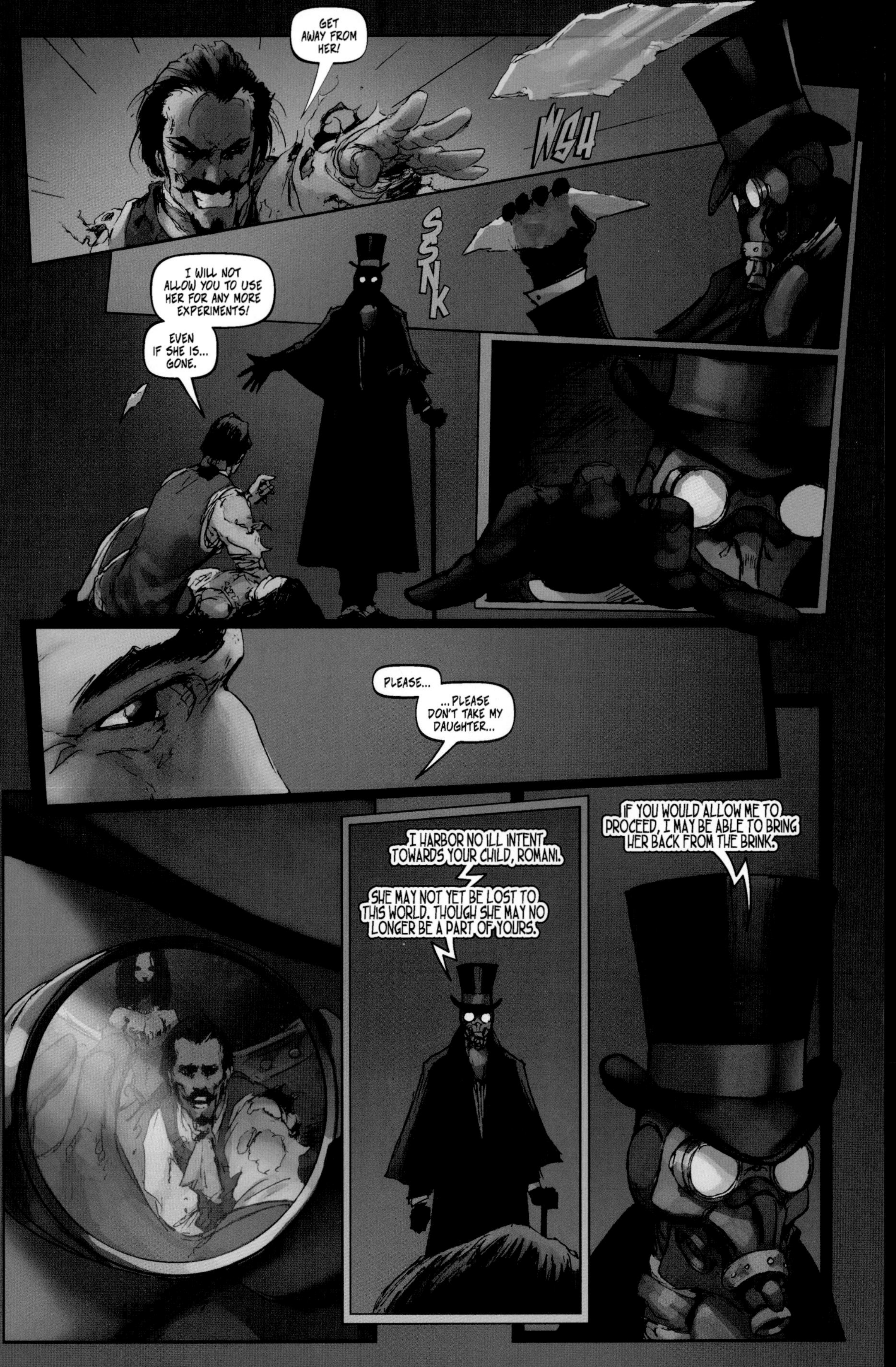
GET AWAY FROM HER!
WSH
SSNK
I WILL NOT ALLOW YOU TO USE HER FOR ANY MORE EXPERIMENTS!
EVEN IF SHE IS... GONE.
PLEASE...
...PLEASE DON'T TAKE MY DAUGHTER...
I HARBOR NO ILL INTENT TOWARDS YOUR CHILD, ROMANI.
SHE MAY NOT YET BE LOST TO THIS WORLD. THOUGH SHE MAY NO LONGER BE A PART OF YOURS.
IF YOU WOULD ALLOW ME TO PROCEED, I MAY BE ABLE TO BRING HER BACK FROM THE BRINK.

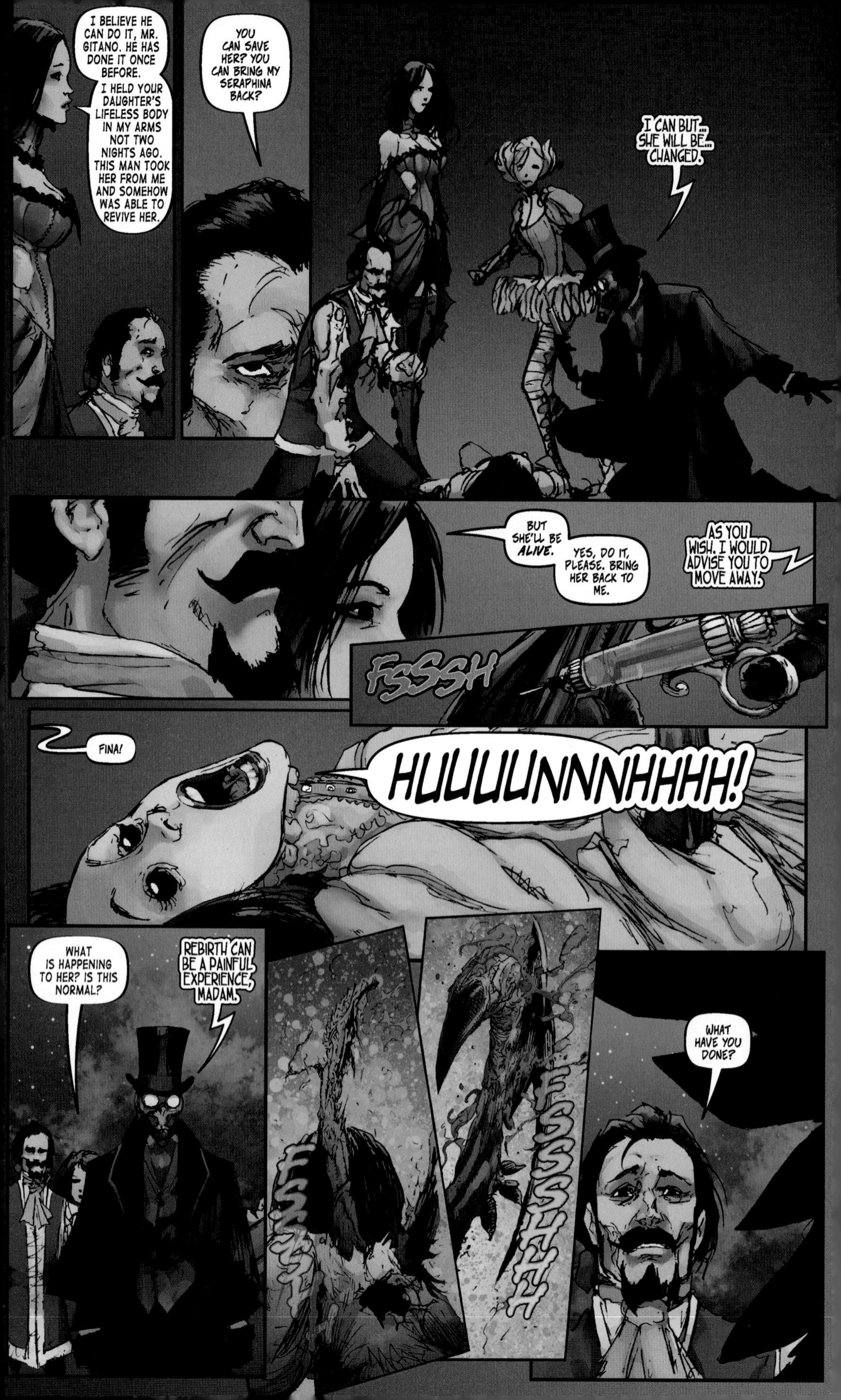
I BELIEVE HE CAN DO IT, MR. GITANO. HE HAS DONE IT ONCE BEFORE.
I HELD YOUR DAUGHTER'S LIFELESS BODY IN MY ARMS NOT TWO NIGHTS AGO. THIS MAN TOOK HER FROM ME AND SOMEHOW WAS ABLE TO REVIVE HER.
YOU CAN SAVE HER? YOU CAN BRING MY SERAPHINA BACK?
I CAN BUT... SHE WILL BE... CHANGED.
BUT SHE'LL BE ALIVE.
YES, DO IT, PLEASE. BRING HER BACK TO ME.
AS YOU WISH. I WOULD ADVISE YOU TO MOVE AWAY.
FSSSH
FINA!
HUUUUNNNHHHH!
WHAT IS HAPPENING TO HER? IS THIS NORMAL?
REBIRTH CAN BE A PAINFUL EXPERIENCE, MADAM.
FSSSH
FSSSHHH
WHAT HAVE YOU DONE?

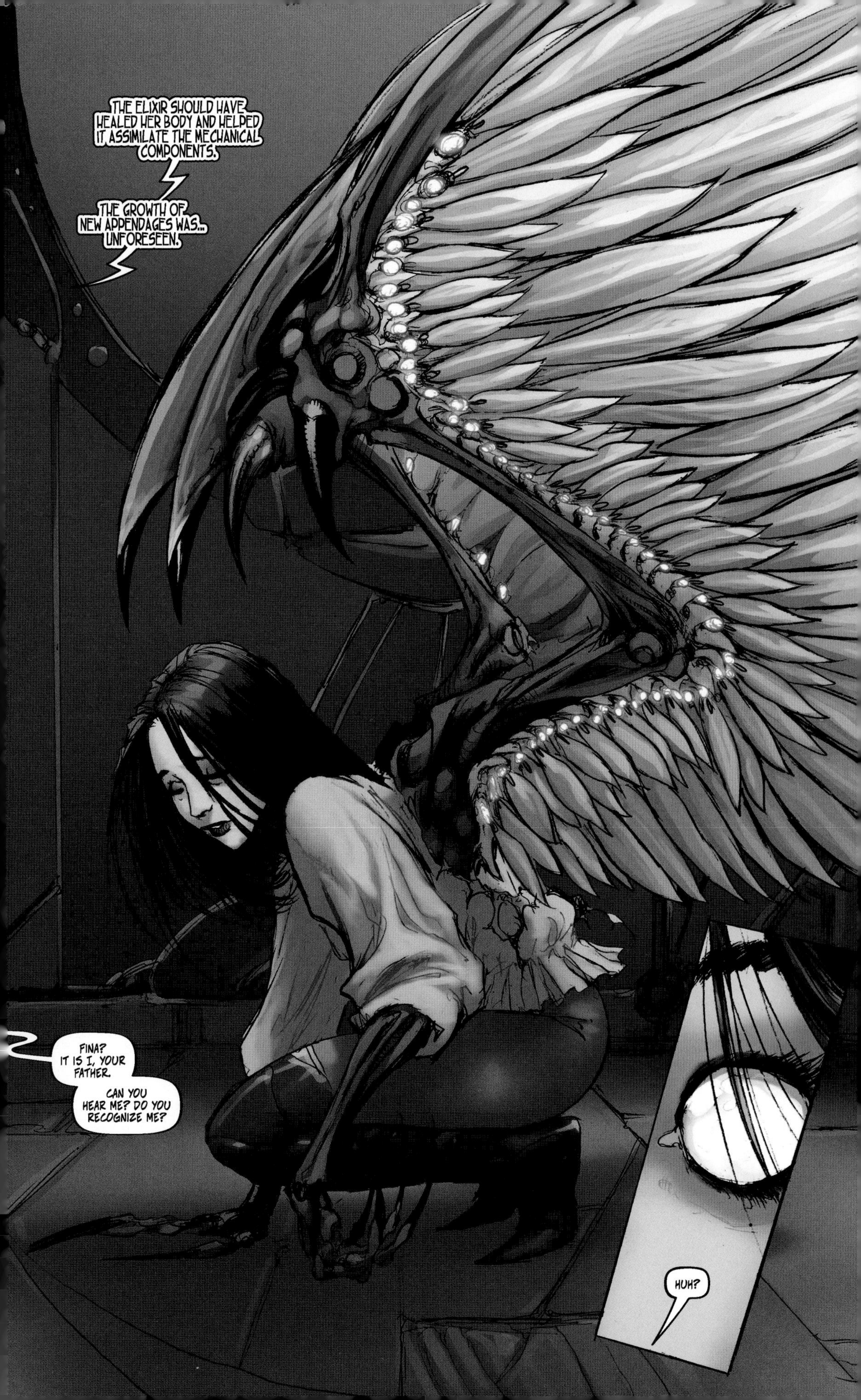
THE ELIXIR SHOULD HAVE HEALED HER BODY AND HELPED IT ASSIMILATE THE MECHANICAL COMPONENTS.
THE GROWTH OF NEW APPENDAGES WAS... UNFORESEEN.
FINA? IT IS I, YOUR FATHER.
CAN YOU HEAR ME? DO YOU RECOGNIZE ME?
HUH?

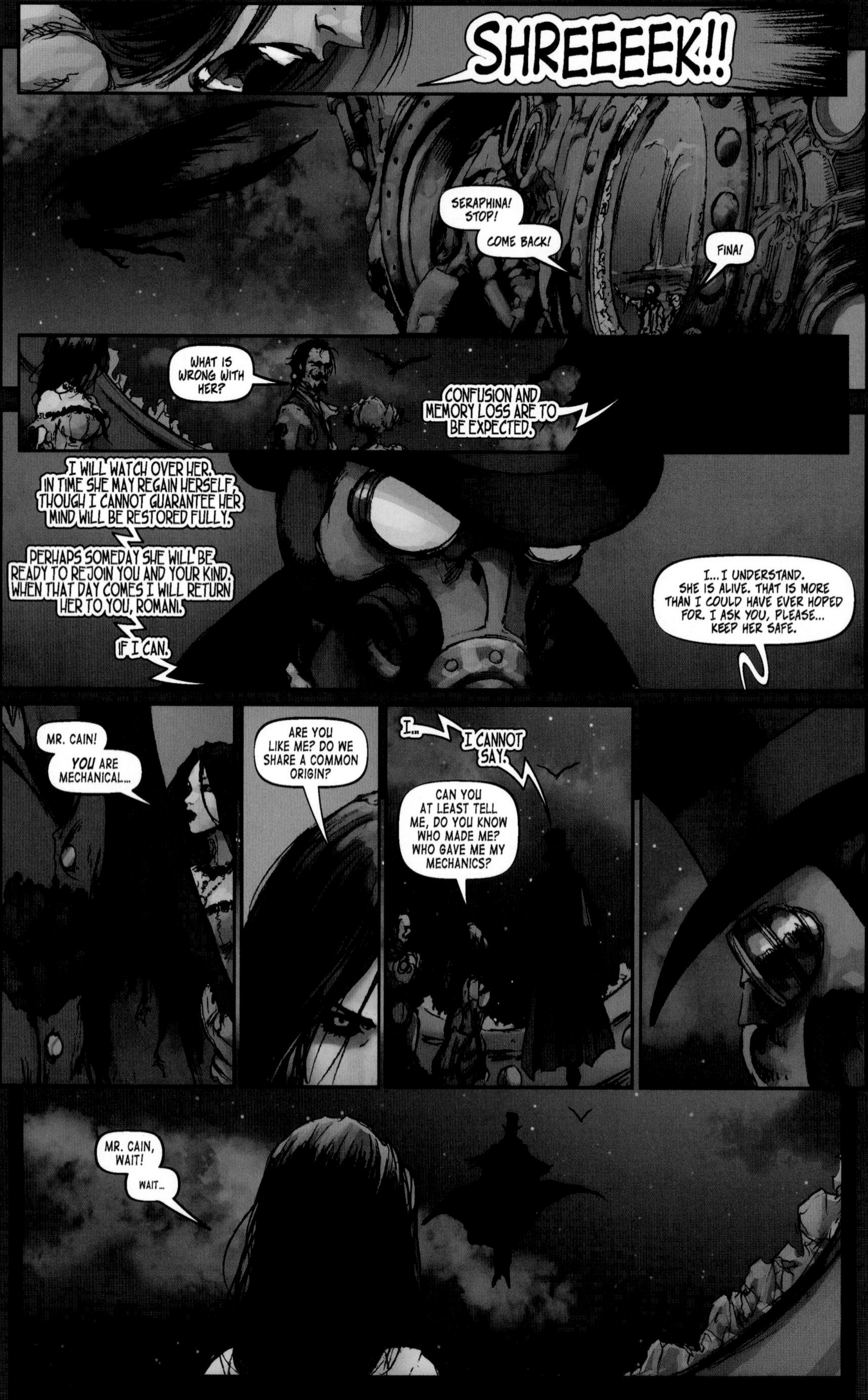
SHREEEEK!!
SERAPHINA! STOP!
COME BACK!
FINA!
WHAT IS WRONG WITH HER?
CONFUSION AND MEMORY LOSS ARE TO BE EXPECTED.
I WILL WATCH OVER HER. IN TIME SHE MAY REGAIN HERSELF, THOUGH I CANNOT GUARANTEE HER MIND WILL BE RESTORED FULLY.
PERHAPS SOMEDAY SHE WILL BE READY TO REJOIN YOU AND YOUR KIND. WHEN THAT DAY COMES I WILL RETURN HER TO YOU, ROMANI.
IF I CAN.
I... I UNDERSTAND. SHE IS ALIVE. THAT IS MORE THAN I COULD HAVE EVER HOPED FOR. I ASK YOU, PLEASE... KEEP HER SAFE.
MR. CAIN!
YOU ARE MECHANICAL...
ARE YOU LIKE ME? DO WE SHARE A COMMON ORIGIN?
I...
I CANNOT SAY.
CAN YOU AT LEAST TELL ME, DO YOU KNOW WHO MADE ME? WHO GAVE ME MY MECHANICS?
MR. CAIN, WAIT!
WAIT...

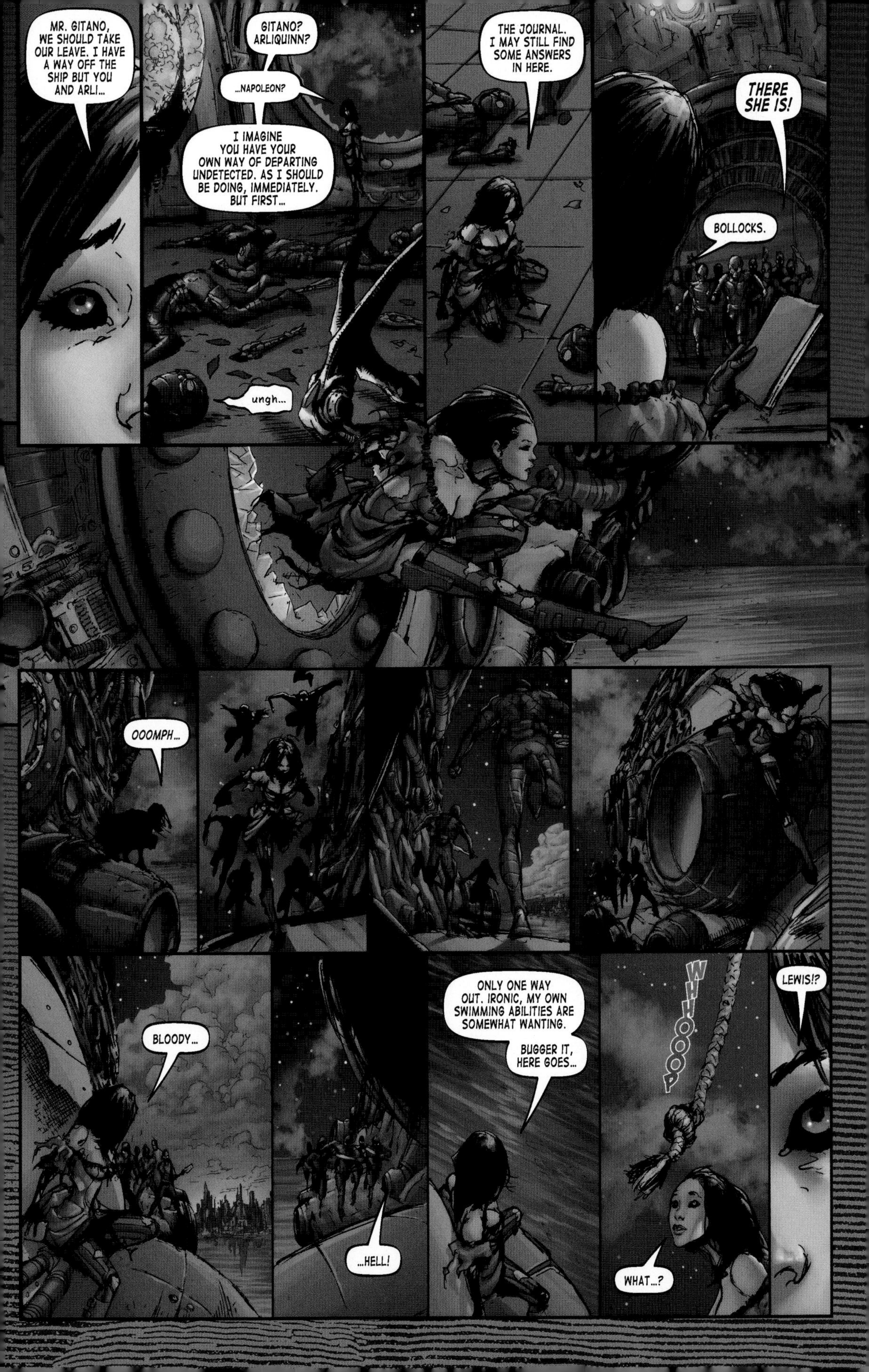
MR. GITANO, WE SHOULD TAKE OUR LEAVE. I HAVE A WAY OFF THE SHIP BUT YOU AND ARLI...
GITANO? ARLIQUINN?
...NAPOLEON?
I IMAGINE YOU HAVE YOUR OWN WAY OF DEPARTING UNDETECTED. AS I SHOULD BE DOING, IMMEDIATELY. BUT FIRST...
ungh...
THE JOURNAL. I MAY STILL FIND SOME ANSWERS IN HERE.
THERE SHE IS!
BOLLOCKS.
OOOMPH...
BLOODY...
...HELL!
ONLY ONE WAY OUT. IRONIC, MY OWN SWIMMING ABILITIES ARE SOMEWHAT WANTING.
BUGGER IT, HERE GOES...
WHHOOOOP
WHAT...?
LEWIS!?

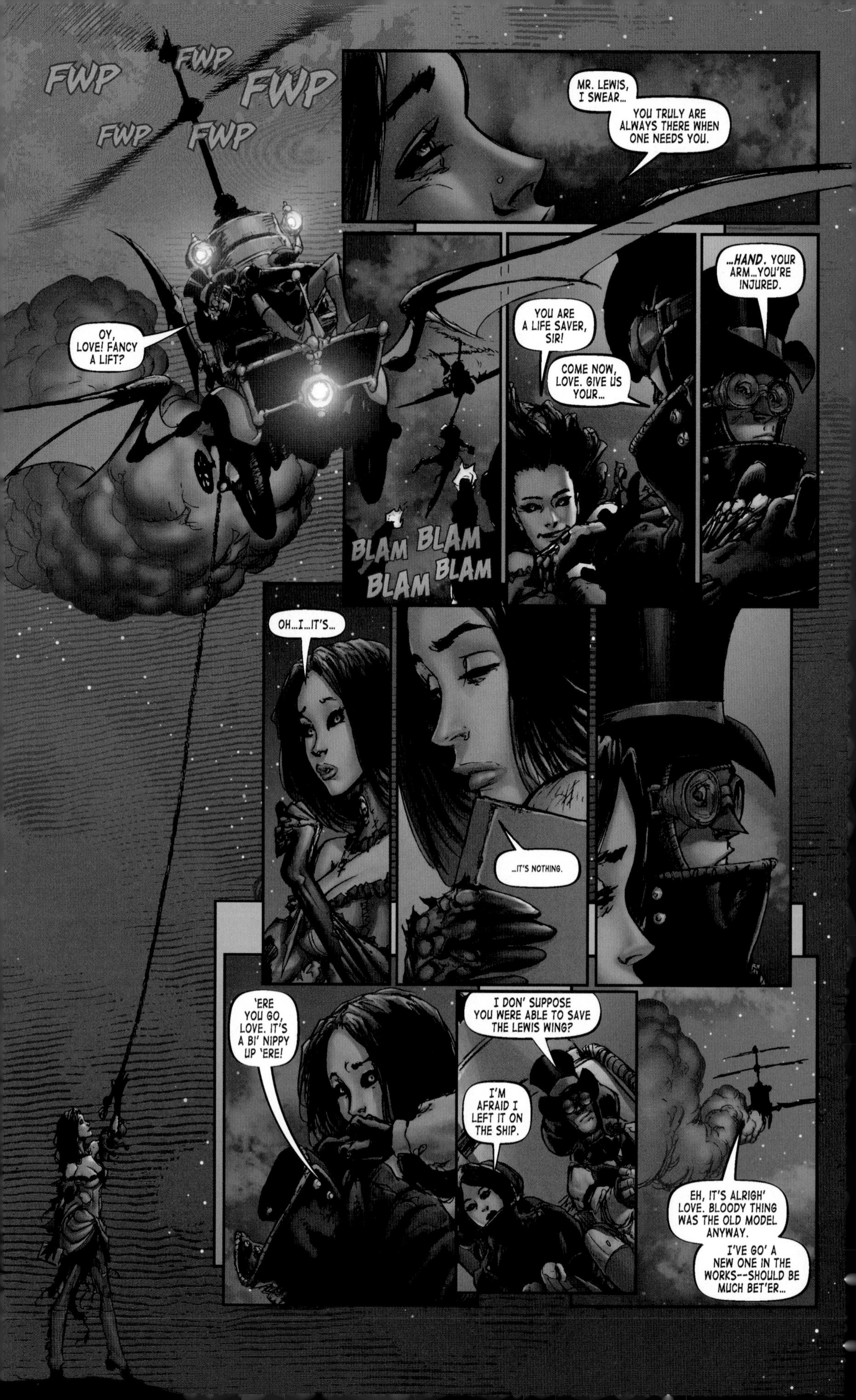
FWP FWP FWP
FWP FWP
OY, LOVE! FANCY A LIFT?
MR. LEWIS, I SWEAR...
YOU TRULY ARE ALWAYS THERE WHEN ONE NEEDS YOU.
BLAM BLAM BLAM BLAM
YOU ARE A LIFE SAVER, SIR!
COME NOW, LOVE. GIVE US YOUR...
...HAND. YOUR ARM...YOU'RE INJURED.
OH...I...IT'S...
...IT'S NOTHING.
'ERE YOU GO, LOVE. IT'S A BI' NIPPY UP 'ERE!
I DON' SUPPOSE YOU WERE ABLE TO SAVE THE LEWIS WING?
I'M AFRAID I LEFT IT ON THE SHIP.
EH, IT'S ALRIGH' LOVE. BLOODY THING WAS THE OLD MODEL ANYWAY.
I'VE GO' A NEW ONE IN THE WORKS--SHOULD BE MUCH BET'ER...

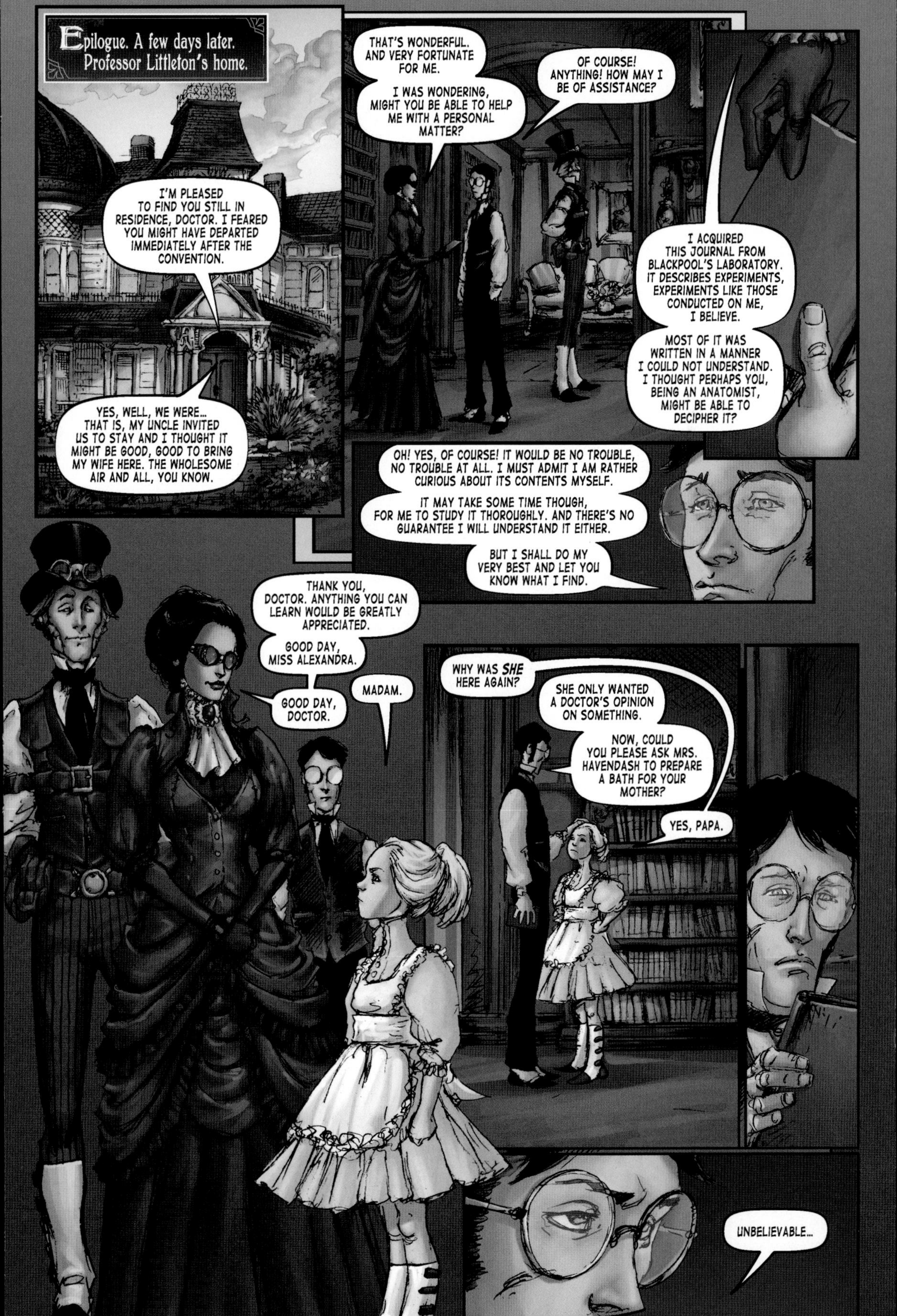
Epilogue. A few days later. Professor Littleton's home.
I'M PLEASED TO FIND YOU STILL IN RESIDENCE, DOCTOR. I FEARED YOU MIGHT HAVE DEPARTED IMMEDIATELY AFTER THE CONVENTION.
YES, WELL, WE WERE... THAT IS, MY UNCLE INVITED US TO STAY AND I THOUGHT IT MIGHT BE GOOD, GOOD TO BRING MY WIFE HERE. THE WHOLESOME AIR AND ALL, YOU KNOW.
THAT'S WONDERFUL. AND VERY FORTUNATE FOR ME.
I WAS WONDERING, MIGHT YOU BE ABLE TO HELP ME WITH A PERSONAL MATTER?
OF COURSE! ANYTHING! HOW MAY I BE OF ASSISTANCE?
I ACQUIRED THIS JOURNAL FROM BLACKPOOL'S LABORATORY. IT DESCRIBES EXPERIMENTS, EXPERIMENTS LIKE THOSE CONDUCTED ON ME, I BELIEVE.
MOST OF IT WAS WRITTEN IN A MANNER I COULD NOT UNDERSTAND. I THOUGHT PERHAPS YOU, BEING AN ANATOMIST, MIGHT BE ABLE TO DECIPHER IT?
OH! YES, OF COURSE! IT WOULD BE NO TROUBLE, NO TROUBLE AT ALL. I MUST ADMIT I AM RATHER CURIOUS ABOUT ITS CONTENTS MYSELF.
IT MAY TAKE SOME TIME THOUGH, FOR ME TO STUDY IT THOROUGHLY. AND THERE'S NO GUARANTEE I WILL UNDERSTAND IT EITHER.
BUT I SHALL DO MY VERY BEST AND LET YOU KNOW WHAT I FIND.
THANK YOU, DOCTOR. ANYTHING YOU CAN LEARN WOULD BE GREATLY APPRECIATED.
GOOD DAY, MISS ALEXANDRA.
GOOD DAY, DOCTOR.
MADAM.
WHY WAS SHE HERE AGAIN?
SHE ONLY WANTED A DOCTOR'S OPINION ON SOMETHING.
NOW, COULD YOU PLEASE ASK MRS. HAVENDASH TO PREPARE A BATH FOR YOUR MOTHER?
YES, PAPA.
UNBELIEVABLE...

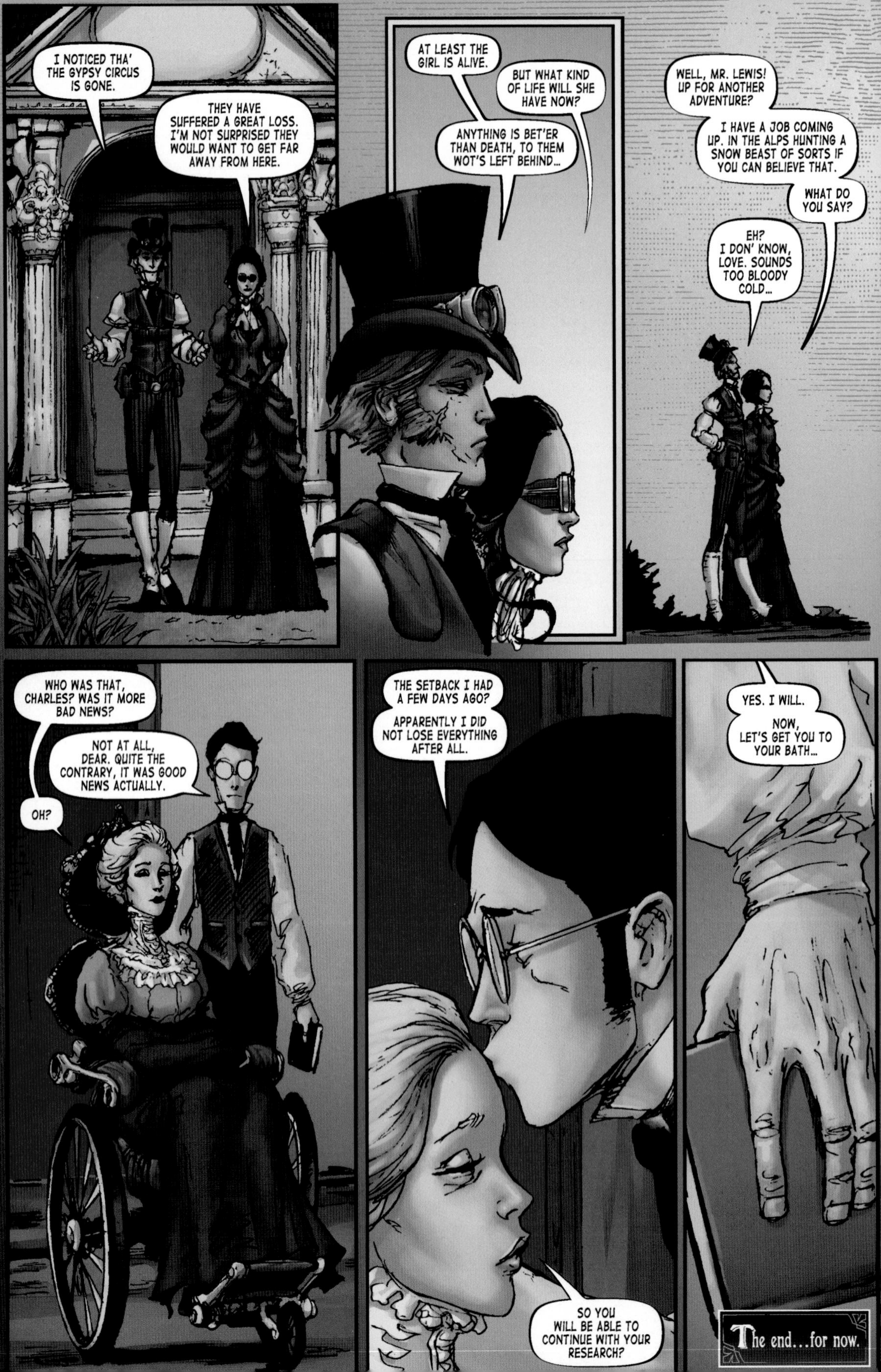
I NOTICED THA' THE GYPSY CIRCUS IS GONE.
THEY HAVE SUFFERED A GREAT LOSS. I'M NOT SURPRISED THEY WOULD WANT TO GET FAR AWAY FROM HERE.
AT LEAST THE GIRL IS ALIVE.
BUT WHAT KIND OF LIFE WILL SHE HAVE NOW?
ANYTHING IS BET'ER THAN DEATH, TO THEM WOT'S LEFT BEHIND...
WELL, MR. LEWIS! UP FOR ANOTHER ADVENTURE?
I HAVE A JOB COMING UP. IN THE ALPS HUNTING A SNOW BEAST OF SORTS IF YOU CAN BELIEVE THAT.
WHAT DO YOU SAY?
EH? I DON' KNOW, LOVE. SOUNDS TOO BLOODY COLD...
WHO WAS THAT, CHARLES? WAS IT MORE BAD NEWS?
NOT AT ALL, DEAR. QUITE THE CONTRARY, IT WAS GOOD NEWS ACTUALLY.
OH?
THE SETBACK I HAD A FEW DAYS AGO?
APPARENTLY I DID NOT LOSE EVERYTHING AFTER ALL.
SO YOU WILL BE ABLE TO CONTINUE WITH YOUR RESEARCH?
YES. I WILL.
NOW, LET'S GET YOU TO YOUR BATH...
The end...for now.

Cover Gallery

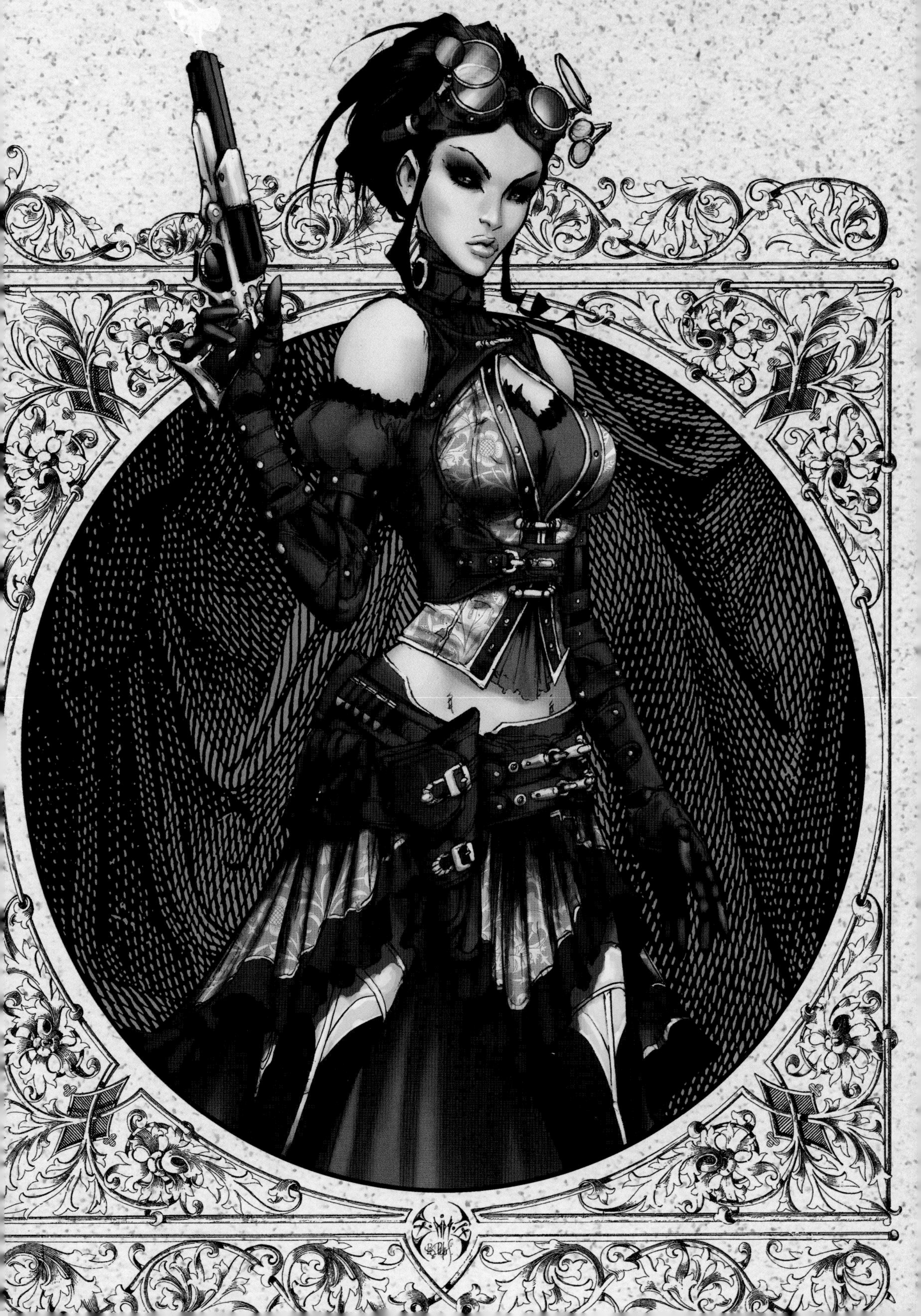

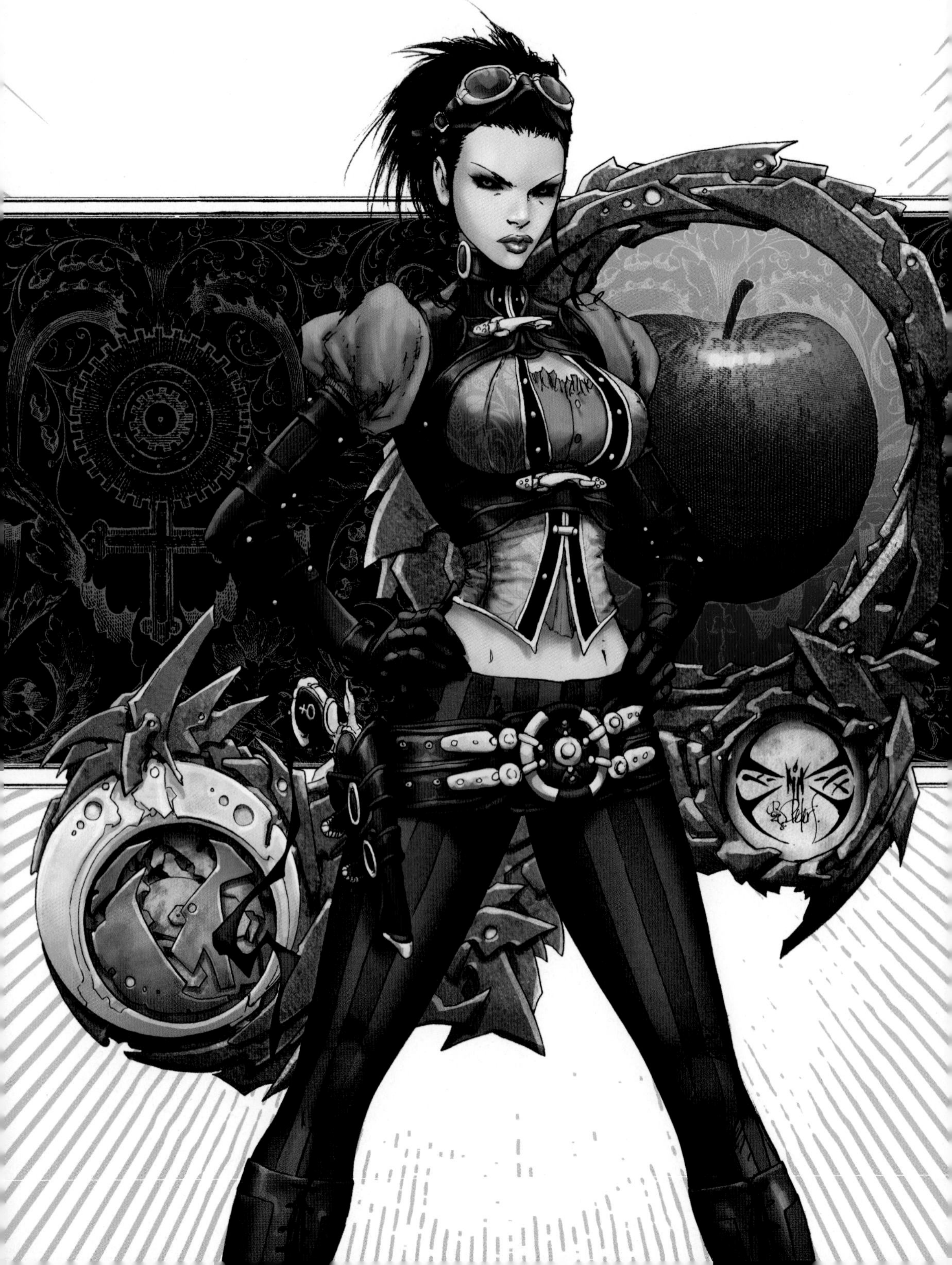

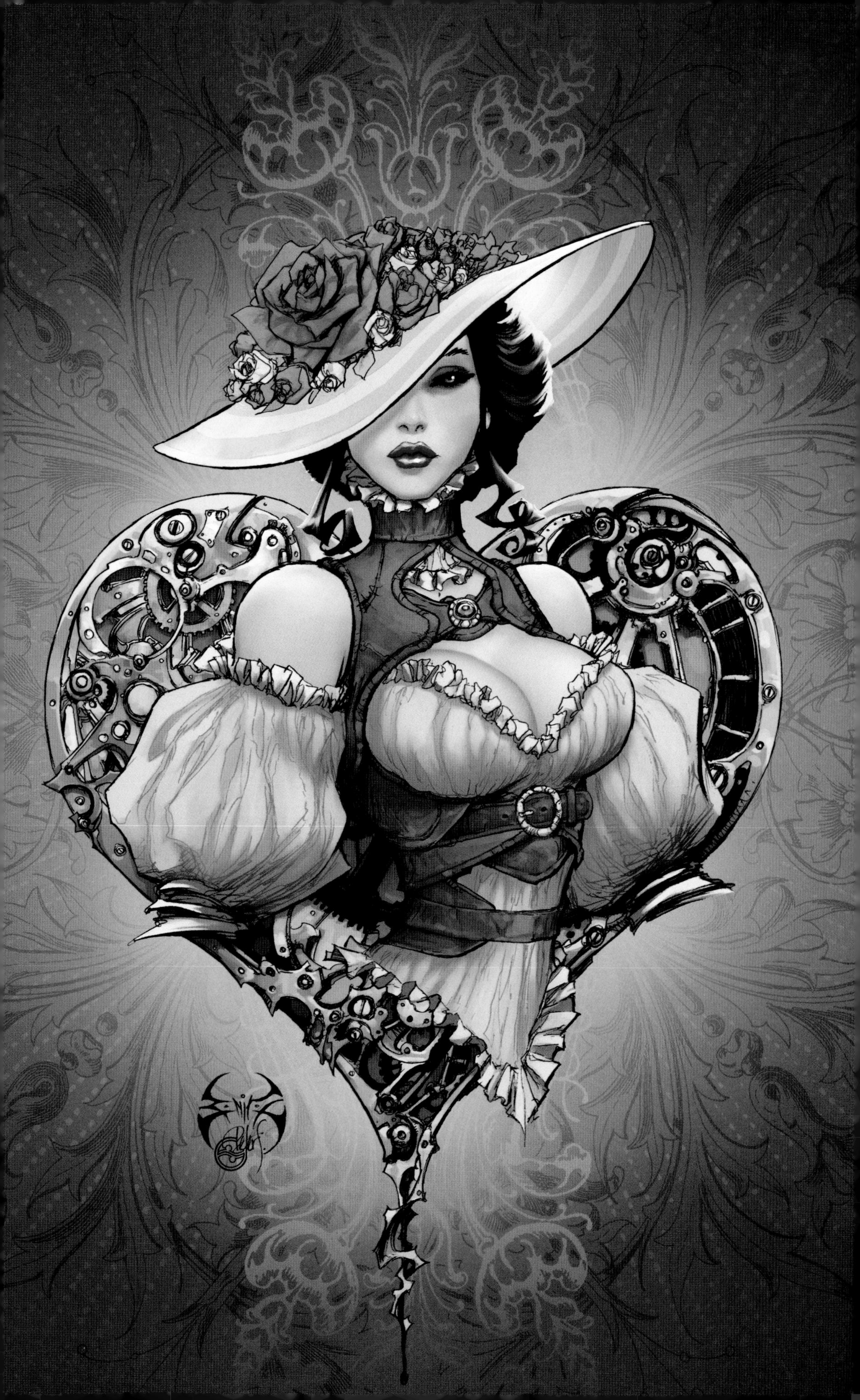

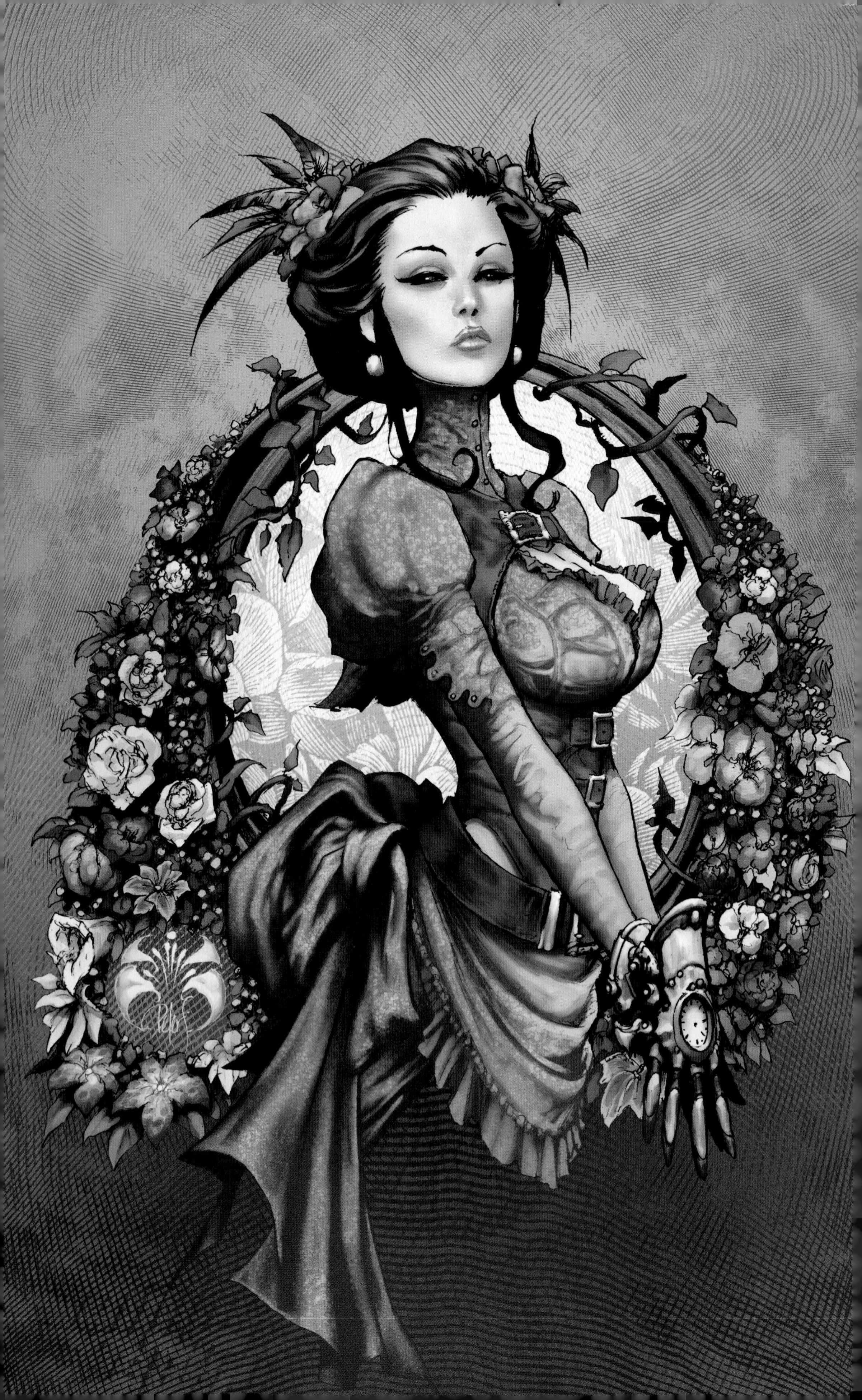

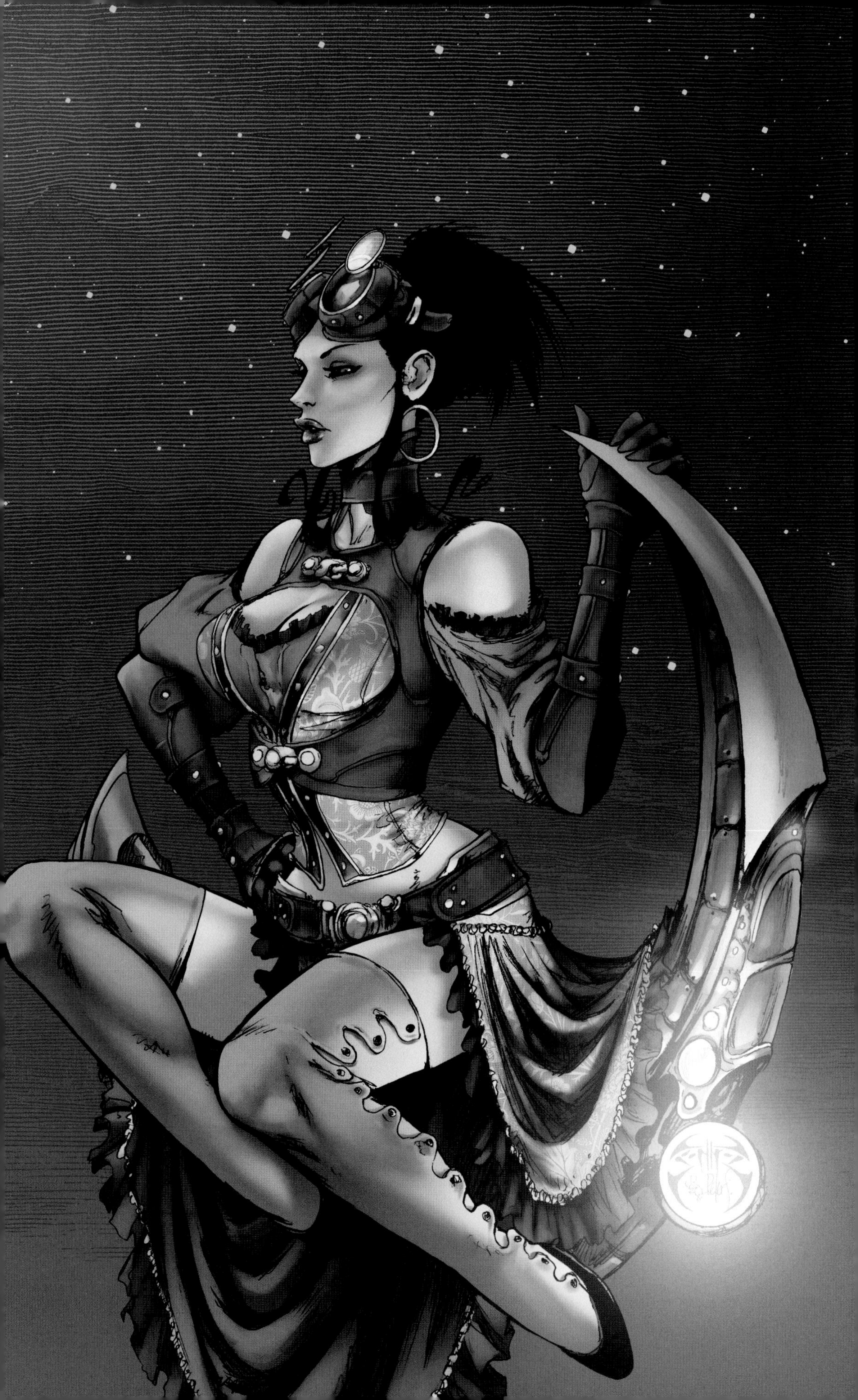

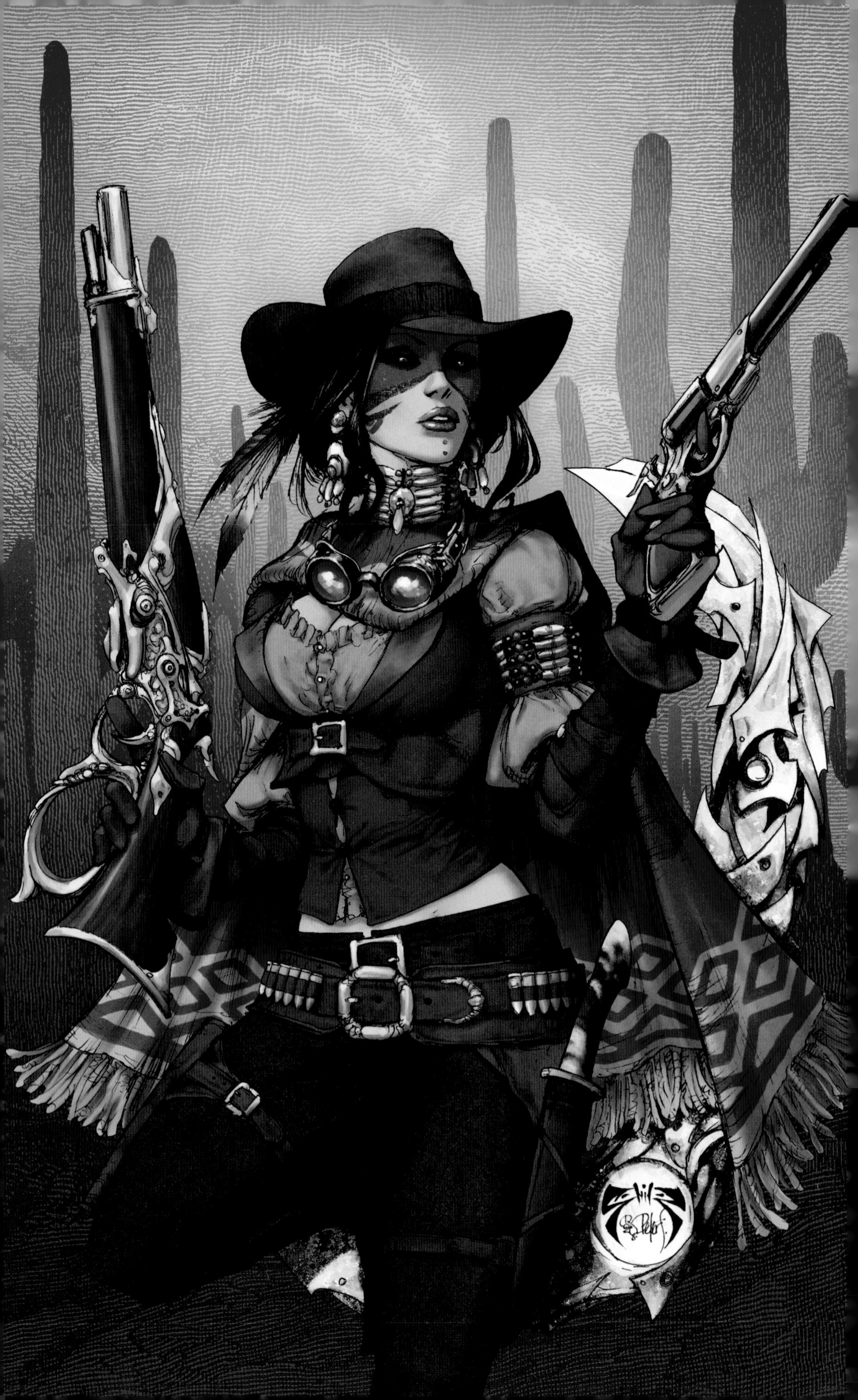

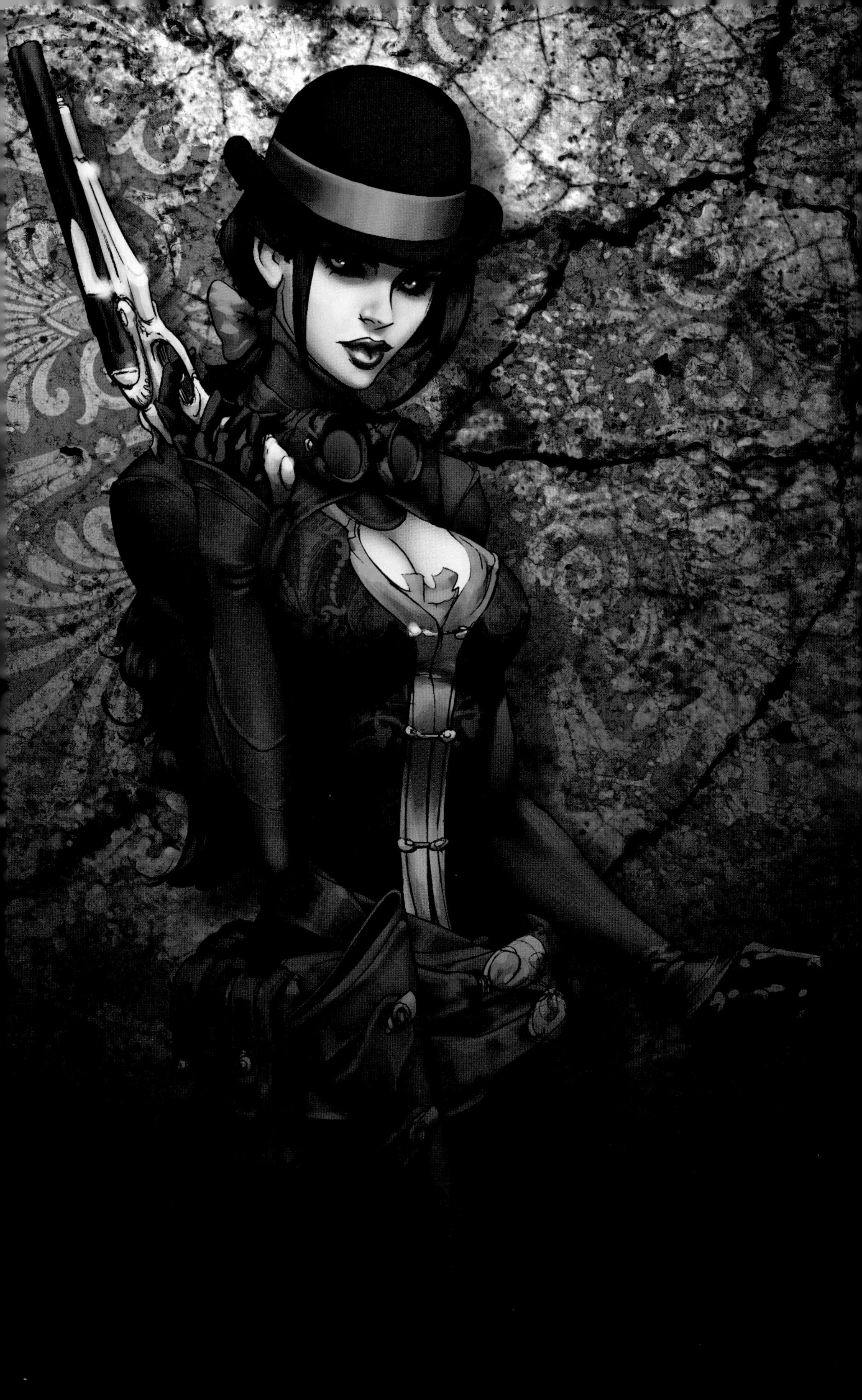

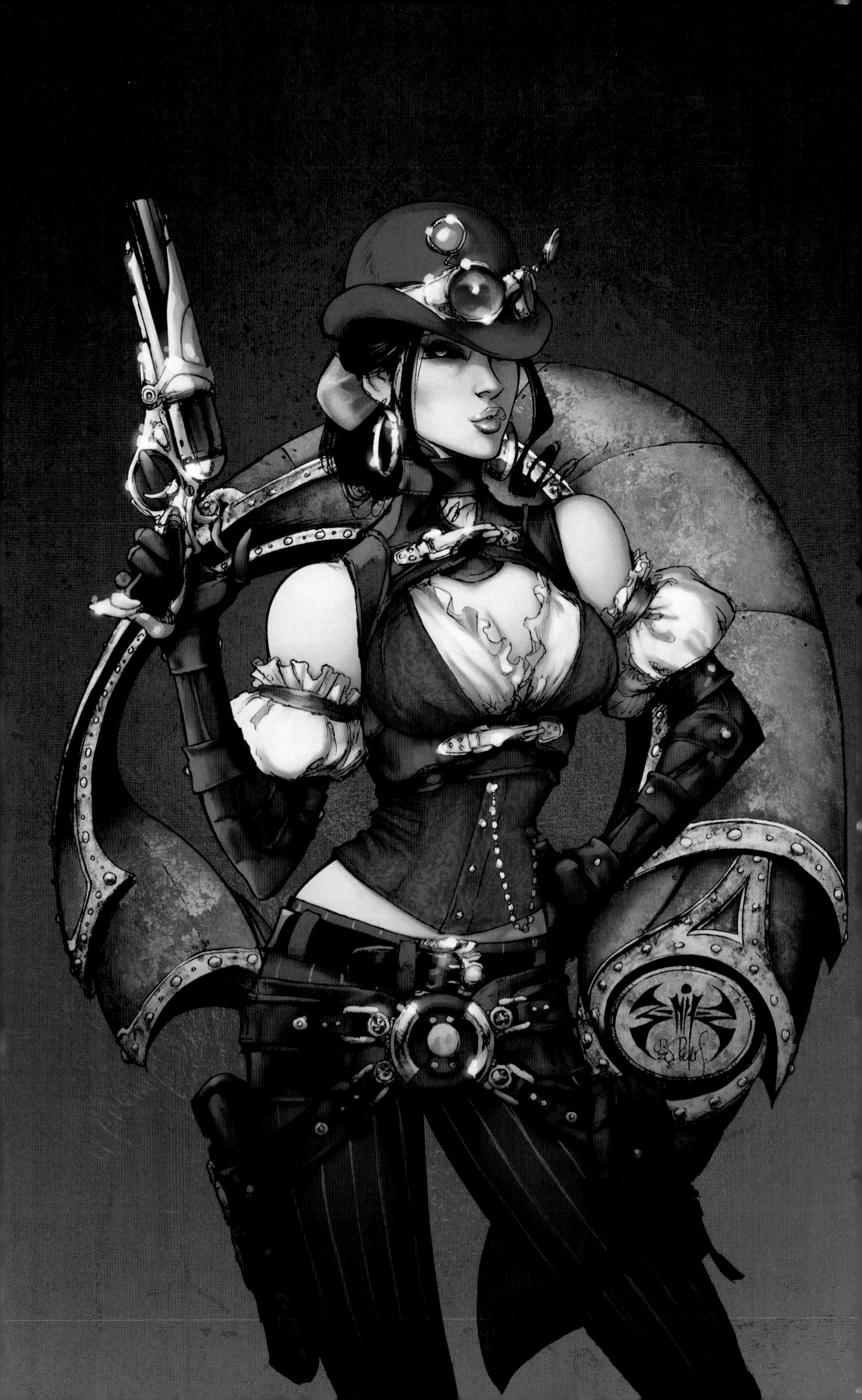

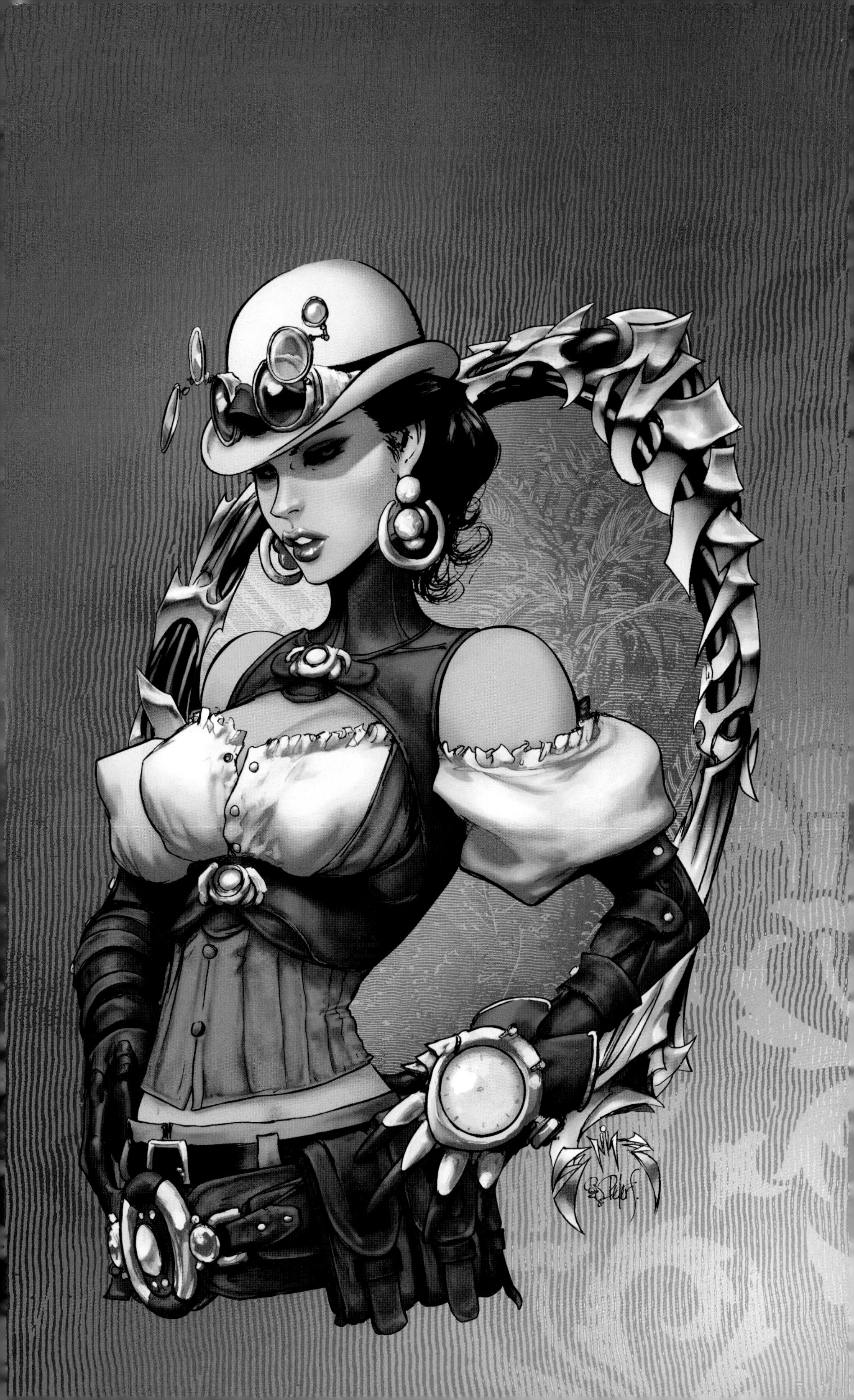

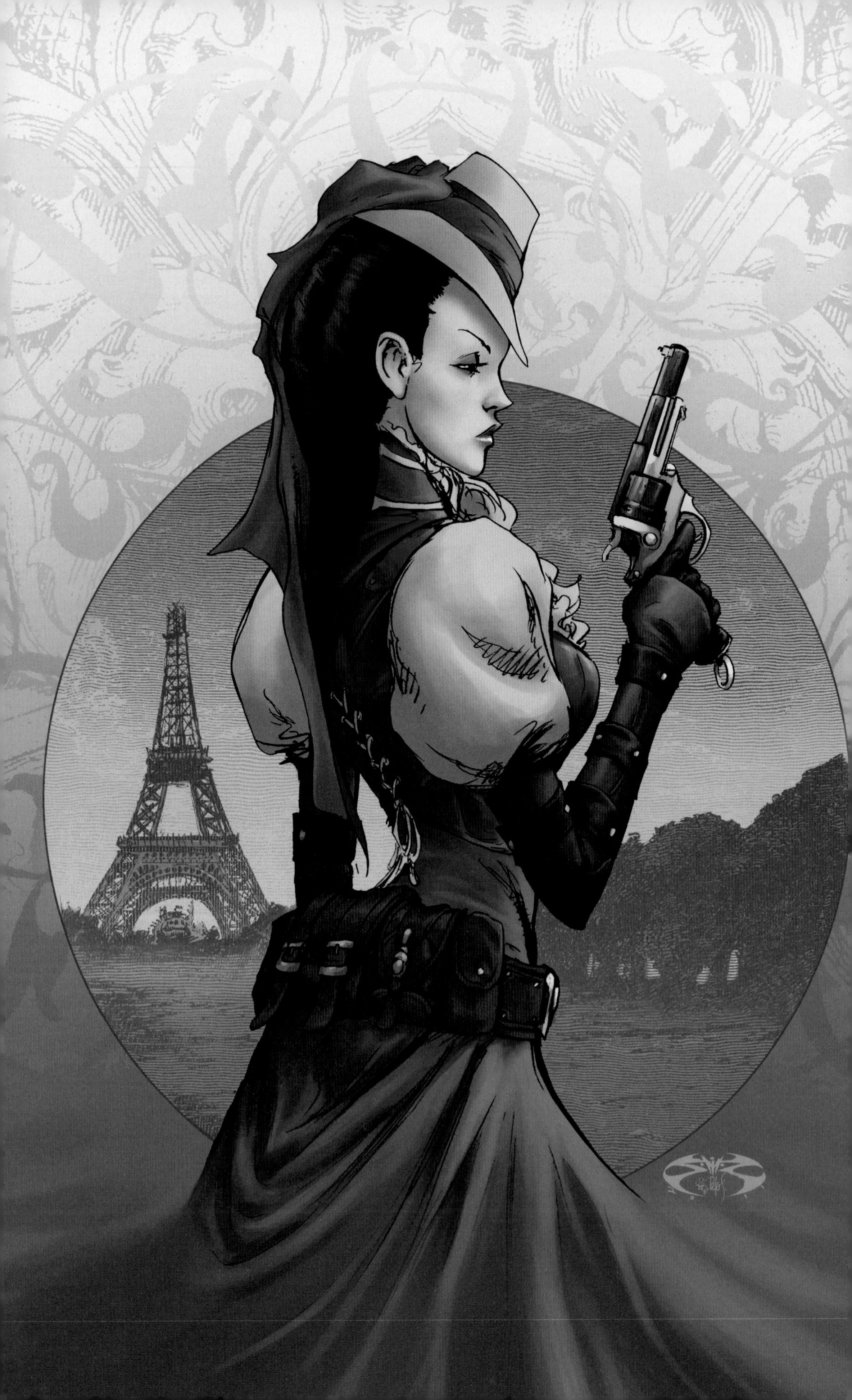

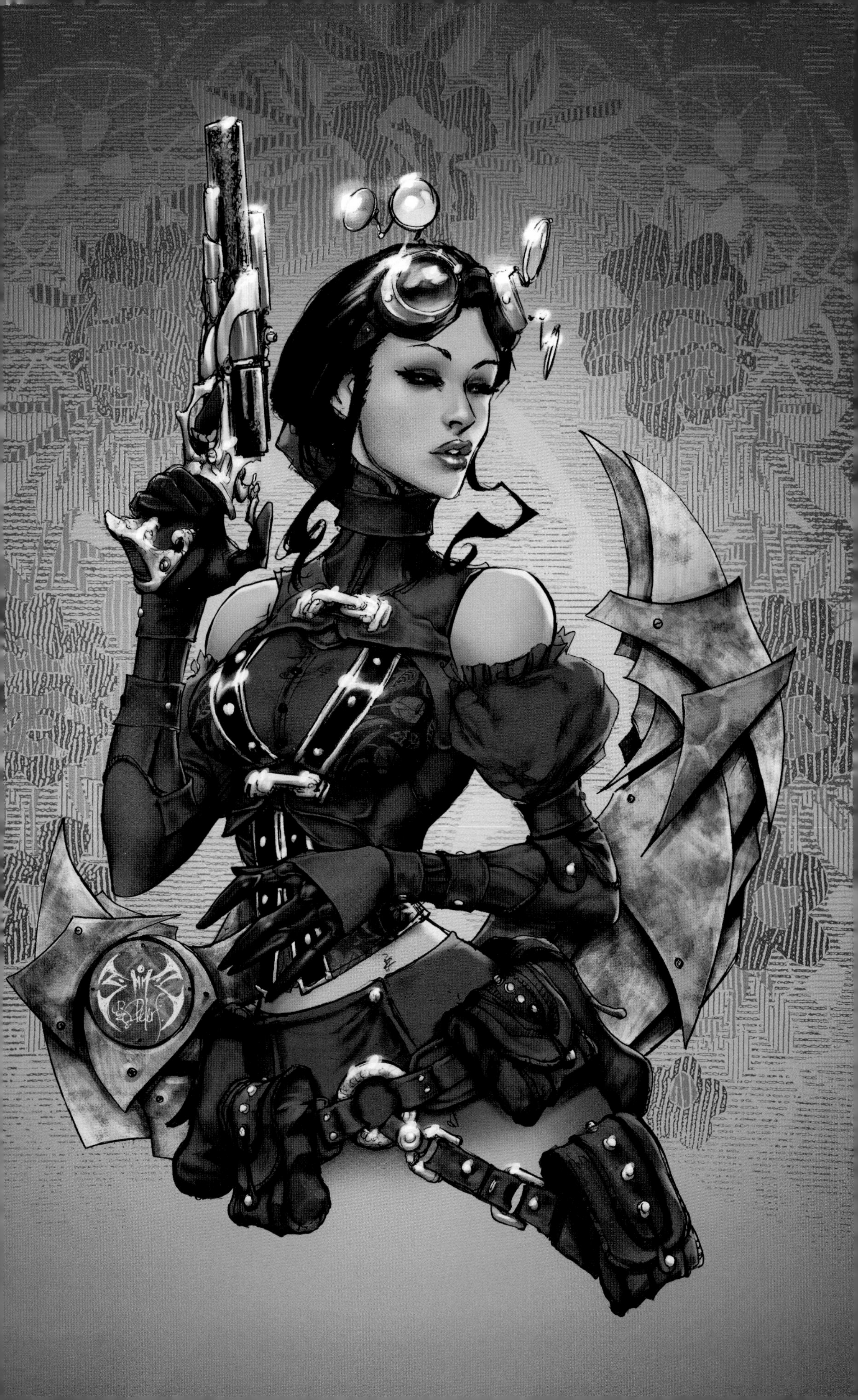

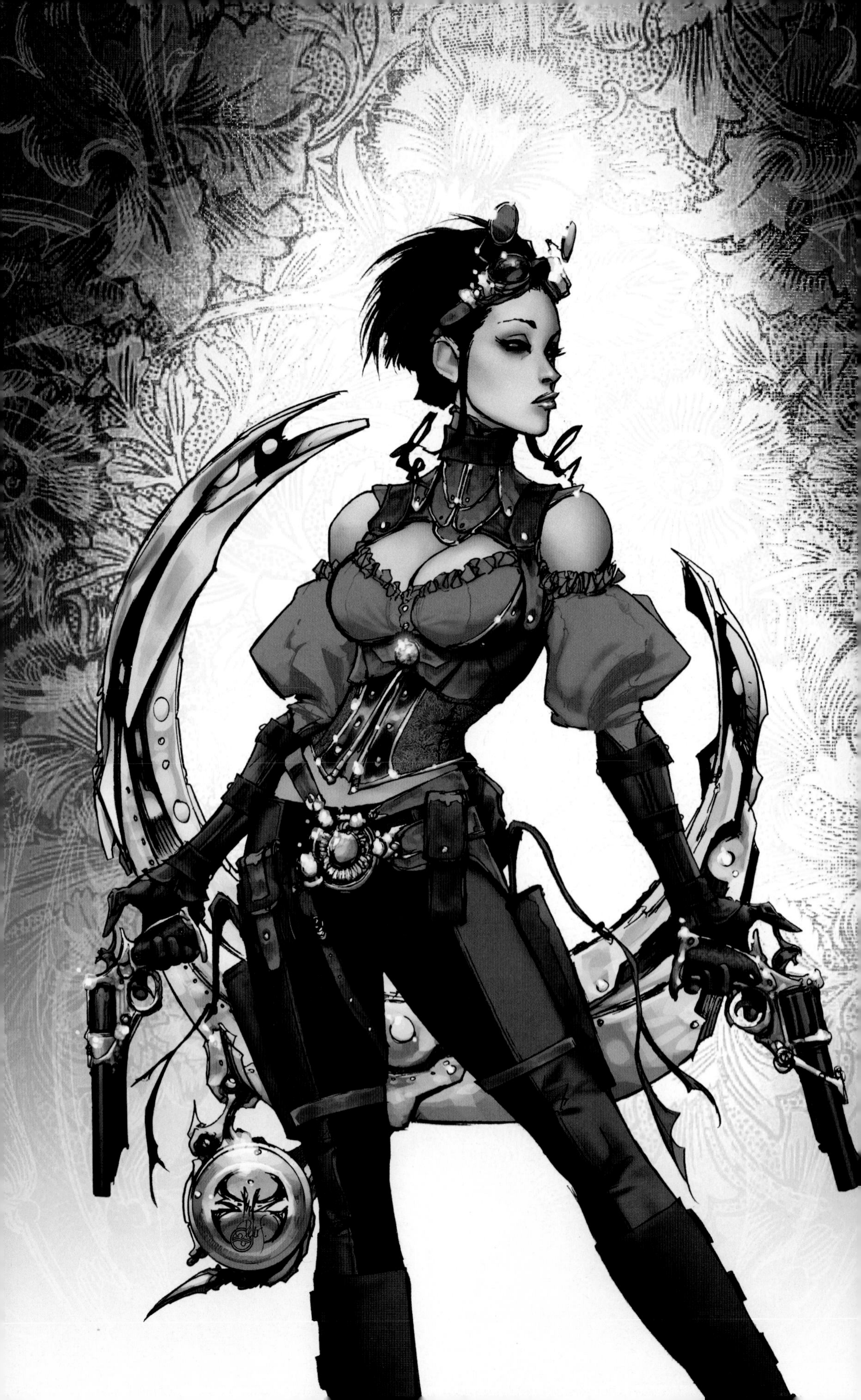

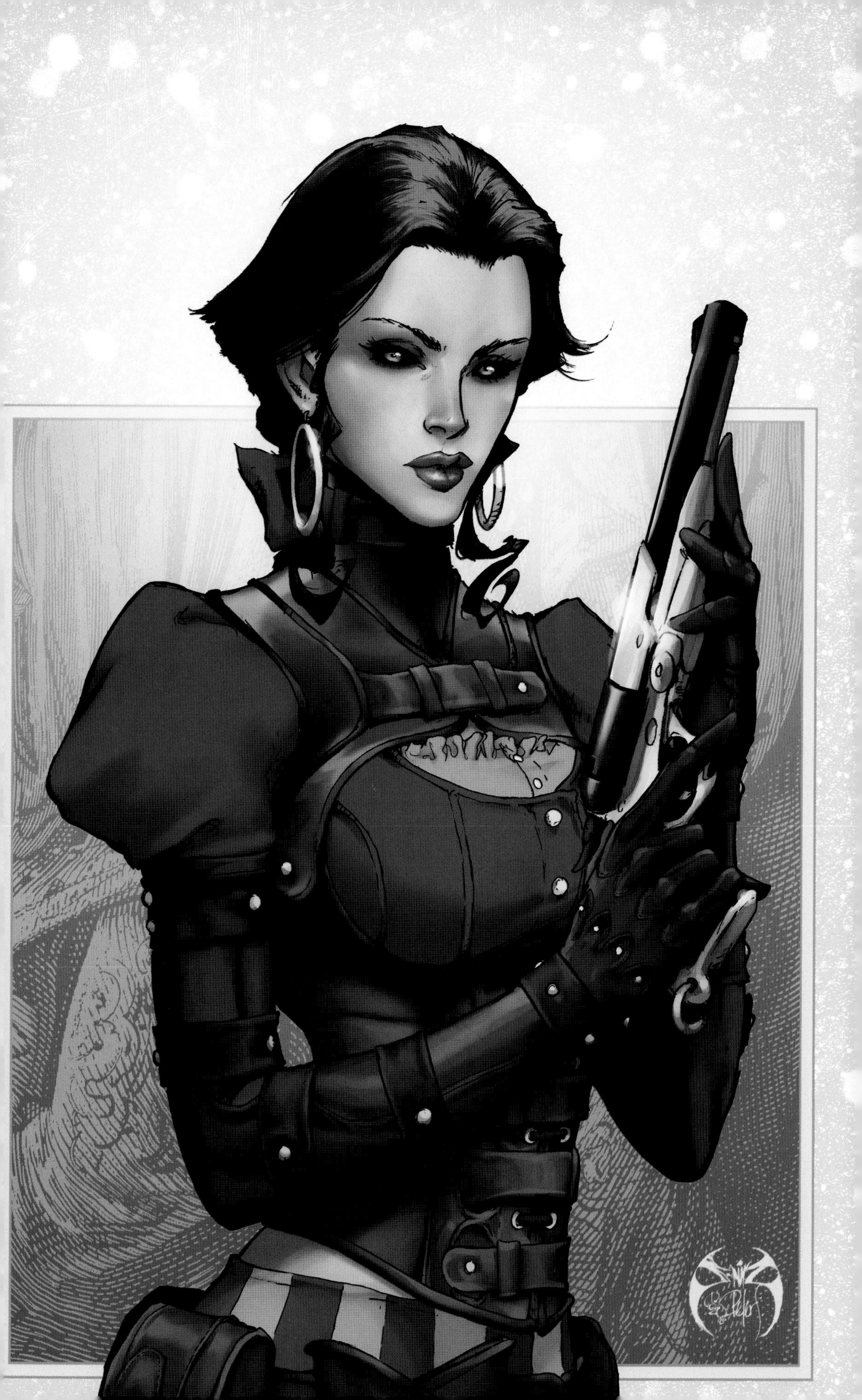

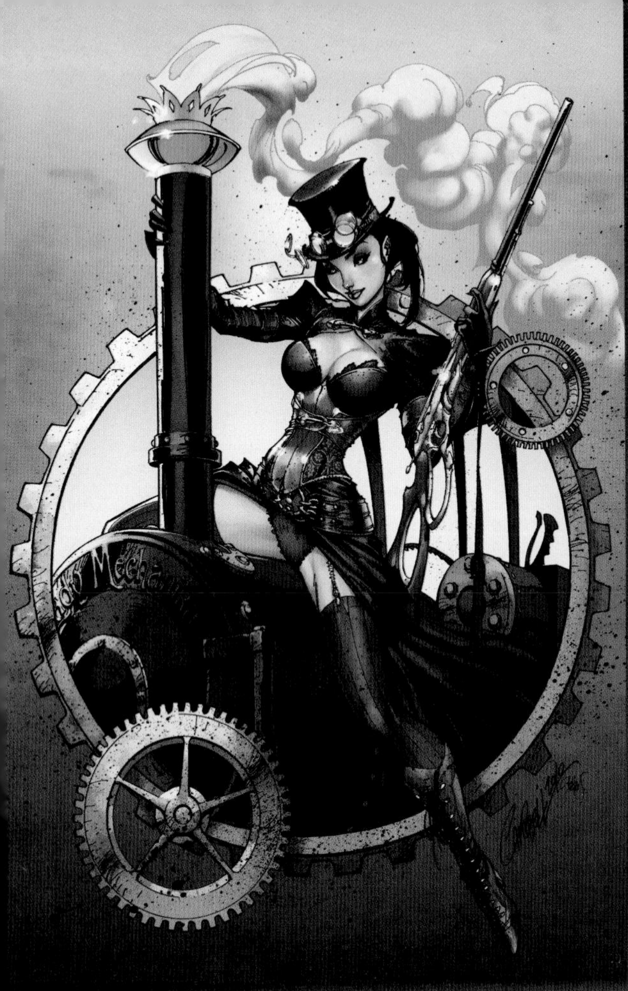

COVER B TO LADY MECHANIKA #2
by ALÉ GARZA & PETER STEIGERWALD

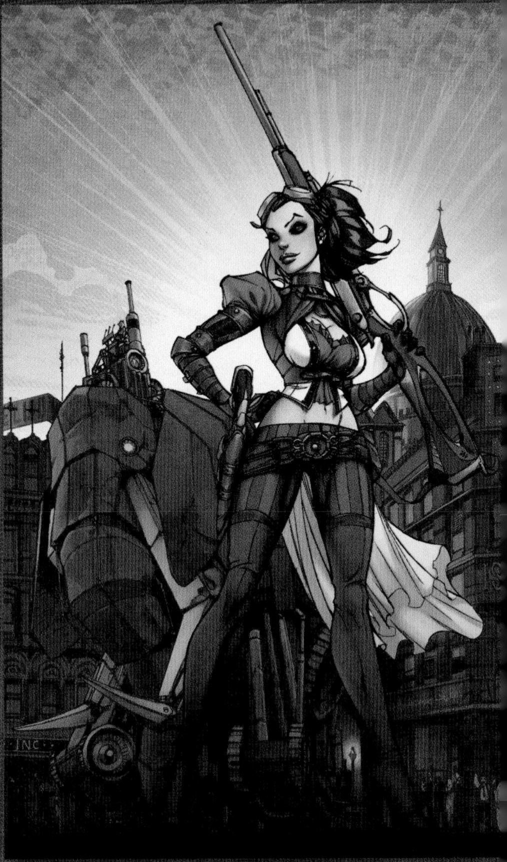

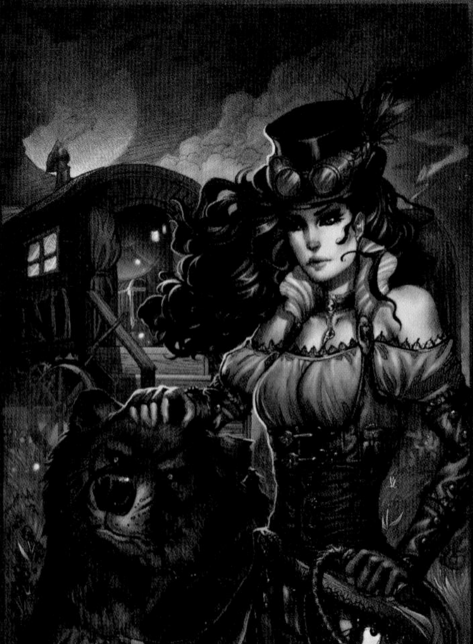

COVER H TO LADY MECHANIKA #2
by NEI RUFFINO

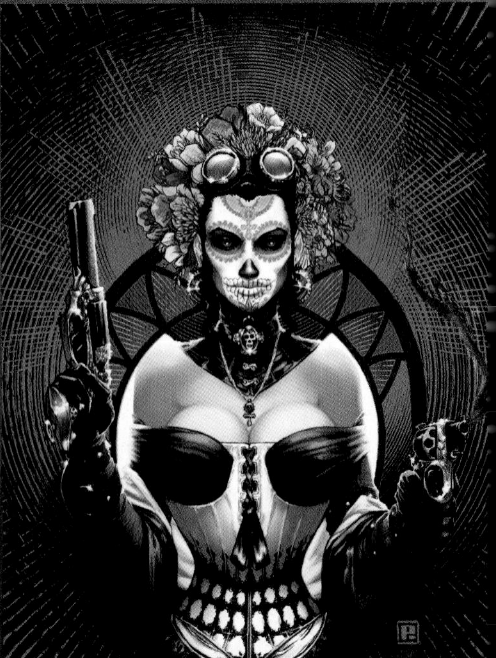

COVER E TO LADY MECHANIKA #4
by PETER STEIGERWALD